Post To Post

Book 1

(Establishing the Way)

By

Rayola Kelley

Hidden Manna Publications

Post To Post
Book 1
(Establishing the Way)

Copyright © 2022 by Rayola Kelley

ISBN: 978-0-9915261-7-8

Cover Design: Pam Wester

Printed in the USA

Except where otherwise indicated, all Scripture quotations in this book are taken from the King James Version of the Bible.

Hidden Manna Publications
PO Box 3572
Oldtown, ID 83822

Facebook:
https://www.facebook.com/HiddenMannaPublications/

CONTENTS

Introduction 5

Salvation 7

The Gospel of the Cross 16

Repentance 29

Redemption 35

Reconciliation 38

The Reality of God 41

God's Will 51

The Light 60

The Truth of a Matter 69

God's love 79

Prayer 90

Hope & Promise 99

Courage & Encouragement 107

Attitudes 124

The Disciplines of a Christian Life 134

The Spirit & Liberty 143

The Church 153

Discernment 163

Grace, Joy & Peace 176

Wisdom & the Fear of the Lord 184

The World 191

Judgment 202

Service & Worship 212

Challenges 230

Adversity & Suffering 242

Character 251

Fighting the Good Fight 261

Faith 281

Righteousness & Obedience 307

Issues of the Heart 320

Waiting & Resting 336

Spiritual Season 349

Preparation 359

The Days We Live In 368

High Calling 383

Time 394

Reaching our Potential 402

Overcoming 412

Resurrection 429

INTRODUCTION

Various people suggested that I put all of my Facebook posts in a book. I accepted the challenge and discovered that all my posts had to be put into two different books. Both books contain over three years of posts that include such events as the Covid-19 "plandemic," and the loss of our four-legged companion, Bell, along with endless protests over rigged elections, our cities on fire, and the exposure of great corruption among world leaders. My co-laborer, Jeannette suggested I keep the title simple by calling these books *Post to Post*.

As I thought about the Word of God, I realized that the themes of it are like corner posts such as salvation, redemption, and reconciliation while Scriptures can be compared to posts and the Holy Spirit is the wire or board that connects each post. We are to compare Scripture with Scripture. In other words, we must not allow one Scripture to stand alone, but we must put others beside it to make sure that each Scripture lines up to the different corner posts of truth in order to hold up the Christian life and maintain the spirit and integrity of the fence.

It is at this time we must consider the significance of putting posts up in the first place. They are to create a boundary that must not be trespassed, a space where order exists, an area of safety and protection, and a type of map that guides or directs the direction one can walk to ensure them of arriving at the right place.

My prayer is that these posts accomplish the same task. It has always been my heart to encourage believers to discover who they are in Christ, align them up to the path of righteousness, bring order to their lives with Biblical instruction, and give them the means to follow in the footsteps of Jesus to their real calling and destination.

SALVATION

Salvation is a helmet,
not a nightcap.
(Vance Havner)

Through the years I have asked people, "What is the Gospel?" Sadly, most answers are vague. I had one person tell me she knew she believed and possessed the right gospel because she had a "burning in her bosom." However, the gospel is not some feeling or vague notion, it is actually a message. As believers, we know the word "gospel" means "good news" or "good tidings."

The Apostle Paul tells us that this message is the power of God unto salvation. In other words, the "good news" contained in this message is that it can actually save a person who believes it and receives it as being so in their heart. To have "good news," there has to be some "bad news." The good news is we can be saved, but the bad news is that we are sinners, transgressors of God's Law, separated from Him, and doomed to taste His wrath.

The Apostle Paul summarized the Gospel in *1 Corinthians 15:1-4.* The first thing he established is that like any message the "good news" must be preached or proclaimed. I may teach you about what the Gospel is, but when delivering it, I must preach or proclaim it.

The Gospel must be preached because people are dead in sin, dull of hearing to their spiritual plight, and asleep to the destruction that is coming at them. Anointed preaching of the Gospel will alert the dead, penetrate the dull of hearing, and awaken the sleeping by the urgent call for them to flee the wrath to come by running to Jesus, in search of being saved by His work on the cross.

Rayola Kelley

When you mention the Gospel, most people assume they know it, but when you ask them to explain the Gospel, the silence you encounter can be pretty loud about the ignorance that people operate in when it comes to the actual message of the "good news" of Jesus Christ. And, yet what is our commission as the church—to preach about eschatology, to proclaim the latest popular, politically correct doctrine, or promote a social conscience?

According to *Mark 16:15*, we are to preach the Gospel unto every creature. In fact, *Matthew 24:14* says, *"And this gospel of the kingdom shall be preached in all the world for a witness unto all nations; and then shall the end come."* There are gospels clearly being promoted, but are they the right gospel? Is it the pure, proven message that was first proclaimed by the first apostles?

If a person's faith is not founded on the true Christ of the Bible, it will be shaken and collapse as waters of judgment take all remaining residues out to the seas of destruction. If a person receives a wrong spirit, he or she will be set up to fall into a pit of complete spiritual ruin, but if a person preaches or receives another gospel, he or she will stand accursed *(Galatians 1:6-9)*.

The Apostle Paul speaks of perverting the Gospel. "Perverting" something points to some type of subtraction or addition to it. In the case of the Gospel, the natural tendency is to subtract from who Christ is (the God-Man, the Christ, and the Savior), while adding to His completed work of redemption. Any time you subtract from the nature of Christ, you end up with an antichrist that is unable to save you and when you add to the redemption of Christ with works, church affiliation, ordinances and etc. thinking you are earning your salvation, you will frustrate the grace of God.

As Christians, our testimony of our salvation experience began with the simple seed of the Gospel taking root in our soul, and from that point it started to produce fruit in us as we built our lives on who Jesus is. As we walk out the hope of the Gospel in obedience, we begin to become a true witness of its authority to stand regardless of the days, its power to save and transform us, and its enduring character to see us through to the end of our spiritual journey. The question remains, can you explain what the Gospel is?

Christians are wrestling with loyalties and responsibilities. As citizens of America many of us feel vexed over what we see happening. It is overwhelming to see pictures of people screaming foul, endless blasphemes in a fit of blind rage, watching our cities burn, hearing about the growing numbers of murders, the cries of parents losing their children to sheer senselessness, injustice happening in the name of justice, and the utter corruptions and insanity of leaders who have sold both their souls and their votes to gain the useless riches and power of this world.

This world is being systematically turned upside down and now is being turned inside out in order to cause an implosion from the bottom up to the top down. Sadly, it has been planned by wicked powers and is part of the mystery of iniquity that has been working in this world ever since Adam's fall, as well as in this nation ever since its inception.

However, at different times this plan has been pushed back by an unseen hand using a few good men to stand in the gap because the timing was never right. As some watch in shock, others in horror, and a few in disbelief, we as the body of Christ, who are also part of our communities and a nation, must stir ourselves out of any confusion and wishful thinking, as well as any attitude of "getting by" until it all "blows over."

We must honestly face the times, seasons, and reality of what is happening, and admit this is not a political problem, not a race problem, and not an ideology problem, it is a spiritual problem of the heart, and as Jesus' Body we hold the key to address this problem with hope, healing, and salvation.

Paul asked important questions in *Romans 10:14-15, "How then shall they call on him in whom they have not believed? And how shall they hear without a preacher? And how shall they preach except they be sent? As it is written, "How beautiful are the feet of them that preach the gospel of peace, and bring glad tidings of good things!"* We are clearly hearing and seeing the bad things, but as the body of Christ, are we boldly carrying out our commission by sharing the Gospel? Granted, we must be prepared, sent, and ready to share the message at all times, which begs the question, do we really understand the Gospel, and if so, are we where we need to be in our life, calling, and gifts to be ready to share it any time the door opens?

Are you seeking that which is alive or dead? Every person has a vacuum in their soul they must fill. For me I initially sought what I perceived would fill that vacuum in the world, but each search led me to leanness in my spirit. Each rabbit trail I ran down to find meaning and add substance to my life left me with greater disappointment, disillusionment, and depression. I finally hit a great crisis in my life, and it was there I was challenged to look up.

The challenge came from two people. One was a woman who gave me Chick tracts. The simple message and presentation in the tracts began to awake a reality in me that I did not understand the true God or the work the Lord Jesus Christ did on my behalf. Another one was a Navy corpsman who was a dental assistant. I was in the Navy at the time, and while he worked cleaning my teeth, he was challenging my soul with the reality that Jesus Christ died for my sins and that I needed to receive Him to be saved.

I have to admit that what I was reading and what I heard as the dental assistant worked cleaning my teeth brought a stark contrast between what I assumed I knew about religious matters and the real message of redemption.

The light of Christ that was penetrating my soul revealed also the darkness of my soul. I realized the issue was not the reality that I failed to do right by doing enough good works to work my way to heaven, but that I could not do right in my present state and only God could resolve the darkness of my fallen condition due to sin. As the reality of my spiritual state came to the light, God's provision was illuminated. I could see the need to receive the light of the world, the Lord Jesus Christ as my Savior.

One of the words I meditate on is the word "deliverance." Deliverance means different things to different people. To the captive it means release, to the oppressed it means liberation, to the weary it means relief, to the lost it points to being rescued, and to those who are facing execution in light of judgment it becomes a means of escape.

For the Christian, it is summarized in one word, "salvation." We are all born into captivity to sin and need to be released from its claims on our lives. We are oppressed by the spirit of the world and need spiritual liberation from its tyranny. We are weary with the endless battles that confront us and need to know there is relief that comes through spiritual rest.

We must also daily face the fact that we are and can become lost in the darkness of the age and need the light of the world to rescue us by guiding us through its terrain. Without the peace of God, we have a sense we are facing the wrath of God, but as believers, we take great comfort because we have found the way of escape through Jesus Christ. He alone delivers us from all the enemies of our soul so we can be delivered to a new life in Him.

Yesterday I spoke of salvation which points to deliverance. Deliverance works in two ways: deliverance FROM something and deliverance THROUGH something. We clearly see these two types of deliverance in operation.

The sinner is delivered FROM death into life, while Noah was delivered THROUGH the flood. Deliverance FROM something changes one's status, while deliverance THROUGH something tests and enlarges one's faith, while refining character and preparing the inner man.

As Christians we must avoid looking at the great flood of darkness that is encroaching upon us and remember God has provided the Ark of Christ for us to hide in, and when we face the massive challenges of the of Red Sea before us and as we hear the enemy behind us, we must not forget that God has provided a way through it and when the time is right, He will enable us to see it. This is why Jesus stated in *John 16:33, "These things I have spoken unto you, that in me ye might have peace.*

In the world ye shall have tribulation: but be of good cheer; I have overcome the world."

The Bible tells us that Jesus is the foundation of true faith, the cornerstone to all that is true and right, and the head or authority that is to influence all matters concerning His Body. He is Lord, the overseer of His household, the king over an unseen kingdom that will be unveiled one day, and the ultimate judge who will judge all matters of the heart and conduct.

As many Bible Scriptures point out, Jesus Christ is the Son of God (deity) who was fashioned as man and clothed in humanity (Son of man), and commissioned as the Messiah (Anointed One) to preach the Gospel, heal broken hearts, set the captive free and heal those bruised by sin. He became the Lamb of God who would take away the sin of the world in order to become the Savior to all who would believe that He was, is and always will be God's solution to the sin problem that truly ails all humanity.

The reason I say this is because *Matthew 7:24-27* states if you do not believe the Word about these matters, then you are standing on shifting ground and when shaken, the religious foundation you have under you will collapse into complete ruin. Jesus asked Peter in *Matthew 16:13-18* who did men say He was and then He asked Peter who did he say He was.

Peter answered correctly because it had been revealed to him from heaven. Jesus is the only way, the only entrance into the promise of eternal life, but there is only one true Jesus who fits all the qualifications as set forth in Scripture. It is for this reason the way to heaven is narrow.

If you don't get Jesus right by building your life upon Him as your sole foundation according to His Word, while lining your attitude and life up to Him as the only cornerstone, you will miss entering through the narrow entrance to life. And, if you fail to come under His authority as Lord, you will miss fulfilling your high calling in His Kingdom.

Was the knowledge of your sin liberating? I tried to be a good girl in my adolescent and teenage years but I knew it was a game that presented a certain façade. It is not that I did anything bad, but I realized my thought process was not always right.

My attempts to be good while struggling with attitudes and wrong thoughts sometimes made me feel like a hypocrite. When I joined the Navy, I found out what I was really made of and I came face to face with the depressing reality that my inward person was far from being "good."

The more I wrestled with my inward state the more depressing and hopeless my reality became. Through a series of God-ordained events, I was introduced to the salvation of Jesus Christ.

One of the most liberating aspects of the Gospel message was that Jesus died for my sin. My inward state finally had a name and a face to it, but did I dare admit the real source of my struggles? When I realized that Jesus came to address my sin by dying for me, it brought a great relief to my soul. I later learned that we have all sinned and have fallen short of the glory of God, and it we say we have no sin, we deceive ourselves and the truth is not in us, and if we say we have not sinned, we make God a liar and His Word is not in us (*Romans 6:23; 1 John 1:8, 10*).

Realizing that my sin was an inherited state from Adam allowed me to understand the problem and with gladness receive God's solution. Today sin is being watered down, adjusted, and practically done away with. The Bible tells us we are slaves to it, which means we need to be liberated from it, but if people refuse to face their sin, own, repent, and confess it while seeking God's pardon, they will see no need for a Savior. My question for those who wrestle with bondage attached to the old life is have you been liberated from the real taskmaster of your soul, Sin?

Have you accepted Jesus' invitation in *John 5:37-39* to come and freely drink of His water? Because we are fleshly and living in the world, we sometimes allow our feelings, emotions, and our opinions to dictate our perception of a matter.

Rayola Kelley

As many believers soon discover, such feelings or activities cannot ensure the quality of their spiritual lives. *Isaiah 12:2-3* states, *"Behold, God is my salvation; I will trust, and not be afraid: for the LORD JEHOVAH is my strength and my song; he also is become my salvation. Therefore, with joy shall ye draw water out of the wells of salvation."* Jesus is the well of salvation and we must draw out the water of His Spirit daily to offer it to thirsty souls.

As believers, the water must be uncapped in our souls as it fills us up every day. The problem is when we perceive or pursue the things of this world or the flesh as being satisfying enough to us, and fail to realize that such satisfaction is temporary and will have no impact on thirsty souls, we end up becoming barren wildernesses. In such barrenness the water is rendered ineffective. It either becomes stagnant because there is no living water coming in to replenish and refresh our souls or eventually we become like empty or broken cisterns.

Living Water only remains active and vital as long as it is allowed to move in and out of our lives like a river. We must not only drink of the Living waters ourselves, but we must be an open channel for it to flow out freely to others.

What stands out the most about your salvation? It clearly means Jesus is in you. God not only sees His Son when He looks upon you, but He sees His Son when He looks within you due to the fact that Jesus' life is being worked in you. This is something you reckon, believe, and trust as being so.

Every time you consider your salvation, you declare, "Amen, so be it for it is so" no matter how much Satan is accusing you and regardless of your feelings or the day. Being saved means we have received by faith in our heart the witness of God concerning His Son redeeming us, and as a result we have confidence that we possess the gift of life (*1 John 5:5-8, 11-13*).

We also know salvation is not based on our decency but on God's goodness in providing us with the source of salvation. We can stand on assurance, and once we receive the gift of life, salvation becomes a helmet we wear that reminds us that we have nothing to fear concerning

14

our life, our present hope, and our future home because it has been secured for us (*Ephesians 6:17; 1 Thessalonians 5:8-9*).

Every believer has believed the Gospel message, put their trust in God's work on the cross, as well as the work He is doing in them, and have learned to rest in the promise of it. This is the essence of our hope that we stand on. Because of Jesus being in believers and believers being in Him, God does not consider what might be or what could be, but He looks at what is. The Apostle Paul summarize the "what is" of Christianity in *Colossians 1:27, "To whom God would make known what is the riches of the glory of this mystery among the Gentiles; which is CHRIST IN YOU, THE HOPE OF GLORY."* (Emphasis added.)

I recently read a book published back in 1968 called, "Voices from the Edge of Eternity." It is a collection of recorded testimonies that span many centuries of people ready to enter eternity. There were testimonies of believers rejoicing as they entered into glory, hearing the sounds of heaven and seeing Jesus, while those who failed to serve the Lord to their fullest calling and capacity died with some regrets. However, those unprepared to meet God met with a frightening, despairing, desperate reality because they knew it was too late to receive God's provision and that hell was their fate.

These people included the French infidel Voltaire and the deist Thomas Paine. The testimonies of this group of people surrounding their last days and hours is very disturbing.

There was no joking about hell, no ranting that there was no God, no denial of who God was, just the dreadful reality of the existence of a place that was void of the reality of God, a place of utter torment. If there is something that you or I are putting off in regards to God until tomorrow or the New Year, we each must see the urgency of responding today, for we are only assured of today to do right towards the Lord and establish a lasting witness in regard to eternity.

As Paul declared, *"today is the day of salvation"* (*1 Corinthians 6:2*).

THE GOSPEL OF THE CROSS

*Shedding the "wrongs" of my life at
the foot of the cross is a liberating
exercise that allows me to discover
my "rights" as a child of God
in His kingdom.
(Rayola Kelley)*

It is amazing how many people start out with a new hope at the first of the year. Some act as if they are beginning with a new slate. Perhaps it is the idea of a brand-new year that encourages people, but the truth is New Year's Day is just another day.

I learned long ago it is not the years that serve as a gift to each of us, but each day is really the true gift of God because we only have today to make our life count *(Matthew 6:33-34)*. Each day is new and will present its own opportunities and challenges and as a result, we believers must be faithful with the day to avoid looking back and seeing wasted years.

I have noticed that most people live in the past or the future, but very few live in the present. For those who live in the past they bemoan the good "ole" days, while missing the opportunities of the present to make a difference in some way and actually experiencing the various gifts that life brings their way.

There are also those who keep looking back, wishing they could change something that will always be. For those who live for the tomorrows being better or when things will finally change, will either become disillusioned or angry. The reason for the dismay over the present is because we so often bring the lifeless, old graveclothes of sins, unbecoming attitudes, regrets, and unfinished business from the last year with us. We can see the drudgery of today too boring, or present challenges too great to endure and wish the day was any other day but today.

As Christians God has dealt with our past so we can face the present and has made mercies and compassions new everyday so we can be prepared to face tomorrow. The cross of Jesus stands to remind us that we have the gift of life for today, His covenant points to the hope we have, and the hope reminds us of the promises that are yet to be fulfilled.

Are you truly becoming identified with Jesus? We declare and sing about how Jesus became identified with us. The incredible miracle of Him coming from the glories of heaven and being fashioned as man in the womb of a virgin in order to become the Lamb of God, the ultimate substitute for you and me on that cross to address our sin and satisfy God's holy Law, stands as a foundation to fundamental Christianity. (*Philippians 2:6-8; 1 John 2:1, 2*).

Believing this leads to salvation, but the abundant, satisfying life is also part of our spiritual inheritance as believers and it is meant to be enjoyed here (*John 10:10*). What does it take to partake of the abundance of the eternal life in us? We must become totally identified with Jesus.

The Bible talks about us being baptized in Jesus' death and buried with Him in the grave so we can be raised up with resurrection power into a new life in Him. Before Christ, we are dead **IN** sin, but because we are in Christ, we become dead **TO** sin so we can walk in the newness of life.

What a glorious exchange of the old with the new. That is the message and hope of the cross that opens the way to salvation.

The one thing that has limited me the most in my Christian walk is my focus. We have the natural tendency to focus on issues, challenges, adversity, emotional chaos, and the every day drudgeries of life. The challenge when it comes to focus is from what perspective that I ultimately choose to consider or examine a matter.

The Bible tells us people perish from ignorance and lack of vision. Ignorance will keep us in the dark and lack of vision will keep us from

17

seeing beyond what stands before us. When I consider the different focuses that can capture my attention and even my affections at times, I have discovered that if they are of this world, they will keep me limited and earthbound, especially if I fail to get God's perspective about them.

For example, issues can become immovable walls that make no sense in the end, challenges often become larger than life, and adversity will serve as a deep pit I fall into or a thick blanket that covers my soul with hopelessness. When it comes to emotional chaos it will bury me with foul moods, torment, and desperation, while everyday drudgeries will put me spiritually to sleep out of pure boredom.

The cross of Christ reminds me that I must first look up before I look down or around. I first must seek God's perspective in prayer and His Word before I try to calculate what must be done. Granted, the cross of Christ casts a great shadow over the things of the world, while blocking out the light from those who are in utter unbelief, but we as believers must remember that the light of the world was lifted up on the cross so we can see, and by becoming identified with Jesus on the cross, we can be lifted up to gain His perspective.

As *Ephesians 2:6* remind us, we are seated in high places in Christ. It is from such heights we gain the right perspective while finetuning our eyesight to see not only beyond the present challenge of the age, but to become an Abraham, *"For he looked for a city which hath foundations, whose builder and maker is God" (Hebrews 11:10).*

The only way to gain life is by way of the cross. So many of us want to hold onto the life associated with this world, but if we do, we will lose it because it is void of what is eternal.

To gain real lasting life, we must cross out the old life associated with our earthly identity and inheritance to gain our new life and a heavenly inheritance. Jesus was clear about counting the cost. One must count the cost of the life attached to this world in order to gain the life that is being formed anew in us by the Holy Spirit, a life that will be raised up on that last day with a new outer covering of a glorified body.

The choice is clear are you trying to keep the life bound to this world or are you breaking the bonds of the present world by being raised above it and seated in high places with the Jesus Christ *(Ephesians 2:6)*?

I've often talked about counting the cost. In an imperfect world, counting the cost can prove to be discouraging. You look at as many facts and requirements you can in order to make an estimation that will fulfill the obligation before you. However, the problem is that there are hidden costs that are thrown at you, unforeseeable costs that arise out of nowhere, and unexpected fees and taxes that are tacked on. In the end, the world proves one thing—that it wants to steal, bankrupt, and destroy what we do have to make us nothing but serfs, slaves, and servants to its ways.

The world wants a person to always be beholden to it in some way, dependent on it for their very existence, and answerable to its demands. This should not surprise us because Satan is the god of these systems that want to enslave us to their wicked tyranny and evil ways.

Jesus instructed us to count the cost because He wanted us to realize when it came to our souls and salvation, we could never satisfy the debt, because the penalty of judgment, wrath, and death was leveled at all of us due to sin. Jesus gave up the glories of heaven and took on humanity in order to identify with our plight. He became the only way to life, and to accomplish this He had to taste death on our behalf.

Out of love He became a ladder, connecting earth with the hope and promise of heaven when He was lifted up on the cross as the Lamb. On the cross He became the avenue of grace to life and the source of mercy to forgiveness, and when laid in the grave He became the bridge of reconciliation, and in His resurrection, He pointed to the heavenly, abundant, victorious, eternal life that was now available to all who would come out of need, brokenness, and spiritual poverty to simply believe His Word of truth, and receive His life by faith. I may not be able to correctly count the different costs of the world, but I know that God's payment for my redemption was complete, and I can trust that when I enter glory and stand before Him, there will be no hidden, unforeseeable, and unexpected costs leveled at me that I must personally pay before I can fully inherit all He has promised me.

How important is it to get the Gospel right? Paul tells us the Gospel is the power of God unto salvation. Clearly, we can't be flippant about the Gospel because a person's response towards it is a matter of spiritual life or death. Why is the Gospel so powerful? Because, at the core of it is not the message itself, some doctrine, or religious affiliation, but a person, Jesus Christ.

The Jesus of the Bible presented in all of His glory, lifted on the cross, alone, is the only One who can save. It is lifting Him up that draws men to salvation, not presenting our best piousness, religious front, or charismatic ways. It is not a matter of intellectually accepting the Gospel, it is a matter of receiving Jesus Christ into our heart as the only One who could redeem us and confessing Him as Lord (Romans 10:9, 10).

Keep in mind, we ultimately have two masters in this world, sin and God and we can only serve one master at a time. It is for this reason that it is important for those who profess to be Christians understand that confession in Romans 10:9,10 points to a binding contract that points to ownership.

As I hear the presentation of the "gospel," it is evident it has been watered down by taking the bad news of sin out of the equation as to not offend those of the world, or it has been made sentimental by emphasizing God's love while ignoring sin's grave affront to His holiness.

There is a "social gospel" which is about "doing good" to change the environment of society rather than the heart of man. In order to capture the people who want to constantly ride on the religious roller coaster of emotions and experiences, a "feel-good" gospel has been devised where one can imagine that since God would not die for junk, they must have some worthwhile and desirable quality in them to offer Him. It is true God did not die for junk, but He did die for lost souls who are at enmity with Him.

When people ask why aren't people being saved, and why is it that those who do come forward to say the "sinner's" prayer never have a real change take place in their life, it often comes down to a weak, heretical presentation of the Gospel. These pseudo gospels are identified by the fruits they fail to produce.

There is no inward change, no outward godly disciplines evident, no real response to service, and no real commitment to speak of. We must remember the power of the Gospel has the power to save us because we are delivered from the claims of sin on our life and given the very life of Christ that transforms us within, producing fruits unto everlasting life.

What is the true Gospel, which as the Apostle Paul declared in *Romans 1:16*, is the power of God unto salvation? The crux of the true Gospel rests and is firmly rooted on an immovable foundation, the person of Jesus Christ. The cornerstone of the Gospel is the work of Jesus on a cross, and the victory of the Gospel is an empty tomb.

Once again, I must iterate, if you do not have Jesus right, you will end up possessing a wrong Gospel. I don't know about you but when I first came to Christ, it was as a lost soul who needed to be saved from what truly ailed my soul and conscience: SIN. It was a wonderful liberating moment for me to realize that Jesus addressed my sins on the cross, but I had to continue to learn of Jesus in order to become identified with the work of the cross.

Most people simply stop with the message of Jesus dying for the world and not the ongoing work of the person of Jesus. Jesus' great act became a means in which man can be saved, but it is the presence of the life of Jesus in us who saves us. Initial salvation is like a honeymoon where people are swinging high on sentimental branches of finding forgiveness for a sin-laden life, but the cross does not simply stand as a symbol, but it casts a line in the sand and like *Matthew 7:13-14* points out it serves as a crossroad for every soul as to whether they will continue to choose the broad path of the world and its ways of destruction or the narrow path to eternal life.

The cross is a reminder that we must bear a personal cross in order to ensure that the old is crucified so the new can be worked in us by the Spirit of God. Many simply stand in the shadow of the cross to receive forgiveness, some come to the light of the cross to be cleansed and healed, but how many come up to the cross of Christ and embrace it in order to become identified with it, allowing them to become completely consumed and hidden in the great message and hope of it?

Today I was meditating on the narrow path to life and the broad path to destruction. The picture this conjures up in one's mind seems black and white, but there is a tendency to adjust the narrow path just enough to fit it into shaky theologies, deceptive narratives, and wishful thinking.

A few years back I realized that the narrow way did not have any adjustable lines because it was a true path designed by God Himself. There was only one such path and we have a map, the Bible that points to the way and outlines the course to show us the way to our ultimate destination.

In studying the map leading to Calvary, it became clear there was no way of adjusting the path because it was truth--absolute, unadulterated truth. There was one entrance to it, but it involved becoming identified with an old rugged cross. Since truth forges the way, its narrow way is hard to accept.

The sharp edges that line the passageway are tough to adjust or hold onto, the narrow curves difficult to maneuver, the ascent into the clouds of uncertainty unnerving, and the distance a true test of character, faith, and commitment. The reason the path is narrow is because it is comprised of the work of redemption, the examples of servitude and suffering, and the teachings of one person, the Lord Jesus Christ.

There is no way of adjusting the way because Jesus Christ is the same today as He was yesterday and will be forever. We must all come in a state of utter desperation to the cross as the only altar where forgiveness for our sins can be found and life obtained.

It is in such a state of need and confession that the Father will positionally place a person in Jesus through the born-again experience. It is not enough to be identified to Christ in His death, we must become identified with Him in a new life and this can only happen if we allow the life of Christ to be worked in us and through us so we can manifest it to the world.

If Jesus Christ is not the essence of the way in which you have believed, chosen, and embraced true life by faith, and walked it out in the simple wonderment of an obedient child, then you are still on the broad path. A person may be standing at the entrance admiring the work of Christ or they may be on a religious odyssey that runs parallel to the path. They might be paving the path they are on with good intentions to do right or establishing markers of good deeds along the way, but such individuals must not be mistaken, they are on a path of their own making, their choice, and their doing and it will lead to utter spiritual ruin.

In 1991 the ministry that God entrusted to Jeannette, my co-laborer, and myself, came to a real defining moment as to our calling and mission. We were attending a missionary school at the time with the idea of being temporary missionaries in some third world country. We sensed we were in some personal and spiritual struggle but we couldn't really see our way through the long dark tunnel.

One Saturday we hit a point of real discouragement and we knew the only thing we could do was look up and seek the Lord's intervention. I will never forget what I said in my prayer, "Lord, our back is up against the wall and we need You to do something on our behalf." It is not unusual in our humanity to feel like our back is up against some immovable wall, but it can prove to be overwhelming and depressing.

Once we finished the prayer, we both felt that in some way He was going to answer our prayer. The next morning, we went to church, and in his usual manner the pastor opened in a word of prayer, but changed up the normal procedure by introducing a special song.

It is important to always take note when something is suddenly changed in such a way and I felt a certain expectation arise in me. I had never heard the song that was shared that morning before, and it would be almost twenty years after the event that I would hear it again. The crux of the song came down to a phrase, "When your back is up against the wall, remember His was against the cross." God changed a schedule and personally answered our prayers.

I learned that day that when your back is up against the wall, all you have to do is change your perspective by remembering that the wall is not your actual cross and that the One who was nailed to the cross is able to lift you above the hindering walls of this world to give you a heavenly perspective of what is eternal, important, and lasting.

One of the challenges I have is changing gears from what I am doing to being available to do what God wants me to do. Like everyone I have my preferences. My first preference is to finish my projects, but God's heart always comes down to one matter, and that is the well-being of others.

I try to make myself available to God at all times, but that means I must make myself available to people. As a minister of the Gospel, a servant of Jesus Christ, I have no personal rights to life on my terms. In fact, I must deny myself of those rights up front and then I have to become crucified to my personal selfish preferences in order to follow Jesus into true ministry.

It is easy to be a willing servant of Christ as long as it does not interfere with my projects and preferences, cut into my personal time, and cost me any real conveniences in the end. As ministers of Christ, we must remember that at our core is selfishness where pride can reign, the flesh proves fickle, feelings must be catered to, and egos must be stroked.

This is why the life of a true servant of Jesus begins with accepting the call to true discipleship that ends with one's life being offered up as a consecrated sacrifice. Dead sacrifices have no rights, ongoing sacrifices are void of carnality, and living as an available sacrifice makes you a living martyr, a witness of Christ's life that is being offered, poured into, and manifested to others.

We must always come back to the true Gospel if we are to be saved. Paul warned that he feared people would accept another gospel and he cursed those who dared to preach a perverted gospel, which he summarized in *1 Corinthians 15:1-4)*.

As believers we are commissioned to preach, proclaim, or share the Gospel. When I ask people about their salvation, I hear about pastors, churches, doctrines, and family ties, but I rarely hear a testimony about how after reading or hearing the Gospel message their heart was pricked to the core about their sin, lost state, and the reality that they were marked for God's wrath. It was in light of the grave darkness of their doomed state that the Gospel became "good news" to them as Christ was lifted up on a cross to become their solution. Instead of dying in their sin, they are now made into the righteousness of Christ for the glory of God. Instead of tasting spiritual death, they now live the wondrous everlasting life of Christ. Rather than being an instrument of unrighteousness, they have become an instrument of righteousness, and instead of facing hopelessness they walk in light of living in unending heavenly glory.

The problem is the Gospel has been perverted. "Perversion" means to add or subtract from something. If we add man's work or religious affiliation on to the gospel, we have just perverted it, and if we subtract from who Christ is, the significance of His great sacrifice, and that it was all a matter of God's grace, we have perverted it.

One of the problems is that we have made the message of the Gospel an intellectual exercise and not a matter of the heart. It is easy to see the intellectual benefit of mentally accepting the Gospel, but we are told we must receive it in our heart to be saved *(Romans 10:9-10)*. In other words, the Gospel seed must take root in our heart and be watered by the presence of God's Spirit residing in our spirit in order for the life of Christ to come forth.

It is for this reason I fear some have deluded themselves that they are saved because they mentally accepted the benefit of salvation, but it never reached their heart where a new birth took place. Jesus was clear that unless a man is born again, he will never enter the kingdom of God *(John 3:3, 5)*.

What current are you in? We are all in the current of life. This particular current is determined by God who often uses circumstances to direct our path. However, there are other currents that intercept, intertwine, and run parallel to the current of life. When man encounters these currents, he determines how he responds to them, and if he is going to allow them to shape the terrain of his soul by deciding which current to get in.

There is the current of sin and the flesh. It can be compared to the Jordan River that borders Israel. The word, "Jordan" means "descended" because it is known for its rapid descent. This river is a little more than 200 miles long and varies in width from 45 feet to 180 feet. It starts from the foothills of Mount Hermon and runs through the Sea of Galilee down to the Dead Sea. Sin also starts out in a small way, but as it takes hold of the flesh, man will quickly descend down to that which is dead and lifeless. It is for this reason the Israelites were told to cross over the Jordan where their inheritance of the Promised Land waited for them.

As believers, we must come by way of Christ's cross and cross over the murky waters of sin and the flesh to obtain our spiritual inheritance. There is the current of the world. It is like the Euphrates River that has served as the lifeline of commerce to great civilizations of the past, but where are they today? Like the world's temporary glory, they have digressed into the sands of time, and now mounds of dirt serve as their silent epitaph that marks the place of their demise.

Another current is man-made religion. It can be compared to the Tigris River which runs parallel to the Euphrates River. Occasionally the Tigris and Euphrates Rivers come together. Much of man's religion runs parallel to the Word of God, but fails to become part of the River of God. It keeps its own identity to maintain its personal kingdom, and if there is any agreement, it will be with the spirit and ways of the world. Both the Tigris and Euphrates empty into the Mediterranean Sea, where their waters cease to bring any real distinction, and likewise, one day all man-made religion will be consumed by judgment and will cease to be.

The final river is the river of God. God's River of Living Water, the Holy Spirit, flows from heaven and it is He who supplies the fountains of salvation to revive the lost soul, puts oasis in deserts for the seeking soul, provides the many tributaries of gifts to enable the willing soul to fulfill his or her calling, the stream of preparation and rest for the weary soul, and glorious pools of promise to the despairing soul. However, to benefit from God's river, we must get into its current, not to merely swim in it, but to trust it will bring us into the abundant life promised to us.

We were about to wrap up our short pause from our regular routine and begin our journey home, but before we hit the road, my two companions wanted me to see a massive tree. It was not just any tree: it was a Ponderosa Pine. It stood tall, and in a sense, alone in the midst of other pine trees. It was as if it stood as a great marker to time.

It was clear that it was old but still strong. Some of its former limbs were now snarly looking but its trunk was erect and reaching high, pointing upward. It appeared almost immovable, infallible, and to ensure the integrity of its significance the occupiers of the land cleared out the space around it. It reminded me of a memorial that reached backward to a history long forgotten, as it stood sure in the present, pointing to the promise of a future due to the ability of enduring the time yet to come. This tree reminded me of the "Old Rugged Cross."

I don't know about you but that one tree that was erected as a form of judgment leveled at mankind's sins became a personal altar to me where I left my sins at its base, looked up in trepidation to only find love personified reaching out to me. It was there, judgment was met with mercy, allowing grace to flow down as a healing balm upon my sin-ladened soul. It was there that hope became a ladder into the heavenlies and peace became a bridge to that which leads to everlasting treasures. It was there that a line was drawn in the sands of eternity, an altar erected and a sacrifice offered all on my behalf.

I don't know about you but I have cleared out a spot in my life of service and worship for that one tree. Its history points me back to justification, its presence reminds me of the ongoing work of sanctification and its endurance points me to a future life glorified by the divine and the heavenly. I realize the reason that the old rugged cross holds such a place is because it lifted up the hope of life that clarified my purpose, and defined my calling.

We know that Jesus Christ, the Lamb of God was lifted up on that altar to attract the seeking soul, the lost sheep, and the wandering spiritual vagabonds of each new generation to Himself. Yes, I cleared a spot for a tree, not as an idol or ornament, but to remind me that it is JESUS ALONE who holds my heart, owns and preserves my soul, and brings everlasting life to my spirit.

If I asked you why did Jesus die on the cross, the quick answer is that He died on the cross for my sin. You would be right, but we must never stop there. I think this is one of the reasons Christians become stunted in their spiritual growth. It is like looking at one side of the coin that has the picture of the cross and redemption on it and saying to themselves "That's all folks, that is all I need to know," but never turning over to see the figure or image on the other side.

Yes, Jesus came as God's Passover Lamb to take away sin, and yes, the redemption of the cross opened the way for us to receive eternal life and be saved, but the way to what? When we look at the cross of Christ, it is about us as to what God had to do for us to save our souls, but when you turn that coin over it becomes all about God and His desire concerning us.

When Adam disobeyed God's one command to not eat of the tree of knowledge of good and evil, sin entered into the world, but it is what sin did between God and man that broke and continues to break God's heart, and that is it caused a separation between Him and His creation. Sin broke the relationship and fellowship that God deserved, designed, and desired.

Here's the other side of the coin, Jesus died on our behalf so we could be RECONCILED back into a relationship with God. Adam, who was created to reflect God's glory in and to creation, walked and communed with God before he rebelled. He not only fell into a soulish state that could only reflect man's ineptness and depravity, the world's fading glory, and Satan's darkness, but his fall would also prevent him from being able to reach his potential that is stamped on the other side of the coin by reflecting God's glory.

We can't reflect what we are not exposed to and it is only in an ongoing relationship with God where there is true fellowship that we can be restored to our original purpose and calling.

28

REPENTANCE

Salvation truly goes back
to genuine repentance.
(Jeannette Haley)

How many of us are looking towards the New Year in the hope of seeing certain things happen in our life, possibly changing something about ourselves we don't like, or meeting a goal that has been put on our bucket list? I don't know about you, but I tend to put off today what I need to do or start, thinking that tomorrow I will be ready or more prepared to do it, which allows me to put off giving up something I needed to in the first place to carry out my plan.

Sadly, this is how it is when it comes to God. Certain people put off all types of aspects of religion which includes salvation, repentance, consecration, and even callings. The Apostle Paul gave this warning in *2 Corinthians 6:2, "today is the day of salvation."* People want to put off the salvation of their souls until the last hour and minute so they can squeak into heaven after tasting the deadly fruits of the age. They avoid turning around in repentance and honestly facing God to resolve the real issue of their soul.

The problem with avoiding repentance that leads to salvation is that we have to resist the Spirit's attempts to bring awareness to our spirits to respond to our need to repent, our plight to be saved, and our desperate need to get real and do business with God to establish a sure witness in our souls. *Genesis 6:3* reminds us the Spirit will not always strive with us and it we fail to heed to Him when He is prompting us to do so, He will eventually withdraw His presence from us, leaving us no place of repentance as Esau discovered after he sold his birthright (*Hebrews 12:16-17*).

The one thing I often think of is empty chairs. This must seem a little strange, but empty chairs represent the people who were a big part of my life but are no longer. Chairs not only fill a space, but a particular place. Whether it is that chair that becomes a place where one finds comfort and rest in the living room, or the chair at the dinning room table that was always filled by that one person, those close to us have always filled certain spaces of our heart with their person (personality) and a particular place in our lives with their presence.

The empty space triggers bygone memories and the hollow place reminds us of the importance a person played in our life. These empty chairs become more so prevalent as I get older and the cycle of life continues as an older generation gives way to a new generation. I am reminded of how our lives are but vapors, the rising of breath that can sometimes be seen in the dark, cold shadows and twilights of snippets of time. They are here one minute and gone the next moment.

In the Jewish home a custom was observed by leaving a certain chair empty at particular celebration. This custom was in reference to *Malachi 4:5-6* to remind the people of Israel that a man of Elijah's calling and status was coming and that they must be prepared to welcome and embrace him and his message. We know that man to be John the Baptist. He came after 400 years of silence from God to prepare the people, but was not always embraced as he called them to repentance for the kingdom of heaven was near (Jesus).

Are you a Christian in appearance only or is your life before the Lord a heart matter? You can have a type of repentance without true conversion, but you can't have true conversion without godly repentance. There are pseudo repentances.

There is the repentance where you comply outwardly, but hold onto your way of thinking, which reveals that your mind has never been transformed. There are those who outwardly reform their actions, but their heart attitude remains the same as they only reformed their outward actions.

Another pseudo repentance is when the person simply performs. This means the individual takes on another image or acting role that gives the impression they are lining up, but they remain unyielded, holding on to independence of the soul and when others are not looking, they are going to do what they want to do.

Finally, you have those who conform outwardly to get people off their back, but their will to ultimately have life on their terms remain cemented in concrete. True repentance involves the change of mind and action, while conversion entails the change of heart attitude as the will lines up to what is true and right.

The truth of the matter is you can give the appearance of repentance, but you can't fake true conversion because it will come out in a right attitude and in honorable actions that bring glory to the Lord

History repeats itself and the problem we are seeing now with pandemics, and etc, has happened before and it would behoove us to find out what they discovered then and the psychology behind it. It is clear we need to understand what we are up against so we can make viable decisions about what do to in regard to our own health and life.

This brings us to the question, who are we looking to, to deliver us? Some are looking towards the medical profession, some to government, others to individuals, some to great causes, and others to wishful thinking, but the truth is none of these institutions, political movements, individuals, or philosophies can deliver us. There is only one who delivers us and that is the Lord Jesus Christ.

Instead of desperately looking around for deliverance, it is time for man to fall on his face in true repentance of his sin, in complete brokenness over his indifferent attitude towards God, and look up to the only true deliverer. Meanwhile, we need to always be open to be part of the solution when it comes to present-day challenges, and not part of the problem because of a lukewarm spiritual life.

I am not always up on terms and when I read "red pill," on certain information, I had no clue what it meant until I asked a brother in the Lord. He shared with me that the term came from a movie, "The Matrix."

In this movie they had a "blue bill" for those who desired their own reality which allowed them to live in the dreamland of sleep, while the "red bill" was for those who desired the real truth of what was going on so they could confront it. The catch with taking the "red bill" is that once taken, a person can never go back to sleep and live in some false dreamland.

Jesus said that in the end days there would be much deception. Needless to say, as believers we must never settle for a false reality, but I must admit Paul's instructions to believers reveals that we can take the "blue bill" of worldly deception along with others because the desire to maintain our own reality can prove to be stronger than loving the truth.

In Rome the Apostle Paul exhorted those asleep to awake out of sleep for salvation was even nearer, while in Corinth, they were told to awake to righteousness, and in Ephesus, they were instructed to wake out of their sleepy state and arise from their stupor and Christ would give them light to walk circumspectly, not as fools but as wise, redeeming the time because the days are evil *(Romans 13:11; 1 Corinthians 15:34; Ephesians 4:16-18)*.

It is human to want to control reality to avoid the unpleasantness of wickedness, and it is understandable to want to direct our personal reality to avoid the challenges and devastation around us, but it is also a matter of pride to ignore, reject, become unteachable, easily insulted, and stiff-necked towards what is true. Sadly, it is obvious that a nation of people (as well as some in the church) took a "blue bill" and went to sleep and now in the midst of what they declare to be a "great awakening," the last thing we must avoid is pointing the finger.

As a nation or a sleepy church there is only one response that will prepare us to face the depth of wickedness that has become a deadly, consuming cancer in every arena of life, and that is personal repentance. We must consider if we love the truth enough to guard it, fear God enough to trust and do what is pleasing to Him, care enough to keep our spiritual edge to discern what is going on so we can warn others, and be ever ready for deliverance to come from above as we walk in the ways of truth and righteousness towards the promises of heaven.

Truth will always cause some type of disturbance. For those who embrace it, it will shake them at different times, to those who become awaken it will shock them, to those who are ignorant it will cause fear, and for those who have a high opinion of self in one way or the other, it will insult them.

The other day I talked about the blue and red pills. There are different types of blue pills that can be taken by those who want to choose their particular reality, whether it is delusion, catering to feelings, denial, fantasy, worldly causes, and/or drug induced stupors to keep fragile realities going, but there is only one red pill. You have to keep taking the blue pill to keep from waking up from any false reality, but the red bill is intended to not only wake you up to reality, but it won't let you go back to sleep because you now know too much, the good with the bad, the bad with the ugly, the ugly with the insane, and the insane with the absolute face of evil.

God is truth and will never offer a "blue pill" to endure the days we are in. In fact, we are told to redeem them. We must make sure that we walk in the truth by ever partaking of the "red pill" of His truth and by faith walk it out. However, to avoid the "blue pill," we must repent of not loving the truth enough to endure the times because we are sojourners who are walking by faith towards what is eternal and true and not according to what our fragile psyches are willing to accept.

It is easy to want to point our fingers at everyone else for the mess we are in as a nation and the church, but we must stop and ask ourselves some tough questions. We must acknowledge that the state of affairs we are in did not happen overnight. The problem with "deep sleep," for any group of people, is that in such a state they are content to assume all is well as they remain clueless and unaware of the watchmen who have been trying to warn them for years of the enemy's advancement.

As a result, the enemy has penetrated the wall, torn down the gate, and is now among us. As you know, people who are first awakened out of a deep sleep are not prepared to immediately respond. They are shocked at what they see, confused by what they need to do, and can easily give into an insipid fear. Those who are awake must avoid judging those who have been asleep.

As believers there is only one red pill and that is truth, but truth must be preserved by righteousness, and righteousness by the disciplines of godliness. Truth is not only a matter of choice, but it must be the sole preference of a person when it comes to facing life. Truth is hard because it is offensive since it will not placate, soften the blow, or dance around what is true and right. It will prove to be uncomfortable due to being sharp, agitating because it will not be moved, and arouse explosive responses due to being absolute, but it is what sets the captive free from any false reality to realistically and honestly face what is, and repent of what is not right in order to walk victoriously through it.

We must remember truth will come back to the Person, teachings, and examples of Jesus Christ. In Christ truth is freeing, reality is hopeful, repentance is cleansing, honesty is refreshing, and promises can be found in abundance.

Clearly, our nation is in a crisis and at a tipping point. Sadly, it takes a great crisis to wake people up who are comfortable and who have fallen asleep in their easy chair and pews. The good news is that that people of this country have been awakened, but we must ask to what and by what?

Many will admit America needs a spiritual awakening but to what? There can be a religious and spiritual awakening, but will it lead people to the right God, to recognize the real problem, and to discern the correct solution to make sure that we are hitting the right mark.

The other day I watched as people were called to come into agreement and pray for this country. It is commendable, but which God are they praying too, what spirit is present, and what are they seeking in prayer? The Word is clear without agreement in the right spirit and coming to the place of agreement as to who we are praying to, there is no authority or power in such prayer.

The authority in prayer is found in Jesus Christ of the Bible, and the power in prayer is that it hits the mark of God's will. Spiritual awakening for Christians will always bring them back to the source of the problem, which is sin and the solution to the problem, which is repentance and brokenness over that sin, in order to line them up to the will of God as to what needs to be done.

We could be very well watching the last days harvest taking place before Jesus' coming, but we must guard our relationship with Him as to the spirit we come into agreement with, guard our life in Him with integrity, and our walk before Him as to whether something is Scripturally acceptable.

REDEMPTION

Our redemption was not by muscle,
but by love. It was not wrought
by vengeance, but by forgiveness.
It was not by sword, but by sacrifice.
(Unknown)

Genesis 3:15 reminds me of God's promise to send a Redeemer. We know it points to Jesus Christ, the blessed Son of God. This promise was given because man lost it all, his relationship with God and Paradise because of one rebellious action.

Since man lost it in a garden, we see where Jesus had to go by way of another garden, Gethsemane, where His journey to Calvary addressed and paid the price for our sins. Man desires to somehow secure his own Paradise of peace and harmony, but sadly he wants to do it outside of God and the redemption He provided through His Son.

As a result, man is always falling into one of the temptations of the serpent. Such deceptive and seductive temptations blind him to his real state, as he fails to realize that he can only find Paradise when he faces his need to be redeemed in light of the great destruction of sin upon his life that can only be addressed by the work of Jesus on the cross.

Rayola Kelley

I am often reminded of how God had to redeem me from the claims and works of sin and death on my life. What a process He had to put forth to ensure such redemption. Jesus had to empty Himself of His sovereignty to reign in order to adjust His nature to take on the disposition of a servant. He then was fashioned as a man in the womb of a woman after a miraculous intervention by the Holy Spirit.

Jesus was born in the midst of grave darkness and remained in obscurity most of His first thirty years in a small community called Nazareth. He started His ministry at age 30 and became a powerful revelation of God in the midst of great national and spiritual darkness. His Spirit and ways caused His life to burn brightly for three years, only to be put out by the darkness of death and the grave. However, this darkness would only reign three days on earth, then the light would be brought forth from the grave in resurrection glory and power.

Being a follower of Jesus has involved ongoing change in the terrain of my soul. Such changes remind me that I am a sojourner in this present world, and my prayer is simple, "Lord, thank You for preserving my soul in darkness, enabling my spirit to soar above this world in praise and worship, and ultimately leading me home."

When we think of the Moabite Ruth, grandmother of King David, we think in terms of her giving up her gods, family, and home to follow Naomi to Bethlehem *(Ruth 1:16-18)*. This sounds noble, but the reality is that Ruth was not pursuing just any god, she wanted to know the one true God of Israel.

What we overlook is that Ruth was introduced to this God and drawn to Him through Naomi. Her steadfast faithfulness and desire brought her to the feet of Boaz, and there she was redeemed (purchased) and placed at his table as his wife.

If we know our Redeemer Jesus Christ, are we like Naomi, seasoned enough to attract the Ruth's of the world to eventually sit at the feet of Jesus as they are placed in the Living Church, His future bride? We must remember there must be a Naomi before a Ruth can find her way to the one true God and His redemption.

Are you standing in the redemption of Christ? Jesus is wisdom, righteousness, sanctification, and redemption to us. As Christians it is easy for us to talk about salvation, but without redemption there would be no salvation. Because of Christ's death on the cross, we have been bought back from the claims of sin on our lives; thereby, possessing the means to avoid spiritual death or separation from the Lord. However, we must be in Christ to benefit from His redemption.

It is in Christ we stand as a redeemed people, but to be placed there we must receive Christ as our only provision to address all sin, knowing that He alone is the only one who could have paid the necessary debt to buy us back from this harsh taskmaster. Jesus made it clear that this redemption was complete when He declared from the cross, "IT IS FINISHED."

Those three words should not only bring great awe to us, but they should cause us to realize we do not belong to ourselves nor are we to do what we please, while somehow sliding into heaven. Slides go one way: down. If we are sliding it will not be into heaven.

Redemption implies we have been snatched out of the clutches of tyranny and ransomed from terrible captivity to be restored to a life we have been called to live. Redemption reveals we have a choice. We can remain slaves to sin, knowing the end result will be spiritual death or we can choose Jesus, and be placed in Him because of His redemption.

Redemption reminds us that if we are to choose the full benefit of being redeemed, we must choose the headship of Christ over the headship of Adam (man). We must choose God as our master over the master of sin, and we must choose coming into agreement with the risen Christ over trying to somehow appease the Law in our flesh and hope we make it to heaven.

It is important to point out we will not know the fullness of our redemption until the day we receive our new glorified bodies *(Ephesians 1)*. May we be among those of *Psalm 107:2* who declare, *"Let the redeemed of the LORD say so, whom he hath redeemed from the hand of the enemy."*

A statement in the Bible that causes me to pause is found in the last part of *Genesis 7:16, "and the LORD shut him in."* There are many doors but there was only one ark with one door. We can debate about how big that door was, but the reality is most people want to enter any other door but the one door.

These individuals may stand afar off and consider the door, get as close as they can, walk in front of it, and even dance before it but unless they enter through that door into the ark of salvation that God has provided, they will not be spared from His wrath.

It is important to note God commanded the ark to be built, and Noah built it and made it available to anyone who would believe his preaching to enter in, but in the end only eight souls entered in. When the time came, God (who ordained the building of that door) was also the one who shut Noah away from His wrath.

God has provided another door for His sheep to enter into, Jesus *(John 10:1-7)*. It takes faith to enter through the door in order to be spared from the wrath to come, and the question is what are you doing about that door? It is not enough to consider it and hope you are close enough that God will accept such a half-hearted attempt.

Today is the day of salvation, the day of entering through the door of redemption, all the way into the life of Christ, remembering that Jesus is coming for His church and those who have not entered into His redemption by faith will in the end find a closed door *(Matthew 25:1-13)*.

RECONCILIATION

*An upright relationship with God
keeps us dependent on Him, teachable
before Him, and honorable in Him.
(Rayola Kelley)*

We start out with life in us. However, the cycle of life ends in physical death. We see this reality all around us as those we love, our friends and acquaintances, prove to be nothing more than a mere vapor when once the breath exits the physical body for the last time, leaving a lifeless shell behind. We wrestle with the idea of death because we fear the unknown. At times we might ask ourselves, is this all life consists of, or is there an eternal dimension that physical death serves as a door to?

The truth is we can't imagine any other existence but the one we are living; therefore, we almost see ourselves as immortal, infallible, and immune from the claims of physical death upon us. If there is an unseen eternal dimension beyond this world, we either avoid looking at it, or we live in a type of denial that it will not happen to us, but when we encounter the reality of life being but a vapor, we encounter the shock of unbelief, the shaking of fear, or the despair of hopelessness.

As Christians we wade through the emotional fallout that comes when a soul parts from this world, but eventually we come to land on the promise of possessing eternal life and a future resurrection in a new body. We have hope because we know that past this world eternal glory awaits us. We have the heavenly breath of God in us because we have been born again with God's very breath, the Holy Spirit. We have been redeemed, placed in the family of God; therefore, we have a spiritual inheritance that will be ours to claim.

In the past there are many who have asked what it means to inherit the unseen, heavenly life, and it comes down to identification with the cross of Christ, embracing the redemption that secures our eternal destiny, being sealed by the Holy Spirit, and resting in the fact that we are indeed children of God, heirs of salvation, and joint heirs of glorification with Christ.

This brings us down to what connects us to this great inheritance which is something called reconciliation. We have been reconciled back into a relationship with God through Jesus' work and death on the cross, and His resurrection. We can get caught up on various aspects of salvation, but what really serves as our witness to salvation is that we indeed have a living, growing relationship with our Creator, our God, our Redeemer, and our Savior.

When we talk about Jesus' death on the cross, it is natural as believers to think of salvation. It is true Jesus died to saved us. However, salvation points to deliverance. Jesus died so we could be delivered from the master and reign of sin on our lives and the claim of spiritual death on our soul, as well as the judgment of damnation that awaits those who fail to receive His provision.

Salvation points to Jesus as our Savior, but salvation was a tool of redemption, a means to buy us back from our harsh taskmaster of sin and our dreadful inheritance of death, while providing a place of justification where our sins could be forgiven and we could stand justified. Jesus' mission was to save us, but it was for the purpose of carrying out His ministry. And, what is His ministry—that of reconciliation *(2 Corinthians 5:18-19)*.

Christ died for the ungodly because God commended His love towards each of us while we were yet sinners that Jesus should become that sacrifice, the payment for our sins in order to provide a bridge between God and His enemies. Enemies are treacherous and will undermine the work, the plan, and the advancement of those whom they oppose. And, who are God enemies? The ungodly and the sinner.

If people are honest, they will have to admit that there are times they act and live contrary to godliness revealing their ungodly state, and when they examine themselves, they can't help but admit that at times their foul moods and ungrateful attitudes, along with their lack of resolve and inward character and rebellious actions have in some way broken the law or covenant of God. But, for many people they can't envision they are an actual enemy of God *(Romans 5:6-10)*.

To be an enemy of God means a person is standing on the side of death, separated from real life, and marked for failure, defeat, judgment, and wrath. Jesus' death has the power to translate the ungodly, take away the iniquity of the sinner, cleansing them, and bringing peace to God's enemies who were far away through reconciliation. Clearly, Jesus' death is not just about deliverance from sin, but reconciling us back into a relationship with our Creator.

We often forget that what Adam lost in the garden because of sin was his relationship with God. We can tout we are saved, but the real key is, are we reconciled back to God in a living, growing, active relationship? It is in a relationship with God that one truly finds complete restoration of spirit and soul.

I often ponder what I refer to as the three R's of Christianity: Redemption, Reconciliation, and Righteousness. Redemption is all about us. It reminds us of the cross where Jesus Christ paid the great price of His life to redeem our souls from the claims of sin and the curse of death upon them. We have indeed been bought with a price and we no longer belong to ourselves, but we are now part of an eternal plan, and we must remember for this plan to be fully realized we must come into line with the will of God.

The purpose of redemption is that of reconciliation. Reconciliation is all about relationship. It is God's heart that we be re-established in a relationship with Him that had been lost in the Garden of Eden. He wants us to walk in the garden of sweet fellowship with Him that will surely bring spiritual restoration to our souls through the work of sanctification that enables us to reach our potential of reflecting Jesus' image in this dark world.

Sanctification is the process of bringing us to a state of holiness so that we will develop the peaceful fruit of righteousness in our life. Righteousness has to do with our attitude in our relationship with the Lord. This attitude will influence our approach, discipline our responses, and ensure our authority in our prayer life and our walk.

As Christians we must make sure we do not stop at redemption because we now have eternal life, or assume much about reconciliation unless our relationship with the Lord is active and growing; thus, falling short of allowing the right attitude to be developed within. This is what will ensure us that we reach our potential by being a reflection of Christ to others, who is the essence of our righteousness.

THE REALITY OF GOD

We are constantly being prepared
to walk IN our life in Christ, be refined
to walk OUT our life for His glory,
and being transformed to walk

THROUGH our life because of who He is.
(Rayola Kelley)

The challenge for every one of us is to avoid putting the eternal God in some theological box because we want to control our understanding about Him, or try to contain Him within unscriptural notions to control the narrative about Him, not only in our lives, but in the lives of others. We also must avoid taking on the self-serving "waiting to see attitude" as to if God is true before we believe Him.

Faith is a choice of the heart and is child-like in response, and people who start from any of these three premises mentioned have already started from a point of unbelief that will cause them to buy a lie and slide into some quasi state where they become indifferent to truth that does not fit into their understanding. Eventually, they reject the ways of God because it will not confirm their narrative, and ultimately end up walking away from the true God of heaven because it will not serve their worldly, selfish purposes.

There is a saying, "Grow where you are planted." As believers, the question is do you believe you are right where you are because God has directed your footsteps to such a place? Perhaps, you believe circumstances have led you there or the choices of other people.

The one question Christians have to settle in their mind in order to grow where they are planted is, "Does God direct all of our footsteps?" God is sovereign. In other words, nothing occurs in His people's lives unless He allows it, but how many Christians understand His sovereignty?

For example, are we bitter, resentful, or angry at the place we are in now? If we are and God is sovereign, in control, and is good all of the time then WHO are we being bitter (hostile), resentful (offended), and angry (irritated) towards? Granted, we often direct such feelings at others to avoid facing who we are grumbling about, frustrated with, and ungrateful towards.

Either God is God or He is not and where we have been planted has been at His bidding and not a matter of circumstances, fate, or other people's choices. Granted God may use circumstances or other people to plant us in certain places, but it is not a matter of fate, it is a matter of God wanting to do a deeper work in us according to calling, a greater work on our behalf according to His plan, and work through us in light of our mission.

When we refuse to accept that God has us at a particular place, we can miss what He is doing in us, what He is doing in our midst, and what He can do through us. If we are focused on our way instead of going with the flow of what He wants to accomplish, we will not only miss His incredible workings, but many times we will fail to see the miraculous.

I have wrestled with God in the past about His choice to plant me in a certain harvest field, move me to a different location, and put me among a variety of "seedlings" I knew nothing about, but in due time I had to humble myself and acknowledge what is so; "God, Your sovereignty is beyond comprehension, Your ways perfect, Your plan on target, and Your character good. Lord, not my will but Your will be done."

The question is are you taking this moment, this time in your life to grow in your relationship with God, and in your knowledge of Jesus Christ, or are you allowing the root of bitterness to take hold, the weeds of resentment to grow up, and the storm of anger to build up in your soul? If so, you will not prove to be a thriving plant in the barren wilderness of this world, but a mere bump on some log that will have no spiritual effect on anyone.

Who do you say I am? Jesus asked His disciples this very question in *Matthew 16:13-19*. It is easy to assume we know the answer but *Matthew 24* warns us that many will be deceived and the greatest point of deception comes down to who we believe and say Jesus Christ is.

For me I learned I had many such assumptions about God before I truly learned who He was. For the most part, my concepts of Him were sentimental at best and very vague at worst. I was surprised that my understanding came from others, and that the problem with words and titles are that they can be surface and lack true substance.

It is easy for people to repeat what is being said about God and the Lord Jesus Christ without any real understanding. For example, it is

43

easy to use the term God but what God and who is the God you believe in?

We have a Bible whose main purpose is to reveal God to us. The problem is people approach the Bible to confirm doctrine, to debate it, and to use it to uphold what they think, but how many truly approach the Bible to believe what it says about God? The Bible is clear what we need to seek in it and why we must seek it, *"Seek the LORD, and ye shall live"* *(Amos 5:6).*

The Apostle Paul was concerned that believers would get away from the simplicity of Christ, and what is the simplicity of Christ? He is the ONLY way to salvation. It is for this reason that when it comes to the unsaved, we are not to preach or promote anything other than Christ and Him crucified.

As Christians we must be reminded that we are heirs of faith (not of certain denominations, laws, or practices) that identify us as the spiritual seed of Abraham whose faith allowed him to see the day of Christ in the figure of his own son, Isaac and rejoice in it as he looked for a city made by the hands of God *(John 8:56-58).* It is that same gift of faith that Abraham possessed that allows us as believers to see who Jesus is and needs to be to us.

The Bible tells us that Jesus is the foundation of true faith, the cornerstone to all that is true and right, and the head or authority that is to influence all matters concerning His Body. He is Lord, the overseer of His household, the king over an unseen kingdom that will be unveiled one day, and the ultimate judge who will judge all matters of the heart and conduct.

He is the Son of God (deity) who was fashioned as man and clothed in humanity (Son of man), and commissioned as the Messiah (Anointed One) to preach the Gospel, heal broken hearts, set the captive free, and heal those bruised by sin. He became the Lamb of God who would take away the sin of the world in order to become the Savior to all who would believe that He was, is and always will be God's solution to the sin problem that truly ails all humanity *(Luke 4:18-19; John 1:29).*

Yesterday, I talked about who Jesus is. The reason I wanted to establish a testimony of who Jesus Christ is, is because if you do not believe that Jesus is God that came in the flesh, the Promised Messiah, and the only Savior, then you are on shallow ground that, when shaken, whatever religious foundation you have will collapse into complete ruin.

Jesus asked Peter who did men say He was and then He asked Peter who did he say He was. Peter answered correctly because it had been revealed to him from heaven. Jesus is the only way, the only entrance into the promise of eternal life, but there is only one true Jesus who fits all the qualifications as set forth in Scripture. It is for this reason the way to heaven is narrow.

If you don't get Jesus right, you will not be established on the sure foundation according to what the Word declares about Him. You will fail to line your attitude and life up to Him as the only cornerstone, missing the opportunity of entering through the narrow entrance. And, if you fail to come under His authority, you will miss fulfilling your high calling in His Kingdom.

I haven't been on Facebook much because I'm still trying to gain my energy back after having what appeared to be flu like symptoms. The truth is, I don't have much energy but I must continue to ignore the low energy in order to maintain a semblance of life.

As stated, we take energy for granted. When we are young, we have boundless energy, but as you get older you easily find out that personal energy is like the tides. It can ebb in and out depending on the circumstances. When I have very little energy, my practice is quite simple, I ask God for every bit of energy I need to get through each demand.

We forget how dependent we are on God until we have to look to Him for what we take for granted. We always think energy will be there when needed, but the truth is man's strength is here one day and gone the next. It is not dependable and can be unpredictable and will prove to be limited.

The Lord has never let me down when it comes to making His strength available to me. I am so thankful that I know the God of the universe and the Apostle Paul stated the obvious *in Acts 17:27 and 28a*, *"That they should seek the Lord, if haply they might feel after him, and find him, though he be not far from every one of us: for in him we live, and move, and have our being."*

According to *Proverbs 6:16-19* there are seven things God hates. The writer of this section of Proverbs was clear that God hated six things and then went on to say, "Yea, seven are an abomination unto him."

Abomination points to "loathing" something. Was the writer adding the last one as an afterthought or did he miscount up front and realize that there were seven things God hates? Perhaps, he wanted to highlight the seventh thing because the first six are obvious, such as pride, lying lips, murder of the innocent, hearts that devise wicked imaginations, feet that are swift to carry out such mischief, and false witnesses, while the last one is more covert, making it a greater threat.

The sins mentioned reveal the iniquity, the moral flaw, and deviance of man's character. Pride is hard to pinpoint because it can be clothed in so-called "nobility," while lies are often covered up by excuses and ruses, and murder of the innocent is overlooked or deemed as being acceptable in the realms of abortion, offering our children to idols and Satan, and oppressing and trying to destroy the righteous.

Our hearts can secretly devise ways to pursue wickedness and those who carry out wicked deeds do so under the cover of darkness to avoid repercussions. And, finally we have those false witnesses, who murder a person's reputation behind their back with gossip, and innuendoes and slander that are falsely labeled with words such as "concern." What is the last sin mentioned? It is "sowing discord among brethren."

Today there are many seeds of discord being planted in homes, among families, and Christians. Seeds of discord divide and a house divided against itself will fall. Agreement among even two or three in God's kingdom can stand and withstand great opposition. This brings me back to the question as to why this last sin was highlighted. Stay tuned for tomorrow's post and see what my conclusion is to this question.

Yesterday I asked a question concerning the seven things God hated. I have wondered why the writer seemed to put an emphasis on "sowing discord among the brethren." I believe there is one big reason for this sin being mentioned last. At the core of this sin, you will find the other six sins present.

There is always pride reigning when there is discord, and those who sow discord are often lying to themselves about the real truth of the matter. Their "concern" or "feeling" about something that made them uncomfortable shows a failure to discern as to whether their concern is really warranted or they were simply imagining some offense, because they were in a touchy state or a wrong spirit.

It is at such moments that man's natural tendency is to look around for some unsuspecting, innocent culprit who is somehow attached to their negative feeling, giving their pride a platform to stand upon as judge. Needless to say, pride or Satan will magnify the offense or so-called "grave concern" that has been mounting the stairs of logic. Once the imagination swings on the branches of pettiness and speculation, the person becomes justified in their mind as to their conclusions, without considering the destructive results of relationships, reputations, and lives. By this time, the individual becomes blinded to the board of arrogance in their eye and to the fact that a critical spirit has just become the jury.

Their next step is to find others to agree with them and confirm their attitudes. Needless to say, the first seed of discord has been planted in the person's imagination by pride, the next seed of discord is being planted in the hearts of others and the result is that often the unsuspecting "culprit" is falsely accused, ending in division where a type of cruel execution, or tearing apart of relationships takes place with the dull knife of suspicion.

The next time you hear the term "sowing discord among brethren," because of something destructive going on among the brethren, know

God loathes it and make sure you are not the one planting the seeds because of moral deviation, vain imaginations, or being in the wrong spirit.

Man has sought the "fountain of youth" where youth and strength remain the same, and I have discovered that fountain, it is called "memories."

I am sure you have been in a situation where your eyes spanned over a group of people and you see a face that catches your attention enough that you stop and actually look at the individual. There is something familiar about that person, but you can't connect them to a name in order to establish any history, time, or place in which you could actually identify who and how you know them.

This happened to me recently and I scrambled to connect all the dots so I would not embarrass myself. I finally recognized the person in spite of the changes. I realized I didn't recognize him up front for a couple of reasons. First, I was not looking for him, and secondly, since I was not looking for him, I was not expecting to see him.

The third reason I didn't recognize him is because his looks were different from the last time I saw him. He not only had matured quite nicely, but he was wearing a beard. My memories were clear about him, but time is the channel in which we observe and become part of the gradual changes that take place to the point that someone is not just familiar to us but we know them.

I don't know about you but I am looking for Jesus because I am expecting Him to come at any moment. However, the question I had to ask myself is will I recognize Him for who He is. Jesus' hometown recognized Him as the hometown boy, but not as the Messiah. The beloved John had laid his head on Jesus' chest the night He was betrayed, but in *Revelation 1*, when the apostle encountered Him as King and Judge, he fell as if dead before His feet.

Time marches on, while memories of yesteryear remain stuck in the midst of shadows and outlines. Today, there are many claiming to be Jesus and as a result my eyes are quickly spanning over the insanity of our time because I will not settle for a false Jesus. However, it comes back to a simple question, "Am I simply familiar with Jesus who remains unchanged because I have failed to grow in the knowledge and relationship with Him, or will I immediately know Him when He comes. *First John 3:2 says, "Beloved, now are we the sons of God, and it doth not yet appear what we shall be: but we know that when he shall appear, we shall be like him; for we shall see him as he is."*

I don't know about you but I get weary with those in Christendom venturing out into the extremes when it comes to who God is. He is either too mushy or too strict. He is either looking the other way where sin is concerned or frowning as He is about to deliver some devastating blows.

When I listen to these people who are operating in the extreme talk about God, I either hear all about His love, but not His chastisement, His mercy but not that He is being longsuffering, His grace but not about His holiness, and His incredible goodness but not about His consuming jealousy or vice versa if one is on the other side of the extreme. The truth is, there is a balance between extremes that Christians must come back to if they are going to present the Lord in the right light, and that balance has to do with the fact that He is Just.

In other words, the Lord is just and fair in His judgments, ways, and responses. When we try to weigh out these different characteristics of God and we fail to counterbalance them with His justice, that which is true, honorable, and right, we will fail to discern His response in the matter.

For instance, God is love, but love does not rejoice in iniquity and as a result He loves us enough to chastise us so we can partake of holiness. God is merciful and as a result He chooses to be longsuffering towards those who insist on walking in their rebellious ways because it is not His will that they perish in their sin. He is full of grace, but He is holy and grace will only reign in our life through righteousness. He is good, but goodness has to do with moral uprightness and He will not share love, commitment, devotion, service, and worship with any other god or idol in our life. When His authority, place, or position is threatened, He can become a consuming fire.

Rayola Kelley

We need to make sure our presentation of Christ is balanced so people will realize His work of love, mercy, and grace on our behalf was so we could be made in the righteousness of God.

Many people are looking to various saviors to save them from destruction. For example, many people are looking to government to save them, but government often is the organization that will oppress and destroy people in the end. Some people look to religious affiliations, but such affiliation has no means to spiritually save a person. The latest is to look to science to preserve man, which is known as "Transhumanism."

Man may worship his intelligence, but he forgets where it came from, God. The roots of this latest science can be found in the practice of freezing the body, head, or brain, because these individuals believe the soul is in the head, so that when science invents the way to resurrect the person with a different body, regardless of whether it is mechanical such as with bionic parts or even robotic, that the person (personality, abilities, and intelligence) will be intact because the brain has been preserved.

We know the brain and the soul are not the same. The brain is physical and enables a person's physical body to function, but the soul represents the will, intellect, and emotions of the person. To me the present pursuit of man is beginning to sound more like the days of Noah where every imagination of the thoughts of their hearts were continually evil and Babel, where the people thought nothing would be restrained from them that they have imagined to do *(Genesis 6:5, 11:6)*.

With this in mind we must remember the Lord destroyed Noah's world with a flood and brought man's intellectual pursuit at Babel to a standstill by confusing their language. And, how will God judge this latest attempt of man to be God? He will do it with a great tribulation that will usher in the second coming of the King of kings in glory, Jesus Christ who will judge all matters and set them right.

GOD'S WILL

Religion is obedience to God,
the voluntary submission of the soul
to the will of God.
(Charles Finney)

Are you struggling with the concept of the will of God? God's will is often nothing more than a romantic concept at best and a vague notion at worst. The Christians I talk to want to do God's will but they do not understand what it entails.

To do God's will mean lining my will up to His will. I was once asked, "If there is a God why do all these bad things happen?" Just because bad things happen doesn't mean that God does not exist and that He is not good.

It is true God has supreme say over everything that goes on in this world, but God will not step over man's will to force him to do right nor will He try to bend man to His will to keep him from doing wrong. The reality is that bad things happen because man has chosen to do it his way and not God's way.

Man's way brings devastation, destruction, and death but sadly he will rarely own the consequences of his way while conveniently blaming God for the devastating fallout. I realized a long time ago I did not want to find myself in the category that the children of Israel were in. *Hebrews 3:10* states, *"Wherefore I was grieved with that generation, and said, they do always err in their heart; and they have not known my ways."*

There are three words that can cause confusion for the believer: surrender, submission, and subordination. When you check out these three words in Scripture, the one that is highlighted and used in light of our relationship with God and each other is submission.

Enemies demand your surrender to their will, and tyrants call for you to become subordinate to their whims, while godly submission responds to that which becomes excellent in action, fruitful in results, and will properly benefit others. It is important to understand these words because subordination is often used in place of submission.

Subordination is where we become dutifully enslaved to totally come under the authority of another, and surrender is not a popular word because it means to "give up" and to become subject to something contrary to one's will. God does not demand we surrender to Him or become subordinate to Him; rather, He asks us to submit to His will, His work, His way, and His plan.

True godly submission points to giving way to something that is considered, counted, and known to be worthy of such action. True submission will not give way to anything that is inferior, dishonorable, or destructive. In godly submission we put aside our personal will in order give way to that which is righteous. We become a humble instrument in the hands of God, a pliable vessel in His service, a willing subject in His kingdom to do His bidding, a faithful servant in His household to carry out His will, and a prepared soldier in His army that will carry out His plan.

For example, Jesus loved us first so we could love Him. As believers we do not dutifully come into subordination to God; instead, we willingly submit out of love because He first loved us. We are not forced to come into line with His will; rather, out of love we desire to do His will because He is worthy of such honor. We do not surrender to Him in reluctant obedience; rather, we prefer to please Him by obeying what we know is morally honorable that will bring Him glory.

It is easy to test our Christianity by our actions alone while failing to test our heart motive by being honest about the attitude behind them. Jesus never stated that we would be known by our doctrines and our actions but whether we truly have love for Him because we have genuine love for others.

Are you following the example of Jesus? Jesus became subordinate to His Father's will and learned obedience through suffering which came by way of self-denial (*Matthew 16:24-25; Philippians 2:6-8; Hebrews 5:8, 9*). Jesus said that doing His Father's will was His meat (*John 4:34*).

Today many religious people stay with the milk of the doctrine because they can maintain a worldly attitude, while some graduate to eating bread by partaking of Jesus (coming into agreement) on some matters but not all, rendering His life into a type of milk toast. However, to partake of the meat of the kingdom of God means one must be doing the will of God.

The writer of Hebrews actually voiced his frustration about Christians' unwillingness to grow up in *Hebrews 5:12-14, "For when for the time ye ought to be teachers, ye have need that one teach you again which be the first principles of the oracles of God; and are become such as have need of milk, and not of strong meat. For every one that useth milk is unskillful in the word of righteousness: for he is a babe. But strong meat belongeth to them that are of full age, even those who by reason of use have their sense exercised to discern both good and evil."*

If not submitted to the will of God, man's will, will be in competition with God's will. You cannot intellectually make a judgment call on good and evil; rather, it must be discerned. Some things considered good have evil intent and some things classified as evil by the world and the flesh, may be of God.

The Bible is clear about such matters. In *1 Corinthians 2:12* and *13* we are told that we have not received the spirit of the world and that the things we speak are not according to man's wisdom but that which the Holy Spirit reveals by enabling us to compare spiritual things with spiritual things. The apostle summarizes it this way in *1 Corinthians 2:14, "But the natural man receiveth not the things of the Spirit of God: for they are foolishness unto him: neither can he know them, because they are spiritually discerned."*

The world is clearly into lifeless degrees, useless positions, and temporary ranks. I have had to honestly admit to myself I do not know what it means to hold certain positions of honor or what it feels like to be in someone else's skin when it comes to being on the receiving end of great honor and recognition.

However, I do know what it means to be part of the great human race in an imperfect world where prejudices become an excuse to spew out hatred, elevated positions are used as a ticket to abuse, extort, and enslave those considered "inferior," injustice the great oppressor, wickedness the dictator, and evil often the victor.

It is easy in such a world to misrepresent a problem in society because someone wants to drown out the obvious to control the narrative, redirect the theme, and change the story line to determine the ending. However, as believers, we know that the core of the problems we face in society have nothing to do with color, race, positions, status, and etc.; rather it has to do with what plagues all mankind: SIN.

The presence, level, and practice of sin is what determines the color of the heart: white (purity) or black (wicked). Sin is what robs man of what he has earned, kills what is precious to him, and destroys what inspires and gives hope. We can hide sin behind fig-leaves of excuses, black robes of so-called "righteous indignation," and masks of opposition, but it remains what it is: a great offense to God and humanity.

As believers we also know the solution: Jesus Christ and Him crucified. For the forty-four years I have been a Christian I am aware that the Lord who knows my days, has been writing in the book of my life with the pen and ink of His Spirit. I already know the glorious ending of my life, but the sweet blessings have come when I look back on the pages of experiences and the sections of challenges and I can see the wondrous work God has done upon my heart, mind, and soul to bring forth His perfect will and plan for my life.

Are you doing it God's way? We are in Jesus but we must remember that Jesus is the Way *(John 14:6)*. We must walk in the Way if we are going to ensure God has His way in our lives. Walking in God's way will ensure us of lining up to His will. God's will, will greatly benefit the quality of our life and the fruit that will ultimately be produced in and from us.

I have done it my way many times in the past and was met with defeat. I have done it others' way to keep the peace only to be swept away by waves of resentment, despair, and disillusionment.

I have learned there is only one right way and that is God's way, and we will come to understand what it means to be in the way when we realize Jesus went before us and became the way to truth and life. His ways are higher than ours and when I encounter a couple who are having some type of wrestling match in their marriage because there is a clash of wills, I recognize that at such times they cannot trust each other's ways to be fair. It is then I challenge them to institute the ways of God in a matter because they can trust His way to be fair in both cases.

God's will leads to His way being done and His way ensures His will, will be done. His Word is the light that reveals His way and His Spirit is the guide that leads us in His way but we must submit to God's will to line up to Jesus as the way. Jesus showed us the way by always lining up the Father's will and walking in the way of obedience.

It is interesting to note how quick a person who takes a stand in light of controversial matters can quickly dig a hole for themselves with others who approach it from a different angle. I have learned my convictions do not always apply to others and their convictions do not apply to me.

We all come from different perspectives depending on history, experiences, and present challenges. What measure is called for in one area is not necessarily called for in another area. In the times we live in, Christians struggle with what it means to put God to a foolish test. For instance, who do I believe during this time? By believing the world, am I showing a lack of faith towards God, but on the other hand, if I fail to do what I am advised to do by so-called "experts" during a crisis like the one we are confronting, and possibly become sick and expose others, have I somehow put God to a foolish test?

Putting God to a foolish test has nothing to do with adhering to the warnings of the so-called "experts;" rather, it has to do with seeking God's face to determine what my response needs to be during such a time. Although the world is untrustworthy and an enemy of God, I can't assume that by tacking Christ's name on something in some show of defiance towards it that I will be blessed, or by presuming that God will automatically agree with me because I am doing something that is religious and seems good or right, that He will actually protect me.

I must know what God's will is in a matter and I must trust Him to work out the details of it in my own personal situation. In some cases, our decision to do something may not matter, but in other situations it could be an eternal issue.

So many times the world gives us causes to stand on or pursue while taking our eyes off of the bigger picture of what is going on, but on the other hand, if we seek God, He is the One who will give us the real picture so that our response can be in light of His will in lieu of the place and time we live in. There will be future crossroads where we, as Christians, must choose the way of God and we must never be surprised that they appear contradictory.

At such times we must avoid judging others to be automatically wrong because they do not line up to personal convictions. In such cases it is not a matter of right or wrong, but discerning whether I am here for such a time as this and therefore, I must stand where the Lord shows me, withstand when challenged to give way to any other current, and continue to stand in light of the eternal picture the Lord has entrusted to me.

I have talked about letting present reality simply be what it is. For many people to let something be is the same as surrendering something that they perceive is right and would prove to be beneficial to everyone, when in reality it is simply an acknowledgement that we are not God, and that any interference on our part will most likely create a greater mess. I had to accept this truth in order to LET GOD BE who He is.

In the past I have tried to dictate to God, influence Him as to what I think needed to happen, and in a sense anxiously "held my breath," like a spoiled child until a matter worked out the way I wanted it to be. Needless to say, I had rendered God into a small box that hindered and oppressed me as I witnessed that such matters never worked out according to my ideas or plans.

When I finally realized that my desires boxed God in, my thoughts rendered Him to be my equal, and my ways made Him appear smaller and less honorable, I began to realize I was stripping God of His honor that is worthy of trust, consecrated service, and worship, while trying to control His power to do my bidding. Without realizing it, I was attempting to not simply share in His glory, but to claim it for myself.

Such knowledge humbled and broke me resulting in true repentance. I was amazed to discover that I could claim His salvation by faith, but I had failed to activate and exercise it by choosing to trust Him with my well-being, while He faithfully and honorably took care of the details, resolved the issues, and brought forth something according to His will, plan, and glory.

The struggle of the heart and mind has to do with the fact we are human, in a fallen state, an imperfect environment, among wicked men, and in an evil world. In our humanity we are natural servants to sin, but we must choose the right master. In our heart, we may be open to the Lord but fail to do right when we are asked to walk an extra mile because we are still quite complacent and do not trust Him with the details enough to risk any inconveniences. And, in our will area, we may desire to be submissive to His will, but we still hold on to our independence to determine where we will submit.

We may desire to serve, but it is according to how it makes us feel and we may want to glorify Him while still desiring glory for ourselves. It is for this reason the Apostle Paul beseeches us to present our bodies as a living sacrifice in *Romans 12:1-2*. For fleshly man he will hide behind religious cloaks while giving the impression of religious compliance, true reformation, pious performances, and outward conformity, and it is for this reason that we offered up our bodies to ensure that we are transformed inwardly by the Holy Spirit so we can discern what is the acceptable, good and perfect will of God.

Are you in the will of God? The work of sanctification will prepare a believer to be placed in this great work of the Spirit in order to walk in the will of God. There is what I call a "general will," a "collective will," and a "personal will" of God.

The general will of God is found in the Bible and is directed towards all. For example, it is not His will that any perish but all come to repentance. It is His will that all believe in His Son to receive eternal life, and that every believer morally sanctifies his or her body to avoid all fornication, and it is also His will for everyone to be thankful in all things because He is God *(2 Peter 3:9; John 6:40; 1 Thessalonians 4:3-5; 5:18).*

The collective will of God involves His body, the church. As the church it is our commission to preach the Gospel and make converts (disciples) of Christ. As the church He wants to perfect us into one Body so in turn we will edify each other as we grow up together into the knowledge of the Head (the Lord) and in the unity of the Spirit *(Matthew 28:18-20; Mark 16:15, 16; Ephesians 4:11-16).*

The final aspect of God's will has to do with His personal will for each of us. We have different callings, gifts, and paths to travel. We must ask Him to have His way in our lives if we are going to come into our calling because we must be prepared for it. We must seek to know His truth before we will ever come into the place where we can properly receive the gifts that will enable us to walk out our calling. We must knock on doors, waiting for the right ones to open so that we can walk through them and walk out our calling in the harvest field of the world *(Matthew 7:7-8 refer to John 14:6).*

Have you learned to obey God's general will and submit to His collective will so He can bring you to the place of doing His will?

Is your great pursuit in life to do the will of God? Yesterday I talked about the general, collective, and personal will of God. In order to be productive when it comes to doing God's will, we must always do it from the heart *(Ephesians 6:6-7).*

We must not ask God what we are to do when it is already outlined in Scripture because that would be putting God to a foolish test. We must not think so highly of ourselves in ministry that we overlook the brethren and fail to properly love and minister to them *(Matthew 4:7 John 13:34, 35; Romans 12:3; Galatians 6:2, 9, 10).* If we fail to do His general will and are not faithful to be part of His collective will, we will not be trustworthy to carry out His personal will for our lives.

The general will of God provides the foundation we are to build from, while the collective will of God are the steps that lead us to understanding what the real heart of God is towards souls. We cannot miss the foundation and the steps and assume God will bring us into our high calling.

Once again, we are reminded that the real work of sanctification belongs to God, but the main purpose of this work is to bring us into the will of God so that the Lord will be glorified in our lives and in all that we do in His kingdom.

Are you doing the will of God? The act of consecration of setting ourselves apart to God comes first in the work of holiness. The main reason we set ourselves apart is to do the will of God, but we must be transformed in our minds in order to discern the acceptable, good, and perfect will of God (*Romans 12:1, 2*).

Sanctification by the Spirit is the means to prepare us to walk in the will of God. It is important to point out that everything that occurs in this world happens within the SOVEREIGN will of God. God's will manifest itself in three ways, His permissive will, His providential will, and His perfect will.

God's PERMISSIVE will is where He actually permits a person or entity to have his or her own way according to his or her will. For example, Satan works within the permissive will of God. He must receive God's permission as to what he is able to do. God will put boundaries on him, allowing him to go only so far when he is inserting himself into the lives of His people. This is clearly brought out in *Job 1:6-12* and *2:1-6* and in the case of Peter when Jesus in *Luke 22:31 & 32* said, *"Simon, Simon, behold, Satan hath desired to have you, that he may sift you as wheat; But I have prayed for thee, that thy faith fail not; and when thou are converted, strengthen thy brethren."*

It is clear that the Lord permits and uses Satan to test and refine the faith of His people, reveal character, and bring them to a place of true humility. It is important to point out people will taste consequences when

59

operating in God's permissive will and everything will ultimately be judged.

God's PROVIDENTIAL will occur when a person declares, NOT MY WILL BUT YOUR WILL in a matter. At this point, God will set into motion events and circumstances to discipline the steps of the person in order to bring him or her into line with His perfect will.

God's PERFECT will does not mean all is roses and sunshine, but what it does mean is that the believer will have confidence to stand in the storms, withstand because nothing can thwart the perfect working will of God in His people's lives, and continue to stand because in the end there will be victory and fruits that will ultimately bring glory and honor to God.

THE LIGHT

The world is a dark, cloudy
mansion. Oh, when will the Sun
of Righteousness shine on my soul
without intermission?
(David Brainerd)

The sun was shining on Saturday. After days of overcast skies, the light broke through to illuminate a dusting of snow on the mountains, while the different parts of creation become more defined on the landscape surrounding us. God's creation is beautiful, His heavens vast, and His plan for His people eternal.

The sun should remind us that the true Light of the World, Jesus Christ, will penetrate the darkness, creation will proclaim God's majesty, the heavens will declare nothing can contain or control Him in His power, and His plan will be carried out according to His perfect will. Even though we live in very dark times, as believers we walk in the light.

At times we can become overwhelmed by the greatness of darkness only to look up and see our real light of hope shining through His Word, taking hold of our souls as it becomes an anchor attached to the Rock of Ages. We can be overcome at times by the darkness, but we know the darkness will not always be and when the light penetrates it, it will recede back into its place. We can feel as if the darkness will always be, but we can remind ourselves that in light of heaven it is temporary. When we think about why we know the light will never be overcome by the darkness, all we have to do is remember that like the snow covering the tip of the mountains, even though *our sins be as scarlet, they shall be as white as snow; through they be red like crimson, they shall be as wool (Isaiah 1:18).*

Jesus addressed our sin on the cross, His blood came forth to cleanse us from all unrighteousness, and now because of His grace and our faith, we can stand before Him as if we never sinned. However, we need to walk in righteousness if the landscape of our lives is going to bring real distinction as to our heavenly connection. And, what distinction will it bring forth? The very image of Jesus.

In these times of great darkness, we need clarity, but we must be careful about what we focus on to gain that clarity. We often focus on the things that effect our emotions, or feel abrasive against our opinions, and contrary to what we understand. We can irrationally react emotionally rather than discern the problem and respond to what is so. And the reason for fleshly, worldly reactions is because we have all been born into spiritual darkness.

We think our understanding is light, our feelings are the measurement of properly discerning something, and our conclusions, truth. The reality of spiritual darkness is we are not aware of it until the true light of Jesus comes on in our soul.

Saul (the Apostle Paul) didn't realize that his light of religion was indeed darkness and opposite to the real light. His darkness enfolded his soul in self-righteousness and anger and when he met the light of Jesus, he found himself left in utter darkness, revealing the great darkness of his soul. He had to be led to Ananias' house where he would receive the truth, causing the scales to fall from his physical eyes in order to receive the power from above to be led in preparation of his calling.

There is only one truth and that is Jesus. The Bible talks about the great delusion coming on the world. It is going to sound right to some, feel right to others, and seem right to the rest, but it will reveal the darkness of their soul because they do not love the truth of Jesus. If a matter does not uphold who our Lord Jesus Christ is, line up to His teaching, walk in His truth, and produce His image in their life, it is not light but darkness.

Over ten years ago, there was a message to the fellowship I was involved with. The message was simple, "Come higher in Christ or you will be consumed by the darkness coming on the face of the earth." It made me shake in my shoes, but sadly the urgency of it passed many by because to them it was religion as usual. Later after the fellowship disbanded, there were families that fell apart, some of them went into a cult, and others into worldly, immoral living and pursuits.

The only way we will survive this darkness is to come higher in the light and truth of heaven so that our soul will not be consumed by the delusion, the destruction, and the culture of death that is now enfolding the world.

It is vital we discern that which is artificial in our spiritual life so that we can properly discern what is real from that which is silly, needed for spiritual growth, or missing because of a wrong mixture of the holy with the profane. In the tabernacle there were three compartments all lit by different lights.

The outer court was lit by the natural light of the sun during the day and the burning embers of the fire on the Altar of Burnt Offering. Both lights were to keep before the people the great cost of their sin.

In the Holy Place of service was the artificial light of the Lampstand that was kept burning by the priests, but there were shadows cast where the priest could hide the quality of their inner character in shadows while maintaining an outward life of religious service, but in the Most Holy Place was the glorious light of God's Shekinah glory.

The High Priest, once a year, entered the Most Holy Place on the day of atonement to sprinkle the blood of the sacrifice on the mercy seat of the Ark of the Covenant. However, before he entered, he had to wave incense from the Altar of Incense into this most sacred place. He could not stand in the glory of God without some covering whether it be a cloud of incense or darkness like Moses.

Jesus' redemption caused the tall, thick temple veil between the Holy Place and the Most Holy Place to be ripped from the top down to signify that there was no need for a veil to protect us from the penetrating transparency of God's glory, and that we now, as part of His priesthood, could enter in.

You might ask what is important about this significance. For many, when it comes to God, walk according to the natural light of their understanding. They may reserve the right to stand in the gate as an observer so they can run into the world when convenient to do so, while staying close enough to the gate to run in and do their religious activities.

There are those who enter into the artificial light of service, while holding on to aspects of their old life and ways. But, when it comes to true worship, the only place that this can happen is away from the world's pull to the temporary and away from mere outward artificial service that lacks heart. And, why do we need to come into the Most Holy Place: to seek communion with the one and only true Lord and God at the mercy seat in order to worship Him in Spirit and truth. This is what ensures our life before Christ remains genuine, grounded upon the eternal, and ever the center of what is true and right.

As believers we are told that before the light comes, we will experience the depth of darkness, whether it comes by way of a crisis of faith or the heavy darkness on our soul. It is important to point out that this type of darkness has nothing to do with sin or failure, but with God's sovereignty.

God sovereignty is that mysterious aspect of His workings that remains hidden from us. It is that great light that translates into darkness because we cannot begin to comprehend the depths of His ways, the heights of His judgments, the width of His love, and the transparency of His holiness in a matter. It is within the sovereignty of His mysterious workings that He does the greatest and deepest work in the life of a saint in order to fulfill His plan in their life while enabling them to reach their potential in His kingdom.

63

God's goal is to prepare every believer for the heavenly. In fact, for the saint the door of physical death is the entrance into His eternal glory, and the transition should be natural due to the pure environment of worship of our wonderful Lord where our ultimate potential will be realized, joyous because one is finally home residing in His glory, and satisfying because the spiritual race is now completed.

As believers we MUST be the children of light. This goes without saying for Jesus is the light of the world, but how many of us understand the light of Jesus?

To the seeking soul the light can be seen penetrating the grave darkness of the world bringing hope to their troubled soul. To the unredeemed sinner, it is darkness to their soul, to the wicked it is an offense that must be silenced, and to that which is evil it is an enemy that must be destroyed.

It is vital as believers that we discern this light and understand its characteristics in order to properly walk in it. First of all, this light is the life of Christ. Without being born again the person will always be groping in spiritual darkness as to God's identity, His work of redemption, and the hope of an eternal inheritance and promises. They may be close to, or walking parallel to the light, but will find themselves far away from God as they take detours and hit dead ends because they have been blinded to the real Gospel by the god of the world, Satan.

This light is the sword of truth that penetrates the darkness, bringing grave offense to those who prefer their own reality. It cuts through the darkness of deception, parts the fog of confusion, and exposes the wretchedness of the soul, while exposing all workings of sin and death. This light is transparent. In other words, it will bring to light all matters that are hidden or belong to darkness and will strip all dross of pretense away.

This light will awaken Christians who are succumbing to the twilight of compromise, challenge those who are becoming comfortable in a quasi-state of religion to stand, and become a source of vivid contrast to those seeking to walk by faith and obedience to the Word of God. It not only penetrates the darkness but it divides as well.

There are those who want religion on their terms and those who want to know the terms of God in order to walk in the path of righteousness. Those who want religion on their terms will walk in and out of religious shadows to hide their carnality, pride, and rebellion, but those who want to know God's terms love His truth. They understand that the light of Christ in them is to enable them to line up to His Word in order to walk circumspectly, knowing that they must redeem the days for they are evil. They know that the main purpose of walking in this light of truth is so God can be glorified and they can finish the course set before them.

As believers we are looking for black and white (clarity) without recognizing in the light of God's truth darkness will be totally consumed. As the wickedness of the times is being exposed, my greatest surprise comes from those who consider themselves to be religious.

I realize being religious can be expressed in outward piousness, self-righteous judgmentalism, and religious snobbery and elitism that is ever ready to scrutinize those on the outside of the "group" to be inferior or suspicious. Religious people can perceive they have some corner on truth or doctrine that makes them part of the "enlightened ones," a concept associated with the New Age and the occult. What is the real test of a true believer of Jesus Christ and His Word? We are told we know them by their fruits, but good fruits do not solely consist of action, but must also be motivated by a right spirit with the intent to uphold truth in love and humility in order to bring the proper glory to God.

We are to walk in the light of God's love which is expressed in humility, His grace which manifests itself gratitude and worship, His mercy which reveals itself in compassionate service, and His faithfulness that enables us to endure to the end.

When people claim to be a Christian but are indifferent to moral conduct it becomes obvious that they are void of a love for truth because love never rejoices in iniquity (moral deviance) but in the truth. If people care only for their comfort and not the plight of their brethren, they are lovers of self more than lovers of God. If people show a concern for the immigrants who are unlawfully trying to flood our country, but show no regard for the sex-trafficking that is happening all around us and unborn babies that are being aborted in the wombs, killed and mangled so the despots of the world can sell their parts, they are double-minded and hypocritical.

If people say they care about the rights of all people but are willing to turn the other way while the abominable and morally depraved scorn all sanctity established by God to justify trampling on the rights of the righteous, the innocent, and the pure, they simply prove they are godless and partakers of the sins of others. I could go on and on, but I think you get the idea.

I realize that some carry around Christianity like an insurance policy, others claim Christianity out of ignorance, while some out of personal gain, and the rest because it is the thing to do for appearance's sake, but we are living in a time of great judgment and a clear line between darkness and light, good and evil, and right and wrong is being drawn by the transparent light of truth. It is clear that people are being awakened and forced to look into the face of the great evil that is being exposed by the powerful light of God's truth. It is ugly, sickening, and overwhelming but it is time to call it what it is and make a choice as to who and what we are going to serve. And, do not be mistaken, the price could be the comfortable existence you know here, or it will cost your soul to try to maintain a worldly, fleshly lifestyle while the wrath of God abides on those who walk in unbelief and disobedience. The light of the truth is that saints will make the necessary choices to put them on the right side of eternity, regardless of personal cost.

We live in a world of bad news and it is natural for us to look at the bad news, while forgetting we possess the good news. We do not have to succumb to the darkness of this age because we have always been walking towards the unending light of the age to come.

It is true, everywhere we turn our spirits become vexed over the events happening in this insane age that is becoming darker and darker due to rebellion, deception, sin, and now a pestilence. It is clear that time is winding down to the prophetic climax the Bible has warned us about, but what can we learn from such darkness?

As Christians, we must constantly remind ourselves that we are not of this world and that the unseen kingdom we belong to is real, operates in truth, possesses and proclaims the Good News of the Gospel, and is eternal. We must not allow ourselves to be bogged down by the hopelessness of this world. We must avoid looking around and continue to look up. We must not trust the bad tidings of this age because they do not apply to us, as we choose to remember we have the enduring promise of the next age.

It is for this reason that God's followers can encourage themselves even in the midst of such insanity and chaos, knowing we are simply passing through this age to our real destination, to our real home.

I have been away from the computer for a couple of days to take care of responsibilities. Yesterday I traveled to the "big" city, by Idaho standards, to take care of some business. This experience made it clear that the Covid-19 issue has changed the atmosphere, mood, and attitude of the people.

I observed that there are three groups of people. There are those who have accepted that masks and shutdowns as the "new normal." There are others who are beginning to break free of the lies and bondage put upon them, and there are those who remain resolute that they will not surrender to the lies and propaganda that has attempted to rob them of their identity.

I continually find consolation in the fact that I am a true citizen of the Kingdom of God and I remind myself of that glorious fact, which causes rejoicing that in Christ He has shown me the way through this propagated ploy, while establishing my faith, and enabling me to walk in the confidence and liberty that He is in control. Because of His sovereignty, I simply need to look to Him and trust Him and He will show me the way through the challenges.

Rayola Kelley

Each time I encounter this present world colliding with my life and inheritance in Christ, I remember that my true citizenship is above and not of this dark age that I am passing through. My first love and allegiance are to the Lord and King of my real home in glory.

As I become increasingly aware of how dark and corrupt this world is, I am glad it has no real claims on me. I don't know about you, but as stranger in this world, it is becoming foreign to me as I get closer to glory. As a sojourner traveling in the world, the world's terrain has grown more unfamiliar and uncomfortable to me as I see the formidable landscape and storms ahead. And as a pilgrim, I will never be content until I reach my destination of a city made with the hands of glory, the unabated worship around His throne, and the liberty to see my Lord as He is.

I am not excited the world is becoming darker and more unstable, but I am rejoicing over the fact that in the great darkness, the light of His life is becoming more defined and real to me.

Truth is truth, and light is light. This simple nugget of wisdom is hard to accept. I started out desiring the truth because I didn't want to believe a lie, but what I discovered is that truth caused my world to turn upside down, especially when it came to my high opinions of self and my surface theology that sounded good but failed to always be applied.

I wanted the light of Christ to bring understanding, but what I found is that the true light not only exposed matters, but it had a tendency to purge what was wrong. In today's world we want truth according to what serves our purposes, and light that will simply placate our lies and pamper our fragile egos; but the problem with trying to maintain our own take on reality is that life is like a big sickle that comes through and cuts everything down that represents man's strength in order to expose true character.

Man's tendency is to adjust truth to establish his own propaganda, and man deceives himself in such a way that his darkness becomes light, allowing him to conclude that what is good is evil and what is evil is good. I realized through the years that truth sets us free from the lies, but for it to do so we must love the truth more than desiring that it somehow placates the ways of lying so I can feel good about myself.

When it came to the light, I had to choose to walk in it instead of hide in the shadows of my own understanding, trusting that it would expose and purge me of what is darkness to the Lord. Truth in these days is a luxury while darkness is becoming the preferred normal and it is for this reason we are told in *Proverbs 23:23, "Buy the truth, and sell it not; also wisdom, and instruction, and understanding."*

THE TRUTH OF A MATTER

The truth that's told with bad intent
beats all the lies you can invent.
(William Blake)

The TRUTH of the matter will never change. Truth will remain standing in the end when all false narratives and philosophies fall into the pit of destruction and leave those advocating them completely undone, without recourse, and trembling at the prospects of the judgment that awaits them.

People can act flippant, casual, foolish, and even jesting towards the sobering truths of eternity, but in the end, they will be used to judge those very same people. The Bible is clear, believing the Gospel is a matter of the heart and not the mind.

We can always logic out why we should selfishly agree with the message of salvation, but the good news that leads to salvation must be believed in the heart as being so. *Romans 10:9-10 says, "That if thou shalt confess with thy mouth the Lord Jesus, and shalt believe in thine heart that God hath raised him from the dead, thou shalt be saved. For with the heart man believeth unto righteousness; and with the mouth confession is made unto salvation."*

We must make sure our salvation is not simply an intellectual acknowledgement; rather, it is an experience of the heart that has not only created a new heart in us, but brought obvious changes to our lives.

Rayola Kelley

One of the challenges I have had in the past is to accept something for what it is. It is clear we wrestle with, fight against, declare war on, and resolve ourselves against accepting reality.

Reality is different things to people, but truth is reality and truth is what we must accept even in its rawest stage. It is true that we must speak truth out of love in the attitude of meekness, but we want truth to be diplomatic when it will prove to be sharp, we want it to be honest without exposing anything bad, and we want to weave some garment around it that will allow the person it is directed to, to maintain their feel-good status when it will offend.

We want love to take the bitterness out of truth's sharpness, humility the rejection of it, and tolerance the fact that most people prefer their reality over truth, but when we use such measures, we strip truth of its authority and means to truly set people free from the deception, lies, and ignorance that oppresses and enslaves them.

We fail to realize we often fight against accepting the truth of a matter for what it is, and accepting something for what it will be. Whenever we strip the truth of its authority, we fail to discover liberation and become more enslaved to a spiritual darkness that will eventually judge, condemn, and consume us.

Too many people perceive that to accept a reality that shakes their understanding, turns the world upside down for them, offends others, and embarrasses them, implies surrender to something that is unacceptable. When it comes to accepting truth, I have learned that it is not a matter of surrendering, but of submitting to that which is greater and more excellent.

I have had to learn acceptance of truth in three ways and in so doing, I was the one that was set free in the end. I first had to accept the happenings in my environment, next I had to accept people for who they were, and lastly, I had to accept the final result.

When I accepted what was happening, I found I could seek God's perspective about it. When I accepted people for who they were, I took the pressure off of them and myself to perform a certain way and left them in God's capable hands, and when I accepted the way things were, I discovered treasures and memories that would have passed me by when I was busy trying to manipulate reality according to my codes.

It has been raining for the last two days and clouds hang on the mountains. As I observed the clouds, I realized that what often hangs over man is like that cloud that hides resistance to what is true. Jesus as truth can only bring perspective when it is present and change what has truly been left in His hands, thereby, bringing true liberty to the wrestling soul.

In these times, when you don't know what information to trust, you begin to realize how valuable truth is. No wonder we are told in *Proverbs 23:23* to *"buy the truth and sell it not,"* along with wisdom as to how to apply it, instruction in light of obedience to His Word, and understanding when it comes to that which can only be seen by the eyes of faith.

Truth is that penetrating light that pierces spiritual darkness in order to set the captive free. I personally know this because it has set me free in many ways. I guess that is why the one thing that often surprises me is how people react to truth. I shouldn't be shocked about how truth is treated and handled in a world where the father of this age is the father of lies. He is also a murderer who does everything from crucifying the truth, intimidating those who stand for truth, silencing those who dare seek truthful answers, and quenching it in any arena he can.

In studying people's reaction to the truth, I have noticed they can be hard against it, insulted by it, or fearful of it. Those who are hard against the truth have set their face against it because it does not serve their cause. Those who are insulted by it want to control their own reality. In essence, they want to do away with the sharp edges of truth so they feel good about their life, they want to smooth out the bluntness of truth to control the narrative, and they want to make it acceptable to their tastebuds to ensure it is acceptable to others.

The Bible tells us we are to speak truth in love and meekness, but neither one of these virtues take away the sharpness, the bluntness, and the contrary taste of truth.

Rayola Kelley

I don't know about you but I can be quite opinionated, dogmatic, and unreasonable at times about the things I feel strongly about. I have to wrestle with myself when I have felt the urge or temptation to stand on some mountain, waving my flag, making myself a target. It is at this point I ask myself is this particular mountain really worth dying for?

I recognize that such mountains are for the most part a matter of pride, a way of bringing attention to the person and not the issue. Truth does not have to wave a flag, because when it is lifted up, it will bring a clear separation between those who desire it and those who want their own reality.

Today as I watch battlelines being drawn as people wave their flags from the top of their different mountains of politics, doctrines, and beliefs, I ask myself what have they accomplished? Some do get shot off their mountain and walk away like a suffering martyr. These individuals try to wear their pride like a badge of courage to show how noble they were on their mountain, but they are the only one attending the ceremony that speaks of their supposedly great feats. Others throw their hands up in complete despair and walk away angry and disillusioned. When you watch some, it is not that they are standing for anything; rather, they are always standing against everything based on their opinions. In a way, they remind you of small-minded people that never can get past the small dot of self-importance to discover the bigger picture. They are contrary and unreasonable, while touting they are experts about the matter at hand. I have learned from past experiences that I am only required to stand for THE TRUTH.

As Christians, we need to avoid trying to be the Holy Spirit or serve as the conscience of others until they see it our way; rather, we need to ensure Jesus is lifted up because when He is, He is the one who will draw people to the truth of God, life, and hope. Keep in mind, Jesus died on a mount so we do not have to die on some ridiculous mountain to prove a point. He established what was and is true, and we do not.

Truth is simple and it never has to be threaded though some presentation to make some grand point as to how everyone else is wrong. Truth simply stands for what is true and as a result will bring a contrast that others can rightly compare.

The Apostle Paul's main concern in *2 Corinthians 11:1-3* was that Christians would become beguiled like Eve. He points out three ways in which this can happen: that they would receive a different Jesus, believe a different Gospel and receive another spirit.

It is important for us as believers to periodically examine ourselves to see if we are missing the mark in any of these three areas. We must always begin with our foundation, the Person and work of Jesus Christ. For example, ask yourself the question Jesus asked Peter, *"Who do you say I am?"* This is not only the million-dollar question we need to individually answer, but it is the ultimate one we need to understand to possess the right answer to maintain the integrity of the true Gospel and ensure we are of the right Spirit. We must not only ask it once or occasionally, but at different times to soberly test the ground we are standing on. After all, this answer is a matter of life and death.

We must not assume we know the answer, we must not presume that we have Him neatly confined in an untested doctrinal box that when challenged will actually collapse beneath us, and we must not be casual when considering who He is. We must do everything we can to come to a sure, unwavering knowledge of Jesus Christ to stand sure in salvation, be establish in redemption, and walk confidently in light of eternal promises.

In my initial Christians years, I knew ABOUT Jesus because of past religious experiences and as I read Scriptures I began to INTELLECTUALLY LEARN about Jesus, but when my theology of Jesus was challenged during a great crisis of faith, I realized I did not KNOW Him. Jesus made it clear that such understanding comes from above.

To know Jesus requires the Spirit from above to reveal Him to your spirit, otherwise you possess nothing but dead letter doctrine about Him. He may be a truth, but He will not be the LIVING TRUTH, TRUTH PERSONIFIED that becomes the essence of all truth to what you believe, understand, discern, and know. Without the living truth, one will be void of the right spirit whose responsibility is to lead you into a greater knowledge of who He is by bringing life to the Word of God.

Without the right spirit you will not be able to discern matters and to make sure all lines up to the righteousness of heaven. The Holy Spirit will always remind you or bring you back to the fullness of the true Gospel. It is clear, if you are deceived about Jesus, you will end up believing a wrong gospel and receiving a seductive, religious, anti-Christ spirit.

One of the things that still shocks me at times is people's capacity to deceive themselves about spiritual matters. There is nothing more telling about a person's standing in the kingdom of God than their attitude and response towards truth.

Truth is absolute and eternal, but the tendency of people is to try to control the sharpness of it that will cut across people's bows and challenge, shake, embarrass, and anger them. I have met people who fall into a certain category, such as those who assume they know the truth, but in reality, they have been deluded by their idea of truth and when truth challenges their reality, they can become touchy and defensive about it.

Then there are others who have religious knowledge and presume they know the truth, but are stiff-necked towards that which dares to challenge their idea of truth. Others see themselves as trying to soften the "insults," or what some would consider the negativity of truth by wrapping it up in some type of diplomacy. However, such attempts take away its authority to make the necessary impact in people's lives that would ultimately set them free in pursuing and knowing the truth, the Person of Jesus Christ.

It is obvious that people want truth on their terms, while serving their purpose, confirming their idea of reality, and making them content in any preferred lie they choose to walk in. Truth will not change, be adjusted, dulled down, or let someone who is operating in some form of delusion to remain unchallenged and content in it.

As Christians, we need to know there is nothing that will make us a bona-fide hypocrite more than an incorrect attitude towards God's truth. We can easily enough profess we believe the truth, but if we live contrary to it others will see us as unreliable, foolish hypocrites.

In *John 8*, we often quote verse *32, "The truth shall make you free."* Oh, how we love that verse but the reality is how many of us want to be set free from our particular reality? How many of us, when we come to the end of doctrine, we admit we know in part and when we come to the end of personal theology, admit we don't know anything outside of who Christ is and what He has done for us?

How many of us are willing to let go of what we think we know in order to come to the knowledge of that which is of spirit, righteousness, and is eternal? How many of us are willing to settle for the crumbs of truth instead of the revelation of it? After all, crumbs will allow us to pick and choose what we hear and believe, as well as how we interpret it to fit into what we understand.

In *John 8*, Jesus reveals the three religious' responses towards truth. There are those who believe His Word, but His question to them was do you believe me? In other words, we can believe aspects about His Word and still not believe Him if we do not see Him as being truth. This points to one understanding that Christ alone, is THE TRUTH, and will be the final authority in all matters.

There are those who believe certain things about Jesus, but fail to believe in Him as to who He says He is and must be to ensure that they are standing on the correct foundation that will withstand all shaking. If one does not believe in Him as the foundation of all truth, then in reality they do not really believe, hold to, or abide in truth.

The next time you pick up His Word, ask the Lord how He wants it used, as a surgical tool to examine within, a knife to cut away the binding cords entangling others, or a sword to put the enemy on the run.

I have been thinking a lot about truth. I make this statement often to people, "Your reality may not be truth, but truth is always reality." The harsh reality is that people have a real problem with truth. It is not that truth is fragile, untrustworthy, and unpredictable; rather, it is that man prefers his own reality as he emphasizes what he wants to believe, while applying his take on matters and interpreting something to fit his own narrative. Needless to say, he ends up deceiving himself about what is. This scenario may be all right when it comes to fantasy, fiction material, and entertainment, but it is destructive when it comes to life.

Truth is the only means in which problems can be properly addressed, challenges faced, and effective solutions applied. The truth can't be ignored away without becoming a tsunami that will leave behind destruction, covered up without coming back to haunt the culprits, or denied without ultimately revealing that these individuals are liars and fools.

We also know truth will not change according to the culture, adjust to acceptable philosophies of the day, or come into line with the elite or the masses. It is for this reason our foundation never moves and remains sure regardless of the changing winds of darkness.

What happens to those who refuse to accept truth so they can realistically deal in and with life? THEY GO MAD!. We are watching people who will not accept what is, struggle to control the present narrative and do everything they can to change what is while going insane as they constantly hit the wall of what is so.

These people have become so stuck in their rut, that all their mental spinning has become a deep hole that in the end will become their grave in which the stench they are leaving will continue to identify the place of its demise. The only thing left to do is to put a tombstone on it, that is if anyone cares enough to do so after leaving the stench behind.

As Christians we know all truth is summarized in one person Jesus Christ. He is the Rock we stand upon, the only premise we begin from, the reality we build upon, and the final judgment we come into agreement with.

As I watch those who try to control and maintain the false narrative around them, I am so thankful for the simple truth of Jesus that gives me a sound mind to face what is, while inspiring faith in me that gives me the hope to walk through what is, as I peer beyond this world to see the glory that awaits me.

It is oftentimes discouraging to me because of the constant debates that go on in Christendom about non-essential matters that have nothing to do with salvation. The reason I say this is because debate is a fleshly activity and proves to be unprofitable. This is brought out by the Apostle Paul in *Romans 1:29* and to some extent in *Titus 3:9.*

When you look up the word "debate" in *Romans 1:29* in the Strong's Concordance it uses such words as quarrel, wrangling, contention, strife, and variance to describe it. Think about the meanings: quarrel points to one who is in the state or spirit to emphasize a particular issue to start some type of conflict; wrangling has to do with controlling something such as a narrative; contention and strife will result in division; and variance simply points to some adjustment that will prove to be contrary. With this in mind, show me where debate at any level or over any matter promotes that which is virtuous and part of the fruit of the Spirit.

In my initial years of being a Christian I loved the debate that would occur over doctrine, practices, and presentations. I had studied enough that I felt I could not be wrong. I later learned my interpretation of something was a matter of pride, being right, and not truth. As you can see, everyone has their opinion that in their mind can't be wrong, and in every debate, people will take sides.

Have you ever noticed that such debates change no one's mind meaning they are still of the same opinion? God never tells us to debate the truth because it is not debatable; rather, He tells us to stand for it and stand on it.

As stated, the truth is summarized in the person of Jesus Christ, and Jesus Christ stated that if He was lifted up, He would draw all men to

Himself. The next time you find yourself in a debate, discern the spirit present while keeping in mind that when Jesus is properly lifted up, all debates will cease.

Yesterday I talked about debate. I get it that we Christians want to get it right, but as a human I realize I have a tendency to swat at or strain at the small things while missing what is important. As a result, at times I have given the impression to those around me that technicalities are far more important than the message. As a result, I have allowed the small things to define my attitude while missing what has the capacity to be life-changing, not only to myself, but others.

As believers, we have the authority and power to define any matter according to the Word of God. Let's face it, the god of this age, Satan has taken everything that is made by God and of God and perverted it. For example, the days of the week are named after pagan gods, and even though God named every star along with the constellations (*Job 38:31; Psalm 147:4*) and speaks of the zodiac (Mazzaroth) in *Job 38:32*, we get into a dither, cry foul and run the opposite direction when such matters are mentioned, and the question is why?

Instead of bringing such subjects back to center, which is God, by reasoning it out according to the truth of His Word, we have allowed Satan to hijack precious truths and practices with his perverted narrative, such as in the case of astrology. We have allowed ourselves to be put into little boxes of theology by the narrative of a wicked world that has taken captive the truths of God, whether it is through such celebrations as Christmas, Easter, and/or tokens like the rainbow. And, the result is truths that should bring joy to us have become points of debate and division.

We forget we have been given His Spirit that allows us to properly discern a matter and the sharp sword of truth to separate the profane from the holy. We are also the ones who have the responsibility to keep that which is from God, pure, simple and true in our own hearts.

I want to challenge each believer to stop and ponder in what way have you allowed the world to define and pervert a narrative that does not even belong to it, and as a result, you have been robbed of any of

78

the joy it might bring to your heart. *"These things have I spoken unto you, that my joy might remain in you, and that your joy might be full" (John 15:11).*

Jesus warned us to take heed in how we hear a matter. When man is born, he is like a white, empty slate. The attitude, biases, and assumptions he adopts are shaped by the environment he is exposed to.

He is often seduced into his present reality by the direction of his affections according to worldly attractions, and he can be indoctrinated into the philosophies of this age if he fails to reason a matter through from its inception to its end.

These influences determine how we hear a matter. It has taken me awhile to identify the conditioning of my past to allow transformation in how I think. I had to replace past assumptions with discernment, and a love for the truth to root out all indoctrination. After all, one never has to be indoctrinated into the truth. I realized this is the only way that I can be assured of properly hearing a matter in its purity when it comes to spiritual truths.

GOD'S LOVE

The love that keeps His commandments
is the only way to remain in His love. In our
whole relationship to Christ, love is everything.
Christ's love to us and our love to Him is
proved in our love to each other.
(Andrew Murray)

The subject of God's love is far reaching because it is eternal. It is for this reason we are told we love Christ because He first loved us.

Jesus proved God's incredible love by giving up the glory of heaven. He became the face of God's love by taking on humanity in order to become the Lamb of God who would take away the sin of the world. He

Rayola Kelley

revealed the commitment of this love by going to the cross. He showed the endurance of God's love by rising from the grave to prove victorious over death, and ascending to heaven to become our High Priest. Jesus' act of love is translated in one word, "GRACE."

We are told that grace and truth came by Jesus Christ and that because of His fulness that all heirs of salvation have received grace for grace. This means grace is ongoing and flows downward from heaven and nothing can disrupt it in the life of those who receive the fulness of it when they receive Christ.

Grace clearly stipulates that we can't earn, deserve, or warrant any aspect of His grace which includes His love. His great sacrifice and His flowing grace revealed the far-reaching tentacles of God's love. There is no width, height, depth, and length to His love. There is no obstacle, challenge, or point of hindrance that can keep God's love from reaching the sin-laden soul, the broken hearted, and the wounded spirit.

There are those who ask if we can't earn love, deserve grace, and warrant forgiveness, then why would God show such great love to lost, underserving sinful man. The answer is simple, He could do nothing else because HE IS LOVE.

Walking by faith has led me to discover untold abundance of God's blessings and promises, and the fruit of this walk is satisfaction in my soul. The question I have for the reader to consider is do you have such satisfaction? If not, why not?

The abundant life promised in *John 10:10* is for NOW. We do not have to allow Satan to rob us of our assurance in God because of lies, kill the joy of our salvation because of personal challenges, and destroy the testimony that the Lord is establishing in us because of sin. Make sure that you have not settled for a desperate state of fake nobility, thinking some challenge or sin is too great for God to address, flinging you into a religious quasi state that has no real distinction or clarity to it.

Perhaps, you live in wishful thinking that God's love will overlook some moral inconsistency in your life, keeping you on the outside of any real victory. You could also be like those who are trying to handle some challenge or sin on their own while thinking mercy is a given without seeking God, followed by true confession of your need for His great intervention to save you from self. You might be standing with those who cling to the idea that what love does not overlook, God's grace will certainly cover. However, grace can only effectively work and be received when it is reigning through righteousness. (See *Romans 5:21*.)

As believers it is natural to make reference to love. We can preach love all we want, but we need to remember the world also talks about love. This is why preaching love may create some type of sentiment, but it never changes the environment. We need to recognize that until there is a distinction made between God's love and the world's love, it may stir up emotions, but fail to change the heart.

I have learned that the matter of God's love never reaches those who assume or take for granted that it will cover up their rejection and mockery towards it. It will also fail to reach a tormented, unbelieving soul who feels unworthy of such love, as well as people who have deluded themselves that they have somehow earned it or are worthy of it. It also does not impact those who operate from wishful thinking that their goodness will prove to be good enough on that great day of judgment. It is what makes the love of God distinct that will impact lives.

God's love is distinct because it is moral, honorable, enduring, sacrificial, and active. It is for this reason, after submitting His will to the Father, Jesus Christ for the most part remained silent as He was being led to the place of the cross. At that point there was nothing more to be said because the love of God compelled Him to show the level of commitment that God has towards all sinners. God's love allowed itself to be led away by a mocking world, stand mostly silent before an accusing religious system, be beaten by a shrewd ruler, and come under the great burden of a cross.

It is God's love that went all the way to a hill, where an altar was lifted up for the world to see. And what did the world see? That out of love for the whole of humanity, the Lamb of God was offered on our behalf on that altar and for our sake so that we could be recipients of the gift of life that was wrapped in grace, bound by mercy, and marked by the reality that ultimately His love will always bring Him glory.

God's love is expressed in honorable actions. We see these actions being outlined in Scripture, but the one place that it will be obvious is in godly marriages. Paul's instructions to husbands and wives in *Ephesians 5:23-31* outlined the attitude and action of God's love. Wives are to submit to the husbands and husbands are to love their wives. These two instructions make up a two-sided coin. There may be different pictures on each side of the coin, but it is the same coin.

Consider the word, "submission." Wives are to submit to the husbands as unto the Lord. When it comes to submission in Christianity, we are told to submit to one another out of fear of the Lord. True submission must come out of godly love or it is not true submission. This act has to do with giving way to that which is honorable and worthy for the benefit of the whole to ensure proper function and order as well as the integrity of a relationship. Keep in mind, that if integrity and moral rightness is not present in love, it is not godly love.

To ensure the integrity of submission on the part of a wife, she must submit as if she was submitting to the Lord. This is the wife's point of great strength, influence, protection, and discernment in the marriage. If her action of submitting does not ultimately honor her Lord, then she foremost must do what is right by the one who loves her soul, died for her, and owns her very life to establish a more excellent witness to her husband.

The husband must love his wife as Christ loved the church. Christ's example showed husbands they must prefer their wife's well-being over their own personal life and desires. Husbands must remember that due to her position of submission, wives have been placed in a weaker position and the example that has been given by Christ and in the church when it comes to weaker parts of the body is to exalt them to a place of preference and honor.

The submission of a godly wife who is exalted to such a place will become a sweet fragrance that will reach the very throne of God, pleasing Him, as well as bringing great honor to the Christian witness of her husband.

It is hard to think of love as a light burden because it can cause sorrow to our spirit, anguish to our mind, fray our emotions, and cause our soul to crumble in despair. However, this is not the burden of love, but love's ability to come into a place of identification.

You cannot come under a burden until you can first identify with it. Jesus could not take on the cross and come under its great burden until He gave up the glory of heaven and became man, and He could not address our sin until He became sin for us. Love must sometimes break us before we can truly come into a place of identification, before we can take up the burden of a matter.

There was a time I had a great burden for the people of the church I attended, but there was a change in leadership. The pastor was a bit immature and problems immediately arose setting small fires of discord in the body. I found myself somewhat in the middle of it and knew that I was walking a fine-line. One day while taking my walk, the Lord instructed me to leave the church because if I didn't, I was about to cause greater discord in the body.

Proverbs 6:14 tells us God hates those who sow discord among the brethren. My heart immediately began to break and I asked the Lord, "Why did you give me such a heart for these people for it to only be broken?" I will never forget what He said, "At least you have a heart that can be broken." He then showed me the broken heart of the Son of God on the cross, a heart that was broken by sin, broken because of lost humanity."

The picture literally almost brought me to my knees. It was one of the moments where the awe of humility takes flight on the wings of hope as I realized that out of the broken heart of Jesus, came life, reconciliation, healing, and restoration. Jesus died as our Savior, rose as our victorious Redeemer, oversees our life as LORD of lords and now serves as our High Priest, our wonderful Mediator in the courts of heaven.

Rayola Kelley

Yesterday I pointed out that it is the identification of love that at times proves to be emotionally unbearable, and the reason is before we can do what is right and honorable, genuine love must become identified with the object of our love. This is why we are told that love bears all things, but the power of love is that it ultimately sets us free to come under the true burden of something.

The real burden of love is that it sees bearing such burdens as our reasonable service. In other words, it is the least we can do for that person; thereby, ensuring that it always remains light and obtainable because in it the power of the Holy Spirit is present. Such love will go the extra mile and to some it may seem to be a great sacrifice, but at such times such acts are not regarded as sacrificial to the one who feels the compelling sweetness of it. To them they still see it as their reasonable service (*Romans 12:1-2*).

This is why we are told real love believes all things because faith and love walk hand in hand. Faith is what allows us to endure a matter and faithfully see it through to the end. It chooses to believe the truth about something, and out of love it has one goal and that is to do right in the situation in order to ensure the moral integrity of love and to bring glory to God.

Once God releases a person from the burden, He gives the individual the grace to see it through to the end at which point the individual feels a complete release of any further responsibility, allowing him and her to let go of it in assurance and hope that God will have His way. It is at this point that hope allows us the freedom to take flight on the wings of expectation (*1 Corinthians 13:7*).

This is the great story of the cross of Christ. Christ was willing to give way to the will of God because it was the least He could do and submit to the cross. Even though it would prove to be a great sacrifice, He knew He would have to go all the way to the grave before the burden could be lifted, allowing grace to flow downward, while hope rises up in resurrection power so that many who are heirs of salvation could be brought forth in eternal glory.

The other day I was watching a difference of convictions between some professional athletes. One man displayed honorable convictions that once were outwardly encouraged, respected, and applauded by society, (before it became about political correctness or racial), while the other lamented and seethed with hatred and rejection of the other one's conviction.

The first man had integrity, the second one acted like a little spoiled boy who lived in some bubble and suddenly discovered he was not the only duck in the pond, and that the world was not orbiting around his particular take on a matter. The sad part about these two responses is that the later stated that he could no longer respect this man or be his friend, as if that was going to cause some great psyche hurt or harm to him.

Hopefully the first man will avoid placating this insanity by apologizing for offending touching feelings that have nothing to do with what is true and right. The truth is the latter one was a fair-weather friend at best who clearly lacked any real professionalism or maturity.

Everyone I meet has a different take on matters, but God's love covers the difference because it respectable towards others, allowing other people to have their own convictions. Don't get me wrong, real love prefers what is honorable, will reject what is harmful, and will not abide by that which proves destructive, while continuing to stand for what is right regardless of the reaction of others. But, the real power behind love is it simply knows how to let things be without taking personal offense. The reaction of many is not against the person, but against their convictions.

The battle is rarely about the differences between personalities and as a result we who love God's truth must not take it personally. Let us remember in this present age that the world's great hate and rage are against God's truth and righteousness and not against us personally.

I don't know about you but at times I have made the Christian life unbearable. I wrestle under burdens that are burying me, feel hopeless due to religious standards that seem unobtainable, and try to adjust to the attitudes and opinions of the religious. At the end of my struggle, I hit a place of hopelessness as I throw up my hands in despair, thinking, "I will never make the grade."

At such times, I am reminded that Jesus' burden is light and His yoke easy. The first time I finally made peace with this truth is when I asked myself what is Jesus' burden and what constitutes His yoke? I had to acknowledge we Christians have a tendency to "ooh" and "ah" at those sayings that touch, inspire, and encourage us without ever really considering what they really mean.

I concluded that I could not properly discern the burden I carried or the yoke I was under until I understood what burden and yoke Jesus was referring to. It was after seeking the Lord, He showed me the burden and the yoke.

The burden is to love God with everything in me and to love my neighbor the same way I regard and prefer myself. Godly love is not a real burden because it comes from God and is shed abroad in our hearts by the Holy Spirit. Our responsibility is to simply share or give this love to others in practical and honorable ways. Because of the Spirit we are empowered to walk in love and because love is eternal there is no limit to it.

As vessels and instruments of the Lord, we are simply the avenues in which love is to flow out to others and what others do with it is neither our burden of responsibility or concern, making it light.

What is the yoke that I must come under? Keep in mind the yoke is the means to yoke together some type of team in work and service. Yoke disciplines the steps of each team member and makes sure the burden of the work does not fall too much on any one of the members.

There is one object we are called to come under and that is our personal cross. As my cross began to discipline my walk, I found myself actually coming into step with Jesus, discovering that Jesus not only prepared the way I was to walk in making it easier for me to keep on the path, but He was also carrying the heavy part of my cross. Next time your Christian life becomes unbearable, stop and examine what heavy burden you have taken on and what yoke you have come under.

What sets God's love apart from the fickle love of the flesh, the unpredictable love of the world, the conditional love of man's religion, and the perverted attraction of Satan's kingdom? What sets God's love apart is that above all else it is moral which means its actions are always honorable.

It also is selfless; therefore, sacrificial, which means it regards and prefers the well-being of others over personal preference, desires, and pursuits, and it is available to WHOSOEVER WILL. Note the last statement.

We often promote the part about God's love being unconditional. It is true you can't earn it, but to experience it, there is one condition and that is a person must receive it by faith.

There are many that I have loved in the past but no matter what I did for them and on their behalf, unless they were willing to receive it, they could never benefit from it. This is true for humanity.

If one does not receive the pure love of God at the point of Christ's work of redemption on the cross, they will ultimately spurn it. It is for this reason that God's love alone does not attract man to Christ, it is the great act of Christ being lifted up on the cross on our behalf to pay the wages for our sins, that has been and always will be the drawing point for those who are lost, seeking a solution, and desperate enough to receive it as being so for them.

We must avoid cheapening God's love by presenting it as being toothless (because it requires nothing to benefit from it), unpredictable (as if it is emotional and sentimental), inept (because it is not worthy of personal sacrifice), and unappreciated (because it can be used, abused, and discarded if it does not serve one's selfish purposes).

We need to keep in mind what *1 John 3:1* shows us about God's love. The Father bestows this incredible, indescribable love upon those who are part of His family.

There is much emphasis on God's love, but the presentation is often shrouded in fleshly practices, whimsical notions, and worldly attractions. It has often been presented as a pinnacle of lustful pursuit, the key to personal happiness and satisfaction, and the solution to the world's problems. After all, "What the world needs now is love, sweet love."

God's love fits in none of the fleshly or worldly notions, ideas, or presentations, and yet how many of us are trying to define God's love within such base confines? In order to make God's love attractive, it is natural to try to spin it according to sentimental nonsense that swings on notions that operate high in the canopy of euphoric fantasy. Such fantasy is void of any reality (safety) net to catch one when they run out of the means to maintain the delusion, nor does it have any real substance to sustain it because it is not real. Since it is fleshly and surface, it ultimately produces fruits of jealousy, disillusionment, contempt and hatred when reality finally inserts itself into its midst.

This brings us back to what God's love is. I have tried to used various words to describe it, but there are none and the reason for that is because God's love is not of this world and it is for this reason God's love is best understood by its action, "For God so loved the world, He gave His only begotten Son."

Christ's death on the cross shows mankind that godly love is an unwavering commitment that is not fickle when faced with disillusionment, is not jealous when encountering insecurities, is not indifferent, and will not be quick to show contempt when others fail to reciprocate in the way they think they should. We need to remember that it is easy to say we love someone or something, but godly love is more than a word, it is action that results in the most excellent way regardless of what is going on around it.

It is from the book of Joshua that the Israelites entered the 400 years of Judges, leaving us an important example. We need to keep in mind that it is not enough to possess the promises of God, you must preserve them to enjoy the fullness of their blessings. However, the only way God's people can enjoy the fullness of the promises of God is by making sure that they keep Him the center of their lives, service, and worship.

The Lord warned the children of Israel that if they followed after idols, they would surely taste the bitterness of such foolishness. Keep in mind that the Lord told them to rid the land of all idols and pagan practices, but the people of Israel failed to do so and as a result the idols tested their hearts as to their devotion to God and became snares to them.

We have many idols that are in our midst, ever testing our hearts as to the love and devotion we have for the Lord. It is easy to think that such idols cannot hurt us and pagan practices will not influence us, but they are effective snares and if we do not keep our heart single in its love and devotion to God, we will end up knowing the bitterness of such captivity to idols and the vanity of, and judgment for, pagan practices.

One of the things I remind people is that your present reality may not be truth, but truth is always reality. We all can have our reality which becomes our concept of truth, but unless it lines up to the Truth, Jesus Christ as to who He is and His work of redemption, we will find ourselves walking in a pseudo light that will blind us to the pending destruction.

There is a great wave of delusion rolling through the world. It will test our love for God and His truth, and to keep from being taken with the great delusion, we must, above all else, love the truth, love the true Jesus of the Bible, and love the one and only God of heaven and earth. The challenge with many of us is that we can intellectually agree with aspects of God and His Word and works, but do we believe Him in all that He says?

If we believe Him that means we believe all of His Word and apply it to our life, conduct, and practices. As previously stated, there are three levels of believing something. The first level agrees with a matter but such agreement will not end with applying it. The next level of belief has to do with believing the source. If we can't trust the source behind something, we will see no need in taking it seriously enough to apply it, and the final level of belief is that not only have we agreed intellectually and believe the authority of the source but we believe in the truth of it making it an "amen, so be it, for it is so" moment in our will area. Believing something to be true means nothing unless we walk in it as being a truth that will be properly applied at all times.

PRAYER

Forsaking all for Christ saves us
from hypocrisy in prayer.
(William MacDonald)

People have their own ideas about prayer, but prayer is personal conversation with God. We must find a common ground in which to approach Him, but Jesus is clear that no one can come or approach the Father but by Him.

We are told in *1 Timothy 2:5* that Jesus, as man and High Priest alone, stands between man and God as our intercessor. The reason we are to approach God by way of Jesus is because Jesus represents our place of covenant that He secured with His blood.

In the Old Testament you see many approaching the Lord on the basis of covenant that was established by the blood of innocent animals. Every time the Jewish people approached LORD, (Jehovah to us, Yahweh to the Jews), they were doing so based on the fact that as LORD, He is a covenant keeping God.

There must be some type of access to approach anyone. For most of us, we approach people based on the type of relationship we have with them and the Lord is no different. Jesus provided the only access to the Father through His redemption, but we can't approach Him unless we have become part of that covenant through faith by receiving His salvation.

Have you ever been overwhelmed when you encountered the Lord in prayer? The first time I encountered the presence of God, I was surprised and overwhelmed. I had a real sense that I would not physically be able to stand long in it because the flesh cannot stand before or in the presence of God for long without fainting.

This was confirmed by what happened to those who came to apprehend Jesus in *John 18:6*. Consider Jacob in *Genesis 28:17* and the Apostle John in *Revelation 1:17* as to their overwhelming sense of

God which caused Jacob to dread the meeting and John to almost faint for fear.

We must be aware of a casual attitude towards God that believes that God's presence would be something to arouse sentimentality or emotional ecstasy. The way God approaches us is based on the type of attitude He wants to create in us towards Him so that we can properly receive what He has in store for us.

When Moses was given his marching orders in the wilderness, the Lord appeared to Him in a burning bush, but when He was giving him the Law, the Lord's presence was dark and foreboding, causing great fear in the people of Israel as to the seriousness as to what was happening on Mount Sinai.

The truth is we can never know how God will approach us, but we must keep in mind that the environment His presence creates has a lot to do with the attitude we must have to come into a place of communion with Him.

When it comes to prayer, we must be persistent and when it comes to a need being met there must be a desperation. For blind Bartimaeus in *Mark 10:46-52*, he was both desperate and persistent.

Jesus had just declared that He came to minister and to give His life as a ransom for many. While He came into Jericho, blind Bartimaeus sat on the side of the highway begging. When he heard that Jesus of Nazareth was coming near, he began to cry out, "Jesus, thou son of David, have mercy on me." The people around him told him to hold his peace but he cried the more to Jesus.

Jesus stood still and commanded him to come to him, and the crowd that tried to silence him told him to be of good cheer for Jesus was calling him. It is interesting to note that Bartimaeus cast away his garment, rose and came to Jesus.

How desperate we are will be determined by how much we cast off the garment of the old in order to come to Jesus to embrace the new. So many times, in prayer we need to cast off the burdens that beset us in order to come to Jesus to be ready to receive what the Lord has for us.

When we consider the blind Bartimaeus in *Mark 10:46-52*, we can see how we must be in prayer. We know in part and see through a glass darkly. Every spiritual search we take must be for the sole purpose of seeing Jesus in a clearer more concise way. We see that when Jesus came by way of Jericho, He did not seek out Bartimaeus; rather, the blind man called out to him and it was upon Jesus' invitation that he came, but first he cast away the old garment.

Jesus has invited all of us to come to Him and learn who He is. It is up to each of us to accept the invitation and seek Him out. It is interesting to note what Jesus asked the blind man, "What wilt thou that I should do unto you?" Jesus knew Bartimaeus was blind but He still asked him, "What would you have me do for you?"

It is important to realize that Bartimaeus' life would totally change if he was healed. He would have to cease begging and begin to take his place in society to provide for himself. To some this may not be a big deal, but to those who have lived life on the streets, it could mean disaster if they are not prepared to walk in a new and different way.

This is true for believers. We may come to Jesus seeking relief or deliverance from a bad habit, a destructive lifestyle, or some great bondage, but are we prepared to walk in a new life? Jesus will first call us to be honest with ourselves, because with this type of change, we must first consider the personal cost such change will bring with it.

One of the purposes of prayer is to seek the God of heaven in order to allow Him to be God in all matters. The big hindrance to prayer and worship is our idea of God and what we think He should do or will do to prove He is God. However, this idea shows that the one who holds such a concept has never really come to a place to trust God to be God.

God will never prove He is God because He already is, and the inward knowledge that God is God is a matter of faith, believing it because the Word tells us so. Remember, faith comes by hearing and hearing by the Word of God (*Roman 10:17*).

I don't believe God is all He is because He has proved it to me; rather, I believe it because the Word says it, and the amazing thing is God has confirmed it as being so by being who He is in situations where I have stepped back and trusted Him with a matter. I don't know if this all makes sense, but the faith I have towards God does not move God; rather, it allows God to be God and at such times I have witnessed His ability to do the impossible.

However, the impossible often reveals that He does not perform great feats to show off; rather, He works the impossible through the most practical means to meet me in my circumstances that, if I am looking for greatness according to some grandiose idea, I could easily miss the blessing or miracle. The one thing I have become very aware of is that God does not do something because He can; rather, He does it because He is faithful to His word, His promises, and His people.

How do we keep our sanity in insane times? We must strive to always come to a heavenly perspective which involves prayer.

Prayer is a privilege, allotted to each of us by redemption. It is the will of God that we pray about everything, knowing that nothing can be done or accomplished without prayer for it connects us to the throne of God. It will part the veil that stands between us and heaven and open the way for us to gain the necessary insight into where we are and the direction we must travel.

As a result, we must learn what it means to pray without ceasing (*1 Thessalonians 5:17*). It means that our heart is always in a state of open communion with God, in a state of abiding in the place of sweet fellowship with the Lord and like any loving Father we can go to Him any time to voice our questions and our concerns.

Let us take courage and learn what it means to approach our Lord in boldness, not because of who we are, but because of what He has done to open such an avenue for us.

I have heard people declare that God answers all prayers, but the Bible indicates differently. If we regard iniquity in our heart, or a man fails to properly honor his wife, or we ask amiss because we want to heap on our lusts the things of the world, or when it comes to the prayers of the wicked the Lord will not hear (*Psalm 66:18; 1 Peter 3:7; James 4:3*).

It is clear that in order to answer prayers they must be heard or regarded. Granted, the Lord may say, "yes" to the prayer because the timing is right and it is according to His will, or "wait" until the way is prepared in which it can be properly received and utilized, or "no" because it would not benefit us in the right way, but this idea that God is ready to hear us at all times to do our bidding is not a correct presentation of God or prayer.

God is not a "Sugar Daddy" that is ready to give us some candy, nor is He a "Santa Claus" that is out there somewhere, but is still able to hear our request, and depending on whether we are good or bad, give it to us. God gave us prayer so we can communicate with Him to find out what is important to Him and make sure we line up to His heart about a matter.

Prayer is to be a type of communion with God where He can share the deep things of His kingdom with us. Effective prayers will never bring God down to our base level; rather, it will cause us to bow down before Him in humility and abandonment so that we can be lifted up into the heavenlies to gain His perspective about those things that concern Him about our lives, His kingdom, and the souls of others.

How important is it for us to be right with others when it comes to our prayer life? The first three commandments of the Ten Commandments have to do with our attitude and worship of God, the fourth one has to do with us putting aside a day to examine and regard our life in the Lord to come to a place of true rest, but the last six commandments have to do with our conduct towards others.

I must state honorable conduct only comes out of right attitudes. We must have a godly attitude of love toward others to do right by them. The debt of love cannot be paid; therefore, it must become our motive when it comes to our life in God and our life before others. Consider this

Scripture, *"Therefore if thou bring thy gift to the altar, and there rememberest that thy brother hath ought against thee; Leave there thy gift before the altar, and go thy way; first be reconciled to thy brother and then come and offer thy gift"* (*Matthew 5:23-24*). *1 Corinthians 11:28-33* tells us we must examine ourselves first before taking communion, and then we must tarry one for another.

Clearly, we must deal with anything that stands in the way of our relationship with the Lord before taking communion and ensure we have a right attitude towards others if we are going to effectively tarry for them. We are to show meekness to all men and instruct those who are fighting against religion in meekness so they may recover themselves from the devil (*2 Timothy 2:25; Titus 3:2*).

We must remember we are called to be intercessors and not stand in judgment of others, and if we are going to be effective intercessors, we may have to become identified with the sins of others to stand in the gap, but we must not be named among those who are in sin because of a wrong attitude towards someone else.

In the last post the word, "meekness" was mentioned. When we read about the nine ingredients in the fruit of the Spirit in *Galatians 5:22-23*, we see that this virtue is part of the abiding fruit that should be present in our lives as believers, but what is meekness?

If we think of this word in terms of our language, it points to those who are wimps and have no real backbone, but the Bible has a different meaning. I was told by a pastor that in the days of the Romans, they had chariot horses that were called "meek." These horses were powerful, but they were considered meek, because all their power was under control, and their master only needed to move the reins slightly and the horses would respond quickly and effectively.

Meekness is "controlled strength that is channeled through humility" that can quickly respond to the Spirit. The example of these powerful horses teaches us that the only way we can have self-control is by being under the control of the Spirit.

The Spirit is the one who inspires, anoints, and prays through us but we must be under His leading if we expect our tongue to be under control, our prayers in control, and the results to be powerful and life-changing.

Do you treat prayer as a means to direct God or are you seeking God so that His Spirit can lead you into a more intimate relationship with Him? I have watched people in prayer attempt to arm wrestle God in doing it their way. Some use certain methods, while others seem to use Scriptures to try to beat Him into some type of submission. God does not direct the world based on our prayers; rather, prayer is His choice of communing with us. After all, prayer is not some blow horn that we use to get God to hear us, but a means to converse with the Lord so that we can share the matters of the heart.

So many hearts are burdened down by issues that are of a spiritual nature and matters that entail life and death, as well as challenges that bring great sorrow. We need to keep in mind that Jesus' heart was broken on the cross because of sin that separates man from God.

Prayer needs to be a means to ensure our relationship with the Lord is right, that nothing is standing in the way of having sweet fellowship with Him. I don't know about you, but as I mature in my relationship with the Lord, I become less and less concerned about getting my way in prayer like some spoiled child, and have come to a appreciate the sweetness, joy, peace, and rest that comes out of being in communion with the Lord.

People sometimes struggle with what to ask the Lord for. They have their list, but oftentimes such lists prove burdensome and become drudgery when it comes to prayer, but is God putting such burdens on them?

This is why it is important to approach the Lord to see what burdens He wants us to come under as a yoke in order to become co-laborers with Him. Once we understand what our burdens should be in regard to His kingdom work, then we can effectively make our requests known to Him.

However, requests and what we need to personally ask Him for are two different matters. In the disciples' prayer Jesus instructed them as to what to ask for personally, "Give us this day our daily bread" (*Matthew 6:11*). I have learned that the cross of Christ is all about me, but 90% of prayer should be about the work God wants to do in the great harvest field of the world.

We are to ask for what we need in order to carry out our responsibilities in the kingdom of God. For me, my prayers in my initial years of Christianity were very selfish and I was missing the mark as to what was important to God. Later I discovered this important prayer in *Proverbs 30:7-9* that puts my needs into perspective that I want to share, "*Two things have I required of thee; deny me them not before I die: Remove far from me vanity and lies; give me neither poverty nor riches; feed me with food convenient for me; Lest I be full, and deny thee, and say, Who is the LORD? or lest I be poor, and steal, and take the name of my God in vain.*"

In my last post I talked about needs. I cannot tell you what a valuable lesson I learned when the Lord impressed me to ask for my needs in order to avoid the trap that came with what I would refer to as "tormenting wants."

As our Creator, God clearly knows what we have need of to properly live and function in this world, but we live in a world that operates from the platform of advertisement and propaganda. The world is forever telling us that we need this or that to make life "easier" or to be "happy."

The life God wants to give us is satisfying because it is based on what has substance and is eternal, but all the world can offer us is a certain lifestyle that will free us up to have more "fun" or to pursue what it promotes as bringing "happiness." I don't know about you but I have observed that people who pursue the lifestyle of the world and not the life God has ordained for them end up empty and miserable.

As Christians we can find ourselves confused as we try to juggle the life God promises and the lifestyle the world promotes. The problem is we can easily end up pursuing the so-called "happiness" of the world, while miserably trying to adjust or tack Christ on to our lives. It is for this reason Jesus stated in *Matthew 6:24*, *"No man can serve two masters: for either he will hate the one, and love the other: or else he will hold to the one and despise the other. Ye cannot serve God and mammon (money).'"*

Prayer that does not lift up God's plan and will in a matter will fail to hit the target; and, what should be the ultimate target of all prayer, service, and forms of worship? As believers we must test everything we do by this one standard: DOES IT BRING GLORY TO GOD.

The Apostle Paul stated in *1 Corinthians 1:29 & 31*, *"That no flesh should glory in his presence…That, according as it is written, He that glorieth, let him glory in the Lord."* It is important to point out that "glory," has to do with what makes something distinct.

There is only one God, there is no entity that possesses like glory that can compete with Him as to the attributes that sets Him apart, and there is no entity that will be able to share in His glory. It is important to point out the world has a fading glory, man has vainglory, man-made religion a false glory, and Satan a counterfeit glory.

The world may put off glitter but it is temporary, man may put forth strength and beauty but it will eventually wither, man-made religion may display self-righteousness but it is false because it has not been wrought by true faith, and Satan is always trying to counterfeit God's glory in order to receive worship from the world.

The world clearly wants to magnify its fading glory, while it is natural for man to compete with God's glory to receive recognition, and false religion wants to replace it and Satan wants to falsely claim it. It is for this reason one of my main prayers has been, "Lord, don't let me TOUCH Your glory."

HOPE & PROMISES

It is not a matter of how much headway
we make in life; rather, it comes down
to how much headway God has made in us.
(Rayola Kelley)

I have wrestled with the idea of entering into all the Lord has for me. I simply did not want to wish for it or talk about it, but I wanted to personally experience His love, know His forgiveness, enjoy His grace, sense His presence, witness His power, and share in His blessings in greater measure.

I have heard great testimonies and wonderful platitudes, but I realized that I must come to terms with this matter for myself. After all, we can only receive such virtues in a relationship with our Lord. The question is how does one start?

As I studied the children of Israel just before they entered the Promised Land, I realized there was an obstacle in front of them, the Jordan River. As believers we must expect and cross over or around obstacles in our walk to inherit what the Lord has for us. We need to remember it is the obstacles that give God an opportunity to show His work and intervention in our lives.

The second aspect was that I needed to trust the great leadership of my Lord. The Lord told Joshua to be strong and of good courage for the LORD his God was with Him and would go before Him (*Joshua 1:5-11*). I realize I had to receive that simple and powerful truth as being so, trusting that the Lord allows the obstacles in my life in order to show Himself faithful to me and mighty on my behalf.

$$\sim$$

As believers, we all have different courses to walk in this age. No two courses will look alike but it will require faith to run the course to the finish line. Faith walks according to the Word of God, while enduring the hardness of the course in light of His promises.

Promises have conditions that only childlike faith will embrace and hold onto as the believer walks out the conditions of the promises in light of the expectation of seeing them come to fruition. Abraham walked by faith in the promises of God in light of seeing the glorious city made by God.

The problem with some Christians is that they have never developed the eyesight of faith to see beyond the glitter of this present age to see the glory of the new world. They walk by the false promises of this age instead of the hope of the next world. They fail to see that at the end of true faith is our inheritance.

This inheritance has nothing to do with gaining the present world but receiving that which is eternal. For me, my goal is to develop the eyesight that allows me to become so caught up with the glory of the promised city of God that the present world loses more of its hold on me. I have long realized my walk in this present age is to prepare me for the glorious inheritance that is awaiting me.

Though the years I have pursued the wrong things out of a false hope or promise. As a young child I pursued ways to gain attention, as an adolescent I desired to be accepted, in my teenage years I wanted recognition, and in my adult life some type of glorification. Each pursuit graduated to another pursuit until I realized such pursuits left me empty, dissatisfied, and miserable.

It is natural for people to search for that which brings satisfaction to their soul, but they look to worldly relationships and activities to find it, only to end up finding themselves in great conflict in the soul. The world can only offer that which brings temporary satisfaction, happiness, and success. The reason is because it promotes lifeless things.

For example, the world promotes wealth through things, man-made religion through works and some type of enlightenment, government through free handouts, and selfishness through lustful pursuits. The problem with such pursuits is that they leave individuals spiritually bankrupt, causing them to become like restless waves that are driven in the oceans of the world by winds of circumstances that hold no hope or real direction.

It took some big failures in my spiritual journey to realize that there is only one thing that enriches my life and that is Jesus and there is only one way to obtain eternal riches in Him. *James 2:5* summarized it in this way, *"Hearken, my beloved brethren, Hath not God chosen the poor of this world rich in faith, and heirs of the kingdom which he hath promised to them that love him?" Hebrews 6:12* tells us how to obtain the richness that comes through faith, *"That ye be not slothful, but followers of them who through faith and patience inherit the promises."*

Each day reminds me of a rainbow, which to this day serves as a covenant from God to man. If there are sins, the blood of Jesus washes them away, and if there are regrets, which often are a result of missed opportunities, the Lord can make them into stepping stones where I learn from them as I step above them to take advantage of the opportunities that are before me.

There may be storms but they settle the stifling dust of drudgery and are followed by a rainbow that reminds me that my present life is a memorial to God and that, like the rainbow, the opportunities to enjoy the moment of the day will fade quickly; therefore, I must note the moments of beauty, the opportunities before me, and the gift of life that God has given me.

God clearly gives us the gift of today so that we can live in the now and walk by faith in it and through it, while experiencing His compassions and mercies that are new every day, knowing that He is writing on our slates and is renewing the inner man in us so we can come forth as new creations. In the end we will gain an inheritance where we possess the promises of eternity and reflect the heavenly glory of the next world.

Last night we had wind, rain, and lightning. The wind was alerting us of a coming storm, the rain followed and clearly left its mark on the terrain, and this morning the clouds hung on the mountains like curtains that would lift at any time revealing God's handiwork. But last night, it was as if God was speaking through the thunder and the sky was displaying its own fire-works in preparation of unveiling the miraculous works of God within creation. Although the clouds created a type of subdued environment, the expectation that the best was on the horizon was present because we all know the sun will always break through.

The event reminded me of my walk with the Lord. The environment we are now in has caused many to become subdued with uncertainty, but the inspired Word of God has already warned the saints of the storms pending on the horizon. Remember, God's Word is His voice and it still can be heard as long as the spirit is able to discern and the ears of faith are present to believe what is so. His thunder and lightning are necessary to cause people to heed the warnings in order to properly respond.

Regardless of the intensity of the storm, the Holy Spirit will bring the waters to revive the spirit, renew the inner man, and bring expectation to the soul. Although the clouds of uncertainty shroud the future for many, as believers we know that the Sun of Righteousness will break through soon enough to reveal that God was in the midst of the storm doing a greater work on the terrains of men's souls. This is not only our sure hope, but a wonderful promise.

It is snowing today, but rain will soon follow, pointing to the fact that we are now in that exciting time of the year when much around us is about to reveal itself in living color. In spite of today's weather, it appears spring is here.

I love when the crocuses rise above the remaining snow, or what appears to be lifeless earth, to make their wonderful appearance. Here is a flower that appears petite but defies the harsh elements. Its petals close at night, but as soon as the sun appears, like other flowers it faithfully opens up to receive the rays of life. This flower is not here for very long, but it is the first flower people look for and the one they let out a sigh over when it is gone. It is a flower of hope because it breaks through the gloom of winter to greet those who are tired of the snow, the gray skies, and the deary landscape. It is a flower that reminds me that in spite of my life being just a vapor, here one day gone another, that because the Sun of Righteousness has risen with the light of His life in my soul, I can still have hope, and I can bring it to the downtrodden, knowing full well it can break through the gloom of any darkness with God's promises. This hope is what causes light to shine through the grayness with truth, while serving as an avenue to share the Gospel that can change the terrain of a man's lifeless soul.

As people, our lives may be a vapor, our impact small, and our time limited, but as believers we must remember that we have what it takes to break through the trying elements of our time, stand distinct from the lifeless landscape, and become a wonderful testimony and blessing of God's abiding grace to others as well as a living witness of His ability to miraculously make a lifeless rod bloom wherever it is located.

Since losing our precious little Chihuahua, Bell, we have kept an extra eye on her companion Tucker. We often referred to Tucker as Bell's pet because in a way she chose him after she lost her companion, Angel. These two Chihuahuas did almost everything together. They went out together, especially in the morning and at night. In the morning they were put in Bell's chair together to sleep.

Initially, Tucker would have to push his weight around in order to secure his spot because Bell was a bit of a "hog" when it came to "her" chair. However, they worked it out and would settle down and sleep peacefully together.

Tucker knows his companion is no longer around and from his responses, the infamous chair now appears big, lonely, and no longer a warm place for him to rest. He seems a bit lost, uncertain, and not sure how it will all translate in the end.

So often we underestimate animals. They have feelings, and we have seen different species mourn the loss of one of their own. Tucker reminds me that when it comes to such things as wading through some great loss, change, and transition that it becomes a personal journey. No matter what, we can't take the pain, the uncertainty, or the distress away from another. We want to spare them, but we would have to become them in order to identify with them in their plight.

When you think about Jesus Christ, you realize this is what He did on our behalf. He became man to identify with us in our plight. He traveled the same path of temptation as we do in this world in order to meet us in our state, and when the time came, He went to the cross and took our place to become sin while tasting death so we could be spared from tasting God's wrath and be able to experience real life.

Even though what Tucker is experiencing is his personal journey, I think he is beginning to recognize that even though we can't take away what he feels, we are there for him, to share with him in his experience. Although our spiritual journey as believers is personal, we can rest assured that the Lord is there to share with us in the experience, for His promise is clear, "I will never leave you or forsake you."

I love the Lord's promises. I hope that when a Christian is asked what is the first promise in the Bible that he or she is able to answer the question. The first promise is found in the first book of the Bible, *Genesis*, and it was given in the midst of great judgment being pronounced because of what happened in the garden.

I realize the matter of Adam and Eve has been a great debate. For example, it is Eve's fault because she talked the man into taking of the deadly fruit, and yet it was the man who was entrusted with the proper instruction and it was clearly noted he was with Eve when she was being tempted by the serpent *(Genesis 3:6)*.

There is the idea being presented that Adam was so honorable that he partook of the fruit to be in the same state as Eve. Such an action is not only dishonorable, but completely foolish and points to idolatry. Besides, if Adam was so honorable and so loved his wife, why did he not rebuke the serpent in the first place and lead his wife away from the temptation?

The debate and the excuses seem endless about the first act of rebellion and it continues to this day. To me the real message of Adam and Eve's failure is not whose fault it was, but what really happened. If we are to appreciate the significance of the first promise, we must understand why it was given in the first place. And, what was the promise, "That a redeemer would come and restore what was lost."

Has God given you a specific promise that has not yet come to fruition? We walk by faith because of who God is, and we walk in faith according to promises He has given. To walk by faith means I am confidently walking towards something that may be unseen, but is sure, and to walk in faith, means that I am directing my steps in light of something that in heaven is so and on earth will be so because God said it.

This is the reason Jesus stated in the famous 'Lord's Prayer,' "Thy kingdom come, thy will be done in earth as it is in heaven." What many people do not realize is that in most cases the God they have erected in their imagination is too small to do much of anything *(2 Corinthians 10:3-5)*. Granted, they have a sentimental attachment towards this god, but when it comes to their faith, they have faith in their notions about their god, but not faith towards the God of heaven.

When these people go to exercise their pseudo faith, they often put the true God to a foolish test by insisting that He prove He is God by complying to their demands and ways. They may even use His promises against Him in an attempt to arm-wrestle Him into compliance. In some cases, these people are teetering on the precipice of insanity because they carry the responsibility of controlling, manipulating, and wrestling with their "false" god to control their reality, confirm their notions about him, and ensure the outcome.

The thing I love about genuine faith is that it simply believes God and walks in obedience to what is so, knowing God is true to all He has declared in His Word. Genuine faith does not try to control God, coerce Him, or manipulate Him; rather, true faith lets God be God and trusts Him with the outcome, knowing He is perfect in all of His ways.

Yesterday, I asked if God has given you a promise that has not come to fruition. God has given me many promises, and I can say that almost all of them have come to fruition and for those that have not, they will be brought forth at the proper time. God gives His people promises so they can stand and not faint even when it looks like He has forgotten, not only the promises, but them.

I remember a story of a woman who prayed for her husband who was a successful businessman to be saved. God eventually gave her the assurance in her spirit that it would be so. However, her husband was killed in a car accident and she was left with deferred hope that took flight on the wings of despair, touching down on the tormenting runway of unbelief, leaving her in a cold state.

She took over husband's business and five years after his death, the secretary brought in one of her late husband's business cards telling her that a young man was there to see him. Out of curiosity she met with him. She asked him how he had met her husband. He shared how he was in the military and had been home on leave, but when he went to return back to the base, he found himself without transportation. He started hitchhiking when her husband stopped and gave him a ride.

She asked him about their conversation. The man began to relate their conversation and brought up how he was a Christian and the opportunity opened up for him to share Christ and the message of salvation with her husband. It was then that the woman discovered that her husband's heart had become receptive to the message and he actually pulled off to the side of the road to receive Christ as his Savior and Lord. When her husband dropped the soldier off at his destination, he handed him his business card and told him that when he was in town, to look him up.

By this time the wife was overwhelmed. She asked him if he remembered the date it all happened. Because of the situation, he remembered it well, and the woman recognized it as the date her husband had entered into eternity. God had kept His word and her husband had actually left his calling card so that five years later his wife's faith would be resurrected in a humbled, repentant spirit for wasted years of unbelief, hope would once again rise up in expectancy in her soul and the joy of her salvation would return.

So many times, we put our hope in the promise instead of the Promiser. Without the Promiser, promises mean nothing. The problem is we want to see the promise instead of simply trusting the Promiser, that regardless of whether we see it or not, the promise is so because God never lies.

COURAGE & ENCOURAGEMENT

*Courage comes after we count
the cost and realize that we have
nothing to lose, but everything
to gain. At that point any
concerns become pinnacles
of encouragement.
(Rayola Kelley)*

One of the challenges I have had is to leave the old life and old ways behind. I am quite acquainted with the old and the new always presents the unknown to me. However, the old represents the wilderness of my soul before entering into the abundance of the inheritance that goes with the very life of Jesus that abides in me.

The Jordan River represented the boundary between the children of Israel's old wanderings in the great wilderness and the Promised Land. They had to somehow pass over or pass through the river. Their leader Joshua had a promise that the Lord would go before him and go with him as he led the people.

The Ark of the Covenant represented the presence of the Lord and the people were instructed when they saw the priests and Levites bearing it that they were to leave their place and follow the ark. Jesus is our ark that we are hid in, the Great Shepherd who leads, the High Priest who carries our burden, and His Spirit, the presence who goes before us. I realize my responsibility was not to figure out how to get around, over, or pass through some obstacle; rather, my obligation was to simply rise up and follow Him as He passes before me.

As the children of Israel witnessed, once the priest placed their feet in the Jordan, the water parted. As believers we can encourage ourselves that regardless of the obstacles that confront us in our spiritual walk it is not our problem to deal with them; rather, we must be ready to wait for instruction and then be prepared to rise up when our Lord Jesus passes before us, calling us to follow as He leads us into greater promises.

In your Christian walk, how many of you felt like you just stepped into it? Walking by faith has occasionally caused me to feel like I am stepping into an unknown territory that is full of many uncertainties and dangers. At times I have felt as if I have just stepped off some cliff, marched into a dark cavern, walked into a hornet's nest, or treaded into the enemy's camp.

When we follow the Lord, we can't see ahead of Him and around Him. My friend, Jeannette, the artist depicted the scene on a painting that best describes it. She has a small lamb following Jesus up a narrow path, with an abyss on one side and the rocky mountain side on the other. We may not always be able to see where we are going, but as long as we see Him in front, we must exercise faith and trust that He knows where He is taking us.

Faith begins where our understanding ceases and we choose to trust the Lord with the outcome. We must take courage in each step knowing Jesus promised to always go before us, that He would never forsake us, and that He knows exactly where He is leading us. Through the years when I have felt like I have stepped off a cliff in order to learn how to soar in His Spirit, I became aware of His hand catching me like a mother eagle swooping underneath her eaglet to catch it before it hits the ground.

When I found myself in a dark cavern, I became aware of the light of His Word that lit the path enough that I could take the next step, and when I encountered some dangerous hornet nest, I had the promise that such things could not harm me. As for the enemy's camp, they had already been scattered.

The great beauty about encouraging ourselves in the Lord based on His Word and promises is it allows us to rise up and truly exercise our faith towards Him.

One of the reasons we must take courage when we are contending with fear towards the challenges before us in our faith walk is because we have to wait on the Lord until He moves. I don't know about the rest of you, but my mind can create all kinds of overwhelming scenarios when I am to wait.

In the past I have had to be honest about the concerns (worries) that I have found myself getting caught up with when fear begins to peak around the edges of my mind. To avoid being pushed or paralyzed by fear I immediately must bring all my thoughts into obedience to Christ, which is always easier said than done (*2 Corinthians 10:3-5*).

In the past I have allowed imagination to run rampant causing the flesh to war against the Spirit creating a tumult in my soul. At such times I have tried to reason with myself to only find my mind fainting. I have quoted promises only for them to be drowned out by the storm that was raging. It has taken a few times around the same mountain for me to realize that the reason I was losing the battle in my mind was because I was holding onto to some right to see a matter turn out a certain way. It was only when I truly humbled myself before the Lord, and from the depths of my spirit declared, "Not my will but Your will" was I finally able to land on the runway of peace to soothe my heavy heart.

Before we can encourage ourselves in the Lord at such times, we must first secure the peace of mind and heart that by faith we are where we are because we are in the will of the Lord and until He moves, everything is still on schedule. I like what the Psalmist said in Psalm 27:14, "Wait on the LORD; be of good courage, and he shall strengthen thine heart: wait, I say, on the LORD."

Intellectually, as a Christian, I know who I can seek when the challenges of life toss me back and forth emotionally, and slam against my resolve with forceful gales to the point everything in my inner being is shaken. I wrestle with holding onto what small semblance of strength that remains as it appears all will be lost in the end. However, I have learned that I must take courage in what I know is true about my Lord and Savior Jesus Christ in order to stand and face the storms of life.

It is only when I let go of my present struggle to hold onto what is left, and by faith fling myself on Jesus as the great Rock of Ages and cling to His faithfulness that I can sense the anchor of joy taking hold in my soul as peace settles over my spirit. We must not forget that even though the Lord may seem asleep in such storms as He did in *Matthew 8:24-26*, He is very much in our boat and nothing can happen to us without it happening to Him.

In the past I felt I could not be settled in my spirit until the Lord rebuked the storm raging in my life, but in this incident, I learned that Jesus does not want us to stir Him up to calm the storms as if He is unaware of it, but trust that He will go through the storm with us, ensuring our safety and well-being until it is time for Him to speak to it.

The Lord is never late, but according to my personal calculations He doesn't always seem on time either. In years past I have tried so hard to be calm about taxing matters that were moving towards me with great speed. I told myself I was not going to become anxious because the Lord was in control. I would try to push down my doubts that began to bubble up and were threatening to overtake what resolve was left.

At such times I learned some important lessons. I can remember one time that I needed rent money. The date was looming on the horizon without any indication of a resolution. As I tried to keep myself in a calm state, I could feel frustration mounting. I went to a wood shed for some fire wood and suddenly the frustration came out in full force.

Amazingly, I felt the Lord waiting like a good father for what was nothing more than a frustrated child that needed to vent. After I calmed down, I asked Him what did He expect from me. He answered me by saying, "Ask me for what you have need of." I simply said, "I need rent money." As soon as it was out of my mouth, I knew it was a done deal and that afternoon we went to the post office and in our box were two envelops with enough funds to pay our rent.

The first lesson I had to learn that has become a great encouragement to my soul was to discern the difference between wants and needs so I could simply ask the Lord for what I had need of, knowing that it is one of His promises to provide it. I have learned that by believing it is done, and then receiving my needs with thanksgiving without actually seeing it, that it always ended up calming my spirit and satisfying my soul.

When I was a new Christian and I thought about God doing something, it was always in a big way. Through the years I have seen God move some big mountains from in front of me, but what touched me the most was when God met me in what many would consider small ways.

Granted, God moving mountains brought awe to my spirit but it was the small things that touched my heart. Perhaps He answered the secret desires of my heart that seem insignificant to others but was a point of great encouragement to me. There were times He met my need in an unexpected way that revealed He is not only all-knowing, but He knows each of us very well. There are times He answered those small concerns that were barely a whisper on my lips, but clearly reached His ears in heaven. I could go on and on but what each small, personal encounter with the Lord taught me is that He is faithful to each and every one of His people.

The Lord is faithful to care about our secret desires, hears the whispers of our prayers, responds to what many would consider insignificant, and meet us in the simplest and smallest ways to show the length of His care, love, and grace. As believers we must beware of always looking for the big things, because in doing so we may fail to see the small things He is doing that will produce the greatest and lasting results in our lives.

It is the heart of our Lord that we be encouraged in Him and because of Him. It is natural to consider the Lord in light of what He can do for us, but as we fall more in love with Him we learn that the way we encourage ourselves in Him is based on who He is and not necessarily according to what He can do on our behalf.

It is true upon salvation God delivered us from the power of darkness and has translated us into the kingdom of His dear Son (*Colossians*

1:13) The Lord's arm is not short in doing the impossible on our behalf, but we must remember it is His heart to meet each one of us in a relationship as He delivers us from the influence of this present age and guides us by His Spirit through the various storms of life.

It is a daily choice for me to encourage myself in Him and I often remind myself of *Jeremiah 29:11, "For I know the thoughts that I think toward you, saith the LORD, thoughts of peace, and not of evil to give you an expected end."*

One of the lessons I learned about encouraging myself in the Lord is that there must be some environment of discouragement. We do not encourage ourselves in the Lord without needing a reason to do so.

As Christians it is natural to want to avoid such places, but keep in mind Jesus was led into the wilderness by the Spirit after baptism to be tested for 40 days and nights. Obviously, none of us want to experience discouragement because of some circumstance that is out of our control. However, the environment of discouragement has to be present in order for someone to take the necessary initiative to stand in faith, remembering who God is, while reminding self of His promises. It is not that the Lord forgets His promises, but it takes faith to stand in the midst of challenges and claim His promises to endure the test.

It is natural to want smooth waters but it is in the challenging times we learn that God is God and we discover that it is His abiding faithfulness and power that keeps us during such times. After Jesus calmed the storm that had caused His disciples to go into despair, what was their response? *"But the men marveled, saying, What manner of man is this, that even the winds and the sea obey him?" (Matthew 8:27).*

As you can see it is in the times of discouragement that awe can rise up out of despair and take flight because of the miraculous intervention of God to save, deliver, and bring His people safely to their destination.

One of the hardest challenges is to encourage ourselves in drudgery. Doing the same thing every day can cause spiritual stagnation. We all would like to avoid tribulation, but to rise up out of drudgery often causes us to look to meaningless future events with anticipation which can cause us to miss present blessings.

It is easy in this uneventful state to settle for sensationalism that will prove to be quite temporary, but take a good crisis and it not only wakes us out of the normalcy but as Christians we are challenged to take the high road that will enlarge our character if we accept it. Consider Peter.

The fact that he failed to catch fish took all expectation out of catching any that day Jesus stepped on the scene. Jesus instructed him to cast his net on the other side of the boat and when he obeyed, his nets became overflowing with fish. The problem with drudgery is we can become complacent in our present state while looking to the future and missing the opportunity to simply cast our net on the other side. For Christians to cast their net on the other side simply means changing their focus.

We need to quit becoming complacent because of what is not, avoid dreaming about what could be, stop looking around for what will never be, and look towards the Lord in order for Him to redefine our present reality in light of our heavenly purpose. We need to do this while trusting Him in bringing forth the hope that is yet to be fully realized as we are faithful with the tasks before us. This type of state allows us to ever look for and seize upon the opportunity to bring glory to our Lord and Savior, Jesus Christ.

Being in these bodies and surrounded by the tides of challenges and problems this present age can bring with it can be overwhelming and daunting. Sadly, as believers we have been encouraged to act as if these different challenges can't possibly affect us because we are either above them or immune to them. However, this presentation proves to be bitter to those struggling with challenging problems, unrealistic to onlookers, and ultimately prevents those who are struggling from looking up and trusting the Lord to lead them through each situation.

The truth is the Lord does not always deliver us out of situations but leads us through them like He did Noah when he was in the ark. We would all like to live on the clouds of spirituality, and swing from the flimsy branches of fantasy that believes the Christian life spares us from the worldly challenges but, we are bound to this earth by our physical bodies and the Lord wants to use such challenges to make us effective ministers of consolation. We can't console certain people unless we have experienced like struggle, sorrow, and loss while experiencing the reality of Christ through it (*2 Corinthians 1:3-7*).

I have had many different challenges that caused despair and sorrow to penetrate into the very bowels of my soul and spirit. I realize that I could become a victim of it, rage against it, or trust the Lord that He is working something in me in order to bring forth something that will be precious to Him that could bring consolation, inspiration, and comfort to others.

We need to always remember we are not here to live our own lives, but to live the life of Christ and impart it to others.

Jesus took on bodily form in order to become identified with us. He experienced everything in His humanity that we could experience except sin. He did not try to hide from challenges, give in to temptations in weaknesses, shake in opposition, whine against false accusations, or avoid the cross. He was not spared from the judgment of sin; rather, He was lifted up to become judgment for sin.

He experienced all of this in order to be our example that we can overcome in this world regardless of what confronts us, but we can only do so in the Holy Spirit as we line up to the will of God through obedience to His Word. We are not here to avoid being touched by life; rather, we are here to enter in with the hurting and lost and touch their lives with the reality of Christ.

This world is our testing ground that is preparing us for heaven and when we are being tested by life, we need to remember that we are simply passing through this present age as strangers and to encourage ourselves with the promise found in *1 Corinthians 2:9, "But as it is written, Eye hath not seen, nor ear heard, neither have entered into the heart of man, the things which God hath prepared for them that love him."*

One of the ways we can encourage ourselves is by remembering God's promises. There are those who have actually counted all the promises in the Bible. According to one account, there are over 3,573 promises in the Bible and another declares there is really over 7400 promises. The problem I see when it comes to the promises of God is that many people quote the promise, but fall short of noting the conditions that must be present for God to honor His promises.

Since people speak of God's love being unconditional, they have a tendency to act as if His promises are also unconditional. It is true God has made His love available to all who will receive it at the place of Jesus' sacrifice on the cross, but one must receive His love to benefit from it. People can use, shun, or reject love and if they do, they will not benefit from it.

God's promises have also been made available to all but there are conditions that must be met before one can receive the promises. I appreciate all of God's promises, but I am also sober when I claim one of those promises. I am aware that if I am not meeting the conditions that go with it, I will not be prepared to receive it in the right attitude and way.

Keep in mind God, is using our present journey on earth to prepare us for those things we can't begin to imagine in our present state. It is great to claim promises, but it is more so glorious when we actually experience the reality of a promise because we have met the conditions that allow us to embrace it in such a way that it truly enriches our lives.

There are various ways we can try to encourage ourselves in our Christian walk. We can try to talk to ourselves, but it is hard to step over self when you come to the same feelings and conclusions about a matter. We can try to reel in our emotions but they often refuse to be silent when our world is out of control or there is overwhelming injustice to confront. We can claim promises but they can seem hollow when we are in the midst of great struggles.

I have tried these different methods but the one way to encourage ourselves is to remind ourselves of who God is. When my friend is struggling with a matter she often goes out and looks at the night sky. When she does, she remembers that the vast heavens cannot contain the majesty of God and that He named each one of those stars.

When we compare the matters of this world with the greatness of God, it is amazing how they become small and our sense of Him becomes overwhelming as we realize He is still in control.

One of the emotions that can rob us of our peace of mind is something called "worrying." When we "worry" we find ourselves running around in dark caverns of hopelessness. The more we worry, the more the walls of the caverns will close in on us, as any type of sanity and encouragement recedes further and further away from us. The Bible refers to "worries" as "cares of the world" or even "little foxes" that can be destructive to the fruit of our lives.

Worries have three springboards to operate from: unbelief towards God, fear that I won't get my way about a matter, and losing total control of something. As you consider the three reasons for worry it becomes obvious why it is sin to God. In a sense, worries are accusing towards Him. They are saying "I can't trust You with certain things," "I know what I want or what will be right to me and Your way may not prove to be the best for me," and, "I must still control the matter because I can't trust You to properly work it out."

I lived in an environment of constant worrying while growing up, and I can tell you that all it managed to do was drive the person who was doing it into an unnecessary frenzy because worrying changes nothing, while pushing others around into utter frustration as they tried to figure out how to bring the sanity of reality back into the picture.

The only way we can combat worrying is to not allow matters to cause us to faint in our minds and look up to the Lord as we choose to encourage ourselves in who He is and His many promises.

In my last post I talked about worrying. When you consider "worrying," it points to an undisciplined mind. Granted, worrying is an emotional response that will escalate until it becomes tormenting, but it begins in the imagination.

The Bible tells us what to think on—that which is true, honest, just, pure, lovely and of good report (*Philippians 4:8*). If you compare the qualities highlighted in this Scripture with worrying, it is obvious that worrying is contrary to this verse. For example, worrying is being concerned about certain things happening according to personal preference and not truth.

It is not honest because its motive is selfish. It is not just because the affect it will have on others is not regarded. It is not pure because the flesh is active and it is not lovely because of the distasteful fruits it often produces for others. Finally, it lacks a trustworthy testimony.

We must discipline our thinking by bringing all thoughts into captivity to the obedience of Christ. After all, when you consider the characteristics of correct thoughts in *Philippians 4:8*, there is only one thing we can think on that possesses each attribute, and that is the Lord Jesus Christ.

It is for this reason that *Hebrews 12:2-3* stated this, *"Looking unto Jesus the author and finisher of our faith; who for the joy that was set before him endured the cross, despising the shame, and is set down at the right hand of the throne of God. For consider him that endured such contradiction of sinners against himself, lest ye be wearied and faint in your minds."*

There are two biggest culprits behind worrying and that is fear and impatience. When I become fearful about a matter, I begin to worry about it and when I become impatient with something, I can easily slide into worrying about it. Clearly, worrying about something reveals that the matter before me is beyond my capacity to change.

The question is, will I allow worrying to cause me to slide into a paralyzing state of despair, or push me into a frantic state that will make me inconsolable and unreasonable, or will I choose the way of faith and

Rayola Kelley

trust that since God is sovereign over all matters that He has allow the situation and has timing as well. Perhaps I am to learn something or maybe I am being tested to be enlarged.

The Lord could also be using me in regard to someone else's life. God never wastes an opportunity and as believers we are to choose the way of faith that when all avenues become closed to us, we must step back and let God open the doors He wants to open while keeping the rest of the doors closed.

I have been a Christian now for over 40 years and I often come to this crossroad of faith, ever learning that fear is a test that requires me to take a step back from it and look up, trusting the Lord to lead me through it, and that in waiting upon the Lord I have learned what it means to be patient due to abiding confidence in the Lord's perfect way of doing something and His perfect timing that produces eternal results.

Worrying is the fastest way to close down all avenues that would allow you to encourage yourself in the Lord. As stated in the last post, worrying finds one of its bases in fear that will cause unbelief to rise up out of the ashes of self-centered concern.

Jesus understood the reason for worrying, but He clearly rebuked the unbelief of it. When the disciples were worrying about the outcome of the contrary winds they were encountering on the Sea of Galilee as Jesus slept in their boat, unbelief took hold of their minds and convinced them that He was truly oblivious to their plight. They looked at the storm instead of resting in the fact that Jesus was in the boat with them and nothing would happen to them that did not happen to Him.

This is true for us as believers. Jesus is in the boat of our life with us and everything that happens to us will likewise happen to Him. We must quit looking at the waves of life that are tossing our boat from side to side and know we are not alone. Even though it seems the Lord is asleep on a particular watch, the Bible tells us He never slumbers. What will we choose to believe because it will determine if we encourage ourselves in the Lord or not: the contrary waves of the present situation or the Word of God?

118

The world is a barren wilderness and the way is hard and it is easy enough to become discouraged. We see this example in the journey of the children of Israel in *Numbers 21*. They were on the last leg of their journey through the wilderness to finally be led into the Promised Land, but they became so discouraged because of the hard way that they began to speak against God and Moses.

The problem with speaking against God, is a person will quickly slide into unbelief towards Him and will not trust Him to lead him or her the rest of the way. God cannot bless us if we become so discouraged by the hard way that we melt into anger towards Him.

Jesus stated that the way is hard but it leads to life. We must accept the fact that the way through this world is not going to be a picnic, while remembering the barren wilderness of this present age does not represent our life. God has given us many promises but these promises will not be fully realized until we finish this course and enter into the glory of the world to come. We can't encourage ourselves in the world or by it; rather, we must look beyond it to the next world to come to a place where we will find the courage to continue on until we finally enter into what the Lord has prepared for us.

For the children of Israel, the way through the wilderness had become hard and they became frustrated, angry, and resentful. They were weary with waiting for the time when they could enter the Promised Land that had been assured them 40 years earlier, but we cannot encourage ourselves in the Lord as long we are angry about the way we must tread, and we will never finish the course unless we have the faith to see beyond this present wilderness of the world to see glimpses of the promises the Lord has in store for us.

We become discouraged and overwhelmed as long as we look at the present terrain and if we begin to slide into unbelief because of it, God will put something in the way to cause us to look up for a solution. In the case of the children of Israel the Lord sent serpents to force them to look to the solution that He provided for them in the wilderness.

Jesus spoke of this solution in *John 3:14-15, "And as Moses lifted up the serpent in the wilderness even so must the Son of man be lifted up: That whosoever believeth in him should not perish, but have everlasting life."*

The next time you feel like sliding into the pit of despair and unbelief because of the circumstances before you, remember to look up because the solution has been lifted up above the terrain, above the problem and above this present world.

When it comes to encouraging ourselves in our walk through the darkness of the age we live in, we must consider what we are looking to for encouragement and looking for in light of inspiration that will take us above the present to consider the eternal. We start out with this idea of what we should see, only to fail to recognize it because it is not what we expected.

I have often overlooked what would have been points of inspiration and encouragement to me because of preconceived notions. It took a few years for me to realize that in my life it has been the small things that often encourage me the most. We all think that encouragement comes when the big things of life transpire, but for me when the big things happened, I was often too tired to get excited about it. Don't get me wrong I was truly thankful, but encouragement often comes off the heels of inspiration.

I can't count the times that I was inspired by something in the Scripture I was reading or the text I was studying. Such inspiration always causes encouragement to rise up in me and take flight. This often brings to mind what happened when John the Baptist was still in the womb of his mother, Elisabeth.

Mary who was pregnant with the Promised One, walked into the house of her cousin Elisabeth, causing John the Baptist to react while still in his mother's womb. *Luke 1:41* tells us the result, *"And it came to pass, that, when Elisabeth heard the salutation of Mary, the babe leaped in her womb; and Elisabeth was filled the Holy Ghost."*

Imagine the simple voice of the Messiah's mother caused John to leap in the womb. We must never overlook the small things because they often contain nuggets that will inspire us, bringing encouragement to a sagging, weary soul.

One of the qualities that will bring encouragement to a soul is thankfulness. It is hard to know the depths encouragement can reach in a weary, downtrodden soul that will allow it to find a springboard that causes it to reach great heights in the Spirit. As I stated, inspiration is a type of springboard for encouragement to gain heights, but what allows it to travel through the depths of despair, only to take flight is thankfulness.

It is hard to be thankful in challenging situations, but we can always be thankful for our status in Christ. People often remain in the depths of despair because they fail to look to the One who inspires thanksgiving and is worthy of the praise that can take flight and lift us above the situation.

It is natural to be buried by trying situations, but Jesus said it best in *John 16:33, "These things I have spoken unto you, that in me ye might have peace. In the world ye shall have tribulation: but be of good cheer, I have overcome the world."* In this world we should expect tribulation, but we can be of good cheer as our thankfulness reaches into the pit with the knowledge and expectation that our life, hope, and well-being is not determined by the tribulation of this world, but of the hope that is yet to be fully realized by those of us who are heirs of salvation.

One of the ways I encourage myself is by exalting the Lord in His proper place. Many people remain in the pit of discouragement because the challenge of problems loom in front of them and these problems are often magnified by fear, uncertainty, and unbelief. It is easy to allow these things to cause a blanket of depression to settle upon our soul because in such a state there is no hope.

Encouragement can't exist unless there is hope and hope will have no power if there is no expectation. Clearly, we can't put hope in wishful thinking that all will turn out right in the end, but what we can do is put our hope in is God. We can have great expectation not because He is able to do the impossible but because of His impeccable character and His perfect ways.

It is when we quit looking around and begin to think on who the Lord is that encouragement can be taken off of life supports and infused with hope that stands and walks according to expectation that is firmly established on the immutable attributes of God.

In what way are you discouraged or overwhelmed by circumstances? This is when our faith towards the Lord can be greatly tested. We try to wrestle our doubts down to a low murmur, push aside our uncertainties, or climb over the nagging logic that causes us to look at the situation and wonder why would God care about me in such a plight. After all, He has the whole world to contend with.

Keep in mind, one of Satan's greatest tools is isolation. He can cause us to feel isolated, insignificant, and hopeless because we are inept to get beyond our emotional pit of hopelessness. At such times of darkness, we fail to see that Satan is behind the doubt, accusation, and what appears to be our insignificant plight when it comes to a big, busy God.

It is in such isolation we need to remember that it is an attempt of Satan to not only isolate us from God, for God is always with us, but to isolate us from putting our faith in practice. It is faith that looks up, grabs ahold of who God is and swings upward with His promises to land in a place of complete rest and confidence in our Lord. It is true we are inept to rise above the pit ourselves, but what is not true is that God is not aware of us.

There is one person that often encourages me in the Bible during trying times because he fell into the typical cycle that many of us as humans can fall into. He was zealous, but fell hard into disillusionment. He had a calling but he fell into utter despair. He had strength, but found himself to be a coward when put up against the wall. He had conviction but ended up denying what he believed to be so, causing him to fall into the pit of despondency and depression. I am sure that most of you will recognize this man. His name was Peter.

It is easy to see how Peter's zealousness was based on ignorance, his calling propped up by pride, and his strength was untrustworthy and fading, causing him to deny that he even knew Jesus. Peter clearly was relying on the flesh and not on the Lord. He walked away in utter defeat.

We can shake our head at Peter, but if we are honest with ourselves, we have probably fallen into a similar cycle or faced certain personal defeats when our character and faith were being tested. It is important to realize we are tested so that the flesh will fail. Jesus actually pointed this out to Peter before the great test came, "*Simon, Simon, behold, Satan hath desired to have you, that he may sift you as wheat: But I have prayed for thee, that thy faith fail not: and when thou art converted, strengthen thy brethren" (Luke 22:31-31).*

We can take courage knowing that it is only when we come to the end of our personal strength and attempts that we can truly be converted to the righteousness of God, knowing that it is not by personal strength a matter is accomplished for God, but by His Spirit (*Zechariah 4:6*).

There is another Biblical person I consider when I need to encourage myself in the Lord is Queen Esther. We know her story, but we need to keep in mind that she had to encourage herself in light of death. Yes, she had beauty, but beauty will not always save you.

You could tell she understood the issues at hand, but understanding a matter will not save you. What will save you is first recognizing that you cannot save yourself. Jesus talked about losing our life associated with this world in order to gain eternal life that identifies us to eternity.

The other factor that Esther realized is that she was placed in that particular position by the unseen hand of God for a reason. In fact, she was prepared for such a time she lived in.

In God's kingdom, nothing happens by chance and we have been designed according to His purpose and plan for the times we live in. The question is, are we lining up to the eternal purpose of heaven as we encourage ourselves that our lives and days are in the hands of God?

We are immortal as long as God deems it so and that our lives are not in the hands of others. Esther came to a place of rest by looking up towards God by faith and to prayer while taking on the right attitude when she declared, *"Go gather together all the Jews that are present in Shushan, and fast ye for me, and neither eat nor drink three days, night or day: I also and my maidens will fast likewise; and so will I go in unto the king, which is not according to the law; and if I perish, I perish"* (Esther 4:16).

ATTITUDES

The more of heaven there is
in our lives, the less of earth
we shall covet.
(Charles Spurgeon)

One of the questions I must ask myself is what is my attitude toward life. Do I see it as a gift or a great burden? Do I see it as a journey of great discovery or my boring or terrible lot in life? Is this unseen life a right or a privilege? Do I see it as an adventure or a bad joke?

My attitude towards life will also reveal how I look at God. After all, God is the author of my life, and my attitude concerning life will reveal if I think God is an indifferent or hard taskmaster, a jokester that simply toys with me because He is bigger, or someone I have to tolerate just in case He is real, serious, and all He declares to be.

When I learned that life was a gift from God that cost Him His Son's life to secure it for me, I was able to appreciate it more, and when I saw it as a journey that was leading me to such immeasurable glory and promises I could begin to embrace it with enthusiasm instead of allowing it to weigh me down. As I regarded my life as a great adventure, I began to discover nuggets of truth and wisdom that so enriched it in ways it brought great meaning and purpose to it.

The big breakthrough for me came when I realized that my life was both a right and a privilege. By receiving Christ as my Savior and Lord, I had the right to become a child of God, but it was as I walked His life out in child-like faith and obedience that I began to discover the privileges that come with it.

The greatest privilege was that of spiritual freedom to not only see Christ in greater ways, but experience aspects of the many blessings that are attached to the excellent ways of God. The right as a child ensured me of my relationship with the Lord, but the privileges have allowed me to mature in His life, while discovering my calling and reaching towards my potential to ultimately reflect the life of Christ to others.

What is your attitude towards life? We often approach the matters of life from the perspective of theology and the matters of God from the premise of philosophy. The problem with approaching life from the perspective of theology is that one can become divorced from the challenges that confront people, making religion seem lifeless and useless to address the real matters of life.

On the other hand, to approach God with a philosophical bent will humanize God to a point He becomes Scripturally unrecognizable. *Colossians 2:8* warns us, *"Beware lest any man spoil you through philosophy and vain deceit, after the tradition of men, after the rudiments of the world, and not after Christ."* Whether we realize it or not we do hold to a philosophy of life which determines our attitude about it. Philosophy is a way of wading through the confusing mess that so often challenges our religious notions about life.

What we need to realize is our philosophy will determine whether we honestly face the real issues of life. At the core of life is tragedy because of toil, sorrow and death due to the curse of sin, but once we honestly face the real matters shaping our life and attitudes, then we can look to the Author of life to see what life was intended to be and can be, thus allowing God to establish the right attitude towards the gift of life.

It was during the broken times of my life that I realized some hard truths about myself. Probably the hardest one for me to face was that, at times,

I was judging what God was doing in others and with others. Imagine, judging the God of the universe, and I trembled at such a prospect, but it was one reality that began to show me the limitations, injustice, and cruelty of my own prideful judgments.

A couple of other lessons I learned was that I often stood passionately for personal causes and not His truth, and what I wrestled for when it came to others was outward compliance and not inward transformation.

I remember once dealing with a couple of people whose language was bad and I wrestled with how to approach them. After all, Scripture was on my side. Finally, I asked the Lord what to do. He posed a very interesting question, "Why do you want them to change their language?"

Being all-knowing and patient, He took the opportunity to show me my motive and it came down to the simple fact that such a change would make me look good as their mentor. He then asked me if I wanted them to comply to a religious outward conformity that might turn into resentment or hypocrisy on their part, or whether I wanted them to be transformed within, bringing Him glory.

It is hard at times to look at the motive behind why we want people to agree or comply with us, but if change in a person does not take place because it is a matter of God's conviction upon their soul and revelation to their spirit that changes the attitude about it, there will be no inward transformation. I learned long ago that I can outwardly comply to please other people to keep them off my back, but it takes the power of God to truly transform me to the point where I please my Creator, Savior, and Lord.

Recently, I posted this statement, "Pride is concerned with WHO is right. Humility is concerned with WHAT is right." We see that the difference between pride and humility is the attitude about what is right and the emphasis as to what is correct and trustworthy.

Many people agreed with the statement and even reposted it. I was thinking about the difference between being honest and having integrity. I have met people who were honest. They are quite refreshing when you are trying to look at a situation in order to come to a place of reason.

The one problem with being honest is that in many cases, people stop there and never bother to go to the next step where they actually walk it out. In fact, for some of these people, they take pride in being honest but fail to do anything about what is needed and right, while consoling and justifying themselves with the idea that at least they are honest about a questionable matter.

This brings us to another aspect of honesty and that is that it may have truth as a basis, but if it lacks true conviction to honorably walk it out, it will prove hollow and delusional. You might say in this case, a person's lamp is half-full and when they admit something that is true but have no intention of doing anything about it, it reveals them to be a hypocrite.

A hypocrite is one who may speak the truth, but it is to create or cover a false narrative to hide spiritual apathy, moral ineptness, and an indifferent attitude. In essence, these individuals have a high opinion of their honesty, but they lack the integrity that backs it up with proper action, whether it is repentance, or choosing the way of faith, and walking in obedience.

Integrity is that grit, substance, or character that backs up what is right with right actions. Integrity is what will go against the grain of what feels good to the flesh, sounds logical to the mind, and has to be right because of pride, to do what is right because it is the right thing to do. It stands erect on truth, humbly lines up to what is right, and demands personal responsibility to do it regardless of the results.

King David was a man of integrity. He had to go against the grain many times of what was comfortable and acceptable to others, and every time he chose the right way in spite of the obstacles in front of him, integrity was established within his character. This integrity served him well as a man after God's heart. He successfully faced the giants, became a victorious leader of soldiers and a king who wanted to do right by his people.

As a Christian, I have to be careful of the spirit I am in. Jesus told the zealous John and James in *Luke 9:55*, they did not know what spirit they were in when they wanted to call actual fire down on the Samaritans.

127

The best way I can test my spirit is by being honest about my attitude and mood.

A wrong attitude towards something tells me I am not in the right spirit to discern or make a righteous judgment call about what is going on. In fact, I am going to probably be touchy, impatient, and looking for something or someone to blame for my imbalance and the foul mood that leaves me feeling sour towards life. After all, I want to feel good about myself, have a positive outlook on life, and believe all is well in my world, and wrong attitudes and foul moods will leave me unsettled and looking for someone to blame for my inward unrest or take it out on.

Jesus warned that we need to beware of how we judge. We judge our environment by how we are feeling and we judge others by our rulers of pride such as concepts, standards, images, and ideas. The problem with being in the wrong spirit is that our pride is the board in our eye that keeps us from seeing we are the source of our problem, not circumstances or someone else.

Jesus' instruction in *John 7:24* is that if we judge, we judge not according to appearances but that which constitutes true righteousness. It is Jesus Christ who is the essence of righteousness. It is His life that is being worked in us so that we can be made in the righteousness of God.

What should our attitude be when our enemies are being judged? We have three enemies of our soul, the flesh, the world and the devil. We can't afford to feel sorry for the "old man" when he is being mortified, we must not be complicit when the world is becoming crucified to us and we to it, and we must not let down our guard when it comes to Satan.

I have made mention about those enemies that offend us, that encourage lawlessness in our society, and practice wickedness in high places. The Bible is clear as to how we are to respond when confronting these enemies. For those who offend us personally, we must make sure that God has not been offended as well.

There are some offenses that do not result in death, but there are others that do. The main key is if a person's offense against us is considered a trespass against God such as adultery and ungodly, dishonorable, unbecoming conduct in matters, we are to go to them personally to contend with them in hopes of restoring them.

A little leaven will corrupt the whole lump, and sin in the camp must be properly dealt with as not only a means to separate the leaven but to serve as a warning and example to others. If they refuse to listen, then we take a witness with us and if they refuse to repent, and they are part of the body of Christ, we are to take it to the body where the body has the responsibility to call them to accountability *(Matthew 18:15-17; 1 Corinthians 5)*.

We must never ignore lawlessness or be casual towards the wickedness in high places. The Bible is clear we are to reprove all works of darkness, whether it is to warn others, contend with those weak in faith, or separate from it.

It is snowing right now but even in spite of it, the many birds that come to our place seeking food and refuge are very busy. These birds vary in colors of yellow, orange, tan, black, and white. They consist of finches, nut hatches, quail, and pigeons to name a few. Thankfully we have a big picture window in our living room to watch them.

The working of God's creation is better than TV, and yet how many of us take time to enjoy it? God's creation teaches us it is the simple things that will thrill a tender heart, the beautiful things that will inspire the soul, and the incredible workings of it that will bring hope, praise, and worship to the spirit. The business of the birds reminds me of the gift of life that has come from God. There is so much life in those small creatures.

As they dance around, you sense they love life; as they occasionally fight with each other, you know they value their life; as they flutter here and there, they enjoy life; and as they lift up their heads and communicate with sweet voices, you know that they have that ingrained knowledge of where their life comes from.

It is clear that within the animal kingdom these different species do not operate within the culture of death, but within the realm of surviving in order to live their life and fulfill their destiny. The only species on earth that operates within the culture of death is man.

129

Man toys with death every time he gives in to sin, he plays with death when playing with lustful temptation, he comes into agreement with death when he practices deception and wickedness, and becomes a child of the utter destruction of death when he prefers the evil darkness of the occult, physical and spiritual fornication, tyranny, anger and hatred.

The birds challenge me to consider my own attitude towards life. I love the life that God gave me, but what I struggle with is the quality of my life. The quality of my life is determined by what I love, value, pursue, and serve. I must always choose heaven, by setting my affections on the Lord, valuing the life and gifts He has given me, pursuing truth and righteousness, and making sure I am solely serving Him.

Like the feathery bundles of inspiration outside my window, this is the only way I can be free as a bird to discover the eternal, glorious life God has for me.

What do you prefer the most: changes, adventures, or sensationalism? It is all about the attitude we take on about life, but some may say none of the above. However, the truth is without changes there is no enlargement, without adventure there are no real challenges, and without sensationalism some people would never be able to get in touch with pent-up feelings.

The one thing my stepfather taught me is that life is an adventure and it can be exciting or it can be a nightmare based on the attitude in which I approach something new. In adventures it is not whether you are successful in slaying some giant or monster; rather, it is the fact that you discovered your strengths, weaknesses, and abilities while facing the giants of ineptness and the monsters of fear, ever advancing forward to confront the next adventure.

As for sensationalism it is a fleshly exercise that may allow some to release the emotional pressure building up, but it can also become a type of addiction that some people must seek and pursue daily and at that point it becomes an exercise in vanity that will lead to utter destruction. When it comes to change, the currents of life bring circumstances that will result in change. Again, how do I look at change?

Our God is sovereign and He allows things in our life to bring necessary change to our inward man. It is my openness to the Holy Spirit that will determine the type of change that happens in my attitudes and practices. Am I willing to be brought low by my human ineptness and failures to discover spiritual heights in God? Will I give way to the Spirit transforming my mind so that I can clearly see what I need to see in order to walk out my spiritual life? Will I take on the mind of Christ so I can have the right attitude towards the matters of God?

In the past I have resented challenges leveled at my character, threw a fit at changes, and swung from emotional branches of sensationalism that caused me to collide with reality leaving me in a miserable state. Changes are happening now and there are more on the horizon, but are those changes going to define me or am I going to define them by making the right choices?

At every crossroad of change I must recognize the opportunity to choose the way of faith and righteousness so I can enjoy the gift of life God has given me, and like Paul rest in confidence that I have believed, and am persuaded that the Lord is able to keep that which I have committed unto him against that day *(2 Timothy 1:12)*.

One of my struggles in life is the attitude I adopt about something. Attitudes are greatly influenced by our affections towards something, our prejudices about something, and our bias concerning something. Some of these preconceptions exist because of our upbringing, but some of them are confirmed in our mind or take hold because of the mood we were in at the time we encounter or experience something that was pleasant or unpleasant.

Depending on our mood we can attach some affection, prejudice, or bias to the matter, producing an attitude towards it. The only way I can identify my attitude about something is to first take on the attitude of Christ about it. Sadly, we can pick and choose what we are going to believe about God's Word based on these notions, and it is for this reason I must be prepared to come into agreement with what His Word says about all matters.

Rayola Kelley

In Christ there are no outward distinctions between us, no one culture proves to be superior over another, and no elitism is allowed when it comes to intellectual degrees or material wealth of the world in God's kingdom. God looks at the attitude of the heart.

The heart attitude can make our souls dark because of sin, an unbecoming mood that makes us unpleasant around others, or it will take on the heavenly light of Christ, but we must constantly choose who we are going to believe, love, and serve. The beauty of this is that it all comes down to simply making the right choices based on God's character and His Word.

We complicate much but I have learned that it is in simplicity that I am able to encourage myself the most in the midst of personal struggles and challenges.

Do you have a prevailing mood that crops up when you least expect it? Moods are unpredictable because they can be attached to something such as a memory, an unresolved issue, an unpleasant attitude, a prejudice, or some type of emotional or mental wound.

It is important to discern a foul mood because until we do, we will not allow ourselves to be consoled when we slide into its grip. I often gage my prevailing mood by the attitude that seems the most prevalent when I am being tested, especially in the area of patience. I was recently struggling with such a mood and my attitude revealed that I had an unresolved issue.

We must not allow any wrong mood to define us; therefore, we must be quick to ask the Lord to turn the light on all wrong attitudes or prevailing foul moods that would undermine our testimony as a believer. The problem with sliding into such dishonorable moods is that we will not have the means or authority to encourage ourselves in the Lord.

We must take responsibility for what we have become and what we are allowing ourselves to become in our Christian life. Our walk must be consistent with our talk so that we can become an encouragement to others.

Are there people in your life who annoy you? Through the years I have met some people that rub me the wrong way, irritate me to no end, reveal my impatience, and make me cringe at the idea of having to deal with them at any level. They greatly cause my humanness to take center stage, revealing my ineptness to always maintain tight reins on my attitude, keep the emotions tempered, and my opinions from serving as a cruel judge and a biased jury towards them.

Every time I encountered such a person, I could feel the temperature escalate within my emotions and I realized that I needed to change something in order to take back my life by taking control of my attitude. The one difficult lesson that the Lord taught me about such people is that they were a mirror to me. The things that rubbed my attitude the wrong way was because they were revealing a like flaw in me, and the irritations they caused in me were the same points of annoyance I also possessed within my character. As for the impatience they caused me, well it was because it was something I needed to patiently face and deal with to possess my soul in patience, and the judgment it brought out in me was because it was a ruse to hide the fact that I had the same inner challenges.

It's tough to look in the mirror others present to us in order to face personal moral deviation, recognize emotional buttons due to unresolved matters of the soul and heart, and realize that we are often judging ourselves when we are harshly judging others. Through the years I have come to realize that I am going to receive mercy and grace based on the mercy and grace I show others. It is also when I am willing to give others a break for being human that I can honestly face my humanness and give myself a break, acknowledging that anything that is marked by that which is honorable, praiseworthy, and eternal is the work of God.

DISCIPLINES OF THE CHRISTIAN LIFE

*The finest jewels are most carefully
cut and polished. The hottest fires
try the most precious metal.
(Unknown)*

The call to follow Jesus seems easy enough, but there is a prerequisite in doing so and that is discipleship. There is no cost to salvation, but when it comes to following Jesus as His disciple, He told His followers to count the cost. If we don't deny ourselves, we can become a predator as we struggle to maintain our life in this world. If we do not apply the cross to the old life, we can become a goat who will follow Him until we are distracted by what we consider is another "goodie" of the world that we must possess and pursue, and if we don't apply the cross to our worldly attitudes and ways, we will become complacent and settle down into the pigpen of the world.

The cost of discipleship is the "old man," the "old way," and our identification with this present world. It is important that wherever we look to find our identity, it will define our person, our character, and the quality of our spiritual life. If we look to anything man-centered including religion, we will become bitterly disappointed, feel betrayed, and become judgmental. If we look to the world for our identity, we will become indifferent, greedy, and skeptical. If we possess a combination by trying to depend on our wit, while looking to the world to define our ethical practices we are going to become indifferent towards the things of God; and, if we lean on past religious experiences to get us to heaven, we are going to find ourselves in a barren spiritual wilderness, wandering in confusion, half-hearted in faith, while teetering over an abyss of utter unbelief.

I have been following Jesus for years. It has been downright brutal to my self-life, humiliating to my fleshly life, and humbling to my conceit, but it brought a decisive separation between me and the world.

However, I must declare I would not have it any other way because I have witnessed the Lord's power to do the impossible, His abiding faithfulness, His gentle kindness, His enduring patience, His willingness to forgive, and His desire to restore us with the presence of His Spirit, His eternal life, and His glory.

When you think of discipleship, what do you think of? The root word of discipleship is "discipline." The Bible tells us that some plant the seeds of the Gospel, but others nurture (discipleship) those seeds to ensure they are brought to maturity in order to be productive.

Christianity is about the disciplined life of Christ being worked in us to such a point that we possess His attitude toward things, display His characteristics, and walk according to His life in us. His attitude was that of meekness, His characteristics lined Him up to the ways of righteousness, and His walk was in light of His High calling, His anointed ministry, and His heavenly mission.

When we think of Jesus discipling His followers, we see where He taught them by using those things that they were familiar with, but His leadership also came through example. Jesus did not preach what He did not live, and He lived in compliance to His preaching and teachings to verify His authority and testimony. His disciples were astonished by His teachings and overwhelmed by His miracles, but what they ended up doing was following His example.

Words that are not backed up by action point to hypocrisy, attitudes that do not result in proper responses will prove to be hollow, and conduct that does not become a true expression of godliness will leave a less than satisfying taste in the mouth of others. To properly disciple others, we must recognize that it takes a personal investment that requires more than just teaching doctrine.

It is easy to fill heads with knowledge, but what is hard is to teach one how to live according to his or her calling. It requires one actually entering in with a person to see where he or she is and be prepared to lead the individual not only through teaching Bible truths, but also with practical and realistic examples.

True discipleship leads believers into a productive life in Christ. It allows them to discover who they are, what their place is, and how the Lord wants to use them in His work. Discipleship is a wonderful way in which believers can discover who God is in Christ Jesus, and come out not only being a true follower of His, but one who reflects Him.

Discipleship comes with a cost. Jesus alluded to the cost in *Luke 9:58-62*. The first cost has to do with walking away from what we consider the normalcy of this life and the world. Jesus stated the *"Foxes have holes, and birds of the air have nests; but the Son of man hath nowhere to lay his head."* The problem with people is we are nesters and the world has become our nesting place. It is what we are used to, depend on, and are comfortable with, and in reality, we are so earth-bound we are NOT PREPARED to follow Jesus into a life of discipleship and service until we are willing to let it go.

The next cost is that of letting go of the customs and ways of the world. One man asked to go home and bury his father, but Jesus stated, "Let the dead bury their dead: but go thou and preach the kingdom of God." We do not realize that we are often bound to the customs and ideas of this present world that will entrench us.

The custom at that time was that once a person died their body was left to rot away until there were only bones left. They would then put the bones in a stone container called an ossuary, and then officially bury the person. It took about a year for the body to be rendered into such a state, and Jesus reminded the man his father was already dead, so let those who are dead in sin bury him so he could take the life-giving message of the Gospel that has the power to raise up souls to everlasting life.

Such people who are waiting in this state may console themselves with good intention towards the Lord, but do not have the LIBERTY to follow Jesus because the demands of the world that hold us never cease to make us responsible to its ways. To fulfill our destiny, we must let go of the ways of the world in order to follow Jesus in a new way to a new life as a means to freely worship Him in all we do.

The final one asked to go and bid his family farewell before following Him, but Jesus stated, "No man, having put his hand to the plough, and looking back is fit for the kingdom of God." Let's face it, families have a powerful influence on our thinking, hold emotional stings that will yank us every which way until we do not know which way is up, and create unseen chains that will enslave us in ways we are not even aware of. The chances of simply following Christ after going back to say good-bye to family members are practically nil.

Family members who do not share the same faith, calling, and heart will use everything in their emotional arsenal from fear, guilt, intimidation, and rejection to keep us marginal in our faith so we do not bring conviction to them, nominal in our walk so it will not disrupt them in their realities, and ineffective in our commitment so it will not cost them in the end to consider their own state.

That is why we are told to set our affections heavenward because until we do, the ties that bind us will never be broken and we will never be emotionally READY to follow Jesus. After all, once we do set out to follow Jesus, we must never look back at the old or we will lose the steadfast focus that is necessary to follow Jesus into glory.

We Americans talk about freedom. What many fail to realize is freedom is not cheap. For those who want to do as they please in the name of freedom it will cost them their very souls. For those who defend the freedom of this nation it may cost them the quality of life or their very lives.

To have spiritual freedom, it cost God His best, His Son Jesus Christ, and required the Son to give His all, His life. The question is what will it cost us to not only possess spiritual freedom but maintain it? Up front it will not cost us anything to possess it except for believing that Jesus has secured it for us on the cross, but to maintain it will require us to carry a cross.

Real freedom requires self-discipline on our part. We must resist coming under any bondage but the sweet yoke of Jesus. We must never compromise the moral integrity of freedom by throwing off all moral restraints under the guise of personal liberty, and we must realize real freedom gives us the opportunity to believe and do right according to our convictions without fearing persecution.

We need to keep in mind that freedom is lost through a slow death as people take it for granted and lose sight of what it is. For example, the best way to lose our freedom is by neglecting the moral aspect of it, while abusing it by using it to oppress others, and mocking it when we use injustice to deprive others of the very rights that freedom allots them.

The Bible speaks about the cost of being a disciple of Jesus. It has taken me years to realize some important points in this regard. One is that the cost (of self and the world) for me is really nothing compared to what I gain in the end.

The second thing I realized is that the cost is all about knowing God in a greater measure. We all declare we want to know God, but are we willing to pay the price to know Him in greater ways? Sometimes it means going into the watery graves of loss, deep dark valleys of despair, facing the storms of hopelessness, becoming weary with the onslaught of challenges, and wondering when it will all end.

Through these times my testimony has grown of God's abiding faithfulness, my awareness that even though I can't see or feel Him, He never leaves or forsakes me, and even though I see such times as great darkness for my soul, they often prove to become times of gaining a greater insight into the Lord.

Admittedly, in the past, I have complained and asked "why," but each experience has taught me to quietly wait, while choosing to trust in the Lord's constant care upon my life, as well as learning what it means possess my soul in patience, knowing that my faith is being refined, and in the end the Lord will be magnified in my eyes and glorified in my life.

I am sure that some of you have heard about mountain climbers that fail to reach the peak of a mountain even though they may be within feet of its top. You would think that with only a few feet more to go climbers would press on, but there are various reasons people fail to reach such peaks.

Peaks for people represent endurance, accomplishments, and victory, and the reasons people fail to reach the top include, 1) they become blinded by the elements and lose focus, 2) they are not prepared, trained, or fully equipped to climb that particular mountain, 3) they make a misstep and find themselves falling down the mountain instead of climbing it, and will not risk doing it again for fear of failure, and 4) there are those who fancy themselves as great climbers who have visions of grandeur, but do not have the heart to endure the rigors.

As a Christian, I have admitted I had to learn what it means to be a mountain climber. I have lost focus in the past and missed the mark of my high calling. I had to acknowledge that much of my failure to reach peaks of personal victory was because I was not discipled and could not properly discerned what path I was to take. However, regardless of my inexperience, my failures, and my fears, I had to acknowledge that my different encounters with the mountain is what was actually preparing me to reach the peak that represents my high calling in Christ.

I had to recognize that to survive the challenges, elements, and rigors that the Holy Spirit was my guide, the Word my compass, my faith the ropes that would hold me steady, hope the anchor that held my rope tight, and my gear the righteousness of Christ. The truth is as Christians we all have the same mountain to climb when it comes to our high calling and position in Christ.

In the valleys we are trained through humility to handle the climb, in the canyons and shadows of despair we learn how to scale the heights, in the plateaus of resting in Christ we learn to get our bearings, and on the crooked paths we learn that it is the Lord who keeps us. The present terrain for Christians could be proving to be challenging to some, frightening to others, and unbearable to those overwhelmed, but take heart because we have been equipped to walk through it. However, we must look up to get our bearings, be still until the Holy Spirit reveals the way, take hold of what is so by faith as we obey the instructions of His Word while reaching up with hope in our heart to establish the first anchor of promise that will put us one step closer to the peak of deliverance, revelation, and victory.

I am the type of person who must schedule disciplines in my life to make sure I do them. For example, I have to schedule physical exercise. It is not something I enjoy, but it is necessary if I am going to keep my body going. My mental attitude, emotions, and complacent body resists such an inconvenient notion, but once I ignore the different reasons and complaints and start my exercise program, my attitude changes.

I realize any discipline begins with the right attitude that only emerges once I put down that "old" man in me. I look at exercise as a type of antidote I have to do in order to keep myself functioning so I can move forward. I know that physical exercise does not profit the spiritual life all that much, but it does allow me to keep my temple in working order so that I can be about the Lord's business. The Bible clearly talks about exercise.

To do exercise properly I must have a plan that works for me for my exercise to be constructive, and in order to adjust my attitude I must deny myself the right to listen and give way to excuses. God gave us a plan that will cause us to develop our Christian life and character. It is called the Word of God and if we walk according to the narrow path it lays before us and run according to the course set before us, we will be spiritually and mentally prepared to run the race and finish the course.

Much of constructive exercise has to do with breathing correctly, and when it comes to my spiritual life breathing points to prayer. There is no way we can develop any spiritual exercise without prayer. It is vital we learn how to breathe correctly so we can develop the necessary strength to endure.

The Bible is clear that we are to walk by faith, which is spiritual exercise that is capable of properly disciplining our spiritual walk. In the physical realm walking and water exercise are some of the best exercises for the body.

When it comes to exercising faith through obedience, it indeed proves beneficial to the Christian life because it makes one an overcomer in the world. Water points to the Holy Spirit.

When we follow the currents of His righteousness, are led to places of promises as children of God, and walk in His abiding presence in our lives, we will be prepared to victoriously come into our eternal inheritance. When it comes to physical exercise it can benefit your whole body, but what about the spiritual exercise?

When it comes to physical exercise some people are looking for a mean, lean body and I am simply looking for a working body, but when it comes to spiritual exercise, the Apostle Paul reveals what constructive spiritual exercise will result in when he states that we are to exercise ourselves unto godliness, and he goes on to explain why in *1 Timothy 4:8, "For bodily exercise profiteth little: but godliness is profitable unto all things, having promise of that which is to come."*

There are three areas that must be disciplined in our Christian walk. They are our tongue, our affections, and our mind. Our tongue often reveals our heart attitude or our out-of-control feelings. Our affections are influenced by the attractions of the world that can entice the eyes, and our mind is where the real spiritual strongholds in our spiritual life exist.

To make sure that our tongue does not discredit our Christian life and testimony, making us appear hypocritical and foolish, we have to guard our heart and discipline our emotions by remembering that our feelings do not constitute reality. In fact, our understanding must line up to the Word of God and not our feelings. In order to discipline our affections, we must remember our affections will be influenced by the type of attractions our eyes land upon. We must keep our focus upward if we are going to be effective in setting our affections on things above.

When it comes to the mind, we must let the mind, or attitude of Christ be in us. In order to do that we have to recognize that great idolatry can take place in our mind if our imagination is not kept in check with reality and lined up to the Word of God in our understanding and conclusions. If we do not keep our mind in check, our prayer life will suffer and we can end up creating a god to our own liking and find ourselves becoming a hypocritical, religious, judgmental prude who must hide our real spiritual condition, while creating a ruse to throw everyone off of our religious ineptness.

We are told how to discipline our mind by determining what we think on. When you look at what we are to think on, we are to think on the person, work, and teachings of the Lord Jesus Christ. It is for this reason that 2 Corinthians 10:5 instructs us to bring every thought into captivity to the obedience of Christ.

What is your main priority? Keep in mind, what you emphasize the most will reveal your priority or what you value, and will naturally pursue the most. Do you emphasize aspects of your life here, whether it be worldly demands, homes, jobs, and etc.? Perhaps like me in my past immature state, you even have some religious emphasis that will allow you to operate in a type of arrogant piousness that all is well with your soul, while soothing your uncertainty about where you stand when it comes to your relationship to God.

There are many people with great goals when it comes to God, but because their priority is selfish, worldly, or arrogant, they find themselves doubleminded. They fail to realize that their priority does not line up to their honorable goal.

People who are doubleminded will encounter confusion about what is important, wrestle with what their first responsibility should be when so many abound around them, and they will often end up on detours that rob them of strength causing them to hit dead ends of defeat in their life.

Wrong priorities reveal a couple of things: 1) there is a bit of the worldly attitude still present in how we judge matters, 2) our mind has not been completely transformed; therefore, we do not possess the complete mind of Christ to discern certain matters, and 3) we have failed to mix faith at the point of opportunities where we choose the right way and walk in it in order to walk out our life in Christ.

As believers, we should have only one priority and that is to bring glory to God in all we do. In these times we must possess clarity and in order to ensure we are not double-minded, and we must discern if our priorities line up to our testimony of Jesus and our calling in Him. This is the only way we can prevent becoming a hypocrite in a time when people, more than ever, need to see the light of Jesus' life in us.

When I study the concept of "meekness," I cannot help but remember Jesus' words. "Blessed are the meek: for they shall inherit the earth." Meekness is an interesting term. It simply points to strength being under control.

Cleary, such strength is not unruly, unyielding, undisciplined, or unmanageable. It does not hide behind some veneer of discipline; rather, it gives way to that which is allowed to channel it in a productive way. For the Christian, it simply means that his or her strength is yielded to the authority of heaven, disciplined by the Spirit, managed by the hand of God, and ruled by the Lord of lords.

Meekness allows me to receive from God. Once the mild spirit of meekness distinguishes that something is from God, the now tempered soul becomes satisfied as it partakes of it. From this premised, the heart attitude takes on a thankful pose for the blessing as it recognizes the grace that has been afforded in the situation.

Strength under control is disciplined enough in its focus that it is able to seek God out in purity and confidence, knowing that in the end the person will see God and live.

THE SPIRIT & LIBERTY

Unless we have WITHIN us
that which is ABOVE us,
we will eventually yield
to that which is AMONG us.
(Unknown)

As we come closer to the new year the tradition is to make resolutions that for many will fall to the wayside after fickle zealousness fizzles out within the first two weeks. There are those things we all would like to change about our looks and life, but I have long learned that we are creatures of habit that create ruts in our thinking and emotional arena that we keep tripping into.

I don't know about you but at the beginning of every new journey my spirit starts out excited, as a sense of empowerment lifts me up to carry out some plan to change a matter, but my flesh is weak and within a short time it has a tendency to slide right into existing ruts when certain circumstances fall into place. New Year resolutions remind me of the song, "One Day at a Time." To accomplish something in this world is not about great leaps but taking one day at a time to overcome the ruts in life in order to accomplish a matter.

It takes discipline at every level and an awareness that when it comes to Christianity it is not by any personal might that something is carried forth but by and according to the Spirit of God. If we are to walk after the Spirit in the ways of righteousness, be led by the Spirit into a more intimate relationship with the Lord as a child of God, and walk in the Spirit to overcome the works of the flesh, then there must be a complete submission to Him.

Submission in this case has to do with giving way to that which is worthy of real consideration and what will prove honorable for the benefit of the whole kingdom of God.

Jesus told the zealous James and John in *Luke 9:55* that they did not know what spirit they were of. Keep in mind James and John were taking offense for Jesus because the Samaritans didn't respond to Him in the way they thought they should. Jesus had set His face towards the cross and was simply passing through the area to get to Jerusalem to carry out His ultimate mission.

What does it mean to be of a wrong spirit? It entails a couple of possible scenarios. One, our MOTIVE is wrong. What we are doing may seem right or honorable to us but if we care to discern it, we might find we are doing it for selfish reasons, which will clearly tell us that we are IN A WRONG SPIRIT.

The second possibility is our INTENT may be wrong. We might be saying all the right things, but ultimately if our intent is in line with some personal agenda that has nothing to do with God's way or some point of self-exaltation, then what we are doing is being done OUT OF A WRONG SPIRIT.

The third reality of a wrong spirit is that it is out of STEP with Christ. The right Spirit will always line up to God's care (love), His Word and Will (way), and His eternal plan. To fail to line up to the things of God simply means one is WALKING IN A WRONG SPIRIT, which will manifest itself in unbelief and disobedience.

The reason we need to discern the spirit behind us is because we must confront the wrong spirits differently to ensure we hit the right mark in prayer and/or service guaranteeing victory.

During WWII, America was fighting on two different fronts—land and sea. You do not use the same tactics on sea as you do on land because they require different responses. This is true when it comes to the natural spirit and the spirit of the world.

They are both wrong spirits, but people often use the wrong tactics to address them. If the natural spirit is in operation, it will use temptation to confuse and ensnare us from within, sin to enslave us, while claiming victory over our will to resist, and defeat to bury us while stripping away all life, hope, and authority. We have been given a way out of temptation, but it calls for us to honestly recognize and confess the error of our ways, and then turn in complete repentance to line up to God's way.

If the spirit of the world is behind a matter, we need to recognize that the temptation comes from without and does not belong to us. Whether it is a lie inserting itself into our thinking, bad thoughts, wrong promptings and voices, we must resist Satan's subtle attempts with everything in us by drawing near to our Almighty God in complete assurance, humbling ourselves before Him, submitting to His glorious protection, and raising up the Sword of Truth to claim our authority in Christ, knowing that the devil has no recourse but to flee.

We live in a noisy world. We are bombarded by many voices. Some of these voices are personal. There is the voice of the intellect that tries to tell us what is logical, the voice of arrogance that is supposedly warning us against what is considered inferior and foolish as we ride high on judgmental waves, and we have the voice of lust that is trying to stir us up to pursue personal happiness. We have the voice of the world that is trying to influence and change our worldview about God and life through seduction, propaganda, and lies.

For Christians, God has one voice, but it manifests itself in three ways. The first one is through creation. Creation declares there is a God and we are told in *Psalm 148* that all creation has the means of praising Him. The second way God's voice manifests itself is through His written Word. His written Word is the revelation of the Living Word, His Son Jesus Christ. However, whether His written Word proves to be living or dead depends on whether one is seeking to believe its witness about Jesus, in order to see God with the main purpose of knowing His Son.

The final voice is referred to as the still small voice. This voice is the voice of His Spirit. The voice of the Spirit manifests itself in three ways. Since He is the inspiration and breath behind the written Word, and He is the one who must unveil it to our spirits to make it living and viable to our life. The Spirit will never step outside of the Word of God; therefore, the Spirit brings life to the Word and the Word simply confirms that what you are hearing or perceiving is from the Holy Spirit.

Another form of His voice is what we call, "impressions." The Holy Spirit is a gentleman and He will not yell, scream, or lecture us. He will speak in a gentle manner to warn, to guide, or instruct us about a matter. However, we must learn to listen for His voice, discern it, and properly respond. Obedience to His voice is the only way to fine-tune our spiritual ears in order to hear Him.

The final way He manifests Himself as the means to speak to and through us is with His gifts. It is for this reason we are told to be still. We must learn to be still in a noisy world in order to hear what the Spirit is truly saying to us for this time and in this day for our edification so we can stand in this darkness, while being prepared for His coming.

In the past I watched a memorable show about a family that was falling apart at the seams. As a wise religious counselor counseled with the family, he discovered the problem in the workings of the family: it was a disconnected husband/father.

When we hear about investments, we think in terms of money and assets, but when it comes to the kingdom of God, the greatest investment is in relationships. Today there is a disconnect going on that is cutting off vital channels of communication, fellowship, and communion in families, societies, churches, and our relationship with God. The missing link in communication has to do with the art of listening. We know how to talk over, ignore what we don't like, and be contrary to what we refuse to be wrong about, but very few know how to listen.

To listen one must first step outside of their preferred reality, ideas, and opinions to really hear what the other person is saying. Without the ability to listen, there is no means of connecting with that individual where there could be possible agreement discovered in order to reason out differences, work on problems, and hear the heart, desires, struggles, and needs of that person in order to minister to them.

When it comes to fellowship there must be a place of agreement. We must hear a person to discern the place of agreement in which we can start to communicate with them and when it comes to communion there must be the same spirit present. The greatest missing link in people's lives is that their relationship with God is missing, neglected, and sought out in desperation as a last resort. Jesus was clear that we need to hear what the Spirit is saying. He is the one who is the connection between man and God through the redemption of Christ.

The Holy Spirit has different responsibilities but they all come back to one centralized point and that is fellowship. He is the one who leads us to all truth in order to have a common ground of agreement. He leads us to conviction of sin where man can be reasoned with and led to the fountain of salvation, cleansing, and the revival of hope. He is our only place of unity and without Him there is no unity among believers or in the Church that will lead us into true communion to ensure worship.

It is natural for man, who is in search of happiness, hope and purpose to try, to fill his life with vain empty things, but until that connection is made with his Creator, he will remain disconnected to real life as he becomes a restless spirit in the barren wilderness of the world, a wandering soul in canyons of darkness, and an empty shell that reflects an empty existence.

Clearly, our nation is in a crisis and at a tipping point. Sadly, it takes a great crisis to wake people up who are comfortable and who have fallen asleep in their easy chair and pews. The good news is that that people of this country have been awakened, but we must ask to what and by what? Many will admit America needs a spiritual awakening but to what? There can be a religious and spiritual awakening, but will it lead people to the right God, to recognize the real problem, and to discern the correct solution to make sure that we are hitting the right mark.

The other day I watched as people were called to come into agreement and pray for this country. It is commendable, but which God were they praying to, what spirit was present, and what were they seeking in prayer? The Word is clear without agreement in the right spirit and coming to the place of agreement as to who we are praying to, there is no authority or power in such prayer.

The authority in prayer is found in Jesus Christ of the Bible, and the power in prayer is that it hits the mark of God's will. Spiritual awakening for Christians will always bring them back to the source of the problem, which is sin and the solution to the problem, which is repentance and brokenness over that sin, in order to line them up to the will of God as to what needs to be done.

We could be very well watching the last days harvest taking place before Jesus' coming, but we must guard our relationship with Him as to the spirit we come into agreement with, guard our life in Him with integrity, and our walk before Him as to whether something is Scripturally acceptable.

Another word I often pause to consider is the word "slavery." Due to the hearts of some, this nation finds itself under siege due to a great moral struggle that took place throughout the history of our country in different arenas.

Slavery is not determined or limited by a particular color, race, or culture, but it has become a springboard for another word to take center-stage, "racism." This becomes an excuse in some minds for everything that ails this nation, but in reality, slavery is what all humanity has been born into because of sin, and is not just a past practice, but a very common and present practice happening all over the world.

According to the book, *"The Miracle of Freedom, 7 Tipping Points that Saved the World,"* fewer than five billion of the earth's total inhabitants have ever lived under conditions that we could consider free, and the population of America of 554 million people since 1780, are included in that figure which shows that the experiment of America in light of freedom is unique and has worked in spite of its flaws and challenges.

Keep in mind, the goal of those who are using this old, lame excuse in our nation as a point of justification to be lawless are demanding all who are outside of their insane fringes to bow before them as a conquered people who now can be brought into bondage by mob rule as the vulnerable and men-pleasers are, for the most part, being coerced to submit to their sick ideology.

All conquered nations of the past and present were and are being made slaves, whether it is to pay sick homage to the despots of the age, bow before their lifeless gods of the times, submit to godless, unjust systems of the day, or give way to the cruel intimidation of the mob rule to keep a quasi-peace. Keep in mind, only those who are already enslaved are the ones who demand you must likewise become slaves.

All real slavery begins in the mind and the only real liberty can be found when the spirit is spiritually awakened in the born-again experience and the soul is set free to reach beyond all past slavery to the excellent heights of liberty in the Holy Spirit. Spiritual liberty gives you freedom to decide who you bow before, national freedom allows you the right to choose who you serve, mental freedom gives you liberty to decide what you believe, and emotional freedom allows you to choose what and how you worship.

As believers we must never cower to the decadent slaves of this world; rather, we must stand against oppression with truth and withstand all fear tactics of tyranny and mob rule with what is Scripturally right, as we continue to stand in the power of the Holy Spirit for what is just in light of what is rightfully lawful and moral.

I have been thinking about masks. Do you realize a two-dollar mask makes you acceptable in today's society or, on the other hand, without a mask you are suddenly a "nuisance" that has no right to personal opinions, and certainly no right to breathe the same air as the "intellectual elite?"

I grew up in a time where bad men wore a mask to cover their real identity, but in our now upside-down society the good guy wears the mask and the bad guy is the one who will be considered guilty because he will not surrender his rights in order to simply fit in. I understand the purpose of the mask, but a mask is to contain the germs of the sick.

Germs come out of the mouth and nose, but not only do they find their way through the nasal passages, but through the eyes as well. How many of us are willing to wear goggles out in public with our mask? Clearly, the most practical and responsible practice would be for those who are sick to quarantine themselves at home.

However, we must consider the sad reality that many in our society are primed to throw any real individual identity away, and become lost in the masses without recognizing the devastating result that, as a nation, we are surrendering our soul to tyranny. The fact that some mask can turn our culture upside down, cause prejudice in small, indoctrinated minds, tyranny in arrogant minds, and insanity in foolish minds, reveals to us that our culture has been primed to betray others while being led to the slaughtering pens to be sacrificed on the altars of totalitarian rule.

As I consider the implication of the mask, I realize that we Christians are guilty of wearing invisible masks. Regardless of what we are trying to cover, all masks are superficial and they are either hiding a deep

150

struggle, or covering up the fact that our religion is very surface and is nothing more than a hypocritical façade.

Moses had to cover his face because the glory of God shining forth was unnerving the people of Israel. We know according to 2 *Corinthians* 3, there is a veil over the minds and hearts of unbelievers, but as believers that veil has been taken away, and we have been given the liberty to reflect the glory of Jesus to the world.

I say let the glory of Christ shine and if it makes the small-minded angry and judgmental, unleashes the tyrant's rage, and give way for the foolish to threaten us, so be it, because such glory declares we are not citizens of this world, bound to an oppressive age of insanity. We must remember that we have been endowed by a glorious liberty that can't be taken captive by those who are slaves to the god of this world.

What or who is leading you during this crisis? It is important to know what/who we are following but many assume they know, when in reality they are like sheep who will be led to the slaughter by the wolves, despots, and harsh taskmasters of this age. For example, how many are being led by fear, how many by wicked people with unsavory agendas, and how many by anger and rebellion? Needless to say, all of these taskmasters will oppress and lead a person to the abyss of personal destruction.

Paul stated, "Follow me as I follow Jesus." Those who follow Christ will be led by the Spirit of God into life where there is peace of heart, mind, and soul. We must keep in mind that there are three choices we make daily, who we follow, who we serve, and who we come into agreement with.

I must follow Jesus and not the ways of the world in order to serve God and not sin, while coming into agreement with the Risen Christ and not the lusts of the flesh to ensure I fall into step with the Holy Spirit. The Holy Spirit will always lead me to the truth about Jesus, where I discover the overcoming life and intimate communion with, and worship of, the Father.

Who are you allowing yourself to become? We are who we are based on who or what we serve; but who we allow ourselves to become is based on what we come into agreement with. As Christians, we find agreement at the place of the Holy Spirit.

He is the One who leads us into all truth about Jesus and is the source and inspiration behind all worship and communion. Spiritually, we can't know the matters of God unless the Spirit reveals it. Granted, we may know about something when it comes to God but we will never personally know it until the Spirit unveils it to our spirit as being true. It is only at the place of truth, Jesus Christ, that we can come into agreement with God, giving us access to commune with Him and worship Him.

It is the Spirit of God in us that allows us to discover our calling and reach our potential, to reflect Jesus. I learned this truth a long time ago. I found that every time I came into agreement with someone, I opened myself up to, not only to be influenced by them, but to take on certain attitudes and traits. As you might surmise, some of the people I came into agreement with in the past were not always beneficial, and the result was me taking on some foul moods, a wrong attitude, or a stiff-necked pose that clearly did not reflect Jesus.

As Christians we must be aware of what we expose ourselves to and what we ultimately come into agreement with. We must always expose ourselves to our Lord through sensitivity and submission to His Spirit and obedience to His Word so we can come into a place of true communion with Him. At the place of communion, we can properly worship Him in order to expose ourselves to His glory, as well as bring glory to Him.

Through the years I needed to be set free from various things in my life. Some of them were associated with my past such as sins, others were a result of bad decisions, and some were the product of circumstances that were beyond my control. My way of handling the aspects of my past were to cover them up with fig-leaves of consolation that I was not that way and therefore all was well.

As for bad decisions that left me tasting the foulness of consequences, I felt by understanding them they had been properly handled and when it came to circumstances, I survived them and felt that was sufficient enough.

I want you to note that none of these aspects of my life were really addressed. My past often haunted me, and it became a means for Satan to use it against me and those unresolved bad decisions still left me with the same attitude about such matters because they were not addressed in the light of truth. And, as for circumstances, I often discovered I was harboring some anger about the unfairness of it all that could easily enough end up judging God for allowing them to happen.

It is for this reason, that we must allow the Spirit to do the work of sanctification in us by revealing Jesus to us as our example in order to establish His life in us. It is the light of Jesus penetrating our best, exposing our worst, and revealing His ways to us that allows us to discover the work, power, and anointing of the Spirit in and upon our lives.

THE CHURCH

Toleration of false teachers in
the church of God is treachery
to Christ.
(H. A. Ironside)

What is true fellowship? The word "church" means "the assembly called out." Clearly, the "called out" part has to do with its urgent commission to share the Gospel and its most holy calling that sets it apart from the world in attitude, conduct, and practices. We are told to not forsake the assembling together, especially as that day approaches (*Hebrews 10:25*).

To some "fellowship" is simply about going to a church building once a week, and in some cases, people come out edified, but personally I do not see where looking at the back of someone's head while listening to the preacher is a type of fellowship. It is for this reason it is the habit of many Christians to go out to lunch after church and "talk" some more.

153

Sadly, the way some religious people perceive or present the concept of "fellowship," is in relationship to more of a social event than real fellowship. As a believer, I am not looking for some social event or social gathering; rather, I am looking for true fellowship where there is a personal, intimate involvement with each other as encouragement is offered during trials, exhortation during challenges, hope during grave times of darkness, and prayers for those struggling or seeking.

To have true fellowship for Christians that result in something called "communion," the Holy Spirit must be present in each person's life (*2 Corinthians 13:14; Ephesians 4:13-16*). He is the glue that brings about identification to each other in the spiritual arena, a place of agreement where authority and power are present, discernment is in operation as to the type of ministry required, and a revealer of those matters and truths that prepare, enlarge, and ultimately edify.

Sadly, many of us have had to accept the moldy bread of social gatherings because the sweet water of the Spirit and the heavenly manna of heaven have been greatly missing from fellowship, leaving our souls feeling hollow and our spirits lean.

I am compelled at times to talk about the Body, the church of Christ. I realized that the Body of Christ, although imperfect but being brought to perfection and one day to completion, represents an incredible miracle.

Like our physical body that is wondrously made, the many membered Body of Christ is being wondrously established by the very power of God from above. Like the members of my body, each member of Jesus' Body is different but necessary for the function of the whole Body. Like the different parts of my body, each member of this spiritual Body has a unique role to play in the successful working of the whole Body. No one member of my body can stand alone and no one member of Christ's Body can function alone.

When you consider the different giftings, talents, experiences, and courses of each believer, you realize just what a miracle this body is. There are some members that are fighting for the soul of the church as much encroaches into its standing before heaven, and others are like firebrands shaking foundations, while there are pillars that bring stability to the church by simply standing on the true foundation, setting forth example and exhortation.

There are also those who are trying to prepare and help members to be established in their calling through discipleship. Other members are working in the highways and byways of the harvest fields seeking out souls, while some wrestle for souls who are on the line through prayer. Some are quietly working in obscure places of service to ensure others are able to serve in more visible roles.

Sometimes, like Elijah we feel all alone in our walk, but the truth is there are those who have left indelible footprints that have gone before us, others who are presently becoming part of the great cloud of witness in this generation, and those who are yet to follow. As members of His Body, we are never alone. The path may be narrow, the process challenging, and the terrain wrought with times and challenges that can bring sorrow and despair to our being, but as members of His Body, we know it will only last a short season in light of His glorious eternity.

I have been thinking a lot about the Church. I am not talking about the religious system, the church buildings, the social gatherings, certain religious affiliations, or the visible church that is dressed up in worldly attractions, performances, or presentations. The Church I am talking about is the many-membered Body of Christ that is universal in makeup, has been redeemed by the blood of the Lamb, is humble, but comprised of lively stones that make up a spiritual building, identified to a spiritual inheritance by the seal of the Holy Spirit, part of the family of God, cleansed, prepared, and refined, and called to be a co-laborer with the Lord in the harvest fields of the world.

This incredible body has encountered the gates of hell coming against it since its very inception in crises, challenges, opposition, and in all out affronts. It has often been declared dead by the tyrants of different ages to only rise up again in greater power. Its light has withstood many contrary winds that have tried to snuff it out, and there are seasons when it may seem on life-support, but it possesses the type of life that is able to be resurrected at any time. It might occasionally be found to be weak and weary, but its strength and healing comes from above and at the right timing it will come forth as a firebrand.

Like many of those who read this, I am part of this great body. We may be miles apart, but we partake of the same breath of God. Even though we might not agree at every theological point, we do agree about what is true, for we have received what is eternal, have been entrusted with that which is excellent, and stand on that which will never be moved by the changing winds of time. Let each of us take heart in this wonderful legacy and in doing so encourage ourselves in these dark times, that when the times are the darkest to this incredible body, it signals that the Light that penetrates the darkness and breaks on the horizon is close at hand.

Yesterday, I talked about the glorious makeup of the true church. Every believer makes up this phenomenal Body of Christ. They are indeed, lively stones specially fitted into this spiritual building by the Holy Spirit.

We are told in *Hebrews 3:6* that Christ is the son over this house. The Bible points out that this church can find itself in four different states: asleep, being tested, compromising, or persecuted.

The Apostle Paul told sleeping Christians to AWAKE. We can't be like Jonah asleep in some hull of a ship while the raging seas of judgment are ready to swallow up souls who are scurrying about trying to save themselves or crying in their misery to be delivered when we hold the lifeline in which they can be saved.

There are those who are being tested right now so their faith can come forth as gold, and others are sitting back on their religious laurels while they simmer in the caustic juices of the world that is dulling them down to spiritual matter, while many are suffering persecution, trusting their resurrection will be greater.

Right now, religious foundations are shaking, testing the faith and resolve of believers. Know that everything that crumbles during such trials is not eternal and will not enable you to ENDURE to the end. We must be willing to let go of anything that hinders us from finishing the course. It is never pleasant to see that which we assume, or presume, will stand fall, but as believers we can take heart that what is founded on Christ is eternal and will stand regardless of what affronts it.

Where or what is your hope founded on, events or Jesus? We are living in interesting times because we can see the sure Word of prophecy playing out in living color on the stage of the world. The Bible tells us Jesus is coming back for a church without spot and wrinkle, which points to cleansing and purging. Some believe a great revival will happen before Jesus returns and there are others, who are putting their hope in events based on their theology and not in Jesus' coming.

It is true that the Gospel will be preached throughout the world, but Jesus also warned us that many would be deceived and if He did not come there would be no flesh saved alive. Paul told us there will be a falling away from the truth which implies the opposite of a true revival.

I realize God is moving on Muslims in a miraculous way, and in spite of persecution in places such as Iran and China, the churches are growing there. As a church in America, what are we preparing for—a revival or Jesus' coming? Does the living body of Christ need to be revived or cleansed? The answer to this question will determine our mode of preparation.

The Bible tells us that when Jesus comes for His church those who remain will be caught up with Him. If you look up the word "remain" it points to those who survive in spite of the destitution around them. What does it take for a national revival to occur? First of all, it is a sovereign move of God that has been seeded by great travailing in prayer over the sins of the church which allows God to bring about brokenness over personal and collective sins of the church and nation.

For national revival to occur there must be a great outcry coming from pulpits against all sin, sexual immorality, worldliness, disobedience, and the lack of love, and at this point I do not hear such outcry coming from the pulpits. For me I need to be revived every day and I know the only way I can be cleansed and purged is through consecration where I daily present my body as a living sacrifice in order to be prepared to do the will of God. We need to be careful as believers not to put our hope in our limited theology and what we hope to see or not see, but we need to put it in Christ from whom all blessings flow and all promises will be realized.

The corruption that has been taking root for years in this nation is now rearing its ugly head declaring victory. The fruits of this corruption have been visible on both sides of the political aisle. I knew a long time ago if a politician did not have integrity, his or her vote was for sale. I have warned a couple of them about this very fact.

This holds true for the leadership of the church as well. If our spiritual and governmental leaders, out of integrity, do not govern themselves with a higher moral standard, they will out of greed, weariness, complacency, complicity, and delusional justification choose the lower road of compromise, greed, and bribery, allowing the sanctuaries and halls of Congress to become a place where souls are merchandised.

The merchandising of souls means that these places become the auction block of secularism where bits and pieces of the very soul of our leaders, nation, and the people are constantly being auctioned off to the highest bidder. Today we use the promise of *2 Chronicles 7:14* to challenge ourselves, but this promise is specifically to Israel whose inheritance is land, and not to the church.

We, as believers, must make sure we don't fall into this trap of merchandising souls instead of contending for them so they can be saved and brought into God's fold as His sheep.

Doing spring house cleaning alone makes the road seem longer and more difficult. For the first week I redid my office space pretty much by myself, but on the second week I had the help of Carrie.

Carrie is young and has more energy. She is taller and can reach places that requires a step stool or a ladder for me to reach. It took four days for me to paint and clean my office and with Carrie's help it took only two days to paint and clean Jeannette's office.

The problem with being human is our need to be independent. We don't want help because it is a sign of weakness, vulnerability, and age.

To admit we need help is to admit we are dependent, which will prove to be an affront against our pride, a wake-up call as to our need for help, and the harsh reality that we are not sufficient in our own selves, infallible in all we do, and capable of finishing a course in our own steam.

Ecclesiastes 4:11-12 talks about how two is better than one and a threefold cord is not easily broken. The truth is we are not meant to stand alone and do things by ourselves. We are a needy people and it takes humility, integrity, and truthfulness to admit and face it. This is why the Bible reminds us God is our helper in times of trouble for He is mighty, ever present, infallible, faithful, and capable of doing the impossible.

Jesus gave us a valuable example when He sent out the disciples in two's, and as believers we are placed in a many-membered body, and we are told, *"Not forsaking the assembling of ourselves together, as the manner of some is; but exhorting one another: and so much the more, as ye see the day approaching" (Hebrews 10:26).* We are co-laborers with the Lord in the harvest field and we are called to come under Jesus' yoke where He carries the heavy end.

Why is it so hard to admit and face our need, dependency, and vulnerability? The answer is simple, it requires humility and our pride refuses to admit we are not self-sufficient. It is easy to ask the Lord to save us from our doomed plight, but it is not always easy to humble ourselves and admit our need for His constant intervention, help, and strength in our daily activities, because sometimes He sends in the brethren to help.

As I have reminded myself, "to blazes with my arrogant pride," I need God, and occasionally I need others of the household of faith to help, and the truth is, it is always beneficial when another comes under heavy burdens with you because at such times you can find yourself having a wonderful time of fellowship.

Evil is a subject that usually is a word to some, but clearly a state to others. It has been hard to recognize or describe evil in the past because it can, and has, worn masquerades in order to hide its ill-intent towards whoever or whatever stands in its way. However, evil is no longer wearing a disguise because it doesn't have to.

Many of those who have the bully pulpits in this nation are calling good evil and evil good; therefore, evil is being glorified. In some cases, evil has removed all religious "clothing" and is revealing that wolves are clearly among us, but many have become so enamored by the false claims and promises of these wolves, that they have willingly offered up their souls to follow them.

Jesus warned of such wolves. Wolves in nature are beautiful animals but they are predators. They prey on the weak, the vulnerable, and the isolated. It is for this reason the animals that are the prey of wolves often stick together in herds as a means to ensure the existence of their species. Christians need to keep this in mind.

Today the basic religious freedoms are under attack in this nation as some cower in homes to try to save their lives, making them weak, hiding their testimony behind a mask making them vulnerable, and avoiding assembling together, causing them to become isolated. Some are probably shocked because they never thought it would happen here, but the truth is, much has taken even some of the church captive through wishful thinking, hopeful assumptions, blinding presumptions, and unholy mixtures.

Holiness has been exchanged with man's best attempts, goodness with man's decency, righteousness with the robes of self-righteousness, service with social works, worship with emotional hype, and the word "Christian" now serves as a veneer over every religious activity regardless of whether it is traced back to Christ and His teachings or not.

It is time for the church to remember that to be prepared it must be refined, to be ready to stand it must be empowered from above, and to maintain its testimony it must have unity and fellowship in Spirit and truth. Such a church is able to stand on the promise that in the end the gates of hell will not prevail against it.

As believers, we must now ask ourselves, what does the state of our nation tell us about the spiritual state of the church? The church is the only one who possesses the voice of truth, reason, exhortation, moral accountability, and righteous standing and practices in any nation. The truth is, the church has had its share of wolves standing in pulpits due to a lack of love for God and His Word, as well as the lack of integrity of faith and character, leading unsuspecting sheep down to pagan altars to eventually be taken captive and auctioned off to the different taskmasters of the age.

In some cases, the voice of the true church has been hidden for the sake of its preservation and preparation. It has been to some extent shamed into silence, buried by oppression, and overwhelmed by vexation, but all of it was being done in light of preparing it to be raised up for this time to become the prophetic voice crying out in the barren wilderness of sin to those who are lost.

The church will eventually become the bright light that shines hope into the darkness for seeking souls to see, the feet that bring a message of peace and reconciliation to every isolated, tormented soul, and the hands that offer the healing balm to the brokenhearted, the blind, the lame, and those who have been bruised and wounded by the sins of this present age.

It is time for the body of Jesus to realize that the oven of adversity in our time has been preparing each of its members to fulfill a greater purpose and calling so the latter will be greater than the former because the presence, power, and purpose of God will manifest itself in wondrous ways. In some countries, the saints have been called to die for Christ, but in this country, we have been called to live for Christ, constantly presenting ourselves as instruments, vessels, and sacrifices that have been or will be purged, purified, formed, and fitted for His use.

It is time that as His body, each of us offer our bodies, our lives, as a living sacrifice, void of selfish agendas, fleshly emphasis, and worldly priorities in order to prove what is the good, acceptable, and perfect will of God with one goal in mind, and that is to carry it out for His glory.

You might wonder why I'm taking time to talk about the extraordinary makeup of the church. I have always known that the Body of Christ is in a great battle for the integrity of its own soul, as well as over the souls of others and in a struggle over truth. This has always been and will be until Jesus comes for the church.

Rayola Kelley

I believe we are in the end days, and the night is encroaching upon us when we may not be able to work for our precious Lord. The time to be about the Father's business appears shorter each day, and I know for me I have not yet completed the race set before me.

Being on Facebook reminds me that the Body of Christ is very much on the frontline and some saints are in the battle of their lifetime as the great darkness of our day seems to be engulfing the light (testimony) of the church in America and Europe. There are other believers who are trying not to be buried by the ongoing onslaught being directed at them by the enemies of their souls. There are also emotional, mental, and physical battles that are being used to refine each member of the Body, ever fusing it together.

I say all of this because we Christians can sometimes hold our callings, gifts, or experiences up as a way to judge other believers as to their effectiveness in the body or we compare ourselves to other believers and feel we are missing the mark. Comparing others to ourselves and ourselves to others is not Scriptural. Our example is Jesus and He told Peter it was not for him to know the business of another disciple. Granted, we are to be part of the edification, the building up the church, but it is the Spirit's responsibility to bring the body to perfection.

I have learned for myself that my main concern is whether I am in His will, my main goal should be doing the Father's business, and my main responsibility is not to make sure other people are doing it the way I think they should be doing it; instead, I need to ask myself if I am doing what I need to do according to the Lord.

We need to quit looking around at each other and keep our focus on Christ and trust His Spirit in other believers to convict, guide, and direct their steps. Meanwhile, we must be quick to discern where we are, making sure we are in the way that leads to the truth about the life of Jesus that is in us.

DISCERNMENT

*Discernment is both learned and given.
To be learned there must be a separation
from the holy and profane and to be
given, there must be a willingness to
be separated from what is considered
acceptable to those of the status quo.
(Rayola Kelley)*

One of the elements God's people can lack is discernment. Discernment is the ability to discern the spirit behind something. Spirit influences environment that will affect attitudes, moods, conduct, and fruits. Discernment has the ability to properly classify something based on the spirit behind it.

For example, a duck and a goose are similar but one is bigger than the other, and they differ in color and sounds. At first there may be some confusion as to what you are seeing from a distance, but if you know what you are looking for you can properly discern what it is.

The problem with some Christians is that they do not know what they are looking for when it comes to the unseen realm; therefore, they do not properly know how to classify what they are encountering. It is important to discern the spirit in all matters because it will determine if you can come into spiritual agreement with it.

For instance, if a person has a different spirit than yourself, you will not be able to come to a place of unity regardless of how religious and good that person may sound. It is important to point out that discernment allows right judgment but judgment based on the flesh is what Jesus rebuked in *Matthew 7:1-5* because it is based on biased, prejudicial opinions that are about how someone is affecting you and not on the spirit.

Satan can come as an angel of light and his ministers as ministers of righteousness, thereby, counterfeiting the things of God, and it is for this reason we must be able to discern what is good and evil and to properly test the spirits. As a believer, I have asked the Lord for discernment to know what I am encountering. I do not want to settle for fleshly judgments based on selfish, worldly attitudes. I want to know what is from God and what is a subtle, clever counterfeit of Satan.

I don't know about you, but being human finds me struggling within a fallen condition, trying to daily mortify a selfish disposition, ever stepping over molehills or around pinnacles of pride, and striving to keep in perspective that I know in part and can't trust personal conclusions about truth, reality, and perception. My struggle to keep everything heavenly focused has forced me to realize a few truths.

The first thing I had to learn is that I must ACCEPT WHAT IS to properly confront what is not right. It is hard to confront what is wrong in our reality in order to take the necessary responsibility for our part in the struggle or conflict that may be boiling under the surface or ready to erupt or has already exploded, leaving a terrible mess behind to clean up. Sadly, some of those messes can leave irreparable damages.

God can only meet us at the point of truth, and that means we must be honest with ourselves about our part in order to be set free from the destructive cycle. The second truth I had to embrace is that since something is a certain way, I must LET IT BE SO if I am going to properly discern what I can do in order to make sure I am not part of the problem.

Today we live in a world of optics. This simply means we can't trust what we see and since our news is controlled by only a few, we can't trust what we hear, which means we must discern what we think we understand, know, and believe.

The world is clearly wrapped up like a mummy in lies and the temptations of this world have only three snares to work with—eyes (see), ears (intellect), and taste (fleshly lust and appetites). It is with the eyes man is enticed as the vanity of this world is magnified, with the ears, pride is engaged with an attractive lie, and with the taste, appetites are enlarged to pursue the very depths of hell.

The Bible warns of great deception in this day and that if it were possible the very elect would be deceived. Sadly, our eyes can tell us that it is not so bad and cause blinders to the real evil, our ears can tell us that we would know a lie if we hear it as we embrace a seductive, destructive reality, and our flesh begins justifying tasting a bit of poison here and exposing ourselves to a bit of naughtiness there, while dancing with the devil in the shadows of compromise.

The Bible is clear we are to come out and be separate from the world and to love the world means people do not have the love of the Father in them. In other words, their heart is far from God and their words of devotion to Him vain and hollow, their ears closed to Him and their affections belong to this present age.

However, as believers we possess the sharp plow of truth to keep us straight, the reality of truth (Jesus) to keep us from buying the counterfeit, and the Spirit to enable us to discern even the slightest smell of poison, corruption, and decay. To me these days are exciting because as a Christian, I know my only reliable source is God's Word, the only place left of reliable dependency is Jesus, my foundation, and the only point of sanity is the Holy Spirit. I have no other option but to get deep into His Word, cling to what is true about my only hope of glory, and learn to hear what the Spirit is saying so that if I am instructed to turn, stop, wait, or advance, I can trust that I am being led through the darkness of this day.

We are living in a world where optics are used to present contrary realities in order to throw us off or seduce us into another reality through indoctrination. Media spews out the same lie to make it seem like the false information must be true, and what we ultimately hear is often based on what we want to hear instead of what is. This is why we must be honest about what we can trust in order to properly DISCERN WHAT WE CAN BELIEVE as being so.

This can all be so confusing and that is why it seems most of us are close to having meltdowns. I have learned that trust is based on the integrity of one's character, hope is based on the sure promise of something and not what I see or hear, and my expectation is directed towards what I know I will see. I know without a doubt I can trust God because He does not lie and I know with all of my heart that I can put all of my hope in His promises because He has never failed me, and I know with great excitement that I expect to see Him part the clouds and come for His bride.

Are you teetering on the precipice to keep from sliding down into the abyss of great disappointment? Are you ready to have a complete meltdown because nothing makes sense, or are you ready to be consumed by utter hopelessness? If so, you need to examine where you put your trust—what you really wanted to hear, and in what you expected to see. If these examinations do not end with trusting God and His timing, wanting to hear truth about a matter, and expecting to see Him glorified, then your truth, hope, and expectation have been misdirected.

It is easy to determine what side someone is on. For example, the wicked work under the cover of darkness, scheming to create an evil plan to rob, kill, and destroy the innocent, the decent, and those who dare oppose them. The complacent work in gray, dark shadows to hide their indifference, while at times giving the appearance of righteousness. The righteous will work according to truth, which often becomes hidden in plain sight to those who do not love it, promote it, or desire it.

The wicked will also create a surreal narrative that never fits, and will ultimately produce bad fruits that end in division, despair, and hopelessness, while the complacent will ignore reality, implying a state of ignorance and an attitude of cluelessness on their part to avoid revealing their true character. In the end, they will produce worthless fruit.

The righteous will step back to discern the fruit, wade through the smokescreen of falsehood in order to get down to the truth of a matter. They may encounter the opposition of darkness and the grays of indifference but they will not be content to settle for anything less than what is God's perspective.

As believers it would be easy to throw up our hands at the dark narratives of this age and the smokescreens that often hide the truth in plain sight, but we need to remember that true discernment must be exercised if we are to grow in it. Such exercise means testing must take place and there will be moments of failure, but in that failure, we can humbly learn to fine-tune our discernment and come into a place where we can discern good from evil in spite of the false optics, the hypocritical narratives, and the attempts of some to play religious games to give the impression of righteousness that is void of substance and power.

Keep in mind, if you love the truth, the Lord will keep you on its narrow path and will never let you slip off of it to fall into the abyss of delusion and destruction. Meanwhile, we need to exercise what discernment we have, risk failing here and there, knowing that the Holy Spirit will lead us through the confusion to what is true, and the Lord will bring us into a place of maturity so that we will be able to discern between the optics and false impressions of evil and what manifests the true goodness of God.

I have been struggling this week with both time and technology. My days seem to go by faster and technology left me long ago in a cloud of confusion and a dust storm of ignorance. Time has its own beat and technology its own language.

I am limited in my strength to keep up with time, left overwhelmed by the tasks that are before me, and often frustrated because of my ignorance towards the things I must use to conduct the business of the age we live in. I know how to use a computer, but I also know because of programs it has a mind of its own and because of its language I am often left in a quandary when I encounter any challenge when things go upside down.

In my latest struggle with technology, I thought about how my ignorance handicaps me from moving forward. I assume all will work right when I turn it on, but I have learned that the combination of any slight change in devices, and ignorance about how things work, quickly become a bog that can consume me.

Many changes are happening in this world and because of disruption, ignorance has become a great veil of confusion due to deception and indoctrination about what is really happening. It has created a certain blindness about the challenges and dangers before many who are being consumed by hopelessness, fear, and uncertainty.

I have learned I can't trust what I see and I must throw out over half of what I hear, and what does penetrate my understanding must be put on the shelf until proven one way or the other. Although I have discussed this very fact in the past, it is important to remember during times of grave confusion I have the real light of the world, Jesus' life in me and that I have His Spirit who is able to properly discern the times, as well as God's inspired Word that will bring understanding.

Right now, I may be too close to what is happening to properly discern it, but if I faithfully continue to walk in what I do know to be true I will be brought to the light and the confusion will part allowing me to discern and understand what is happening around me.

There are many things we have to develop along the way. For instance, we develop likes and dislikes in every area from what we watch to what we eat. If we like something, we expose ourselves to environments or situations that allow us to enjoy it and if we dislike something, we avoid exposing ourselves to it or refuse it when someone offers us. Let's face it, much of what we like or dislike is based on the influence of others in our life, such as our family or peers and not necessarily on personal preference.

We have to recognize how much of our preferences have been conditioned in us by the environments we are exposed to in order to recognize or discipline our preferences. It is important to realize that what we prefer may have been influenced by others, but we are still responsible for such preferences. Through the years my likes and dislikes have changed based on what kind of environment I expose myself to. I learned long ago that I choose my particular environment according to my preferences such as the people I expose myself to, the TV shows I watch, the books I read, and those things I pursue.

The problem we often face when it comes to preferences is that we can remain childish in them. In other words, we selfishly consider preferences according to our moods, feelings, and desired reality and not according to whether a matter is true, right, and moral. The one indication of spiritual growth is that it doesn't matter how we feel about something; instead, we must do a "smell and taste" test of all preferences and see if they line up to the salt of truth, the fragrance of heaven, and the clarity of righteousness so that in the end we will truly end up tasting the sweetness of God's goodness.

Can the Jesus you believe in save you? The Apostle Paul warned us about our minds being corrupted from the simplicity of Jesus so that when another Jesus is preached to us, we cannot discern it and we end up receiving another spirit and gospel (*2 Corinthians 11:4*).

There are many different Christs being presented today, but there is only one Messiah who can save us, and that is the Lord Jesus Christ. There are different spirits in operation, but only one Holy Spirit (*Ephesians 4:4*).

The Apostle Paul in *2 Corinthians 11:13-15* speaks of false apostles and deceitful workers, transforming themselves into the apostles of Christ and why should we marvel at such a reality since Satan can transform himself into an angel of light. Therefore, it would be no great task that false ministers would transform themselves into the ministers of righteousness.

These spirits include familiar spirits who become a substitute for the Holy Spirit, interjecting perversion in all religious arenas, religious spirits that play off of the religious notions of the natural spirit producing self-righteousness, seducing spirits that create a false reality in order to condition one towards receiving a delusion while indoctrinating him or her into lies, and the antichrist spirit that takes the place of the real Jesus, while denying the one true God of the Bible.

"Spirit" can only be discerned when operating in the right spirit; therefore, any attempt on the part of man to try to intellectualize the activities of the unseen world, logic out its affects, and deal with it in personal strength will be met with utter failure.

How can we discern a spirit? The Holy Spirit will only speak of Christ, lead people into all truth about Him, and reveal sin in lives, point to the example of righteousness in Christ, and remind us that the world has already been judged. The reason for the emphasis on the work of the Holy Spirit is because it is not God's will that man perish in His sin, but to come to true repentance and receive by faith the only One who can save man's soul, the Lord Jesus Christ.

What is your agenda? Agendas are inspired by our motives and motives determine the spirit in which we operate. This may not seem important to most people to discern their motives due to the fact that most people do not decide each day to be bad or do wrong, but the truth of the matter is that if the spirit is wrong, then the fruit will prove to be unacceptable to God, and mediocre or unpleasant to others.

When a wrong spirit is present and the source of inspiration, there will be no real lasting results because God's Spirit is not behind a matter, and what has not been touched, sanctified, or anointed by the Holy Spirit can't be used by God for His glory. It is important to point out that there is a spirit behind everything that is associated with the working of this present world. In other words, people do not do something without some agenda as to the environment they want to set up and how it is meant to influence people.

Everything that is not inspired by the Holy Spirit, will be inspired by the carnal spirit of man or the spirit of the world, Satan. Consider the agenda of the carnal spirit. We sometimes refer to this spirit as the "old man" in us. In the case of the "old man" a matter must benefit self and even though the agenda may sound caring as to how it will benefit others or innocent enough that there is no malice in it, it will prove to be treacherous, indifferent, and tyrannical in the end.

When the spirit of world is on the scene it may come across as attractive and show itself as a benevolent source of enlightenment, but it hides darkness, rebellion, deceit, death, and destruction.

It is important to discern the spirit in every arena. If we have a wrong spirit, it will drive us, set us up for a fall and ultimately delude us, and if we are operating in an environment with a wrong spirit, it will dull us down, and seduce us into another reality with the goal to indoctrinate us into an utter lie. In this darkness we must let our light so shine before others that the Father is glorified, and it is for this reason we must discern our spirit to uncover our motives to ensure they line up to heaven's agenda.

Jesus warned us to beware of deception in the last days. It has always amazed me that religious people know about this warning but seem to have very little concern about it. It is natural to assume in our fallen condition we have a corner on truth and there is no way we can be deceived.

As a former cult member, I can tell you it is natural to walk in deception. In fact, if we do not choose to love the truth, seek the truth out in the right arenas, and walk in true humility that allows us to be wrong, we are vulnerable to not only buy some lie but walk in it thinking it is truth.

People can be deceived in four ways. They can be deceived about the absolute authority of God's Word, who God is, what the Gospel is, and their spiritual condition. Each of these points of deception are clearly addressed in the Bible, but how many believe the complete counsel of the Word of God as being true and eternal and how many pick and choose what they want to believe, exalting them to be judge where they are the ones who interpret, decide or determine what they believe?

It is hard for people to perceive they have been deceived because it is contrary to their desires and attempts to rightfully understand, but we must recognize that due to our pride, it is not a matter of being right, but the unwillingness to be found wrong. Unless we recognize that if we start from the premise of the old man that we are naturally starting out wrong; therefore, we must truly discern the way we are walking, while honestly examine the fruits our lives are producing, we will never know it we are on the right side of eternity about a matter.

Rayola Kelley

Satan's first attack in the Garden of Eden was against what God said. If you do not believe God's Word to be absolute truth about all matters pertaining to God and life, how can you believe what it says about God? Sadly, the Bible is not believed, considered, or regarded as the complete, absolute inspired truth of God even by religious people.

If a person does not consider God's Word as the absolute and final truth to all matters, it can't serve as a point of authority that will silence arguments, conflict, and debates. I remember a woman telling me if I showed her husband something scripturally, he would believe it and submit to it. However, when he was challenged with the Word of God concerning some questionable attitudes and practices, he ignored it and continued on his way without any real concern for the destructive fruits his witness was leaving behind. Who was deceived, the man or the woman? To me the man chose the contrary way because that was his heart preference. He could have been deceived as to how God regarded his way, but the woman was deceiving herself about the character, level of religious commitment and conviction of her husband.

Jesus stated his truth will offend those who prefer their own reality. This is not my evaluation of peoples' response towards truth; rather, it is His. For me, His truth has offended me when I was walking contrary to His ways, it has proven to be painful when poured on my wounded pride, and it has shaken me to the core after I insisted on my own way, only to have my way end in failure.

Before we can discern if we are being deceived in some way, we must first ask the Lord to show us our attitude towards His Word. Without first knowing whether we are properly regarding, honoring, and handling the Word of God, we remain incapable of discerning any point of deception that might be operating in our lives.

We must discern our present enemy, whether it be the old man (self-life), the world, or Satan in order to ensure victory. You might ask, if the enemy is the self-life, what must I do to become a trained soldier? It's simple: you must truly repent of your selfishness to have life on your terms. You have been bought with a price and do not belong to yourself.

The more the decaying rags of selfishness of the self-life cling to you, the more confused you will become about what is true and right.

If the world is your present enemy, as a soldier you must become seasoned by ceasing to be dependent on it for your desired lifestyle that will always prove temporary and hollow. This requires you to separate from it as you nail your fleshly, worldly affections and loyalty to a cross in order to gain the life God has for you. Keep in mind the world will constantly entangle you with demands, unrealistic responsibilities, and false promises as a means to cause you to take detours, trip you up, or bury you.

When it comes to Satan, to be a victorious soldier you must recognize his devices and confront them with the Word of God. Satan is foremost the father of lies and his kingdom is built on nothing but lies that enfold his systems, man's mind, and the present age in darkness.

Sadly, the old man prefers the world's lies because it serves as a cover for his sins. It is important to realize that Satan wants to create a surreal reality that is divorced from truth and it is easy to step outside the narrow perimeter of truth. For example, propaganda is often half-truths that dull people down, evil agendas are covered by twisted truths which delude a person as to his or her state, false narratives are upside-down truths that have been perverted in order to indoctrinate people, fanaticism can be a truth taken to extremes that will produce insanity, and worldly diplomacy is nothing more than political correctness that is a ruse that redefines moral worldviews while covering wicked intentions.

As believers we know that it is the person of Jesus Christ and not philosophies, doctrines, theories, or theology that comprise THE TRUTH. We also know that anything that takes the sharpness (moral clarity), the teeth (the decisiveness and absolutes), and the sole authority away from the truth of Jesus Christ and His Word is a ploy of Satan. It is truth that sets us free from the grave oppression of Satan's lies, but we need to choose to love it in order to stand against the great affronts upon hearts, minds, and souls.

Recently, some of you may have noticed that I was away from the computer for a few days. This inanimate object serves as a connection

173

to people saved and unsaved, and gives us the opportunity to be world-wide evangelists without ever leaving our homes. It is for this reason that, as believers, we must adjust to modern technology in order to take advantage of the opportunity to communicate the great message of hope and salvation to the whole world.

Remember, before Jesus comes again, the Gospel will be preached throughout the whole world. Obviously, it must be noted that through modern technology it is easy to create an artificial environment in which man can develop any image, direct any narrative, and operate in the worse type of insanity and convince himself it is sane and right. It was nice to take a break from this environment in order to somewhat land on what is in order to gain the right perspective to discern what is going on.

As Christians, we need to take time out from what is artificial, man-controlled, and worldly inspired to be certain we do not accept the nightmarish, godless, narratives of our age. We must make sure that if we have not veered off center (God and His Word) and if we have, we need to come back to center.

We must discern the attitude we are taking on because of the darkness around us. Is it the attitude of Christ or the world? Keep in mind, what we fail to discern in times of self-examination becomes the judgmental board in our eye that will keep us from seeing where we are spiritually, while we harshly judge those with like challenges. As believers, we must make sure our spiritual stake has not moved from the Rock of ages and that our focus remains steadfast on Jesus as we follow Him into the life He has called us into.

ه‍‍ـ‍ک‍ـ‍ـ‍ب‍

Yesterday I made reference to artificial environments. As most of us are aware, we now have artificial intelligence capable of running everything, pointing to its capacity of bringing all of Satan's systems under a one-world dictator. At times, these artificial environments are useful and necessary, but they must be kept in perspective in order to properly discern all other environments around us.

It is important to remember what constitutes that which is artificial because it is can easily become a substitute for what is real and genuine. The first thing we must ask is what constitutes an artificial environment. The answer is simple, anything that is attached to man's ingenuity or involvement.

Consider the stores. Children in cities think milk comes from cartons from a store instead of from cows. Cities are clearly an artificial environment because man perceives he is only subject to himself and not God. As I have stated before, Cain built the first city but he had to depart from God to do it.

Artificial environments allow people to become divorced from what is real. They are one step removed from the source and reality of the real origins of something. This brings me to another artificial environment: that of man-made religion.

Man-made religion finds its origins in man, which means the light (beliefs) is limited to one dimension, proving to be powerless and lifeless, or it is false light and based on the lies of the one who comes as an angel of light, Satan. Satan clearly orchestrates his religious lies through those who appear to be ministers of righteousness (*2 Corinthians 11:3-15*).

It is also easy in our church buildings with our orchestrated worship, and our controlled religious activities to become somewhat divorced from our life in Christ as we substitute it with religion. Our homes are also an artificial environment and that is why we are the temples of the Holy Spirit where the very light, life of Christ resides. For saints, devotion, worship and service is a matter of the heart and true fellowship in the Spirit. As believers, we must beware that our light is not some poor substitute that hides the life of Jesus in us; rather, it is His life in us that is permeating our devotion, inspiring our worship and establishing our service for His glory.

According to *1 Corinthians 2:10-14*, there are three major spirits in operation: There is the Holy Spirit who reveals the mind and heart of God to His people, the natural spirit who operates according to the lusts, philosophies, and preferences of the age and there is the spirit of the world, Satan, who oversees the kingdom of darkness and the godless systems of the age. It is for this reason we are to test or discern the spirit in operation and respond accordingly.

175

When it comes to the Holy Spirit, as believers, we give way to His leadings, instructions, and promptings in order to come into line with God's righteousness and will. When it comes to the natural spirit, people tend to go with the lusts of the flesh, while coming under the conditioning and indoctrinations of popular, anti-God philosophies and chasing after vain preferences that will supposedly make them happy, but leaves them empty and frustrated. When it comes to the spirit of the world, Satan, people are prone to believe his lies, allow themselves to be seduced into another reality, and do his bidding to thwart the work of God as they come under greater oppression.

The Holy Spirit promotes freedom to pursue and know God, the natural spirit offers gratification, that is if willing subjects will eat the poison fruit of the age, and the spirit of the world offers his disciples the world if they will only sell their soul. The reason we need to discern what spirit is in operation, is because we must determine if we are able to come into agreement with it. The Holy Spirit is the only one who can open the door to the matters of God but the natural spirit opens the door to the world, and the world opens the door to Satan.

GRACE, JOY & PEACE

*Unfathomable oceans of grace are in Christ
for you. Dive and dive again—you will never
come to the bottom of these depths.
(Robert McCheyne)*

As we begin to close this year out and enter a new one, I look back to see if I stayed the course according to my election and calling in Christ, and I look forward to see if Jesus is before me and the glory of the next world is still in my sights. I have always tried to stay FOCUSED on what needs to be before me, Jesus; do right as to what has been Scripturally SET before me, and LINE up to the magnificence that has already been promised me.

As believers we must avoid being bogged down by the quagmire of this world, being consumed by it lies, and buried by its hopelessness. We have a sure course set before us. Granted, it is narrow at times, rough in places, requires endurance, entails battles, and includes a personal cross, but it is in preparation to enter and embrace what has been promised us.

I understand that as this world gets more insane, the natural response is to sit down in the middle of the path and throw our hands up and wait for something to put us out of our misery, but we must not give in to such despair because at the end of our journey is the full realization of our faith, our hope, and our redemption: the JOY OF OUR SALVATION

What must we do to ensure that the God of peace shall be with us? *Philippians 4:9* gives us a simple task to carry out to ensure such peace: whatever we have learned at the feet and table of Jesus, whatever we have received by faith from the throne of God, whatever we have heard as to the instructions of God's Word and the revelation of the Spirit, and whatever we have seen as far as godly example, we must DO.

Jesus never called inactive people; rather, He called those who were in the middle of some task because they were ready to respond. The big challenge to much of Christianity is that we have a tendency to wait, look for or expect some greatness to fall before us before we will carry out some function for God's kingdom, but it is clear if you give water in His name to a needy person, you are doing it for His sake.

Much of ministry is practical, which requires us to be willing and faithful to do practical service to those around us. The more we are faithful to simply do what is Scriptural, right, and godly, the more we will sense the anchor of peace in our spirits which is joy. There can't be true peace until there is true joy abiding in us, and what did Jesus state about joy in *John 15:11, "These things have I spoken unto you, that my joy might remain in you, and that your joy might be full."*

How many of us are seeking for peace? We must determine what peace is. There is peace of the flesh that is temporary and only comes when the lusts have been satisfied for the moment. There is an emotional

peace where people have a sense all is well because it looks like everything is working out according to their design, and there is an intellectual peace where we make a decision about something that causes the war of doubt and uncertainty to cease.

There is also a worldly peace that promotes a type of environment that is without conflict, but when you consider each of these types of peace, we must recognize that they are temporary at best and for the most part unrealistic in a world that is shrouded in constant conflict. However, the greatest conflict man has is taking place within his soul.

The Bible calls it the war between the flesh and the Spirit, which reveals man's great struggle is with His Creator. Jesus Christ came to provide the way of peace between God and man through redemption that leads to reconciliation with God. The truth is until man is at peace with his Creator, his world will be filled with conflict, chaos, and wars on every front.

For the most part man wants to be left alone to live his life as he sees fit, but conflict reveals and reminds man he is not ruler of his world and that he must make peace with the one who is Sovereign over all. The next time you have conflict, make sure that there is not something amiss in your relationship with the Prince of Peace.

Mankind desires one of three things: to be loved, have peace, and experience happiness. Many times, people will give away what is happening in their personal environments when they tell you what they desire the most. If they desire love the most, you will find their environment has indifference or hatred in it. If they desire peace, it is because much unrest and conflict rules, and if they desire happiness, you will find misery, despair, and hopelessness are prevalent.

The problem with desires is that they are based on fleshly expectations and worldly ideas. Fleshly expectations set a person up to where they may desire love but it is self-serving. This self-serving idea of love ends up looking for it in the wrong places as it seeks to be adored and worshipped by others in an unrealistic way.

They may want peace, but their idea of peace has to do with the outward environment that is subject to them and not an inward state that is under the control of the Holy Spirit. And, when it comes to happiness, most people's concept of it is worldly, and proves to be a fleeting sense rather than an abiding reality.

God put these desires in man to cause him to seek them out, but man needs to realize that all three of these desires can only be found in a relationship with our Creator who designed us. God is love, but if man's idea of love is self-serving, he will never be receptive of God's love which is selfless, honorable, and sacrificial. God is the source of peace, but God's peace is based on being at peace with Him through reconciliation that comes by way of Jesus' redemption and maintaining that peace through the ways of righteousness that are wrought by faith. As far as happiness, believers realize it is an attitude of the heart and that it is the joy of the Lord that serves as the real anchor that keeps them steady in a cursed world of toil, sorrow, and dismay.

Happiness is mentioned in the Bible, but always in relationship with God being God in a situation. One of my favorite verses on happiness is found in *Psalm 144:15, "Happy is that people, that is in such a case: yea, happy that people, whose God is the LORD."*

I have been talking about what constitutes true peace. In these days the one sure thing you can bank on being prevalent is utter chaos. Chaos must be a reigning factor if the globalists are going to bring in a one world-government, religious system, and leader.

The last man to be the leader of this world will be the anti-Christ. He will offer peace and sadly many will sell their soul to have a semblance of peace in this world, but he will prove to be nothing more than a tyrant that will bring anything but peace. There are three reasons why real peace eludes man.

The first reason for man being void of peace is due to anxiety, which is a form of fear. People worry for one reason and that is they will not get their way. They think their way is the best when the Bible states man's ways may seem clean in his eyes but in the eyes of God they are perverted, unacceptable, and destructive, resulting in spiritual death. The solution to anxiety is setting one's mind on Christ while applying faith.

The second reason peace is illusive to man has to do with his pride. Pride will comply, reform, and perform, but it will never line up to that which does not serve its purpose, agree with it, or placate it. Anxiety robs a man of peace while causing him to be in conflict with reality (truth), while pride kills the attempts of having order to ensure peace, causing man to be in conflict with others.

The final reason man has no peace is because he is at war with God. People in their desire to be independent from their Creator, call their own shots, and rule and manipulate their own life will find themselves walking in the ways of defeat, misery, and death. Their lives, homes, and society will be shrouded in conflict, despair, and judgment. Being at war with God destroys any hope of real peace in the inner man, in his home, and in his world.

Today we see the chaos created by Satan and rebellious and wicked man. We see the darkness of delusion, the sorrow, the lawlessness, and death, revealing that the world will never have or know real peace. But as believers we must remember that as long as our mind looks up to our real Hope, our heart seeks the Lover of our soul, our faith holds steadfast on what has been established as truth, and we walk in obedience to God's Word, we will be assured of possessing the peace the world can't begin to understand.

I have been thinking about a few words lately. One such word I have already used is "privilege." When it comes to the concept of "privilege," people have different ideas of how it looks.

If you are on the low end of a scale in some way in society, to you it would appear that even those in the middle who barely get by are privileged. The point is that it depends on if you are looking up from a point of vulnerability, looking sideways as an observer or looking down from some arrogant pinnacle as to what you might consider to be privileged.

There was a point in my life when I lived on what they called the "other side of the tracks" where you don't fit in because your name is not found among the elites, your dress speaks of your below average financial status, and your address puts you into the low-class part of society.

During that particular short season of my life, such forms of identification made me a target of bullying, name calling, and mocking, allowing me to feel isolated, depressed, and oppressed. To me such feelings of rejection and prejudice are not limited to one color or race, and to act as if a certain group of people have a corner on such emotional challenges is naïve at best and self-centered at worst.

There was a time I also felt like the richest kid in the world because of family and stability but according to NBC news, I was a poor kid as far as financial standing. The truth is "privilege" is a matter of opinions that are based on anything from standards to some type of social status, but in reality, we as humans are all in the same boat, and if you don't believe me, visit a graveyard.

As a Christian I have long ago learned that there are two prominent equalizers in this world, death and the cross of Christ. I have found that the low place of humility is the best way to gain perspective because it will always cause me to look up in the right direction towards the One who has the right perspective and has it all under control.

I have become cautious about looking around as an observer to judge or compare myself to others because it is a futile exercise, and I have fallen off of enough religious pinnacles to try to avoid them. As a believer, I have come to realize that I am privileged because I belong to a kingdom that is not of this world, but I keep such privilege in perspective by remembering everything I have and receive is a matter of God's grace.

It was His grace that provided the avenue to me, a spiritual pauper on the wrong side of eternity, to gain a new identity, a spiritual inheritance, and a sure future. This avenue has been on display in a profound way to anyone who will come in childlike faith and receive it. This avenue comprises the Gospel which is summarized in the death, burial, and resurrection of God's only begotten Son, Jesus Christ.

I don't know about you but I have acquired or carried heavy burdens that buried me in the past. I remember an incident when I asked the Lord to show me the needs of a certain community. He gave me a glimpse into the spiritual plight of many. I felt overwhelmed as the burden of it began to wear heavily upon me.

The Lord allowed me to feel that burden for a couple of days and then He lifted it. I suddenly realized that He was not asking me to carry the burden of everyone because I could not; however, the burden He would give me would be light because He would enable me to carry it.

It is easy to take on burdens along the way that we are not called or ordained to carry. We must discern the difference. I have to admit that carrying an ordained burden has probably taught me more about God's grace than any other instrument.

My sin made me aware of how I needed God's grace, but God-ordained burdens taught me how to be an instrument of grace. I can remember there were times that God lifted a burden in my life but I knew the mission was not yet completed. As I wondered how I would complete the mission without the burden, I became aware of God's incredible grace flooding my soul, bringing both peace and confidence that what was set before me would indeed be completed because the sufficiency of all matters rest with Him and not me. The beauty about this revelation was the knowledge that in the end the Lord would receive glory for the work He accomplished and continues to do on everyone's behalf.

Let us be mindful each day to cast off cares as we discern what we can't change, as well as which burdens to carry that will identify us to the true work of God. We must always be freed up to come under yokes that will bring us into step with the Lord when it comes to the matters of His kingdom.

Joy, a three-letter word that has been defined in different ways. For example, one description of joy is the flag that flies over the palace when the <u>King</u> is in residence. An interesting way to spell joy is Jesus—first, Others—second, and You—last.

It is clear that if Jesus is not first in our lives, we will become lost and miserable, and if others are not second, we will become judgmental and indifferent in our attitude towards them, and if we are not last, our small worlds will become insipid. Joy is one of the ingredients in the fruit of the

Spirit and it is important to note where it is located in the ingredients because the preceding one serves as the source for the product to take root, allowing it to become a platform for a byproduct.

For example, love is first, followed by joy then peace. The order of words points out that true joy comes out of godly love. Without love there is no joy and the byproduct of such joy is peace. Let me ask you a question, how much joy do you have when you feel secure in a relationship with the one you love?

As Christians we are secure in the love of God and if that security is missing, the fault will not rest with God. Joy that comes out of love that is pure, sweet, and abiding produces contentment in the spirit and satisfaction in the soul. Christians have joy because they have experienced and received the love of God in their spirits and the joy produces peace because one now has a relationship with the Lord.

It is a tendency to hide behind the love of God, but to know joy we have to walk in that love by having a growing relationship with the Lord. The more mature our love becomes for the Lord, the greater the joy, and the more peace we will know as we rest in assurance of our salvation and our place in the Lord.

We Americans have our ideas as to what constitutes personal happiness. However, the words that are stressed in Scripture are "joy" and "blessed." "Joy" is a state, while "blessed" is an attitude.

Jesus stated in *John 15:11, "These things have I spoken unto you, that my joy might remain in you and that your joy might be full."* Clearly, joy comes from being anchored in the Lord's Word by faith and through obedience to it.

We can have such joy because His Word contains promises that brings hope and assurance and His commandments clearly show us the way of righteousness. The problem is we claim the promise while ignoring the condition that would ensure it and we admire the wisdom of His commandments while adjusting or excusing them away to pursue what we think would make us happy.

The truth is God calls us to holiness not fleshly happiness, because without holiness we will not see Him (*Hebrews 12:14*). The word "happy"

is used but it is used in relationship to knowing and serving God, being corrected by God, fearing Him and walking in His ways, and observing His commandments.

As Christians we need encouragement that can be found in true joy, but to embrace such joy, we need to line our idea of "happiness" up to the excellent presentation of it found in Scripture.

WISDOM & THE FEAR OF THE LORD

He who prepares for this life
but not for eternity is wise for a moment
but a fool forever.
(Unknown)

It is easy to hide excuses and irresponsibility behind the fact that one can't possibly understand someone else's plight, but such an excuse will never justify wrong attitudes, decisions, or actions. We all have a history and if you have lived very long, there is a combination of the bitterness of tragedy, loss, and sorrow mixed with the sweetness of love, blessings, and joy.

The world serves mankind in various capacities, much like a circus where different activities are taking place but can become redundant, overwhelming, and/or scary. Or it reminds one, of a courtroom of endless debates as to what is real, just, and fair, or/and a classroom where lessons must be learned, but when tested, some end up with different grades depending on the level of moral uprightness, integrity, and wisdom.

The truth is regardless of our cover, we are made up of pages of different experiences, sections of diverse challenges, and chapters where we have hopefully recorded wonderful discoveries made about life along with the beautiful gems of wisdom that were uncovered. It is for this reason I have asked the Lord to write on my slate to transform my mind, paint the canvas of my life with His life, form me as an acceptable vessel for His use, and shape me as a fine-tuned instrument for His glory.

A controversial subject in the religious arenas is "the fear of the Lord," because it can prove to be a bit unnerving for those who do not understand the holiness of God. The fear of the Lord is a healthy, godly attitude of those who understand that God's holiness makes Him a consuming fire that will purge and separate any profane thing from that which is holy (*Hebrews 12:29*).

Such fear produces wisdom because it wants to avoid such consequences and will ensure a right standing in the Lord. Like Jacob's encounter with God in *Genesis 28*, it will create dread for those who understand that they do not want to meet the Lord outside of His mercy and grace that was secured through Jesus' redemption.

For Isaiah in *chapter 6*, he felt totally undone before the Lord and admitted he was a man of unclean lips who dwelled among an unclean people, unprepared to stand before Him in His holiness without being purged. Like the Apostle John in *Revelation 1*, such fear came upon him that he "fell at his feet as dead," because he saw the Lord Jesus Christ as the great judge who came to set matters right. Fear of the Lord also entails an awe that produces godly reverence towards Him (*Hebrews 12:28*).

I fear much of the flimsy presentation of our Lord today strips Him of who He is in the minds of many, thereby taking away the attitude of fear and trembling before Him and His Word, as some also fail to see their Scriptural responsibility to work in their salvation in the same attitude through submission to Him and His Word, and work it out in obedience towards others (*Ephesians 5:21; Philippians 2:12*).

It is easy for people to flit here and there about the matters of God, while picking and choosing what will serve their narrative, their sentiment, their ideas, or their fragile reality, but be assured, God's Word means what it says and says what it means. In short, the "Fear of the Lord" means exactly what it says and *Hebrews 10:31* put it in this perspective, *"It is a fearful thing to fall into the hands of the living God."*

Rayola Kelley

Today our society is drowning in a cesspool of lawlessness due to the corruption in high places such as government, the justice system, and the educational system. When it comes to the lawless, they rebel against authority and the law, and we must never stand in the way of them rightfully paying consequences for their actions. We must not show mercy if they ask for none, we must not be tolerant when they are being stiff-necked and unrepentant, and we must not allow our Christian compassion to set us up to be seduced or deluded by their con games as they look for means to beat the system.

When it comes to those in high places, they must be brought low, and we must not pity them when they hit the depths of the pits they have dug for others. It is important to keep in mind that love never rejoices in iniquity and that the main reason people are enemies of righteousness and God is because they have no fear of God. They fear neither consequence, judgment, or wrath, and it is only the knowledge of paying possible consequences, facing judgment, and tasting wrath that people learn to truly fear the ultimate judge of their souls, God.

The other thing we must remember is that our goal is not to outshine God to prove how great a Christian we are when it comes to His just disciplines and judgments, but we are to reflect His heart, and that is to see a soul truly saved as they received God's grace upon repentance, come to the true knowledge of spiritual healing upon forgiveness, restored by His redemption, and established in a relationship with the Lord through reconciliation.

Knowledge and ignorance are both a choice. Wisdom is the result of knowledge put into practice, and ignorance reveals itself to be nothing more than an indifferent attitude. I choose what I know because I choose what I want to pursue as far as understanding, perception, and preference and anything outside of such knowledge is a point of ignorance.

I often choose my take on knowledge based on what will best serve my ideas, preferences, and goals. Therefore, knowledge simply becomes a platform that will direct me in the direction I desire to go. It will become my scope that will influence my focus, while determining the boundaries of my peripheral vision.

In many ways anything outside of my limited scope becomes what we know as the "blindside" and depending on how stiff-necked I am, it will determine how I react when I am blindsided by the unexpected. Anything that blindsides me will disrupt what I do know either causing confusion, resentment, anger, or hate.

This brings us back to knowledge. What we THINK we know is based on opinions that perhaps have some facts intertwined with it, what we DO know becomes our premise in how we judge all other matters, and what we NEED to know to balance out our knowledge can elude us because it is often outside of our box of what we want to know.

This brings me to what we SHOULD know. It can become quite optional based on arrogant opinions, fickle sentiment, and foolish notions. One of my favorite epistles is *1 John.*

The Apostle John makes it quite clear what we NEED to know, and that is Jesus, while pointing out that we CAN know who Jesus is because we have a sure record of His identity and work, and we SHOULD know who He is because of what He did for us, and we BETTER know who He is because our eternal destination depends on it.

The more I learn of Jesus, the more I realize I do not know much and that it is only at the point of true humility that I CAN truly receive revelation from above that makes Him living and real to my spirit.

Proverbs *29:18* tells us people perish without lack of vision. What vision is this Scripture talking about? Is it physical eyesight? It is true without physical eyesight you can put yourself on a dangerous path, but this scripture is in relationship to the unseen and unknown.

In *1 Samuel 3:1*, we are given insight into the type of vision we need, *"And the child Samuel ministered unto the LORD before Eli. And the word of the LORD was precious in those days; there was no open vision."* "Vision" has to do with revelation.

Knowledge operates in three arenas: facts, revelation, and enlightenment. Facts are based on what is so, revelation on spiritual growth, and enlightenment on understanding. Facts are based on what is obvious, revelation on faith, and enlightenment on the Word of God becoming living.

In reality where there is no spiritual vision there is nothing being uncovered by the Holy Spirit in relationship to forthtelling (exhortation) and foretelling (warning in light of preparation) (*John 16:13*). The Lord is remaining silent at such times and is not bringing clarity to what is hidden in shadows nor is He bringing life to His truths due to rebellion.

Sadly, for many they have no vision past this present life. They can only know the smallness of their selfishness, the false, shallow glitter of the world, and the short-sightedness of their pride. The problem with such vision is that people will not be prepared for what is coming and will perish in the floods of judgment.

As Christians we are able to see beyond this world into the age to come, and those who have developed their heavenly vision are like Abraham, always looking forward towards that which is unseen, ever focusing on the eternal city of God while becoming restless in the spirit as they wait to enter into the unhindered glory of that which is everlasting.

I must admit, I become a bit concerned about my spiritual vision at times. I'm aware of how limited I am in what I see and understand. The hindsight I possess came from past failures and missteps and the foresight I am presently gaining comes from stumbling around matters that are hidden in obscurity of the unseen, or in shadows.

Our vision can be hindered by darkness, conflicts, wrong judgments, and obstacles. For Moses he was hindered by what he considered his ineptness as to speaking and he ended up with Aaron who proved to be more of a thorn in the side than a helper. There was David, a man whose heart was after God and for the most part a straight shooter when it came to the matters of God, but he was not at the right place at the right time and fell into temptation and great sin as his eyes landed on forbidden fruit and he pursued it.

As for the three disciples they were overwhelmed by seeing Elijah and Moses on the Mount of Transfiguration, while one greater stood before them, as well as walked among them. As I consider these individuals, I realize that Moses had to lose his initial vision in the wilderness of preparation, step over his own ineptness to carry out God's vision for him so he could be a deliverer and shepherd to Israel.

It's clear Moses had to take the focus off of himself and place it firmly on God. David lost sight of his calling because he should have been fighting a battle on behalf of Israel instead of losing a personal battle on the home front that cost him in unimaginable ways.

As believers we must remember that as long as we press forward to our high calling in Christ Jesus, we will not fall into such traps. Concerning the three disciples, they had a revelation of Jesus but their example reminds us that there are those things (and people) that may seem to shine even brighter than Jesus that creates excitement and enthusiasm in us, but we must remember at such times that no matter how bright someone's star may shine, the real Light of the World, Jesus, is the Bright and Morning Star that illuminates, highlights, and reveals what we need to see.

We must also remember another simple truth and that is if anyone stands in the light of Jesus, it is His glory that they are reflecting; therefore, all glory belongs to Him.

The fear of the Lord is the only correct response to the holiness of God. God's holiness represents His pure transparency in which nothing that is perverted will remain. In such transparency all wickedness will be exposed, whether it be self-serving agendas, lustful pursuits, or self-righteous piousness.

When man encounters God's holiness his best becomes great darkness and bitterness to his soul. And, when it comes to his personal piousness, it becomes the precipice from which he falls into sorrow and hopelessness and either cries out in desperation for mercy or whimpers, "O wretched man that I am who shall deliver me," because everything seems defiled and untrustworthy; while the passions of his lust are utterly consumed as he finds himself a broken, worthless vessel before the Lord.

Saints who have truly encountered the holiness of God are clearly identified by their sobriety because it is a fearful thing to encounter His holiness. It clearly results in a state of humility where brokenness is realized as one sees that maybe in the world's eyes he or she may not be so bad and in the eyes of self, he or she may be pretty good compared to others, but in light of God's holiness, the best of any man is filthy rags, his fleshly ways will prove to be wretched, and his high opinions of self vulgar.

Through the years I have learned one thing, there is nothing that will cause one to gain the harsh reality that worldly, selfish measurements mean nothing because holiness is not about how bad man is but how holy God is.

The Bible speaks much about the fear of the Lord. It is not unusual to see in Christendom people trying to take away the harshness of this fear as a means to make it more acceptable to fragile, politically correct taste buds. This is a grave disservice to God's Word and kingdom.

Man needs to understand the seriousness of his spiritual plight of being lost, under condemnation, and heading for hell. To make the things of God acceptable to man simply means you are making him dull to his real spiritual plight while causing him to enjoy his delusional slide into hell without any challenge or disruption.

What are the fruits of the fear of the Lord? The first one is wisdom. In the case of sin, wisdom of this type will see the destruction it brings upon one's soul, the reproach it brings upon God, and how it ruins relationships and will develop a healthy hatred for it that will not allow the person to be flippant towards any sin. It will create discretion that will prove to be honorable in its dealing with God and others. It will show understanding by being able to discern a matter in order to make right judgment calls. Finally, heavenly wisdom knows how to allow mercy and judgement to come together that will produce grace that shows itself in love, compassion, and pity.

We must never try to soften the concept of the fear of the Lord in order to make it acceptable to those of the world who are sitting in church pews, for it is intended to wake up people to their plight as a means to cause them to flee the wrath that will come upon all who are disobedient to the Gospel. It is for this reason we must do as Paul instructed each of us as believers in regard to our Christian walk. *Ephesians 5:21* states, *"Submitting yourselves one to another in the fear of God,"* while in *Philippians 2:12* we are told, *"Wherefore, my beloved, as ye have always obeyed, not as in my presence only, but now much more in my absence, work out your own salvation with fear and trembling."*

THE WORLD

If the world is to get back on its feet,
the church has to get on its knees.
(Unknown)

It seems the world is under siege from the weather. The type of weather and the foundational changes that are happening will often signal what is going on spiritually. For example, drought speaks of a spiritual drought, flooding points to contamination of the holy, and earthquakes to the shaking of the foundations.

These events are nothing new except it is happening on a greater scale and frequency, and I wonder how much of it has to do with the land spitting us out due to the abominations taking place. The awareness of these weather events could be because of living in a world where technology allows you to see what is happening all over the world. We know that the earth slightly tilts and all of creation moans because of sin.

Today we live in a world that is going mad because of unabated sin ruling with a vengeance, and the more insane it becomes, the more everything becomes tilted in every arena, creating chaos. It is clear that believers need to be standing on the Rock of Jesus which serves as the center to everything of truth, what is right, what needs to be valued, and what is eternal. However, in this world of depravity, it is easy to drift away from the Rock and become confused, overwhelmed, and lost in it all.

Believers need to make sure that they are not becoming tilted like the earth, insane like the world or getting off center like many churches seemed to be because they have left their first love. We need to hold tightly to who Jesus is, stand on what He said, cling to what is true, and have that assurance that we are standing on the right side of glory and one day we will be living in the incredible bliss of His presence that will last forever.

My question is what is the world demanding from its inhabitants? The one thing I hear the people of the world calling for is "compliance." We need to consider this word. Much of what we hear is a matter of propaganda, making the truth a luxury that must be sought out in spite of the deception, and a rare gem that must be prized and obtained regardless of the cost.

It is clear that a minority in this country are trying to control the narrative through censorship and bullying in order to advance wicked agendas, but the eternal truth of God will not be silenced and will ultimately stand and bring judgment. When you consider the word, "compliance," it points to the idea of being conditioned to the point a person will ultimately surrender his or her will and mind without question.

Sadly, such surrender makes people like sheep that can easily be used to advance wickedness, while being led to the slaughter and ultimately sacrificed for the sake of the agenda. Compliance innocently begins as a simple outward act, but it becomes a means to identify and indoctrinate those who can be easily controlled with fear, shame, and intimidation from those who will maintain their autonomy in spite of the pressure being exerted around them. Its goal is to divide people in order to control the masses, take captive the fearful, cause suspicion among families that results in betrayal, and elitism among neighbors that produces arrogance and judgmentalism. This division is necessary to prevent the masses from rising up in opposition against the agenda and isolating anyone who refuses to bow before the "altar of Baal."

Independent thinkers want to evaluate a matter before they submit themselves to any master, cause, or agenda. As believers, regardless of what is going on around us, we must avoid acting without first seeking the counsel of God's Word, discerning the real intent of something, and praying about what our response must be. The Word is clear we are not to conform to this world, but be transformed by the renewing of our mind. We must always strive to have the mind of Christ in all matters to ensure God's authority in our life and liberty in the Spirit. This is necessary if we are to avoid being oppressed or taken captive by the age in which we live.

The Bible mentions that if it were possible even the elect would be deceived. Every time I read this warning, I wonder just how great the lie is that if it was not for the grace of God, His power to preserve His people, and a love for truth that even the elect would be deceived. We are told in 2 Thessalonians 2 that God will send a great delusion as a test to the hearts of men, and those who do not love the truth will be taken away into judgment. We call such falling away "going apostate."

As I consider this warning, I begin to wonder how great, how clever will this delusion be? I have been hearing about holograms, doubles, clones (in some cults it is the clone of Christ who will be coming back), the blue beam (hologram of Christ coming back to claim His people), the false alien invasion, and so on. For example, people in the limelight have doubles, some claim they have clones, and I delved into the information enough to simply be aware of it, while avoiding becoming too informed or familiar with it to the point my spirit becomes totally vexed over it.

It is important to realize Satan's world is not only dark with deception that is based on a complete lie, but the reality that surrounds his workings is surreal and bazaar causing it to look unbelievable to any sane person. However, we must not forget the insane reality around Satan has been made possible by the fact that he is the god of this world and has power to bring about the most bazaar happenings.

As the prince of the power of the air, the devil not only has the power to perform lying signs (happenings in the sky) and wonders (miracles), but his mystery of iniquity has been working through each generation, being fined-tuned, repackaged for the time and culture, and adjusted to use different technologies to create the false illusion of such things as

193

the expected "rapture of the church" and the invasion of aliens from outer space. This may all seemed fictitious to us, but I have one title of a book to put this in perspective, "1984."

We must not give Satan too much credit, but we must not underestimate him. As believers we can discern the counterfeits because we know the real Jesus of the Bible. We can also avoid the endless, insane detours as long as we keep in the narrow way of truth and righteousness, and we can be at peace in our inner man as long as our mind stays on the Prince of Peace and we avoid looking for it in this world. As Jesus instructed, when you see these things happening, look up and keep your eyes open for the only true Redeemer to come back to set things right.

One of the great principles in the kingdom of God is found in what it means to gain Christ. It is clear once we obtain something we never want to lose it, but the things of the world quickly lose their luster and what we call "normalcy" once again settles on our life as the "something new" becomes familiar and blends into the landscape of things that usually become old, while cluttering up our lives.

We attempt to always inspire ourselves to continue on as before with obtaining this accomplishment, possessing this thing, and finding some niche of satisfaction and contentment in this world. Sadly, what we discover is that the temporary luster of the world may begin with great expectation, but ends in becoming lost in the midst of what Solomon would clearly classify as vanity in Ecclesiastes, for all of this world is vain and useless, proving to be empty of any real substance. However, many believe there is some small corner in this world where lasting happiness can be obtained, but that in time proves to be a foolish notion.

In a world of empty things, how can we gain Christ, who is the essence of all that which is eternal and valuable? The answer is simple, you do not look for Christ, everlasting life, heavenly blessings and eternal promises among vain, lifeless, useless things of the flesh and the world. To gain Christ we must lose all silly notions, fleshly ways and worldly pursuits to find some semblance of life in this world, and turn from its many empty promises to pursue the promise of heaven, Jesus Christ.

Today many people, including some believers, are trying to preserve their life in this world as they wait to get back to what they consider "normalcy." However, God is exposing the stagnation of normalcy to reveal its emptiness. He is shaking foolish notions to try to awaken people as to how such notions are nothing more than a house of cards ready to collapse, and He is trying to show that worldly pursuits lead one to the edge of an abyss where all can easily become lost. Jesus was clear, if we are going to gain what is heavenly, we must be willing to lose this present life the world offers, entices us with, and falsely promises us.

I am sure you have heard about the "Fact Checkers" in the world of technology that are "supposedly" setting the record straight about everything. If your opinion is not in line with theirs, they will put a warning on your opinion that it does not check out with their facts. First of all, opinions are opinions and not a matter of "facts." Opinions may be landing on the right target about something but they are more about personal conviction than facts.

What criteria does a "fact checker" use to determine if a matter is a fact or not? It is simple, the criterion is that you have to be in agreement with their narrative and agendas. First of all, facts do not constitute a truth. Facts are tangible, but they are one dimensional and are nothing more than bits and pieces that are often used to interpret a matter instead of properly fitting each fact into the whole picture of something, thereby, confirming what is true.

Facts can be accepted or rejected. For example, facts show there is a God and He created heaven and earth, but how many people reject these two facts while labeling the theory of evolution as a fact? Are facts trustworthy? It depends on whether they lead a person to the truth, truth that can't be controlled, adjusted, or changed according to personal narratives, preferences, and indoctrination.

We live in a very conflicting world and it is hard to wade through the rhetoric of those who often talk out of both sides of their mouth. In fact,

195

for some individuals, all they can do is lie. Truth will set people free, but many people are not interested in the truth because unlike facts, it will not adjust to fit their narrative. Such individuals want to stick to their false reality, while swinging from limbs of wishful thinking. The tragedy is when the truth, and not the facts, finally comes out, their flimsy limbs will break, allowing them to taste the bitterness of betrayal that comes when they realize they have been lied to, leaving them to look like chumps.

My goal is not to line up facts, but to come to truth so that I can be lined up to what is so. The desire to seek, know, and come to terms with truth has left me looking like a spectacle to the "fact checkers" of our times, but it has never left me feeling betrayed and looking like a bewildered chump that has been caught up in a delusion.

Yesterday I mentioned "Fact Checkers." Oswald Chambers made an important observation about facts, He pointed out that when you think you have all the facts, you will discover there is still one more fact you do not know, and it will completely change what you thought was so.

The Bible is clear we know in part and see though the darkened glass of our humanity. We can't trust what we know because our knowledge is very limited and we must remember there are other facts out there we are not privy too. In fact, what we can't see and what we really don't know is what ultimately affects the outcome of something. We can't trust what we see because our vision is clouded and will end up perverting what we do see. It is for this reason, I seek, desire, and will not settle for any reality that has not been confirmed by heaven as being so.

Many times, I put facts on the shelf until the Holy Spirit takes them and reveals their caliber. It is the Spirit who takes the right facts at the right time and glues them together to reveal the truth of a matter. The Holy Spirit is the only one who leads us into all truth about all things pertaining to God, life, and what is truly happening in the world, and until He reveals, confirms, and verifies a matter is so, I hold such facts lightly.

In order to hold lightly the possibility of what might be, good or bad, I must avoid the traps of arrogance and conceit. These two seductive idols of the mind will set people up for a fall, leaving them looking like utter fools. As we wait to see the outcome of the times we are living in, we must be wise and avoid letting this present age interpret for us what is happening. We must never let the voices of this present, wicked world define reality, nor can we accept unfounded, untested, and unwarranted facts or claims.

In spite of the claims, rhetoric, and celebrations going on, I wait in expectancy as my ear is open to the heavenlies. I have to admit what I am hearing is a bit unnerving because it points to JUDGMENT. So, what am I hearing? SILENCE. In fact, I don't know if anyone has noticed but there are two sides and distinct groups that are involved with the major event taking place in our nation right now, and the leader of one side is eerily silent.

Knowing the caliber of this leader, I can tell you it is not because he is on the run, playing dead, or licking his wounds. I understand He is being greatly censored, but as the saying goes, "the shoe has not yet dropped to signal the beginning or end of something." We can get caught up with the voices of the world, but as believers, we must wait to hear what the Spirit is saying before we accept any conclusions. After all, GOD alone is the final word to all matters

Saturday, I took a day off from technology to do spring work in the yard. There are always plenty of projects to do both in the house and outside of the house this time of year. It is a time of regeneration that reminds each of us we are part of a cycle of life. My heart is always to keep centered in what is important.

So many times, our priorities cause us to major in unnecessary activities and our agendas cause us to focus on dead-end activities. We live in a world that chokes out what is important with the insignificant and promises glowing results with that which is void of any life or substance.

Working out in the yard reminds me that since my body came from the earth, I need to come back to it to remember I am but dust. It helps me to become grounded as I recognized how small of a footprint I will ultimately leave. Once I am gone, my footprint will quickly be lost when the dust is stirred up by the winds of changing times and cycles. When

I looked around, I remembered God made all of the beauty I was beholding and that it is His blessing on a matter that ensures life and blessing.

As I am reminded of God, I can't help but look up to the heavens above and remember that none of it can contain His presence and His power. During these days it is so important for believers to become and remain grounded in God's Word as they remember they are but dust, but that God knows their frame, holds their days in His hand, and that the work He desires to do in their soul is eternal and the work He is doing through them, because of the great work of redemption, will become part of the great cloud of witnesses that will testify of God faithfulness, greatness, and power.

A term I have heard lately seems an oxymoron to me, and that is the term "white privilege." As Americans we have certain inalienable rights that come from God and certain privileges (what is permitted within certain guidelines) that are allotted to us from the government such as "driving a car." We can abuse rights and give them up, while governments can take away our privileges for some discrepancy because they have allotted them to us through licenses and etc.

As I thought about the above term, I realized it is not only contradictory but insane because I was born into my race without any choice or discussion on my part, and being white does not mean I am automatically part of the group that is truly considered privileged. As a result, I will not be shamed for being something that is beyond my control or bullied into feeling guilty because I possess things that others might not possess.

The truth is if I am guilty for being privileged, it is not because I am white, but because as an American I have taken advantages of the opportunities that have come my way, and all we need to do is look around and see that regardless of how small or great these opportunities might be for some, other races have likewise benefitted from them.

The idea that things should simply be handed to you because you are a certain color or that you deserve something because of past offenses done to your race is irrational at best and plain wrong in every possible way. The just Judge of the universe clearly stipulated in *Ezekiel 18:4-22* that we will be held accountable for our personal sins and not the sins of our father or prior generations.

It is obvious that we can't change or reverse what has already taken place, but as far as the present, we can't make it right for others by playing along with their deluded insanity in order to keep a quasi-peace. If I had one of these unsettled souls tell me to bow and apologize for something I had no control over, I would ask the one demanding to bow with me before a holy God to openly intercede on behalf of the wicked people of this nation who have gone astray from truth, morality, and righteousness, while asking the Lord to forgive the ignorant, the rebellious, the bullies, the angry, and the violent, for they know not what they do.

If matters are settled in heaven, why debate them on earth? It is simple answer, man's soul is like a restless wave on the ocean of life. He is in search of what was lost, trying to find what can never be in this present life, and desires to know his scheme in a world that makes no sense in light of a barren soul that never can find satisfaction and purpose.

His soul can never rest because he is in search of paradise that was long ago lost because of our first parents' disobedient actions. It is amazing how man seeks some utopia, but like our first parents it is without any regard to God and outside of His authority.

Man doesn't mind God being around to serve his purposes, but he wants to be ruler of his kingdom and world. He does not want to answer to anyone or bother with something that seems insignificant, immaterial, or fails to serve his narrative. Like our first parents, man so often misses the point of what made Eden special and a garden: God was in the midst of it.

Without God, man will always be a restless wave, ever debating his purpose for being, ever seeking real meaning and satisfaction, and always wanting to come out on top of the narrative. Sadly, man fails to realize he needs to quit running away from what ails him while seeking that which is lifeless and vain, turn and honestly face his Creator in repentance, brokenness and submission. When he does, he will be delighted to discover that Jesus is the sole solution and antidote to what ails him. In fact, Jesus is the real answer that will end every debate concerning life, truth, and liberty, allowing one to discover his or her calling and purpose in this present age.

$\rightarrow\!\!\!\sim\!\!\!\sim\!\!\!\rightarrow$

I am sure like me you have become very disturbed by the recent images seen on the news. It is clear that battle lines between light and darkness are being drawn and the war between these two kingdoms is escalating. This war has been going on for mankind since the Garden of Eden and therefore should not be surprising to a believer. Granted, it may be disconcerting but not surprising.

What is surprising are those who wonder how we possibly could arrive at this place and time, while they are still waiting for it to go back to "normal" so they can go back to what? I hope I am wrong in a way because life will never go back to "normal" and in a sense it must not go back to "normal."

"Normal" is different for different people, and will produce grey areas of compromise but when it comes to society the godless practices taking place that are being promoted as being "normal" are anything but normal. The "normalcy" of a matter for societies was established by the Creator of mankind. Normal to our Creator takes on the heights of the heavenly and not the base, sick ways of the world.

The wicked voices of this world would have us believe that "normal" is abominable and demonic, and not what is excellent. These "normals" are extreme and destructive, and not honorable. The "normals" of today promote hatred, are lawless, end in destruction, and are not moral. The practices today are about fun, pleasure, and sensationalism, and not that which is of Spirit and truth. The "normal" of today has allowed many to avoid facing the dangerous precipice American society is teetering on because of godless attitudes, immoral practices, and insane, oppressive realities that are being pushed on everyone.

As believers, we know that "normal" concerning God are the extraordinary, righteous ways of heaven that are far above the base, demonic, pagan, and immoral practices of a world that has already been judged, and subject to condemnation, and will taste the wrath to come.

The question is, are we confused because we operate in the grey areas of compromise, are we taking on the attitude of the world, or are we constantly choosing the excellent ways of heaven to ensure our "normal" is extraordinary and operates above this world?

Jesus warned us to beware of how we hear a matter. It is easy to pervert, adjust, and ignore the truths of God. We have a tendency to hear only what we want to hear and if it does penetrate our understanding, we still have a tendency to adjust it to what we want to believe.

Notice the word "want." "Want" is a type of preference that has been developed. For the world, it uses advertisement to convince you that you "want" something because you "need" it. To "need" something becomes a point of great justification to pursue it regardless of the cost, the logic or common sense behind it. Sadly, for Christians "want" has to do with personal conditioning. In other words, what person, denomination, or religious influence has conditioned you? Once you understand the source of your conditioning, you can trace the doctrine you uphold back to the idea that this is what you need to believe to be right or get it right.

In this case a religious "need" can easily become a point of indoctrination. Granted, some of these beliefs are not wrong, but if you can't discern that it is not a revelation of the Spirit, your belief could end up being an assumption and not truth. As I traced some of my conditioning, I realized that my responses came out of assumptions of what I understood was true, and in some cases, they became presumptions that such beliefs had to be so because they sounded true.

Many people claim they WANT the truth, but how many understand that to stand, endure, and possess the promises of God that they NEED the truth to do so. Through the years the Lord has shaken my assumptions so I could identify them and allowed my presumptions to fall of the pinnacle of arrogance to a place of humility.

I have learned that no matter how scriptural or logical a belief may sound to me, if the Holy Spirit has not revealed it as a truth to my heart, used it to transform the carnal perception of my mind, and bring life to my faith through confirmation by walking it out, then it is simply an assumption that I take for granted is true. In the end, if such assumptions

201

remain standing, they are bound to teeter or collapse when challenged, and if they don't, they will take on an attitude that makes them into a presumption that keeps me flying high on the fragile trapeze of wishful thinking.

JUDGMENT

*It is impossible to keep our moral practices
sound and our inward attitudes right
while our idea of God is erroneous
or inadequate.
(A.W. Tozer)*

Are we about to be astonished? There is a shaking taking place, and from what I understand it is not only happening in this country but in many other countries. After the shaking, what follows?

I have always been fascinated by the way God interjects and intervenes in the world. You can actually see a pattern. For example, when He goes to judge a nation, He first shakes it to awaken the people. This shaking is a type of chastisement, and it often involves a subtle tyranny that leads to humility and unbearable oppression. This oppression becomes so great it causes His people to cry out to Him. It is then that God sends in a judge or leader to push back and expose the wickedness of the oppressor. You can see this pattern in the book of Judges.

This book clearly shows man's **rebellion** that causes **repercussions**, which are designed to result in **repentance**, at which time God is able to **redeem** and **restore**. However, the problem with many nations is not necessarily the majority of the people, but the leadership.

God first awakens the people because they have been put to sleep by complicit leaders at which time they must be prepared to stand against wicked leadership and stand for that which is righteous. God will never send in another nation to deliver His people from the oppressor because He alone will be recognized and acknowledged as the only true Deliverer.

Sadly, many people are looking to government to deliver them, when in reality they prove to be the real oppressors because of corruption. As believers we must remember that those who know the Son of God will be set free indeed, but to know Him we must first seek Him as the only real solution to physical, emotional, and spiritual bondages.

As the wickedness of the times is being exposed, my greatest surprise comes from those who consider themselves religious. I realize being religious can be expressed in outward piousness, self-righteous judgmentalism, and religious snobbery and elitism that is ever ready to scrutinize those on the outside of the "group" to be inferior or suspicious. For religious people they perceive they have some corner on truth or doctrine that makes them part of the "enlighten ones," a concept associated with the New Age and the occult. What is the real test of a true believer of Jesus Christ and His Word? We are told we know them by their fruits, but such fruits do not solely consist of action, but must also be motivated by a right spirit with the intent to uphold truth in love and humility in order to bring the proper glory to God.

When people claim to be Christian but are indifferent to moral conduct it becomes obvious that they are void of a love for truth because love never rejoices in iniquity (moral deviance) but in the truth. If people show a concern for the immigrants who are unlawfully trying to flood our country, but show no regard for the sex-trafficking that is happening all around us and unborn babies that are being aborted in the womb, killed and mangled so the despots of the world can sell their parts, they are double-minded and hypocritical.

If people say they care about the rights of all people but are willing to turn the other way while the abominable and morally deprave scorn all sanctity established by God to justify trampling on the rights of the righteous, they simply prove they are godless and partakers of others sin. I could go on and on, but I think you get the idea.

I realize that some claim Christianity out of ignorance, others out of personal gain, and some because it is the thing to do for appearance's sake, but we are living in a time of great judgment and a clear line between darkness and light, good and evil, and right and wrong is being drawn.

It is clear people are being awakened and forced to look into the face of great evil that is being exposed by the great light of God's truth. It is ugly, sickening, and overwhelming but it is time to call it what it is and make a choice as to who and what we are going to serve. And, do not be mistaken, the price could be the life you know here or it will be your soul to try to maintain a worldly, fleshly existence while the wrath of God abides on those who walk in unbelief and disobedience. True believers will make the necessary choices to put them on the right side of eternity, regardless of personal cost.

One of the questions I ask myself is will it stand? Will what I believe to be true stand in the time of great shaking? Will what I understand about God and His kingdom withstand the massive waves of trials that are bombarding the shorelines of this world and our lives? Will who I am in Christ remain standing when all else collapses?

I am sure some of you know that Challis, Idaho had a 6.5 earthquake that we felt up in Northern Idaho and it was noted as far away as Billings, Montana. Even though I felt the land roll beneath my feet, it reminded me that if I am not grounded on the right spiritual foundation, I will be caught off guard and pushed off balance, and then I will fall when the real shaking begins.

The Bible is clear that everything there is will be shaken. We all know the warning in *Matthew 7:24-27* about building on a faulty foundation of shifting sand and not on the eternal Rock of heaven; but, how many of us are examining our foundation and checking out the spiritual structure of our lives to see if it is lining up to the Cornerstone, to ensure that we are able to stand when the rolling begins, withstand when the shaking begins, and continue to stand because we are founded and lined up to the eternal, immovable Rock of Jesus Christ?

When it comes to God's judgment there is the PRINCIPLE of it, the HOPE of it, and the REALITY of it. God's judgments are true, wise, just, and perfect. Since you can't do anything against the truth but for it, all of His judgments will stand. Since He is all wisdom, He will have all the facts in place to ensure just judgment that will prove to be perfect in all of its ways.

The PRINCIPLE of judgment is you reap what you sow. This shows that you will rightfully reap the fruits, rewards, or consequences of the type of investments you put into this life, especially in relationship to God and others.

The HOPE of judgment is that if you belong to God, He will chastise you when you stray from the right way. Someone pointed out that the hope and beauty of chastisement is that when the Lord leans down to correct us, that is when we are closest to His heart, allowing us to sense His love, know His real desire towards us, and experience His caring and just ways.

Christians act as if they are immune from the tests that exposes character, the adversity that forms it, the suffering that refines it, and the chastisement that lines it up to holiness. However, God uses each tool in order to bring us to full age when it comes to making right judgment calls and to avoid experiencing the heavy hand of God upon our soul.

I have been talking about judgment. This is not a popular subject for many. We want to hide behind God's love that will overlook sin, not judge it. We want to claim God's grace when in sin and ignore that grace reigns through righteousness and is not a ticket to sin and get away with it. Some people want to claim mercy without truly repenting, but without true repentance it is nothing more than worldly sorrow that will lead to destruction.

Judgment does separate. For those who pay consequences, if they do not truly repent, their hearts will become hard towards God's truth, intervention, and leading, setting them up to be separated unto wrath.

Chastisement is to clearly line God's children up to partake of His holiness because without holiness man will not see the Lord. This brings us to the fact that the goal of judgment is to separate God's sheep from the corruption of this world unto His holiness.

Everything will either be exposed, refined, or burned up by the fire of God. Within this fire is God's holiness that will consume the profane, His jealousy that will burn up all idolatrous and unfaithful ways, and His wrath that will devour that which is a stench and an abomination to Him.

God's wrath has been described as a reservoir and it is people that will fill up their personal reservoirs with evil intents and wicked practices. The only thing that keeps this reservoir from breaking forth is God's longsuffering. It is not His will that any perish but all come to repentance. However, when the reservoir begins to fill up and spills over, God's longsuffering will be pulled back. Once the reservoir of God's wrath is let loose, it will quickly overtake and devour as a person is swept into the abyss.

As Christians we have such a glorious past because it points to the redemption of Jesus Christ, we have a sure presence because of the work of sanctification taking place in us by the Holy Spirit, and we have a glorious future because we have indeed been spared from His wrath so we can partake of the hope, glory and promises of the next age to come.

When I consider the matter of God's judgment, I must ask myself at the appropriate times, why are you living like some person who is lost to God's promise of life? Why are you dancing with the profane when you can know the cleansing work of sanctification, and why do you fail to live soberly, in the fear of God, knowing that the Lord is a consuming fire?

I grew up with sayings such as, "If your friends decided to walk off the cliff, are you going to follow them just so you can fit in?" It is too bad the crowd that yelled for Jesus' crucifixion didn't possess that particular nugget. Here is another one, "Two wrongs never make a right."

I have to admit I did not appreciate that particular saying when I first heard it like I do now. Two wrongs will never equal something being right. It is a mathematical impossibility to try to make it so, and yet man is forever trying to disavow this simple equation. How does a person take a wrong, add another wrong to it and declare it is suddenly right?

There are a couple of ways that we human beings continually end up with a wrong answer to this equation. First of all, we convince ourselves that if someone has done wrong by us, we have the right to reciprocate in like manner, but another wrong simply adds more fuel to the fire until it becomes a searing fire of indictment and judgment on the reciprocating party.

In such cases, we will end up standing without any recourse when the day of reckoning comes. We will find ourselves standing in the path of the fire that separates, purges, and consumes because we were on the wrong side.

Another way we justify a wrong is through excuses. We actually excuse ourselves from doing right because at that point we become an exception in our mind rather than being subject to the rule like the "peon" next to us. Any time we have to make an excuse for our attitude and conduct, we can pretty well conclude that we are in a wrong spirit and starting from the position of being wrong.

We do not have to justify or explain right attitudes and actions, for they will stand on their own. The problem with becoming the "exception" or "elite" in a situation is that we will come under a double standard that will expose our deep hypocrisy.

The final problem is that people rarely pay consequences up front for wrong attitudes and conduct. Many times, they are given a false sense that everyone else is doing it; therefore, it is alright for them to do it regardless of whether it is honorable or not. However, there is a day of reckoning coming and it will not matter whether it is your first offense or your 1000th offense, you will be on the wrong side and end up reaping what you have so foolishly sown.

Every time we choose the wrong of a situation, we will find ourselves on the broad path that leads to detours of defeat, canyons of despair, and the abyss of destruction. I love what Joshua stated when he told the children of Israel to choose whether they were going to serve the idols of their fathers or Jehovah, but for him he was going to choose to stand on the right side of eternity by choosing to serve and worship the one true Jehovah God.

Have you heard there is a possible meteor that will hit us just before election time? How much information is true and how much of it is propaganda that has been spun with wicked agendas can prove to be hard to wade through in these times. I have a couple of scenarios I want to challenge you with.

Imagine if you were on a plane and it was being hit by lightning and a terrible storm was shaking the plane to such an extent that your life flashed before your eyes because it looked like it was going down. Would you emotionally react with utter terror or would you choose the way of faith by putting all in the hands of God?

Here is another scenario. A big wave is coming at you, will you look for something to hold on to or run as fast as you can? Keep in mind there is nothing you can do about either event and you can't get off the plane or outrun the wave; therefore, what are you going to do?

The answer will be determined by whether you are going to allow yourself to be driven or paralyzed by fear or whether you reason with yourself mentally as to what the Word of God promises you. Today the world is like that big plane and each of us are facing not just one wave of judgment and destruction, but many. Are we going to give in to fear because of the giants standing before us spewing out arrogant threats, or become like David in 1 Samuel 17, who knows there is One greater than all the giants and He has already won the battle?

Are we going to look at the successions of waves coming at, not only us, but the whole world and cower in some corner awaiting our terrible fate, or run in the opposite direction without any real instruction, or stand in denial and delusion that somehow we are immune from being hit by them? Or, will you be like David in *1 Samuel 30*, when his city was burned, his family taken, and his men threatening to take his very life because of the great anguish of losing their families, he encouraged himself in the Lord and then sought Him as to what He was to do?

It does not say much about a person's Christianity when their reaction causes them to lose all semblance of reason, instead of choosing the way of faith towards the Lord. Regardless of how much the present world is shaking around us, we can trust the Lord with the details and land on the runway of faith where peace of mind awaits us so we can receive proper instruction to make sure we are hidden in the place of His will.

And, what about the waves? If you know Jesus, then believe He is the great eternal Rock and cling to His promises, knowing that regardless of how great the waves are, they can't move the Rock, destroy its presence, or its strength to withstand the forces of hell itself.

It is sad to watch the present rebellious generation rage against God, His truth, His ways, and His servants. Regardless of how vexing it is to our spirits to witness it, it must be so to bring forth both judgment and contrast. Those who call themselves Christians must come out and be separated from this dark, evil age, so that like Noah the judgment that abides on the world can come.

The need for this separation is vital. In America, the visible church's witness seems to have become blended with the world, thereby, leaving no real distinction as to the life of the church, which is Jesus, and the lifestyle of the world which is empty. If distinction is missing, there will be no contrast. Without contrast there will be no way in which man can discern, recognize, or experience the necessary shaking to awake him to the destructive path he is on.

This brings us back to a very important point. Why does man rage against God? Years ago, a witch who admitted she had married Satan came to us for relief. It is important to discern such matters because those who want relief do not want to get real. They just want the torment gone, while still holding on to the power of darkness.

The woman was possessed and it was clear she had to change masters if she was going to be completely delivered, healed, and set free. The conclusion of our ministry to her came when she refused the lordship of the only one who could deliver her, Jesus Christ. It was at that point I made it clear there was nothing more that we could do for her. However, I did ask the woman at one point why she hated God. Her answer was quite revealing.

She told me she was happily living her life as she saw fit when she was challenged with receiving Christ or face the consequences of hell.

The fact that she had to somehow live a life she was not attracted to avoid dire consequences made her angry at God.

Man wants to be supreme ruler in his home, society and political and religious arenas without paying the consequences for such idolatrous ambitions, immoral and corrupt practices. Such individuals do not want to be held accountable for their wrong, wicked decisions, judged for destructive philosophies, heretical beliefs and presentations, and face that in the end there is a day of reckoning before the Great Judge, King and Lord of the Universe where all that is within man and done by him will be judged.

As believers we must avoid falling into the ruse of our day and call out the real problem of this time. It will always come back to man's relationship with God, his attitude towards truth and whether he has faced the real issue that plagues each living soul: his or her heart attitude towards God and His Word.

How can we properly examine ourselves? You might notice I begin many of my posts by asking questions. So many times, we are busy running the race of life. We are thinking ahead, racing around some unseen race track to accomplish things, and trying to avoid staying in the "pit stop" of "maintenance" and "repairs" brought on by challenges before frantically entering the race once again.

At that point everything becomes a blur and we don't always recognize that we are failing to connect to what is happening in our lives. When a question is put to us, we must stop to properly connect to what is being asked, and what has been going on to honestly answer the question. It is for this reason I ask myself questions because, for the most part, I can assume all is well and presume that unless something trips me up and turns my world upside down, that all is running smoothly.

I have learned that as long as everything is in order, one does not have to ask questions because there is clarity, but we do not live in a world of order. It is interesting to note Satan asked the first question in the Garden to disrupt the perfect order, and God asked the second question because man was no longer in order. It is for this reason I personally own the questions in the Bible to scripturally answer them while examining myself. Consider God's first poignant question to Adam and Eve and see if you can answer it in light of your present relationship with the Lord, *"Where art thou?" (Genesis 3:9).*

⌇⌇⌇

We are sadly watching some of our cities burn. At one time our nation was great and it stood for greatness, but godless, greedy despots want to destroy what is pure and right in this nation in order to enslave the masses to do their bidding.

Let's face it, America is where she is today for various reasons: 1) The wicked, corrupt powers have been allowed to kick God out of every system, leaving society without any moral compass and resolve; 2) the sanctity of life (the innocent, unborn babies), ordained family structure, and morals have been offered up on the altars of selfishness, vain imaginations, pornography, and unspeakable abominations in the name of such idols as greed, perverted rights, and godless pleasures; 3) much of the visible church has become more worldly and accommodating to adjust to the world in order to attract it, and as a result is more willing to parlay with the devil and compromise with the present corruption and wickedness of this world to keep up the show to maintain personal kingdoms; 4) we have emphasized convenience and fun more than the family unit, moral responsibility, and accountability, and 5) untold numbers have relinquished parental rights and responsibilities to Hollywood to serve as our children's babysitters, entertainment, and psychologists; thereby, conditioning them to embrace godless ideologies that will seduce them into a false reality.

Sadly, this change of worldview that is subtly taking place is in preparation for their indoctrination by communistic educators who hate the freedom of religion that made this country preferable and great. The question is where will it end? The answer is judgment in the form of grave chastisement and wrath.

As a nation we need to see the seriousness of the hour to confront the challenges, as a people we need to repent, and as believers we can praise God for His longsuffering because we are not receiving what we deserve because of our national sins, giving us time to correctly respond in humility and repentance. But at such times, we must also remember, there will be a clear separation of the wheat from the tares, while fence riders will have to jump off to one side or the other, and the remnant will come out and be separate from all false lies and entities.

The true church is called to be a powerful army of soldiers, not spectators. As a result, believers in many cases will have no other choice but to stand in their armor to confront the real enemies, while standing up with the sword of truth lifted high to knock down all darts of lies and heresy, and continue to stand, sometimes on humble knees of intercession, or at other times in light of great defeat, knowing the war has already been won, and continue to stand in grave weariness of their soul, realizing that their spirit is secured in the Rock of Ages.

SERVICE & WORSHIP

Who we serve is a choice of the will.
Who we follow is a choice of the heart.
Who we honor is a choice of the mind.
Rayola Kelley

The big question for the upcoming year is who are we going to serve? There are those who believe they can walk a thin line between two masters and never really have to totally consecrate themselves to the one or sell their soul to the other. Needless to say, this is a lie, but it is one that can spiritually dull a person down to believe that they can have the best of both worlds and not come out any worse for it.

Jesus was clear you can't serve two masters at the same time. The reason is simple, the middle of the road attitude is nothing more than conditioning the person to ultimately sell their soul while rejecting the idea of consecrating their life to the one master who rightfully deserves total devotion, Jesus Christ. This conflict will take place in the soul, often ending in resentment or raging against a master that will not settle for half-hearted devotion.

The thin line clearly divides the masters. On one side is liberty, truth, and moral uprightness and on the other side, tyranny, lies, debauchery, and total bondage. Those who love truth understand that true liberty affords them the moral uprightness and the means to maintain a quality of life that gives them the opportunity to reach their potential. These individuals will not betray the calling that distinguishes real liberty in their life.

On the other side are those who hate such liberty and will rage against it because they know nothing of it. These individuals are in total bondage to a dark, sick world that causes them to rage against the light of truth, hate that which advocates liberty, and try to destroy that which is righteous.

As the days become darker, those who have walked this fine thin line will find themselves becoming more confused and uncertain about their lives, and the reason is simple, we live in the days of testing and judgment. The darkness will test our devotion and the judgment will shake all religious concepts we hold, including about ourselves, until we choose who we are going to serve.

There will be no half-hearted devotion, no thin line of compromise to balance on, and no shadows of gray to operate within that gives an appearance of righteousness, but lacks the power to stand in darkness, withstand the rage of it, and continue to stand in the midst of its hatred.

I often meditate on child-like wonderment due to that fact we must come to the Lord with a child-like simplicity. Recently, I read about the great evangelist Gypsy Smith. He was called to preach at age seventeen, was trained in the school of the Holy Spirit, and ran the race for his Lord until his death at 87.

This man maintained a freshness and vigor throughout his ministry and some wondered what his secret was. His statements give insight into his devotion to the Lord. One statement he made was, "I was born in a field; don't put me in a flowerpot."

As believers we are called to the harvest field of the world. However, the tendency for organized religion is to try to put us in some flowerpot that is placed in a theological box that will fit in with its program, or some pew for appearance's sake, or put on a shelf labeled "ministry wannabes" to be forgotten, causing zeal to dry up and devotion to wither away for lack of water.

Galatians 5:1 instructs us to maintain our liberty. We must remember unsaved man is oppressed in some way by some fickle, tyrannical, and even religious master, and have no real sense of liberty, thereby, only capable of bringing those around them in bondage.

Yesterday, I mentioned a man named Gypsy Smith and liberty in relationship of being prepared to work in the harvest. We must never settle with being planted somewhere, but we must be about the business of planting the seeds of the Gospel.

We are called to the world and the Spirit of God must have the freedom to move us where He so wills as He gives us the means to plant the seeds of the Gospel and water them in discipleship, knowing the Lord will bring forth the harvest.

In another occasion when Smith was advised to learn how to sing from his diaphragm, he replied that he didn't want to sing from his diaphragm but from his heart. We have made much of Christianity about professionalism, presenting the perfect show in the perfect pose to attract most of the people of the world, but the problem with putting forth the perfect image is that the perfect man, Jesus Christ is not being lifted up in order to draw seeking, lost souls, not numbers, to His cross where they will find redemption that will save their souls.

Gypsy Smith knew if a matter did not come from the heart, it would never reach God. No doubt he understood that if it was not from the heart, it would be the greatest betrayal to his calling and a most profane sacrifice to God, leaving behind the stench of hypocrisy. Finally, he was asked in his old age how he maintained such zeal. His answer was simple, "I have never lost the wonder."

Vance Havner said it best, "A preacher should have the mind of a scholar, the heart of a child, and the hide of a rhinoceros." Smith had the heart of a child and he saw the majesty of God everywhere he looked. Whether it was in the creation around him, in the small blessings about him, or in the vastness of heaven, it caused wonder to rise up in his heart, followed by pure unadulterated praise and worship.

Jesus stated unless we come to Him as a child with a heart of wonder, simple trust and a sincere curiosity of discovering Him, we will fail to discover Him in His majesty and glory.

It is not unusual to become a potted plant that sits in church pews, a dark cloud who simply sit in the same place at home, or become a thorn on some great bush of God's work that instead of bringing pleasure to someone, instead brings discomfort. Perhaps you are a flower that is dried up and has been placed between pages of lifeless words, or fading because of partaking of lifeless doctrines, waterless cisterns, and stagnant waters because the rivers of Living Water has been missing.

If you have become a religious "thorn bush" that pricks people instead of blessing them, a dried-up flower in the middle of much religion that has allowed the ground around you to become hard, or a withering flower in the midst of skepticism, know that somewhere along the way you have lost the wonderment of a child.

Perhaps you have looked around instead of up, inward instead of outward, and backward instead of forward. If you have, turn back to God in repentance, fall broken before Him in sincerity, and ask Him to renew your love for him by making your heart once again child-like in faith and wonderment.

What will Jesus say to you when you stand before Him? I struggled with this matter while trying to establish my life in Christ. In my initial Christian walk I wanted to do good things for Him, but failed because it was in my own strength and according to my understanding.

The problem with "good deeds" is that they may not be a point of service but of meritorious work where one can expect or require something in return, whether it is feeling good about self, receiving some type of recognition, or being exalted. At such times "good deeds" cease to be a blessing of God and quickly become a terrible oppressive burden to those whose goal was to be a blessing.

Rayola Kelley

The crux of the problem is motivation. We are either motivated by God's love or pride. God's love is eternal but man's pride can only demand interest on a matter because it has no real sense about accepting a mere principal payment for such deeds. It will always feel that it holds the deed to personal rights and it will never relinquish such rights because pride is an insatiable master who can never be pleased or satisfied. That is when I began to understand what it really means that all I do is unto the Lord.

It was in my failures that I learned what true service to the Lord entailed. For it to be acceptable it could not be about me and it had to be about honoring Him. It was then that my goal changed. I simply wanted to hear, "Well done good and faithful servant." However, one day a minister told me, "He wants to call you friend."

Good attempts will lead a seeking heart to acceptable service to the Lord, but true service will open the door to communion where our Lord can entrust the important matters of His heart to us, which in the end will produce true worship for and to Him in all we do on His behalf.

So many times, we as Christians, test our spiritual worth according to the world and not according to the life of Christ being worked in us. We sometimes forget it is not the work we do for God that counts; rather, it is the work that we allow Him to do in and through our lives that will ultimately count in eternity.

We often fail to look for small changes in our attitude, test the quality of fruit we are leaving behind, and consider the real character behind our motives and agendas. We find ourselves being worn out by the escalation of battles we are being drawn into, ducking the friendly fire of those who arrogantly judge us from pinnacles of self-righteousness, and trying to maintain a proper balance between our earthly responsibilities and our spiritual calling.

It is natural at times to feel like a juggler by profession, but as a Christian I have learned to step off the merry-go-round of this world and seek the Lord's perspective while quietly waiting for His leading, whether it is opening some door of opportunity, allowing circumstances to direct my steps, or through His Word. As believers we must not be caught up with doing, as much as becoming what the Lord has called us to be. We must become increasingly less concerned about what we are doing or trying to accomplish in this world for Him, and become more concerned about being prepared to carry out the real purpose of our calling for the sake of His kingdom.

We can make Christianity more about religion and activities than relationship and worship. We can become surface in all we do because we are burnt out, instead of becoming burnt offerings where the fragrance of Christ's life is ascending to the very throne of God, bringing pleasure to Him.

The truth is we can major in the minor activities of religion while minoring in the major concerns of God's heart. And, what are the major concerns of God's heart? There are a couple: 1) the quality of our relationship with Him and 2) the souls of mankind. Our relationship with God means nothing unless we love Him with everything in us and our service to God will mean nothing unless we prefer others over ourselves, which only comes out of a love for God.

What are you focusing on? The eye is an incredible creation. It is able to take converging rays and bring them together in order to produce clarity as to what or who a person is seeing.

It is natural for us to take our eyesight and our hearing for granted but both are fine-tuned instruments when it comes to interacting with our environment, and it is only when we begin to lose clarity in our seeing and hearing, do we begin to realize how wonderfully God made man, how unique each member of our body is for the complete function of the whole body.

The present challenge is that much of what is going on can't be seen by the naked eye or picked up by the physical ear. We are greatly affected by an unseen world and the Lord has provided the means in which to see and hear what is going on. To see what is taking place in the unseen world He gave us faith and to hear what is going on He gives His Spirit.

Faith walks by what it Scripturally believes and knows to be true about God, His work and His plan, while trusting that He is the one who will walk each of us through all darkness. To hear the Spirit, our spiritual hearing must be fined-tuned to His voice. We must ask and seek to hear, or I should say discern, what the Spirit is saying as we learn to wait for Him to open the door that has been prepared for us to walk through in order to walk in the Spirit.

The key is that genuine faith towards God is what brings us through the darkness and the Spirit will lead us through confusing shadows, unknown terrain, and through enemy lines to the light of Jesus who will become the point of conversion. This conversion is where the Spirit and truth come together as a greater unveiling of Jesus, thereby, bringing clarity to our spirits.

Faith is a great subject and everyone has their personal experience with it, but faith's main purpose is that it will bring you to places where you experience the eternal, glorious aspects of God's character and working. We can get excited about the power of the Spirit, but the work of the Spirit is to gently woo a person to the bridegroom, cause the new zealot to rise up and follow Him in the ways of righteousness so that they can be led into an intimate, growing relationship with the Father. Communion with the Father points to true worship that inspires acceptable service. True service comes when one begins to discover what it truly means to walk in the Spirit.

What does it mean to offer a real sacrifice to the Lord? Two words that have made me stop and ponder real sacrifice are "reasonable service." These two words are found in *Romans 12:1-2*. To discover reasonable service, I must first offer my whole body to serve the Lord. This includes spirit, soul, and strength.

My first mission must be to get self out of the way so my mind can be transformed by the Holy Spirit. This is what allows me to discover what is the acceptable, good, and perfect will of God, permitting me to offer all for His good pleasure and glory. As long as self sits on the throne, my will is going to supersede the will of God. Granted, I may be seeking His will but as long as mine is engaged it will win out, whether through carnal logic, worldly calculation, or fleshly feelings.

Then I must sincerely seek God in order to discover His will in a matter. Regardless of the cost, all service must be in line with His plan, allowing it to become a form of worship that displays gratitude to be part of His kingdom workings that will ultimately bring Him glory. Everything I do as unto the Lord is my REASONABLE SERVICE, the least I can do. It must line up to His Word, be in agreement with His Spirit, uphold godly principles, and produce fruits that bring real glory to Him.

For something to become a sacrifice that reveals that the true fire of heavenly approval has been put to it, the pure fragrance of Jesus' life, that is void of all self-life and effort, must reach the throne of heaven, bringing sweet pleasure to God. The pure fragrance of Christ's life that is produced in true sacrifice happens when regardless of feelings, self is denied in order to do what is right, and when personal strength is no more, the spirit proves willing to endure all the throes of hell to see it through.

What is left is what we are actually needful of to survive, and as the widow proved with her mites, that must be sacrificed as well and that is when the best, Jesus' life, is offered up in all purity and sincerity to ensure God's will is carried out to the last detail. It is at such a time that the life of Jesus becomes the pure fragrance that rises out of the burnt offering smothering on the altar of consecration, and ascends to heaven, bringing with it the sweet savor that pleases God.

We have a choice today that I refer to as the two "W's." Are we going to look at circumstances and WORRY or are we going to look up and WORSHIP the God of all creation?

Our natural tendency is to worry about what is out of our control, but as believers, we are not called to worry but worship. We have been created to worship and the Father seeks those who will worship Him in spirit and truth, but our heart condition determines whether we worship from a distance out of duty, try to find a crowd that will inspire some type of fleshly, emotional worship, or seek out the place where we can be close to real worship in preparation of coming into that time of intimate, sweet communion with God.

Ultimately, intimate worship is personal and entails a journey that begins with presenting an acceptable sacrifice, that of praise or of true brokenness. As brokenness causes us to look up, praise will lift our weary minds above the present world and we will begin to soar in the spirit above the circumstances as thankfulness for our God's greatness and great work of redemption fills our souls and we begin to glorify our Lord with adoration.

Worshipping our God is the antidote to fear, worry, and weariness. It will bring us into a different state of mind and once again resurrect hope out of the swamps of despair, giving it the wings of expectation to rise above the decay of this world to once again rest in the knowledge of who our God is.

The other day I talked about fellowship. True fellowship can only be done in a place where there is agreement in spirit. For Christians, there is no other place of agreement to be found outside of the Holy Spirit. To come into agreement with another spirit such as the spirit of the world will cause the Holy Spirit to withdraw or lift from the environment.

The main purposes of the Holy Spirit are to lead us into all truth about Jesus, to fit us into the Body of Christ in love, unity, and function, and to establish an environment of communion with God that leads to true worship. There is also confusion about communion. What is true communion?

In the church we have the ordinance of "Communion," where we take of the symbols of the bread (Jesus' broken body) and the wine (Jesus' shed blood) in identification as one body in remembrance of what He did for each of us when He took the judgment of our sin upon Himself (*1 Corinthians 11:23-33*). At such a sobering time of personal examination to see if we are even prepared to take of this solemn ordinance, we are reminded that we have a history with the Lord that started with His cross where justification was established on our behalf.

Justification allows us to walk by faith with one another towards His promises, while looking forward to His coming. However, communion is more than simple fellowship. In the tabernacle of the Old Testament, there were two places of communion: The Table of Shewbread and the Mercy Seat on the Ark of the Covenant.

At the Table of Shewbread communion was about partaking of the holy bread as a means to enter in to true service, and at the Mercy Seat, it was a place of atonement that prepared the way for the priest to enter into true communion with God in the form of "worship."

We are told we are to partake of the divine nature of Christ to take on His likeness and that the Father seeks true worshippers to ensure sweet fellowship. Fellowship is about identifying with someone, while communion points to entering in with someone. There can be no real communion, until there is identification. This is the life of the saint, seeking to always identify with the Lord by taking on His attitude, conduct, and ways towards all matters pertaining to life and godliness with one goal, and that is to bring honor and glory to Him in pure worship.

Last night we had an incredible storm move through, with crackling thunder and a lightning show. No doubt the dry ground was gladly receiving and soaking up the torrent of rain that fell. This morning I was greeted by mist rising like vapors of stream from the ground.

It reminded me that our lives are nothing more than a vapor rising up out of frail humanity in the midst of a spiritually barren wilderness. Even though the life we have here is temporary, there are different things that impact our soul for eternity. And, just what affects our soul? It comes down to the type of life I choose to live here.

The quality of life is determined by the type of air that I am breathing. The breath of this life may be a vapor but can be moved by breezes or even dissipate as the storms of this world move in and out. And, when the dark nights come where our life is being buffeted by the winds of our age, they may seem like eternity, but all that is attached to this present life only lasts a season.

However, what I do with this present life determines my course and destiny in light of eternity. The life we each live is determined by the breath we live by. For instance, does the breath we inhale and exhale simply belong to this world or is it maintained by the very breath of God's Spirit that identifies every believer to the next world?

221

Is the water that our souls desperately need come from stagnant waters of this world, broken religious cisterns, and poisonous waters of heretical presentations or does it come from the wells of salvation? Do the personal storms that pass through our soul test the character of our faith in order to strengthen the roots of our resolve or do they cast us about like a leaf that will end up on some burn pile? Does the dark night of our soul cause us to throw our hands up in the air in complete resignation of unbelief or do we throw our arms around who God is as we tightly cling to His promises until the darkness gives way to a greater revelation of Him?

I've learned that it is as my spirit is quickened to the great hope of Jesus in me, that my soul is set free to rise above the restraints of that which is temporary to catch glorious glimpses of that which is eternal. A soul set free in such a way will become like a vapor in which praise and worship floats upward, to be temporarily consumed in the vastness by the reality of God.

I have mentioned intercession. Some have a ministry of intercession, while others are called to it at different times. As part of a priesthood, this is our highest calling in many ways, and we have the golden altar (the Altar of Incense) in the tabernacle that stood before the veil, testifying of this very fact.

We are told in Psalm 141:2, "Let my prayer be set forth before thee as incense; and the lifting of my hands as the evening sacrifice." Ezekiel 22:30 says, "And I sought for a man among them, that should make up the hedge, and stand in the gap before me for the land, that I should not destroy it: but I found none." All great battles are first won in the prayer closet, but to have authority to stand in the gap and hit the target, one must make sure there is nothing defiling their life as far as having right standing before the Lord, defiling their high calling as far as unholy agreements, as well as their garments of holiness that sets them apart (unholy mixtures).

Jesus, our High Priest has already provided the necessary sacrifice so we can go boldly to the throne of grace, but we are told in James 4:8-10 to draw near to God with clean hands, a pure heart, a sound mind, in affliction and sorrow in a state of humility. It is in authority that we can effectively intercede, and we do so as soldiers standing erect as we trust the Lord to fight the battle while preparing a way for us to march to victory and our destination. We do this knowing that Abraham interceded on behalf of Lot and Sodom, David on behalf of Jerusalem during a plague, and Daniel on behalf of Jerusalem and the people returning to the Promised Land.

Right now, the battle that is raging is not between political parties or ideologies but between good and evil. As Christians we need to properly discern between both good and evil to ensure we are on the right side of the conflict and to identify that which is evil to be sure we are hitting the right target.

I am inside my office listening to the wind. Wind has always fascinated me. You can hear it, feel it, and see the results of it but you can't actually see it. The wind represents the unseen breath that moves the air around us. It is an invisible source, and this invisible source makes itself known by the environment it creates, often revealing its intention in the clouds. It can reveal its anger in the darkness of clouds, warn of storms on the horizon, and a new front coming in.

As I consider the clouds, I am reminded of the pillar of cloud in the wilderness that marked the presence of God to the children of Israel. We know, like the unseen wind and the pillar of cloud, that both represent the presence of God in the midst of His people, and the presence of God is the Holy Spirit.

As wind, the Holy Spirit points to the born-again experience, where the very breath of God revives our spirit and begins to gently blow upon the terrain of our soul to bring forth life. The pillar of cloud points to our need to be led by the Spirit through the present age of darkness, but it also reminds us that His presence sets up the environment where praise floats up on its currents to the throne of God, while thanksgiving becomes a fragrance that is lifted off of the altar of our heart to reach God in adoring worship.

As I consider the environment of our times, I have to wonder about my personal environment in my spirit and soul as well as my home. Does my personal altar contain the fire of His Spirit and does the personal sanctuary of my home have the environment of worship? Does the body I work among contain the love of God and the salt of truth that identifies all that is being done, while the incense of prayers remains pure and unhindered from hitting the mark of God's heart and will?

The truth is that in these days we cannot afford to have lifeless spirits, barren souls, altars where there is no fire of the Spirit, and ineffective churches that fail to hit the mark of eternity with a living witness, a powerful message, and worship that allows the winds of God to set the tone and pace within the sanctuaries that will produce the fruit of everlasting life.

One statement that often makes me cringe is when someone states that, "God needs us." God is all inclusive and needs no one. He has those around the throne who worship Him, the angels of heaven to do His bidding, creation to praise Him, the demons of hell to do the testing, the donkeys of Balaam to set the record straight, and if necessary, the rocks will rise up and honor Him if man fails too.

Inventors invent that which is most needful to others and when it functions properly will use it for their benefit, but if the invention falls short of what it was intended to be used for, it will prove useless to everyone. God created man to bring glory to Him not because He is needful of it, but because He is worthy of it.

I have often wondered why man wants to believe that his Creator needs him unless he sees it as a bargaining chip or from the perspective that if God needs him, He surely will accept whatever crumbs he throws at Him. I remember struggling with this very issue because the Christian walk can prove hard and challenging. I couldn't understand why God was allowing the hard way to buffet me sorely, especially since I was trying so hard to serve Him.

It was then that the Lord broke through my temporary morbid state of self-pity with this simple statement, "I do not need you—but I desire to use you." I also knew if He used me, it would strictly be according to His terms. Salvation of our souls is His miracle and the work of sanctification is a matter of His ongoing grace, but to be used by God for His glory, well that is a matter of His will and His choice, but for us it is an opportunity to share in the heavenly, to become a blessing to others, and serve as a living witness to both the seen and unseen worlds.

The next time you hear that lie or entertain it, remember God has both the unseen and the seen worlds at His beck and call, and in light of that simple reality we are rendered back to nothing but a very small dot that may be good at ending something like a sentence, but not capable of generating that which is beneficial to others or to bring glory to God. After all, the matters of His kingdom were, are and always will be a matter His work.

We had gale force winds come through yesterday. It blew down trees and power lines. Winds remind me of the work of God that is done by the Holy Spirit. There is the sweet breath of God that causes a person who is dead in sin to be raised up in newness of life. There are the north winds that produce cold air of preparation, paving the way for the south breeze that brings forth resurrection life. But there are other winds as well.

We have the tempest winds of testing, the powerful winds of judgment, and the hurricane winds of destruction. Right now, there are various winds blowing through Christendom and the world. Each wind is separating the Body in some way to bring about a desired effect.

It is clear that the Body continually needs the fresh wind of the Holy Spirit to continually blow upon, in, and through the church. Lips, giftings, and hands need to be anointed to effectively do God's bidding. I recognize that the Lord has provided me with the necessary gifts to carry out my calling, but I must make sure I allow Him to prepare me and put me in the right place.

Think about this. If every member was in the right place, being filled daily with the anointing oil of the Spirit, how bright the Body would shine in this world. If every member of the Body was surely tending to the business of the Father and ensuring the health of His Body through proper edification, the church would possess such power that nothing could thwart its advancements and victories.

The other aspect about the great unhindered work of the Spirit is that the church would be fulfilling it highest calling. And, what is that calling? Every member fitted in the Body and functioning in accordance with the Spirit as a complete unit, would reflect the incredible light and glory of Jesus Christ.

One of the big challenges for people is to recognize the idols in their life. It is natural to think of idols in terms of an image formed from some material such as wood, stone and etc., but the idols are different for each age, and we Christians must discern them, whether in our lives or in the lives of those around us.

For example, where do lifeless objects get their importance and where does worship originate from? Idols are first given identity in the mind. Minds magnify the importance and significance of something to the point that it ensnares emotions to feel some type of devotion or affection towards it.

Even though the idol may be lifeless, as we begin to emphasize it, our affections escalate causing us to pursue it even more, whether to possess it, please it, control it, or adore it. Today the idols of America are materialism, wealth, and power. Money is pursued, souls are sold to possess power, ambition becomes treacherous, and success is used as an elusive carrot that leads people down the road of spiritual bankruptcy, despair, and destruction because personal satisfaction cannot be found in any of it.

The Bible is clear, we are to bring down every imagination that exalts itself against the real knowledge of God and bring all thoughts into obedience to Christ as we set all affections on the things above and not of this earth. Before there can be any real revival and acceptable worship, all personal idols must be identified and brought down before the feet of Jesus.

It is a tendency for man to worship something, and without repentance and salvation, he will end up worshipping some aspect of creation instead of the Creator. Sadly, for many they think of idols in terms of some stone, wood, or some other man-made image, but every culture has their own idols and for America they are not actual images, but man's accomplishments, intelligence or abilities, and the greatest idol of all seems to be intelligence.

When man worships intelligence he worships what he thinks he knows while bowing before altars of rationality. However, the Bible assures us we know in part and that the carnal mind is at enmity with God, but in spite of our limited understanding, we still see people who are living in the heights of their intelligence or swinging from limbs of spiritual fantasy in the false light of the demonic world.

As believers, we need to keep our feet grounded in the truth of Jesus and His Word, while ever keeping centered to who God is to keep from being taken away with the great delusion the Apostle Paul warned about in *2 Thessalonians 2:10-12*.

Are you being grounded in the Word of God to ensure that your mind is being transformed and your inner man is being conformed to the very image of Christ?

What do you look to or for when trying to gain the right perspective when it comes to the Christian life? It is easy to see the Demises who run back to the world, while failing to see the Joshua's who have come as far as they dare as a means to personally experience God.

We see the Aaron's of religion erecting the golden calves of idolatry in the sanctuaries of churches, and not the Noah's who are hidden in the ark of Christ. We see the children of Israel dancing around the altars of idols but do not see the seven thousand who have never bowed their knees to the idols of their age.

Like Jonah who was asleep in the hull of indifference while the storm raged above, we see those who are asleep in the pews of churches as the darkness of the present age slams against the doors of complacency, but we do not see the ones who are hidden in the secret chambers of communion or the obscure caves of God's abiding protection.

Rayola Kelley

Are you merely carrying around some token of Christianity or are you being a Christian in your relationship with the Lord, your attitude, your practices, and your conduct? The Jewish men carried around a visible token of the covenant the Israelites had with God, but many failed to live according to the terms of the covenant. This can be true for Christians.

It is man's tendency to claim titles, wear certain clothing with a statement, or even wear a cross, but such things mean nothing if they are not backed with right living. It is easy to tack Christ onto a matter and believe that such a surface overture will suffice the holy, just God of heaven, but it will not. He demands worship from the heart, righteous attitude, and holy living. He will never lower Himself into the pigpens of this world or receive any crumbs man is willing to cast His way. The reason He does not have to accept such profane ways and sacrifices is because as our Creator He deserves the best from each of us.

It is vital for each Christian to realize that we likewise must be circumcised. The Apostle Paul spoke of those who are the circumcision which worship God in the spirit, rejoice in Christ Jesus, and have no confidence in the flesh *(Philippians 3:3)*. Clearly, our hearts have been circumcised by the Spirit so we can worship in truth (Jesus Christ), recognizing that there is no good thing in the flesh; therefore, it must be put off.

In *Colossians 2:11*, the apostle states this, "*In whom also ye are circumcised with the circumcision made without hands, In putting off the body of the sins of the flesh by the circumcision of Christ.*" The old has been circumcised by Christ's sacrifice and now we have the Spirit within us to enable us to live according to the new covenant. Accepting this responsibility to line up to the New Testament Covenant will mean that we choose the excellent way that will bring us into the heights of holiness.

John 4:23 reminds us that that Father seek those who worship Him in Spirit and truth and we must consider if we are truly worshipping Him in a way that allows Him to find us and accept it. In order to come to terms

with worship, we must rid ourselves of any assumptions or notions about it that are not Scriptural; therefore, we must consider what real worship is.

As I stated many times to others through the years, my initial idea of worship was singing three songs during a church service because that is what my church bulletin called it. However, worship is a personal matter that entails heart, attitude, and action. In order to worship the Lord our heart must be tender towards knowing, communing with, and pleasing Him. Our attitude must be one of awe and great appreciation, and our action must end in service that brings Him glory.

Real worship can't happen unless there is a preparation to meet with the Lord. To ensure an inward environment of worship the Holy Spirit must be present to reveal the truth about the beauty and majesty of God so that our minds will be lifted up above the daily pulls and demands of the world in the sacrifice of praise. True praise allows our heart to follow in sweet adoration of the only One who deserves such recognition, such worship: Lord God Almighty, which was, and is, and is to come.

Luke 13:25 warns that many strive to enter in through the narrow gate but will fail to do so, and *John 10:1* speaks of those who try to enter in every way but the right way. The truth is many people are on the outside of the court looking for a way into salvation that leads into the Most Holy Place of communion with God, but there is only one gate into the outer court of salvation and can only be entered through by way of the cross of Christ and His redemption.

There is only one door into true service and that is by way of Jesus' work and example as Servant, and there is only one veil that opens to sweet communion and that is through Christ as intercessor and as the ultimate sacrifice that provided the blood and the way to the Father.

The problem is people try outward reformation, religious compliance, surface performances of good works, and conformity to some righteous standard, but each act is void of true repentance from the old man's outward best, carnality's finest performance, pride's greatest presentation, and the heavy robe of conformity.

Jesus stated, "repent or perish." People must repent of or turn from of their ways, wrong attitudes, lifeless practices, and self-delusion about personal goodness so that they will not perish in their sins. The one thing that separates the real believer from those who are riding on the wave of wishful thinking when it comes to salvation, is that he or she has entered in and through the only door to eternal life, The Lord Jesus Christ.

CHALLENGES

Spiritual complacency is more deadly
than anything the devil can bring against us
in our upward struggle.
(Unknown)

Every New Year reminds me I am about to see another birthday. My earthly tabernacle is showing its years of weathering the stress and challenges of life. The Apostle Paul talks about how death works in the members of our body. Most would agree that we spend much money and time trying to keep our earthly tabernacle of our bodies together.

Many start out trying to keep the outside of our temple looking pretty good but then as inward functions begin to start malfunctioning, much effort is directed towards keeping the inner workings working so that one can accomplish the tasks before him or her.

Some know I had to give up my excessive coffee drinking to save my pancreas and many foods because of being gluten intolerant and discovering various allergies such as to eggs and onions. I have to fight much inflammation within, and now I am battling Rosacea that has marred what was considered a good complexion for years. I have struggled to keep the outside somewhat presentable and declared war on the inward challenge of my health to simply maintain some semblance of life to finish the course before me.

As I consider my life, I realize that in spite of the present struggles with my earthly tabernacle, I rejoice that my inner man is being renewed, my soul is being prepared for a new tabernacle, and my spirit can be found soaring in the ongoing revelation of Jesus Christ. We can make many attempts to maintain the outer man, but each year challenges me to consider how much am I investing in the inner man to be prepared for my final destination.

∂⎯⎯⟋⎯⎯∂⟋

The real challenge for mankind is that we all are prone to fall into some type of deception because we start from the premise of a fallen condition, a limited perspective, and a carnal mindset that can pervert our understanding of God and life, even when we are reading God's Word.

The biggest culprit that sets us up for deception is pride. It is natural for the pride in us to make us a judge that will interpret such things as God's Word according to personal agendas, exalt us as a jury who will decide the right or wrong of a matter based on unsubstantiated convictions, prejudices and biases, and convinces us we have become experts on all matters we take an interest in or put our focus on.

We have conceit that will make us elite in our understanding, arrogance to make us superior in our conclusions, haughtiness that makes us snobs in our way of thinking, and enough selfishness that will insist we are right in our own minds and ample amount of self-righteousness that will assume, presume, expect, or demand that any other human being with any kind of intelligence will naturally see it our way. This is the mountain we must recognize in our own character and the board in our eye that highlights the faults of others while blinding us to like faults in our own character.

In light of *Isaiah 55:8-9* telling us God's thoughts and ways are higher, we must realize that we need to climb over any mound that elevates personal knowledge in order to come to a state where we are open to the truth. We must desire God's truth enough that when we are wrong, we will quickly slide down our pinnacle of elevated knowledge to come into line and agreement with the eternal truth of heaven.

It is when we quit swinging from branches of unabated vain imaginations, looking inward at the molehill of self-importance, and settling for the natural ridges of what we think we know, and truly humble ourselves before the true God of heaven that we will realize that in light of God's eternal truth, we know nothing and can only know something when the person and redemptive work of Jesus Christ is the essence of all truth to us.

Are you choosing life or the cursed way of death? In *Deuteronomy 30:19,* God called heaven and earth as a witness as to what the children of Israel would choose. They had a choice between life and death, blessing and curses. When given a blatant choice, most people would make a right choice, but sadly our environment often conditions us into a lull, where instead of continuing to make the right choice, we simply give in and flow with the currents of the times.

Today we live in a culture of death where people's preference is that of the darkness of deception, the ways of wickedness, and their practices are born out of iniquity. Each avenue leads to destruction, but such individuals cannot see where they are going because they have been blinded by the god of this world, Satan, to the light of the world, Jesus Christ *(2 Corinthians 4:3-6).* They refuse to hear as they put their fingers in their ears and rage against truth and righteousness. They are being driven like cattle by the unseen dark forces around them as they are being used to promote wickedness while being led to the slaughter.

Meanwhile, heaven is taking note, the earth is bearing the scars of wickedness and groaning beneath the sin of mankind, and when these people stand before the great Judge at the Great White Throne of Judgment, they will have no recourse but to face their sentence of death, eternal separation from God.

As Christians we have chosen life, but we must daily choose to walk that life out in obedience to His Word, and continue to REMEMBER who we are in Christ, what we have because of Him, and what awaits us because of His glorious promises.

A recent article in a magazine reminded me of the ballast of a watercraft. I served as a helmsman on a utility boat when I was in the Navy, and during that time I experienced how the choppy waves of the ocean could throw you from one side of the boat to the other, as well as the rolling waves that could make you seasick. Regardless of how the waves affected me, I knew that the small vessel from the World War II era I was on would remain unaffected by them because it was designed to withstand.

Most know that the ballast is what evens out a vessel as the rough waters of the world hit it. Without the ballast or means to bring the vessel back to center, it would not survive the rigors of the rivers, lakes, and oceans. This is true for nations, families, the Church, and ourselves.

We all need a ballast to ensure we do not capsize when the waves of destruction come our way, but sadly it appears to be missing in our nation and it has put us in harm's way of the destructive waves of wicked agendas, tyrants, and evil schemes.

The reason our nation is in such dire straits is because it has lost its moral compass, the family unit has been redefined, counted insignificant, and in a sense brutally dissected to the point it has become unrecognizable. It is also clear that some of the Church has lost sight of its true calling, and individuals have lost their way in a culture where absolutes are evil, righteousness is a joke, and justice a farce.

As a believer we only have one ballast and that is Jesus Christ, and His Word is our compass that helps us avoid the storms or navigate through them. The Holy Spirit is like the engine that prepares us to meet each wave and overcome it with victory. It is obvious the waves of our times are becoming bigger and more challenging, and if we fail to maintain our relationship with the Lord, stay true to the compass and allow the Spirit to do His sanctifying work in our lives in preparation for each storm, we could easily find our faith becoming shipwrecked on the rocks of despair.

The next time you see the big waves of the times we live in come at you, remember your life is hid in Christ. He is our ark and nothing will ever capsize Him.

The one thing I have noticed in my years of ministry is that Christians who are struggling with challenges, losses, and personal failures often end up falling through the cracks of indifference and becoming silent casualties. In many cases, they are afraid to share their struggles

233

because they feel they will be judged. As a result, they struggle in isolation without the benefit of intercession, encouragement, and comfort of the Body.

One of the reasons for this scenario is the way Christianity is being presented by some. There are those who give the impression that if you are a Christian with the right amount of faith, that nothing bad or challenging will happen in your life. Jesus clearly taught differently. He said we would have much tribulation in this world but to be of good cheer for He has overcome it. We also have Scriptures such as *Acts 14:22, "Confirming the souls of the disciples, and exhorting them to continue in the faith, and that we must through much tribulation enter into the kingdom of God,"* that clearly reveal the great struggle that will occur in the Christian walk.

When I hear Christians skip over, or swing on some fanciful branch over the issue of tribulation with their brand of immunity that such things dare not happen to one of the faith, I realize that they have avoided or refused to face what is, to truly become a minister of Jesus Christ.

We are called to be ministers of consolation in *2 Corinthians 1* and it is only by experiencing like challenges, losses, and failures can we develop the humility to be used in a proper way, empathy to relate, the compassion to enter in, and the wisdom of discretion to know when to speak, listen, or be quiet. I for one rejoice in the lessons of my past tribulations, come to a place rest in Him in light of my present tribulations, and know He will prepare me for any future tribulation, knowing I will not get out of this world without it.

In one of my posts, I talked about how some "gospels" are soft-pedaling or have done away with what ails mankind, SIN. I do not know what Bible they are reading, what message they are hearing, or reality they are clinging to, but sin has been, presently is and will be man's great challenge in every arena of life. It breaks all fellowship with God as well as destroys relationships with others.

In a recent post someone stated I needed to let people know what sin was and then proceeded to quote scriptures. It is true that Scriptures tell us about sin, but for many they do not believe or understand

Scripture; therefore, reading Scripture seems obsolete or silly to them. It must be noted Scriptures about sin mean nothing unless the Holy Spirit uses them to convict a person of personal sin and their lost state. This is why if there is sin in the camp, pastors and leaders must personally call the particular sin out in order to give the Holy Spirit the tools to convict or prick the conscience of the person. There are three words used to describe sin.

There is the word SIN itself. Sin is a great offense when it comes to God and His holiness. Your sin and my sin greatly offend God who is the great judge who will judge it as so. There is TRANSGRESSION. This is where man transgresses, trespasses, or breaks the law, commandments or covenant of God. Such offenses are known as sins of commission. For the most part, because of man's conscience, he knows what is morally wrong and when he commits a transgression by trespassing into such forbidden areas, (such as "tasting the fruit") of adultery and fornication, his conscience will be there to condemn him regardless of how he might rationalize it *(Romans 1:20-21)*. It is for this reason many will sear their conscience and rage against righteousness because man wants to be as morally depraved as he chooses to be without consequences.

Then there is INIQUITY or moral deviation. Moral deviation has to do with the inclination and tendency to toy with, partake of, and give way to profane thoughts, self-serving motives, and wrong, immoral practices. This moral deviation often results in sins of omission where the spirit (or intent) is defiled in some way *(Proverbs 16:2)*. This is where man fails to do what is right, leaving a vacuum to be filled by what is wrong *(James 4:17)*. Wrong action is the result of man rebelling against God's authority and Word, and inaction is a matter of unbelief.

The final definition I will give where sin is concerned is very simple, "Sin is doing it my way." Any way outside of God's Way and God's truth will always be a grave offense against God's nature, character and will. *(Proverbs 14:12; 16:25; Hebrews 3:10)*.

What are you desperate for? Today, there are people who desperately want this crisis of the "plandemic" over with, but as Christians what do we need to be desperate about? Sadly, without a crisis there is no real desperation present because for the most part man feels self-sufficient, is content to simply get by, or has become complacent due to comfortability with the way things are.

No one likes a crisis because it reveals that man is not sufficient enough to take care of a matter, and that simply getting by will not do because it requires so much more. A crisis is also like a cannon that will shoot us out of our comfort zones as we come face to face with who we are as far as character, our source of strength in relationship to our faith, and what we truly value.

I do not ask for a crisis, but through the years I have learned to embrace them. As I trace back the different crises through my spiritual journey, it was the reality of sin that produced an inner crisis that caused me to seek out Jesus as my Savior, a religious crisis that made me seek out the person of Jesus in a greater way, and a crisis of faith that made me reach deep into the sovereignty of God and His promises, developing a greater trust in Him while embracing His Lordship.

Finally, there is the crisis of spiritual leanness that made me realize that desperation caused by a crisis will only prove temporary, but desperation for the Lord because of who He is, is lasting and sustaining. It was then that I realized sustaining desperation can only exist when we truly love the Lord with all our heart, soul, mind, and might. It is when the Lord is the center of our heart, we will seek Him, it is when He is the lover of our soul, we will desire to know Him, it is when He is ever on our mind, we will always look to see Him, and it is when we put everything in our relationship with Him, we will know the real sweetness of communing with Him

Fear is a monkey on the back of many people. They do not know what to do with it. Since we all will experience some type of threshold of fear in our lives, I have come to realize that I have the responsibility to decide what will serve as my greatest point of fear. Will I fear being found out by God's penetrating light or will I fear not being exposed in the light so that I can properly address that which keeps me from enjoying the liberating truth of His light.

The first type of fear will end in delusion until the person faces God's light or fiery judgment. The second type of dread will cause a person to fear the prospect of the light never penetrating through his or her obstinate disposition to bring conviction of the Holy Spirit in regard to sin, repentance, reconciliation with God, and restoration of relationship with Him.

I must honestly examine what kind of fear I maintain when it comes to God's penetrating light exposing the darkness of my soul and ways. My prayer is simple, "Lord, You have not given us a spirit of fear that prevents us from knowing Your overcoming power, Your abiding life, and clarity as to Your commitment to save us from that which causes fear. Give me the fear that dreads displeasing You so that I can abide in Your grace.

One of the great struggles Christians have in this present world has to do with "rights." Growing up in America most of us have been told that we have rights, but what are rights? It is simple, it means I have a right to something or a right to do something.

For example, in America I have a right to pursue life according to my religious conscience and I have rights to partake of opportunities that I have the initiative and willingness to pursue. This brings us down to what our rights are when it comes to God.

The first great right we have is to do right by obeying God and loving our neighbor as ourselves. The second right we have is to give up our present life in this world in order to gain our life in Christ. The third right has to do with choosing who or what I am going to serve. We either will serve God or sin. The final right I have is determining where I spend eternity by what I do with Jesus: heaven or hell.

It is important to remember true rights are attached to moral obligations and if morality is missing in the equation, it is no longer a right. It is for this reason we must be aware of what we are serving. If we are serving God, we experience the liberty that such rights afford, but if we are serving sin, we become a slave who has been stripped of liberty by sin and all that can be allotted to me is death.

One of the things I have looked for in Scripture is how the Lord steps into time and introduces Himself to someone. It is not that He is not known by the person, rather It is because the Lord wants to enlarge the person's understanding of Him.

The more we understand who the Lord is, the greater our relationship with Him will grow and develop. We see this example in *Genesis 15:1*. Abram knew the Lord but we see the LORD coming to him and what did He say to him, *"Fear not, Abram, I am thy shield and thy exceeding reward."* Clearly there are three aspects to what the Lord stated. The first one is "Fear not." The Lord used this statement to encourage His servants to not become overwhelmed, discouraged or hopeless in light of the testing, or challenging terrain that lies before them. Abram's big challenge turned out to be a test as to whether he would trust the Lord to bring about the impossible.

Perhaps, you are facing what seems like an impossible challenge. For Abram it was trusting that the Lord would bring forth the son He had promised Abram, who was now 100 and Sarah his wife who was 90 and past child-bearing age. Promises of God will only follow after the challenge has been met, and preparation for challenges will often begin with the Lord introducing Himself in a certain way.

Have you ever wanted to simply give up because you felt you didn't have the means to finish the course? Your strength was gone and your emotions spent. At the time you were exhausted from the battle, overwhelmed with what seemed like a string of defeats, and feeling hopeless in your present plight. I remember hitting such a place.

I saw myself sitting in the middle of the road waiting for some event of life to run over me. Since it was obvious that I was not going anywhere, I was challenged by the Lord to make a decision. In fact, I was given two choices: the plush valley of Sodom and Gomorrah in *Genesis 18* and *19* or the fiery ovens of Shadrach, Meshach, and Abednego in *Daniel 3*.

It would be natural for me to choose the valleys of the world, but I would do so knowing that it was under judgment. I considered my choices and chose the ovens because the Son of God appeared in the oven and walked with the three men.

It was at that time that I learned that when I am at such a place, I simply need to make a choice, thereby, changing my plight. And, to gain the necessary strength, I need to follow Jesus. Whether He leads me to the ovens or not was not the important point, but what was important was knowing that to gain the necessary strength to finish the course, I needed to be where He was. I had the assurance that He would lead me to places where my inner person would not only be refined, but revived.

Who do you naturally look to for help? One of the most comforting thoughts to me during some of my most challenging times is that God is my helper. This points to one who aids and protects.

As our helper the Lord is not above us, below us, indifferent to us, or fickle in what He does on our behalf. As our God, Creator, and Redeemer, He is beside us to encourage, comfort, and guide us through rough waters. His goal is to lead us to a place of rest, but in order to come to the place of rest, we must trust His words, instructions, and promises.

Although it is natural to look to those close to us in overwhelming times, the next time you encounter rough waters, remember the only One who can completely surround you with His abiding aid and loving protection.

In the area I live in I am surrounded by much wildlife which includes an assortment of birds. We have watched the eagles soar, the Ospreys swoop down, and the wild turkeys strut around. We have also witnessed one such turkey become easily confused and frantic because it found itself in a small fenced area.

Rayola Kelley

This turkey would not use its wings to fly to the top of the fence and it was in such a state it failed to see the way out. I remember thinking, "Why you dumb turkey, you have wings to fly and the entrance is within a few feet of your pacing."

I suddenly realized I have been like that frantic turkey at times when I focused on problems instead of looking up to the One who is the solution, putting my wings of faith out so I can be caught up by the wind of the Spirit.

I simply needed to choose to remember that God has provided the one entrance that gives me a way out of my plight and rut, Jesus Christ, our Lord and Savior. Since then, I figure it is my choice whether I am going to be an eagle or a turkey.

Where do you turn when you are confronted by an overwhelming challenge? It is not unusual for people to look to what they know to figure the best way around a matter. Some look to others or to methods and formulas.

My natural tendency was to look to reason, but the Lord Jesus Christ showed me that HE IS THE ONLY SOLUTION! I have since learned for the Lord to be my solution I had to quit looking to the world as even an option and realize that where my understanding ceases, my faith to simply trust God to be God must be activated.

Are you limiting the Lord? One of the questions I had to answer for myself is if God enables those He calls, why did I feel hindered and frustrated in my Christian walk? As I wrestled with the hindrances I encountered, I was reminded of *Galatians 3:28, "There is neither Jew nor Greek, there is neither bond nor free, there is neither male nor female; for ye are all one in Christ Jesus."* In other words, as vessels and instruments there was to be no distinction of pride and prejudice when it came to who or what God uses to advance His kingdom on earth.

I realize that certain things may hinder me, but God is not limited in using my hindrances to do a work in and through me. As vessels of God, we hold the same priceless substance and as His instruments we share in the same commission. Granted, there are different callings and giftings that are distributed by the Holy Spirit to each member of Christ's Body, but they are given to enable the person to carry out his or her calling and commission.

This brings us to what is the defining factor in believers. It is simple, how sweet is the fragrance of the life of Christ coming out of your life and are you speaking the truths of God in authority, power, and anointing? What will always set any Christian apart is the level of Christ's glory they are reflecting and whether they are properly delivering His inspired truth in purity and authority.

The challenge is always the same for God's people, choose who you will serve. The children of Israel were in the Promised Land. The Lord had called them to be special, delivered them out of Egypt, preserved them in the wilderness, and went before them in the Promised Land.

They had witnessed one miracle after another as well as one victory after another, but in spite of all they had experienced and gained because of Jehovah, they still needed to choose who they were going to serve: the gods of Egypt and of those in the land of Canaan or Jehovah.

Joshua lays out what it will take for them to make the right choice in *Joshua 24:14*. First, they must have the fear of the Lord. I don't know about you, but I had fear, or I should say, respect for my parents. They believed that I needed to own my actions, be responsible for the attitudes I adopted, and pay the necessary consequences for wrong actions.

I will admit, I avoided doing some things because I knew I would not get away with it. My fear or respect for my parents brought some much-needed discipline in my life. We only have the power to choose something when we realize that somewhere down the line, we are going to reap the rewards or consequences of it.

Without such fear towards our righteous God, we often prove to be foolish and throw all caution to the wind in order to do what we feel like doing regardless of how our Lord looks at it. The question is are you serving that which serves the self-life or are you choosing to serve and worship the true God of heaven?

ADVERSITY & SUFFERING

The secret formula of the saints:
When I am in the cellar of afflictions,
I look for the Lord's choicest wines.
(Samuel Rutherford)

There was a story about a flower in a pasture that grew up in spite of cows trampling it under and being covered with a cow pie. The reality is that the adversity it encountered was what caused the flower to become a beautiful creation in the end.

As believers we need to keep in mind that in spite of the adverse challenges around us that God is using them to make us into beautiful flowers and healthy trees while preparing us to become precious stones in His crown.

It is natural to try to want to avoid adversity, but God knows how to properly use such measures to make us into His special people, a royal nation, and a holy priesthood.

As many know, I worked in the seed potatoes. It took the first frost to cause the skin around the potato to start maturing but if the frost actually worked its way down to the potato before it was harvested, it would cause it to rot within.

God uses different challenges to bring spiritual maturity. These challenges if left to run amuck would eventually destroy us, but we can take heart because God is in control of the elements and knows exactly how to bring us to a state of spiritual maturity for our benefit and His glory.

I have been told you can never go back to what was so as far as your past. This statement is true. The reality is you can't go back, not because the terrain changes, but because the journey of life will change you as a person.

Life is a current, and it is natural to grow into something because of the present current that is shaping the people and terrain around you, but once your grow out of it, you can never go back because you will not fit into the scheme of things. It is clear that people grow with the current and changes of their communities as they find or develop their place in them.

The one thing Christianity has taught me is that it is all about growing into the life the Lord has called me to. As I walk through this life by faith, God uses different tools to shape me, whether it is adversity, challenges, or tests, He is fitting me into the scheme of His kingdom's work for that time.

I have never looked back longing for what was, but I do look back to see how far I have come in my walk with the Lord. The truth is I never want to go back to what I was, settle for where I was in my life, or be content to be in the current I have not been prepared to grow in.

Some people mourn their past of WHAT WAS, while failing to get into step with WHAT IS so they can grow into WHAT CAN BE. It is occasionally nice to revisit what was, knowing you are passing through this present world as nothing more than a humble sojourner.

As sojourners we are never meant to comfortably fit in or settle in this world for long, and because of this attitude we keep in mind that we are just passing through to another destination, keeping our focus steady and our steps sure as we walk towards home where we have been prepared to take our place for eternity.

Before Jesus was crucified, He warned His disciples that the night would come when no man would be able to work. His disciples encountered that long night beginning on the night Jesus allowed Himself to be taken into captivity so He could go by way of the cross and accomplished His real mission of redemption.

Currently, because of this virus, America is experiencing a type of darkness where no man can effectively function or continue on as normal. It is proving to be a long night, but the reality is that darkness has been on this nation for quite a while, but many have failed to recognize it.

The darkness, of course has to do with the grave sins of this nation that range from idolatry and abortion to abominable lifestyles and practices. Such darkness, however, serves as a great opportunity for the true light to shine. As Christians we are to reflect the light of Jesus' life and when there are various shades of grey due to unholy agreements and numerous worldly compromises, the light is not that clear or decisive. However, in this darkness of despair, uncertainty, sorrow, and loss, the light of heaven can penetrate the darkness and bring hope, direction, healing, and restoration.

It is during such darkness that, as believers, we must make sure that we are not expressing the same despair, uncertainty, sorrow, and loss because our focus is on the troubled waters and raging waves of circumstances instead of on the One who is sovereign over all storms and waves of every age.

Crises reveal how dependent we are on the people around us and the world we live in. It's natural to think as long as everything is going our way, that we are in control of our lives and destinies. The truth is we are in a sense in control of our destiny but it depends on the choices we make concerning the Lord, His Word, and His Gospel. However, we are never in control of the circumstances and events that disrupt our lives.

They are like the waves on the ocean. Some will leave a simple wake that hits the shores of our lives, but since we can hold up under such tides, they simply become small irritations. Sometimes the waves can be formidable, but as long as we are ready to brace against them, we can withstand them; however, let an unexpected rogue wave come in and that is another story.

Giant waves will ultimately cost those that find themselves in their path. This Corona virus is a rogue wave. We saw it coming at us from a distance, but we had no idea how large and all-encompassing it was. We had wise leadership that turned the bow of the ship to face it as a nation in preparation to minimize its effects, but the truth is rogue waves will leave a large swath behind them. It is clear when such waves hit us, we are not in control.

These waves will change the landscape of our soul to reveal if we are situated in Christ, but we will ultimately define how we will allow it to affect our attitude towards life based on our faith towards God. To me this crisis reveals how dependent I am or have become on Jesus. He is the foundation upon which I can clearly brace myself regardless of the stormy waters or giant waves, the Rock I can become anchored to that can't be moved, the refuge I can hide in that will withstand, and the high tower that will lift me above the destruction it leaves behind.

There is much suffering going on in this world and it varies. There is physical suffering in the body that causes pain, trouble, and restlessness. There is emotional suffering that causes despair, mental suffering that causes anguish, and spiritual suffering that causes sorrow and isolation.

Jesus experienced every type of suffering there was. For the physical He offered His body up as a sacrifice, for the emotional He used the Word to anchor Himself to truth, for the mental He submitted His will, and for the spiritual He committed up His spirit for the glory of God.

We must consider all suffering not only in light of Jesus' great examples but in light of the promise of *2 Corinthians 4:17, 18, "For our light affliction, which is but for a moment, worketh for us a far more exceeding and eternal weight of glory: While we look not at the things which are seen, but at the things which are not seen: for the things which are seen are temporal; but the things which are not seen are eternal."*

May these sweet words bring comfort for our minds, healing for our bodies, rest for our souls, and peace in our spirit.

Like most people, through the years I have had various struggles, but the ones that prove to be the most humbling are physical struggles which can take a great emotional toll on a person. Due to being gluten intolerant, I also found a variety of other problems associated with it.

When you are struggling physically, you are aware of not only losing your quality of life, but your strength to run the race. The emotional pit I eventually found myself in was a pit dug by uncontrollable circumstances with great tenacity. I described this pit in this way, "The spade of opposition has taken great chunks out of my resolve, while the shovel of weariness has left me tasting the depths of despair."

The pit was dark and overwhelming for me but it was in that pit of depression that I discovered the abiding faithfulness of God. Even though I could not sense Him, I knew in my heart He was there, ever ready to walk with me in that shadow of the valley of death. I have always wanted to gain the Lord in greater ways, but each dark valley has taught me that in order to come higher in my understanding of the Lord I must be brought down into dark valleys where I learn more about the depth of His commitment towards me.

So often our struggles cause isolation in our lives, but I have discovered those times of isolation is when I am aware of my great need for the Lord, giving Him the opportunity to draw me closer to Him. Encouraging ourselves in who Jesus is serves as the wings in the deep, dark valleys of despair that will lift us above such despair to rest in our hope in Christ.

In the last post I talked about my experience in the valley of despair. There is no way that any of us can get through this world without experiencing such valleys. There is a tendency of some to present a Christianity that is immune from these challenging valleys, but if we are to have a ministry of consolation that is able to enter in with others, we must experience similar challenges (*2 Corinthians 1:3-7*).

We need to keep in mind that the Lord is entrusting and enlarging our testimony about Him so we can stand, withstand, and continue to stand, while walking or running through whatever terrain is before us.

246

The problem with running the race is that Satan, the self-life, and others want to hinder us from running it. It is for this reason we will find ourselves being knocked emotionally backwards as we face different challenges.

I wrote this about my own race back in 2011 when I was faced with some grave situations, "In order to run the race, I would jump out of each hole of despair, only to fall into a ravine of utter distress. I would climb out of the ravine in order to take up the torch to continue my journey, only to fall into a chasm of depression. I would crawl up out of the chasm in an attempt to continue the race, only to find myself tripping over the challenging rocks of problems. Each fall would cause me to roll down the slopes of defeat into the canyon floors of hopelessness."

Although my description was for that time and temporary, many have experienced this as well. We need to keep in mind at such times that God still sits on the throne and at the right time, He will lift us above our situation and give us a wondrous perspective of the work He is doing in us (*Philippians 1:6*).

Does the idea of suffering appeal to you? I don't know about you but I don't look for or welcome suffering, but the reality is no one will get through this world without it. The Apostle Paul understood that if he was to become identified with Jesus in a deeper way that he had to know the fellowship of his suffering.

Suffering comes in different ways. For the body it is illness and pain. For the emotions it comes through hurt, despair, loss, and depression. In the case of mental suffering, it manifests itself in anguish, and spiritually it comes by identifying with others in their sufferings.

Such spiritual suffering actually points to vexation of spirit because of the spiritual climate or compassionately entering in with people where they are in their crises. Jesus was clearly vexed on the cross over sin and He also encountered all aspects of human suffering and that is why in *Hebrews 4:15* it tells us as our High Priest, He was touched with all of the same infirmities as us.

He was emotionally distraught in the Garden of Gethsemane, physically tortured on His way to Calvary, and in mental anguish as He cried from the cross so He could ultimately serve as our High Priest. Suffering can refine a person's character or cause a person's soul to become shriveled up in unbelief and bitterness towards God.

Suffering is a scalpel that is meant to go deep into our character in order to bring out valuable treasures or as some would say the "finest wine" for the Master's good pleasure. When we go through suffering, we must remember *Hebrews 12:3, "For consider him that endured such contradiction of sinners against himself, lest ye be wearied and faint in your minds."*

What do you look at when you are suffering? It is easy to look at what is causing the suffering, and it is natural to wrestle with it in your mind, grapple with your emotions because of it, and become angry over the hopelessness or unfairness of it. It is also true the intense physical suffering is forgotten once it is over with, the emotional suffering can leave a scar on our heart, and the mental anguish can create a psychological rut that is not easily overcome.

But suffering has its purpose and must have its way in our lives. The Bible is clear in *2 Timothy 3:12, "Yea, and all that will live godly in Christ Jesus shall suffer persecution."* For Christians suffering is a type of graduation, where the Lord takes them deeper in refinement of character and the fiery test of their faith in order to bring them higher in their understanding of Him. I don't know about you, but I have experienced a few of these graduations. However, there are people who go into deep places because of suffering, but never allow God to go deep in them, and their Christian life remains surface and ineffective because they never really graduate on a personal level.

In my graduations, I did not come out with a diploma; rather, I came out with a greater awareness of God's abiding faithfulness to meet me in my darkness of despair, lead me by gently guiding my footsteps through the nightmarish maze, and faithfully bringing me to the light of His glorious love and grace. I may have always wanted to avoid suffering up front, but I have never regretted the eternal benefits I have received from it after being given beauty for ashes, the oil of joy for mourning, the garment of praise for the spirit of heaviness that I might be established among the trees of righteousness *(Isaiah 61:3)*.

Have you had to drink fully from the cup of suffering? When Jesus mentioned the ordeal of the cross ahead of Him to His disciples, He referred to it as drinking from a cup in *Matthew 20:22,* and asked if they were able to drink of the same cup. He went on to say, *"Ye shall drink indeed of my cup."*

The Lord is talking about the cup of suffering. He was completely immersed in it and as a result His suffering serves as an example to us according to *1 Peter 2:21*. The question is must we suffer?

A person must care and have a heart in order to suffer, and if you have such a heart, you will suffer as you become identified with those who are hurting and struggling. The Apostle Paul wanted to enter into that fellowship of suffering with Jesus in a greater way. He understood what awaited him in such fellowship.

Paul stated in *2 Timothy 2:12a, "If we suffer, we shall also reign with him."* In *Romans 8:17*, he made this statement, *"And if children, then heirs; heirs of God, and joint-heirs with Christ; if so be that we suffer with him, that we may be also glorified together."* It was Paul's heart to be glorified with Jesus, but he knew it would have to come by way of suffering. His attitude was, "so be it."

The one thing that becomes obvious is that life is fragile. In our initial years of childhood, we are optimistic about life because it seems that we have much time to explore, experience, and discover what life is all about. When we become young teenagers and adults, we begin to see our strength come to maturity and have a sense of infallibility as we start plowing our way through the terrain of life to take hold of it and wield our environment to our will, dreams, and vision.

As we become older, we realize that we do not conquer the terrain; rather, we must wisely choose the way we walk through this world in order to finish the course set before us. There is nothing that brings the hard cold reality that this present life is fragile, uncertain, and temporary more than death. Needless to say, God does not look at the death of a saint in the same way we look at it.

To heaven, the death of a saint marks a gain, a completion, but to us on earth the absence of the presence of someone we love points to loss, sorrow, and mourning. It is clear the Lord understood that mourning was necessary for He established a time of mourning such as in the case of great leaders like Moses.

Mourning allows one time to come to a place of facing the emotional fallout of such a loss as a means to finally let go, which allows the individual to move on. As many know, we lost our little four-legged companion, Bell. We recognize that God graciously took her because it was time to do so. She left many pawprints on our hearts.

As I waded through the bitterness of loss, I was able to taste the sweetness of what this little creature had added to my life. I had to admit that the sorrow I felt was determined by what Bell had added to my life; therefore, the gift of her life would eventually far outweigh the sorrow that in time would subside.

At such enlightenment, sorrow becomes its own special footprint because you would not have traded the time you had with such a life in order to avoid the sorrow you presently feel. It is at such times that sorrow can become a treasured memorial of how that life enriched yours.

As I thought about the impact Bell made on my life, I wondered what kind of impact I was leaving. It is true we leave footprints. As children, we leave them on hearts and as teenagers and young adults we sometimes selfishly walk on hearts as we become lost in activities and remain so until we step out from among the masses and the normal, popular trends, and seek our life according to some calling and destiny.

I realized as a Christian, my present walk of faith leaves footprints, but where are they leading? My heart desire is that they are leading others to the very glory of heaven, Jesus Christ. However, once I leave this earth, what will remain? Time will wipe away the impact of footprints, but as I considered the footprints of those who went before me, I realized that once I step into glory, I will become part of a great cloud of witnesses that will confirm the precious faith of those who dared to follow in the indelible footprints of our Lord and Savior, Jesus Christ.

CHARACTER

*Many people know
how to be a "character" in life,
but how many of us possess
true character?
(Rayola Kelley)*

In a world where imperfection clearly exists, evil often reigns, wickedness more often holds the power, corruption is the practice, and the silent grave the end, while being human adds the final strike against finding some place of sanctuary for the tormented soul in an insane world, we as believers must remember that one touch of heaven can change the status of something.

I would love to do things perfectly, but I recognized a long time ago my imperfect touch is what allows God to reveal Himself to me and through me by putting His signature on a matter. It is His touch of heavenly perfection that brings surprises to flawed attempts, helps the imperfect to graduate to a place of excellence, and gives hope to those who find themselves residing among despairing bits and pieces of unresolved matters of the past and the uncertain challenges of the present.

The imperfection of His people is what allows God to show His perfection, while failure is what gives God the perfect opportunity to reveal the mercy of heaven; our struggles His grace, in despairing times a way of deliverance, and hope to anything that appears to end in a grave.

The greater the stormy waves are that hit the shoreline of our resolve, the greater the opportunity for God to do a deeper work in us in order to bring forth that which constitutes perfection in our life, the image and reflection of our Lord Jesus Christ.

We must remember it is not just about the journey through this world but the work that will be done according to the type of terrain that is set before us. It is not about the hardness of the journey, but the type of character it forges in us. It is all about the Lord having His way in each of us to bring us to a heavenly perfection that will shine brightly in this dark world, ever serving as the light to the hopeless, a place of sanctuary to the weary, and a witness of heaven to the lost.

What do you do with the different challenges of life? In life there are irritations, points of frustration, testing, and crises. God uses each point as a type of tool to deal with our inward character. For example, irritations reveal our level of patience, frustration our temperament, testing our endurance, and crisis the depth of the integrity of our faith. However, the one point that God is not in when it comes to shaping our character is something called, "drama."

If you are part of a family, there will be drama occasionally occurring. At the core of this production will be someone that serves as the "drama queen or king," who, like soap operas on TV, takes the smallest of matters and develops a script that creates misunderstanding, suspense, and tension among the cast of characters that find themselves caught up with some aspect of the story.

In every story you have a variety of characters that naturally will fall into their part. For example, every good drama such as a soap opera will have the patriarch or the matriarch that must keep the lid on the drama so it doesn't unfold too quickly so as to expose that the image of their good family name is nothing more than an illusion, the hero or heroine who quietly suffers and must always be cheered on because they are always misunderstood, the gossiper that plants the seeds of suspicion, the conniver who must cause enough mischief to keep the story line going, and the "drama queen or king" who must take the simplest of offenses, gossip, and innuendoes and makes it into a great mountain of lies that will take months to unravel in order to expose the foolishness that has propped it up.

Not all family dynamics are like a soap opera, but drama crops up at different times. I have experienced this drama in my life and even fell into a role, but as a Christian I realized that such drama only feeds the emotional sentimentality of silly notions, and that I did not need to be part of such foolishness.

As a believer, life may not usher in a daily diet of sensationalism, suspense, and tension, but it brings the right challenges to enable us to discover what constitutes that which is inspirational and lasting to the spirit, satisfying to soul, and beneficial to our person.

Instead of falling into such a script, we must quickly discern it, and then douse the contents of it with the water of God's truth to prevent it from becoming a huge obstacle that hinders personal advancement on our part.

I was thinking of the song, "Growing Up Is Hard to Do." I have met people who have fought, avoided, and escaped the idea of ever really "growing up," but we must come to terms with what it means to "grow up."

After all, if one is spoiled, they believe they should not have to face certain realities and if they are emotionally weak, they want to be kept from having to walk through unpleasant situations that would challenge them to grow up emotionally, actually preparing them to rise to the next occasion regardless of how great it might prove to be. In other words, they want to be pampered, protected, and kept from facing the harsh realities of life.

If they are self-centered, they do not feel they should be bothered with such inconveniences. The result becomes obvious, when the responsible must forget about their part in the scheme of things by picking up the dropped ball and running towards the goal line in spite of obstacles, the strong must allow their strength to be used up, poured out, and abused as they take on burdens that are not theirs, and the ones who are being realistic must sometimes become the sacrifice (so the self-centered can remain clueless in their fragile realities) to make sure that the results are not a disaster down the line.

Age, rank, degrees, wealth, and position do not determine maturity; but the willingness to own personal actions, take responsibility, and take charge of one's life by making the right decisions is what marks real maturity in a person. The greatest sign of spiritual maturity depends on the level of true humility present in one's life.

When I was "growing up," the concept of maturity pointed to becoming a responsible adult in society. It was like taking your place in society and being a productive part of it. When I was a teenager, I realized that growing up had to do with emotionally meeting crisis with some wisdom as a means to test the level of calamity as to whether it was a molehill or a mountain, and that the test of maturity was the ability to keep a molehill in perspective while being realistic about the mountain.

As an adult, I realized that real maturity was not based on age, but constructive experience that built character. As a Christian I began to understand that maturity in the walk of faith was coming to "full age."

"Full age" has a lot to do with coming to completion. In other words, we take responsibility for how we respond by making the right choice. Right choices are what establishes inner character and true character is what strengthens emotions to stand instead of cowering, whimpering, or having a meltdown in some insipid corner.

The problem with "maturity" in the flesh is that it does not want any part of "growing up" if the situation challenges it to deny self. The problem escalates because many prefer their fantasies over reality, their compromising idea of character over the absolutes of the Bible, and their excuses for emotional weakness over sobriety that faces what is happening, while accepting what is, and taking responsibility as to how it will affect and impact them.

The truth is we are living in a cursed, dying world that can promise nothing but loss and sorrow and that the only place where we can be assured of coming to "full age" is when we are hidden in Christ, depending on His strength, walking according to His Word, and knowing that it is the maturing of His life in us that will cause us to know the excellent way and enable us to reach our high calling and potential in His kingdom.

⤞ ✓ ⤚

I shared in the past how the Lord has shown me that people in my life, or the ones I cross paths with become one of three things to me, and on rare occasions all three: 1) they are a TEST to my character, 2) they are a MIRROR to my character flaws, and 3) they are a BURDEN that will stretch my character beyond all measure.

As I stated, we must discern if we have REAL character or whether we are CHARACTERS. When people serve as a test to my character it shows the level of my commitment, convictions, and my conversion towards the matters of righteousness. When they are a mirror to my flaws, they show me the reality of my standing in Christ, the source of my real inward struggles and the need of repentance where I have not overcome, and the places where personal revival must take place for me to have the character to stand with assurance in Christ, withstand with the authority of His Word, and continue to stand with endurance. This is also why we are told not to judge others because we will end up judging ourselves, because those same characteristics we are the most critical of in others can also be clearly identified in our character.

Finally, if a person is a burden, I must seek the Lord as to whether He has placed that person as a burden on me. If He has not, I must offer that individual back to Him and trust Him; but if it is a burden He has entrusted to me, then I must come under His yoke to carry it, seek His face as to what my responsibility is in being faithful in it, and know that no matter how heavy it may feel and how long I must carry it, that it is His love that serves as the strength to carry the burden, His grace the endurance to carry it, and His faithfulness that will see me to the end.

As Christians, we must remember that it is our relationships, our attitudes towards others, and our commitment to others that show the real depth of our character and since we are here to live the life of Christ and not our own, that, regardless the test, the cost, and the endurance required, our response will always be nothing more than our reasonable service in light of Jesus' redemption.

255

Rayola Kelley

I once heard that it takes intelligence to have sense of humor, but some would probably debate such a statement. However, I have learned a few things about a sense of humor, and it is good for the soul.

The Bible even tells us a merry heart does good like a medicine. You can either laugh at something funny or cry to release pent-up emotions. I, for one, prefer to laugh until I cry at something that warrants it. You can learn to laugh at yourself in order to keep the seriousness of life and little embarrassments in the right perspective or succumb to some morbid reality that everything is an ongoing hopeless drama.

Another benefit of a sense of humor is that it can let matters simply be what they are and as the saying goes, "actually make lemonade out of lemons." It is natural to meet with irritations along the way, encounter overwhelming crises, and experience some very deep sorrows, but God gave us the gift of laughter that allows us to make light that which is irritating, find something to smile about in crisis, and during times of great sorrow be able to still appreciate the many little surprising gifts that can cause our heart to find a bit of encouragement here, pieces of hope there, and comfort in the midst of tears.

The other observation I have had about having a sense of humor is that those who lack this precious gift possess a fragile reality and are often teetering on the brink of insanity.

As you know, I spent two weeks spring-cleaning. The first day of spring-cleaning always represents the starting gate. On that first day I was up and ready to go but I was also honest, it is not the first day that is the hardest, but the last day. My thought process was will I make it over the finish line?

Don't get me wrong, I could see the finish line, but did I have the energy and the wherewithal to complete the race. I have enough years behind me to know that on the second day of such a process that I am going to be a little tired, while on the third day I going to become a bit weary and on the fourth day I will be irritable because I am probably passing the weary marker and am ready to throw up my hands and

256

forget it but at that time I am in a terrible mess and have no other choice but to go on.

This is true for the Christian race. As a new believer we have zeal and are ready to run, as a Christian that has been knocked down a few times, we still have strength to get up but not as fast as before. As a soldier who is becoming a bit weary from the battles it takes resolve to keep going, but one must if he or she is going to victoriously complete the course. Eventually, there are those who come to the crossroads where they either sit down in a foul mood and complain, cry, and have a pity party because the way is hard and getting narrower to travel or go on to maturity.

I have asked God to give me strength, send His helpers and help me run the course because I don't have what it will take to complete the exercise before me. Zeal, strength, and resolve never gets the person across the finish line; rather, it is the stamina that comes from inner character that trusts God's strength will be there, His grace will prove sufficient in weakness, His commitment strong in weariness, and His faithfulness sure at all crossroads.

We must remember it is not about our abilities to complete the course, but God's work of the past done on the cross that prepared the way, His work of His Spirit in us that enables us, and His work of bringing forth His kingdom and promises before us to show us the way when we lose sight of our destination.

Today the sky is overcast with gray clouds. Gray points to a subdued day where there is no light of inspiration and no intense darkness that requires us to sleep. It speaks of clouds that are threatening to drop some kind of moisture on the ground, which is necessary to ensure growth when the sun does shine.

Most of us prefer the sunny skies that not only inspire us but allows our spirit to soar, but there are those who prefer darkness because their activities are wicked and they can't afford for others to see them and expose them. As someone has pointed out light is able to purge that which is done in darkness and as Christians, we are instructed by the Apostle Paul in *Ephesians 5:1-13* that since we are children who walk in the light, we need to shine it on such darkness with the goal of reproving or rebuking it.

Gray in the spiritual realm points to different things such as complacency towards spiritual matters, listlessness in the spirit, indifference towards the ways of righteousness, and a mixture where the flesh and worldliness are being more predominate in our attitude and practices. I have learned that it is in the gray days of my spiritual life that I am being tested. Perhaps I do not feel inspired at such times, but I possess that which is able to inspire me, the Holy Spirit no matter what I feel.

Spiritual darkness may be upon me, but I possess the light of Christ's life and Word to walk through it; therefore, I must not allow myself to go to sleep. The key is that when there are the days of inspiration, I must prepare for the darkness by ensuring that the oil of my lamp is filled up and when the gray days come, I must remind myself that I have the wonderful opportunity to continue to be about my Father's business until the darkness comes when no man is able to work.

We are living in a time of great spiritual darkness, but as children of the light we must not give in to it but see it as an opportunity to let our light shine. Perhaps all we will see at first are the gray clouds, but we must remember that the water of the Spirit will send droplets of truth on seeking souls, allowing our light to penetrate the darkness with inspiration, hope, and life.

The great question we Christians find ourselves wrestling with is what is our responsibility when it comes to wickedness and evil. Do we submit to the wicked ways of government and do we lay down when evil is reigning? Do we remain quiet when injustice is taking center stage, as well as ignore or close our eyes to the wrongs being committed against the souls of man and a nation by those in power?

The Bible tells us to pray for our enemies and to submit to those in authority, but in what context do we submit to anyone in authority, and how do we pray for our enemies? The first thing I can tell you is if there is a difference between God's Word and government, we are to submit to God and obey His Word. We must soberly maintain the integrity of righteousness at all times.

This means we must not to partake of any sin or ignore it, because God is holy. In the Old Testament God is clear that all rebellion had to be put out from among His people. A rebellious unrepentant son had to be stoned, those found committing idolatry, adultery, and murder were killed, and it was for this reason that King David admitted in *Psalm 51:16-17* there was no sacrifice he could offer to satisfy the Law for his sins of murder and adultery except a broken spirit over sin and a broken and contrite (repentant) heart.

God has not changed His mind about sin, His ways of dealing with it, and what it takes for us to address it. We must allow the Lord to reveal all rebellion in us from the sin of indifference towards righteousness and all outward independence and defiance.

Yesterday I mentioned God in relationship to His attitude towards sin. Some of you may be yelling, "We live in a time of grace." It is true we do, but grace was as much present in the Old Testament as in the New Testament, but we are told in the New Testament grace reigns only through righteousness.

In the example of the Jews in Babylon they were told to submit and pray for the leaders in the sense that they could live in peace, which would allow them to worship and serve their God, but if our leaders are God's enemies, making them our enemies as well, we must stand as soldiers and pray that God will have His way with them whether it is to scatter, judge, or destroy them.

The more we understand God's attitude towards any sin, whether it is the corrupt state of evilness, the perverted practices of the wicked, or complacency towards righteousness, we will begin to understand that in evilness we are to be a voice of warning, in wickedness we must become the light that brings the contrast, and in indifference towards righteousness, we must challenge it by raising up the truth to bring clarity. This means we are not to come into agreement with evil and act as if wickedness is alright or not all that bad.

Rayola Kelley

We must never sacrifice integrity and righteousness in the name of preserving wicked institutions that are corrupt and under judgment because such standing will put us on the wrong side of truth and righteousness. We must wait on God when it comes to evil to know how and when to stand, stand before Him when it comes to wickedness to wait for instructions, and remain standing in faith and prayer until God's enemies are under His feet.

Yesterday I had one of those busy Saturdays outside. We have a cement patio that was not put in correctly and the result is that there are big cracks in it and during the winter time the frost heaves it up to the point where one can risk injury by tripping over it. We all knew we needed to do something about it, but what?

The three of us, Jeannette, Carrie, and myself had the same idea, lay a patio deck over it. That is what we were doing yesterday with the help of a dear Christian brother, prepping for it and preparing the frame to lay down a deck. I realize that we humans can't be perfect in what we do, and we will always have corrections or redoes along the way. It is true there are some people who never see a matter through because they don't know how, they don't care or they lost their emotional enthusiasm to do it, leaving others to pick up the pieces, but the truth is we are not perfect and do not live in a perfect world.

Our lives are always under construction, our ways being adjusted to line up, and our high opinions of ourselves brought down by the reality that we are incapable of being right and doing right without the intervention of God's grace. For many years I lived a life that left big cracks in my character, forced some people to pick up some unpleasant pieces, and left a few to complete a job, but when I found Christ, He began to fill up the cracks in my character, and as I learned who I was in Christ, I began to wonderfully discover that He had gently redone and corrected my ways to keep me from tripping over, or into, the old life that always left me devastated and undone.

Meanwhile, we need to remember that the Holy Spirit is ever prepping us for the glory of the next world, while preparing us to be brought forth in perfection.

FIGHTING THE GOOD FIGHT

It seems many Christians would rather put on
their spiritual diapers of foolish expectation
and suck on the pacifier of untested doctrine
by standing on feelings and emotions
instead of putting on their armor and standing
on both the Rock (Jesus Christ) and
the Word of God.
(Rayola Kelley)

Truth is the most powerful weapon we have against all enemies of our soul, but we must know how to probably use it. We must allow it to be used as a surgical tool by the Holy Spirit to show us what is happening in our inner lives before we can effectively use it to help others.

We have to also know how to use it as a knife to carefully set the captive free and not as a weapon to put them in their place, thereby, wounding them. We need to use it as a sword to whittle down the power of our enemies and stop their advancements, and a bow and arrow that will hit the right target to ensure victory.

When used properly, the sword of truth has set me free in many ways and I have watched it set many people free, and at such times it became a wonderful source of edification to me. Truth clearly challenges, divides, and separates. It shakes, cuts, awakens, and insults.

Is truth shaking you now and if it is are you waking up to what God wants to accomplish in your life with His sword?

Recently I asked if we were ready to be shaken by the events around us. No doubt we are in the midst of great shaking. In such times people will become fearful, indifferent, and angry as they look around to point a finger at someone instead of holding on to what is true and look up to the One who is the solution.

From past experiences, I've learned that it is after all misdirected hope lies shattered in the shallow ground of doubts and insecurity that our real Hope, the Lord Jesus steps on the scene and brings forth what He has declared. Meanwhile the great shaking goes on and people must come to terms with what they really believe.

Recently, I was asked how are we to respond to the wicked. Jesus said we are to pray for our enemy, but what enemy? We have personal enemies, civil enemies, and national enemies. Personal enemies are those individuals who have personally offended us. Jesus' response to such enemies from the cross was, *"Forgive them for they know what they do."*

Clearly, these enemies rarely realize that they offend us because as humans we can be quite touchy or clueless. This is when the love of God covers a multitude of such offenses and allows us to become peacemakers that regard the well-being of our enemies as of the utmost importance to God; thereby, allowing us to be sensitive as to how we are to respond: intercession or ministry.

One of the obvious fruits of our times is the lawlessness reigning with an iron fist in society. Whether it is stealing, killing, or destroying, they prove offensive to the quality of life. In some cases, their offenses may not directly touch us but eventually they can cause a collapse of society.

Our response is if the lawless have touched our lives personally, we must forgive them and pray that God keeps our attitude right towards such an individual in order to be sensitive to how the Lord might direct us in ministry. As a body, we must pray for their souls as we avail ourselves to be a source of ministry whether it is through an organization or personal involvements. Our goal is to expose these individuals to the Gospel for the salvation of their souls.

Another enemy are those in high places who encourage lawlessness to tear societies apart. Do we pray for such enemies and if so how? Let me respond by asking, can we pray that God blesses Satan? These individuals are often the tools of Satan. We can't pray that God blesses such an enemy, but as soldiers we can pray that if any be heirs of salvation among them that they be turned over to Satan for the salvation of their souls, but if not, that God exposes their schemes, scatters them, and nullifies their wicked ways, so in the end God will be glorified.

It is clear we need to not only know how to use the sword of God, His Word, but how to use the place of authority, and our prayer life, in order to be effective in our intercession.

Good news, I'm feeling better today but I'm also aware of how fickle my energy is. When you don't have a lot of energy, you have to show a bit of discretion when it comes to the demands on your life. The one thing that amazes me is that the Bible speaks of those things which takes limited energy, whether it is waiting before the Lord, standing in the power of the Lord, or holding onto Him.

Granted, these exercises can take some strength, but to stand before the Lord points to that fact that He is the One who fights the real battles, which makes us conquerors. Waiting for the Lord reminds us He is the One who must move, and once He moves, we will naturally move in His power not our own, which points to accomplishing feats.

Holding on to Him often points to the awesome reality that He is the One who is holding onto us, which means we have nothing to fear. The real battle for the Christian comes down to trusting Him. Our pride does not want to take a back seat when it comes to recognition and our flesh does not want to be denied taking a bow for successes.

The big battle is always between the Spirit and the flesh and when there is no pinnacle of strength to stand on, pride will take on an indifferent attitude, and when the passion of the flesh has become subdued with complacency it will display an "I don't care" attitude. To be at this point does not mean you have overcome self or the flesh, it simply means it has no energy to care.

As Christians, we need to offer our bodies as a living sacrifice while neglecting pride, and crucifying the flesh to make sure we use our personal resources in a way that our lives become an open conduit for the grace of God to work and His power to flow.

Rayola Kelley

We are in a battle and we must avoid becoming philosophers about what to do and theologians about what not to do, and as good soldiers do what the Word of God instructs us to do. One of the problems we have as soldiers is that we have not learned to discern our Commander's voice and properly discern His orders (His Word). We debate rather than advance, we argue over interpretation of insignificant details rather than carry out the obvious instructions, and we complain about the way instead of trusting that it leads us to the overcoming life.

Through the years I have often been surprised that God managed to use me at all. I can't count the times I stood in the way of what needed to be done because I first wanted to make sure I was ready, or that I felt right about it, or that I would certainly come out the victorious "heroine" that saved the day. It took me years to realize that it was not about me being ready, but being willing to respond to the call of my Lord and obey the instructions He has given me. It clearly was not about me feeling right about something, but knowing that something was right because God established it as being so. It was not about my person coming out looking a certain way, but about being humbled enough to regress to avoid coming out at all and touching what rightfully was God's glory and complete doing.

We are in the days where the battle rages and we need to keep in mind that soldiers are seasoned on the battle field and not sitting behind some desk, in some pew, and hiding behind fig leaves of excuses that sound noble, but are, in all honesty, being dishonorable to the soldier's calling.

When the battle rages, the orders are clear, we are to stand, withstand, and continue to stand. There is no room for retreat unless we are being called to the prayer closet, no time to get technical about the strategy that has been given to us, and there is no running away unless we want to become a casualty. It is easy to talk or sing about being a soldier in God's army, but unless you are willing to risk all and go into battle, you can't claim you are a real soldier of Christ and that you are part of the army of God.

In WWII American soldiers fought two different enemies; therefore, they had to develop strategies according to the enemy. This is true when we are confronting our different enemies. The three main personal enemies of Christians are the flesh, the world, and Satan.

To conquer the enemy of the flesh, we must deny self and apply the cross daily in order to follow Jesus to the overcoming life. When it comes to the world, we must come out from its influences in order to become crucified to it and it to us if we are going to have an overcoming faith that endures the world's many temptations and challenges during our sojourning. Satan is after our faith, and to overcome this enemy we must submit to God's authority and pick up the sword of the Word and stand on it to prevent Satan from finding any inroads into our lives. However, there are a few traps we must be aware of when confronting enemies.

We must never feel sorry for them when they meet with their just judgment. If you feel sorry for self when the flesh is being crucified, the old man will come out a noble suffering martyr; rather than a coward who will do anything to avoid the cross that will silence him. If you feel worried that you are missing something when it comes to the world, or bad that you have to cast what seems harmless to the side in order to overcome it, then you will become entangled with it once again. This entanglement will dull you down spiritually, render you ineffective as a soldier, and end with different defeats plaguing you.

When it comes to Satan, you can't underestimate his abilities, ignore his presence, be ignorant of his tactics, or be flippant about him or with him. It is only by properly discerning his presence, standing in the authority of Jesus by faith and effectively using our sword that we will overcome Satan.

It is vital that we understand the target and the tactics of our enemies if we are to ensure we overcome them instead of them overcoming us.

We are talking about the war we are in. The one thing we must always keep in mind is we do not fight against flesh and blood; therefore, the battle is with the unseen. Since it is an unseen enemy, we must correctly discern what enemy is posing the greatest threat to us at present because it will determine the ground that must be taken back or defended to ensure victory, along with the strategy required.

There is the enemy of the self-life (old man) who is against God, the adversary of the world with its many anti-God systems that opposes any furtherance of the kingdom of God, and Satan who opposes God by oppressing the one who was formed to reflect His glory, man, from reaching his potential, receiving the promises, and inheriting his true heavenly inheritance.

As soldiers we can't leave our inner sanctuaries vulnerable while we go out to face an enemy in another arena. We can't leave our homes unprotected and go out and expect to stop the enemy at the gate and wall because they have already beached it and have laid siege to our lives in some way.

It is easy to muster up a bit of patriotism here and there about the kingdom of God. It is also easy to become zealous about marching off to some "foreign" soil with noble goals when it comes to defending great causes, but what is hard is maintaining the integrity of the home front because of arrogant assumptions that nothing will happen in our backyard and presumptions that if it does, it will be easily enough put down. Both attitudes will become a breach in our wall of protection when it comes to our homes. We must not leave our sanctuary unprotected because we are doing our own thing and not waiting and listening for orders from headquarters.

Let me first state, that all great battles for the Christian soldier are first won in the prayer closet. It is in the prayer closet that you can kneel before your holy, Almighty God to seek mercy, while standing firmly on what you know to be true about Him, in order to gain perspective, instruction, authority, and empowerment to proceed. Too many times a soldier is driven by emotions (undisciplined zeal), moods (unpredictable waves that are easily driven), and fear and confusion.

A trained soldier is disciplined enough to push all personal agendas aside while waiting for the command, a seasoned soldier is prepared to meet the enemy that is posing the greatest threat, and the victorious soldier is the one who counts the present world completely lost to him in order to gain the higher ground that is marked by eternity.

As believers, we are all soldiers, commissioned by our king to fight in the battlefields of this world, but the question is, have you identified the enemy that is presently threatening to defeat you right now?

The other day I made reference to Satan's devices. His greatest device is lies. This is the foundation he establishes underneath all matters pertaining to God, life, and his systems. His poisonous lies become a means to redefine reality by mixing them with a bit of truth to dull man's mind down, creating a seductive reality that will take man's soul captive.

When it comes to the self-life of pride all he has to do to gain inroads is to send an accusing, or condemning, half-truth that will cause man to look at self and within self instead of upward, which opens him up for the lie to take root, producing the oppressive fruit of depression. When it comes to the world, he simply uses the lure of false promises of happiness and success to take captive man's affections.

These can create obsessive pursuits that leave a person tormented, angry, and driven, and it is for this reason we are instructed to set our affections on things above and not on this world. This brings me to another effective device of Satan and that is fear.

There is a natural fear, a spirit of fear, and the fear of God. A spirit of fear operates from platforms of superstition, intimidation, and the idea of losing life, livelihood, and well-being. Such fear will either paralyze or drive a person. It will confuse the mind, numb the emotions, and paralyze him or her from spiritually moving forward.

The reason fear is such a powerful tool is because it is afraid of the reactions, consequences, and fruits that may follow. For example, one can be afraid of experiencing failure, rejection, ineptness, and losing control; therefore, the individual will do nothing. Perhaps such a person will comply outwardly with that which seems contrary to conscience, while avoiding being honest with him or herself, causing resentment, bitterness, and anger to take root.

On the other hand, fear may cause the person to fling all aside and rush headlong into destruction. As you can see, fear creates a frightening reality as it successfully closes down one's ability to reason, discern, and show discretion.

The question is, how many people are becoming victims of fear at this time, and as a result they are experiencing the bitterness of oppression, the fruit of utter frustration, and the miserable state of hopelessness?

Divide and conquer is the name of Satan's game. If he can divide and isolate people, he can pick them off one at a time, but if a group of people stand together, then it is harder to defeat them.

We have a virus that has isolated people and those who dare stand together are labeled in the worst way, and sometimes charged and handcuffed by a law system that is letting criminals go free, but picks on innocent people who will not continue to play the insane game.

We are living in Satan's system and must expect such bullying tactics and injustices to take place, but as Christians, we must not allow ourselves to be isolated from the truth or like-minded believers. We must, as the Bible states, be quick to exhort one another especially as the day approaches *(Hebrews 10:25)*. I am not talking about going to church where we look at the back of someone's head, but entering into real fellowship with each other in the unity of the Spirit and in the bond of godly love.

We know if God is for us that there is none that can be against us, but we must be standing with God in agreement to ensure we are in the majority and on the winning team. Where there are two or more people in agreement the Lord is with them, but there must be agreement in Spirit and truth.

The problem is that the body of Christ has been divided by doctrine, denominational pride, and practices. It's members have been isolated by petty non-essential issues that have nothing to do with salvation that comes only by Jesus. The great challenge for the church, (the body of Christ) is to take stock of what constitutes the faith that was first delivered to the saints and embrace it. As believers, we should know the fundamental truths that will enable each of us to stand in the darkness, as well as adhering to pure, sound doctrine that ultimately serves as a visible living testimony of our faith.

Let us avoid the religious detours that isolate us, the pettiness that exalts us onto lonely pinnacles where we become sitting ducks, and the incessant doctrinal debates that profit no one except feed pride. Let us become the church we have been called to be, knowing that the gates of hell will not prevail against it.

The Lord did not give us a spirit of fear, but of power, love, and a sound mind *(2 Timothy 1:7)*. John tells us perfect love casts out fear in *1 John 4:18*, while we know as believers that the power from above can raise us above fear and a sound mind enables us to discern and recognize when a spirit of fear is in operation.

One of the greatest fears man must overcome in his life is the fear of death *(Hebrews 2:14-15)*. Death is part of the cycle of life and serves as a door into eternity, and eternity is an unknown factor, especially to those who are unbelievers.

There are those who wishfully think that this door leads to one way— up, regardless of how a person lived his or her life, but in reality, this door leads downward as well. Not all fear death, but they might fear the events that lead up to their death. The ideas and possibilities of their death not being noble, peaceful, and painless will cause their commitment to the Lord to waver and their mind to be clouded by fear, causing them to faint in their minds *(Hebrews 12:2-3)*.

Satan made this statement to God in *Job 2:4, "Skin for skin, yea, all that a man hath will he give for his life."* In summary, man will sell his soul to preserve his physical life. I say all of this because the fear of losing one's life is a driving force behind much of what is going on in this world today.

If people care to check out the facts surrounding the latest health crisis, most of it is nothing but pure propaganda, a means to dehumanize people by isolating them behind a cheap mask. Quarantine is for the sick, not the well.

Rayola Kelley

This "plandemic" has caused me to realize how easy it is for people to look to some aspect of man for a solution, and the result is they find themselves oppressed and ultimately curse just as *Jeremiah 17:5* warned us about. To take control, the wicked powers take something that should be a person's responsibility and make it a right such as health. I have taken responsibility for my health and have quarantined myself as initially requested, but I refuse to give in to the fear and intimidation tactics based on the wicked agendas of a few. Don't get me wrong, what was unleashed on the world was serious, but it was also a test of the powers to be to see how fast they can bring the masses into compliance if they create enough fear through lies and intimidation.

The idea of death has caused many people to become fearful, compliant sheep, ready to fling all aside to save their lives, while giving up their freedoms, personal identity, and a sound mind as they surrender to Marxist tyrants, unconstitutional edicts, and thugs that can't save anyone. Jesus stated any attempt to save our life in this world means we lose our life in the next age to come.

For this reason, I refuse to bow to the lies and the fear of the present systems of the world. I choose the way of faith to conquer fear and disburse the lies propping it up. God holds my days in His hands and I am immortal until He calls me home. I also choose to remember what *Revelation 12:11* tells me about overcoming Satan, *"And they overcame him by the blood of the Lamb, and by the word of their testimony, and THEY LOVED NOT THEIR LIVES UNTO THE DEATH."* (Emphasis added.)

Let it not be said of this day that believers were driven recklessly to slaughtering pens by the lying voices of the age they lived in; rather, they waited on the voice of their Shepherd, knowing HE would lead them through the dark terrain of this present age to green pastures and still, refreshing waters.

What does it mean to be a watchman? It seems like a simple question, but perhaps it would benefit us to consider this term in light of the days we live in. The watchmen of old fell into two categories: the watchman on the wall who watched for enemy attack against the city and the watchmen of God who waited on God as a means to either foretell or forthtell the message the Lord would give them to deliver to the people.

There was also another type of guard, it was the gatekeeper. There were different gates leading into Jerusalem, but almost all were designated for a certain use, but the main gate is where Jerusalem was open to the outside world. The gatekeepers had the vital responsibility to oversee the activities that took place at the gates.

As believers, we are to serve as watchmen over the integrity of our communities and home, as well as gatekeepers over our churches and personal sanctuaries. It is obvious that our nation is under siege, some of our communities caving under the weight of corruption, some of our churches silenced, many of our homes have been looted by an unseen enemy, and the lives of the innocent ransacked. The question is, what is a soul to do?

Well, as for believers, there is nowhere in Scripture where we are told to surrender and become doormats to the enemy as they rush in to destroy everything. We are part of a universal army, given vital access to our commander (prayer), and provided with an armor and an effective weapon (God's Word), which will enable us to stand, withstand, and continue to stand.

The next question is, are we standing or are we asleep, indifferent, operating in wishful thinking, or living in denial. Keep in mind, the reason our sword is so sharp is because it is truth.

Truth awakens those asleep, it challenges indifferences, it cuts away wishful thinking, or it shakes anyone out of their place if they are hiding in the basement of denial. Truth will not let each of us, as believers, to remain in ignorance about the battle, the enemy, or what must be done to stop the destruction.

When was the last time you checked out your weapon to see if it was sharp enough to defeat the enemy affronting your life, your home, your church, your community, and your nation?

Yesterday I talked about watchmen and gatekeepers. As believers, we are responsible to serve in both capacities. Watchmen warn about the enemy coming, while gatekeepers keep the people safe within. The watchmen guarded the wall to ensure there was no breach occurring that would put the city at risk, while the gatekeeper had to be vigilant to identify any covert activities that might come in under a false guise. The watchmen were to alert the people, while the gatekeepers were to be ready to identify possible trouble and close the gate if necessary.

Today it seems like our nation is in grave trouble from within and if so, why? If we, as soldiers, have been vigilant and sober as the Bible instructs us to be, we would have been prepared to fight the enemy at strategical points identified by our Commander or even from the wall, instead it appears we are now in more of a hand-to-hand combat.

Clearly, we have the kingdom of darkness raging against the kingdom of light. When did the breach in the wall happen that allowed the enemy to take hold in this country and our communities, and where were the gatekeepers that would shut the gate at the least sign of trouble?

The church for the most part, was and is, entrusted to be the gatekeeper and what have we, as a body of Christ, let into our communities, churches, and homes? The truth is we have had watchmen like David Wilkerson who warned us as a nation that we would find ourselves in this present mess because of unholy, idolatrous agreements on both the international, national, and religious scenes, thanks to the corruption in leadership at all levels. We also had gatekeepers like A.W. Tozer who pointed out that such things as entertainment would prove to be a grave affront to the church's calling and integrity, and if allowed into our sanctuaries, would render the body ineffective.

The truth is that the watchmen and the gatekeepers have been sounding the alarm for years in our nation, but where was the church, the body, the army of Christ? Were they asleep in the pews, leaning back on their pious laurels, fighting make-believe battles to appear victorious with their paper swords of other men's religious opinions and interpretations, assuming all would be alright, and presuming that the alarms were too radical or extreme to take seriously?

It is important to realize that in the army, soldiers are involved in different warfare depending on where they meet the enemy. In the fields

Post To Post

the strategy is offensive in the sense that they push the enemy back, and at the wall it is to keep the enemy out. But once the enemy penetrates the wall and gate, at that point all the remaining soldiers can do is stand, but stand they must to push back and take back the city.

Whether we like it or not, the church was called to be the first line of defense in every community to protect the integrity of the home, and somewhere along the way we have dropped the ball, maybe not individually but as a corporate body. Now as soldiers we must stand our ground on all that is true and right with our sword (God's Word) lifted high, and protect what has been entrusted to us: our communities, our churches, our homes, and our testimonies.

I have been talking about Christians being the watchmen and the gatekeepers. One of the parts of the Christian armor that allows for protection, advancement, and victory in conflict regardless of the type of battle is the shield of faith. Jesus asked if He would find faith when He came back.

From what I read about Jesus' day the Roman soldier had three different sizes of shields to use depending on the type of combat that was being fought. They had a big shield they could actually hide behind. It could deflect the onslaught of the spears of the enemy. These shields not only protected the soldier, but it allowed a front line of soldiers to form in order to push back the enemy lines.

The medium sized shield was used in advancement as the battle intensified. It could be used to protect the head and the torso from swords and other weapons as the soldier advanced forward through the enemy lines.

The final shield was a smaller shield that was used in hand-to-hand combat. It was small enough to allow quick movement, but capable of protecting the soldier from a weapon.

I fear the different presentations for the last three decades of what constitutes real faith in Christendom has left Christians holding inept shields that will not enable them to stand in conflict, as well as advance forward and withstand a face-to-face meeting with the enemy in the different arenas of the world. The pseudo faiths are nothing more than props used for outward show, but genuine faith is what truly allows us as soldiers of the cross to confront the enemy.

First of all, all true faith comes from God but we must exercise it. We learn to stand in the confidence of faith because the Lord is our Shield, and we advance forward in faith because instead of fainting, our mind has been persuaded that He is true to His Word as we guard our hearts from being pierced by the lies of the enemy. We continue to stand regardless of how intense the battle becomes because we know we are on the right side of eternity and that in spite of what the world may consider defeats or casualties, we already know we are on the winning side.

I must at this point reiterate, God does not equip us with a shield to cower behind; rather, to advance forward. He did not give us the shield without giving us a helmet to protect us in what we know is true about our standing in the Lord, a breastplate to guard the essence of our life, footwear in order to march forward, and a weapon to put us on the offense as we forge forward in expectation of truly seeing the enemy defeated.

The question is do you possess the shield of God to advance forward in victory or a silly prop that will fail you and leave you open for utter defeat?

The one thing I wrestle with is being human. Let's face it, we would all like to be perfect and get it right the first time around without having to run around the same mountain looking at the same scenery until we finally realize what we need to learn.

Most of life is unlearning what is not beneficial or relearning what is necessary because of assuming that since we know something that is enough, when in reality intellectual knowledge may be a notch in some unseen belt of information, but it will not be truth until it reaches the heart and is proven in practical ways.

We need to keep in mind that knowledge does not constitute truth. I remember an engineer stating that he spent four years in college learning his profession and the next four years unlearning it because it was not always applicable when he was working in the field.

Knowledge will impress our arrogance, but if it fails to prove to be practical when tested in the fields of experience, it simply means it falls more into the category of theory instead of truth. Truth never changes and is applicable at all times. It is not a theory based on unrealistic and untried practices, but on what is.

The truth is we are born in a fallen state, living in an imperfect environment, and walking through a temporary, doomed world. We can't expect perfection in life, in our works, in this world, and from others. We may dream of heroic feats of the likes of a superman, but that is why such heroes are cartoons because they are not realistic.

This is why in the real world for Christians it is not about doing great feats, but learning along the way to be good soldiers in the battle when it comes to the Word of God and our enemies, good mountain climbers when it comes to overcoming the world with faith, wise strangers when it comes to knowing our place of refuge, and restless pilgrims that are not content to settle for anything until we reach our final destination.

As someone once said, it is not a matter of what we see along the way, but the journey itself and what we discover along the way that will truly enrich our lives. May we discover that in our imperfection we can know perfection in Christ, in our world of imperfection we are being brought to a place of perfection by the Spirit of God, and ultimately, we will acquire perfection or spiritual maturity by obeying the Word of God.

Are you in a battle? There are many battlefronts a person can zealously and passionately get caught up with. Some are noble causes, and others are honorable because it requires sacrifice, while the rest of them may come down to intangible ideologies which are a matter of opinions and beliefs.

I realize I could be spent out by fighting on too many fronts and not have the strength to fight in the most important battles. As a Christian I realize I need to choose my battles wisely; therefore, I set up some criteria: 1) Remember what army I belong to and who is my Commander;

2) Know I am being called to fight on a particular battlefront; 3) That I am standing on truth, not opinion; 4) Does it require me to put my honor on the line for the sake of others' well-being, and 5) Will it call for excellence on my part that will end with me being a good-will ambassador of who and what I am representing.

Remember, there is no honor in being dishonorable towards those who prove to be the enemy.

The problem is that as people we look for blessings in this world, physical rewards, and protection from our government, law enforcement, and the people in our world, but in *Genesis 15:1*, the Lord makes it clear that He is the one who blesses and that He is our reward and protector.

"Shield" has a couple of implications. It can point to "anointing" that empowers or a tool used in war. There were three types of shields used during the Roman times depending on the warfare that was taking place. There was a small shield that was used in hand-to-hand combat, a medium shield that was used in advancement, and a shield that could practically cover your whole body that was used when protecting the soldier from an onslaught of spears and arrows.

God is clearly our shield but it takes faith to apply His protection in the right place at the right time. By faith we can advance with our weapon, the Word of God and by faith we can lift up the authority we have in Christ to deflect Satan's attacks while standing, and it is by faith that we can hide behind God when all hell is coming at us, knowing He is our refuge.

Faith is the key and God is our invisible shield that is ever before us, to the side of us and even behind us.

There is always a battle raging. Sometimes we may be aware of it while at other times there is a calm but it is before the storm. Rebekah had such a battle going on in her womb in *Genesis 25*. She inquired of the Lord what was going on.

The Lord told her that there were two nations in her womb that would produce two manner of people and one would be stronger than the other and the elder would serve the younger. We know that the battle that was going on was between Esau and Jacob.

Esau grew to be a man of the earth, a hunter, while Jacob was content to dwell in tents, meaning he was one who would work the land as well as tend flocks. The word used to describe Jacob was that he was a "plain man." When you look up the word "plain" in the Strong's Concordance, it says it means complete, pious, gentle, and when it is used with "perfect, it means undefiled, and upright.

Regardless of how Jacob handled the matter of inheritance based on his mother's advice, he was very interested in spiritual matters. This is confirmed when he wanted the birthright, which was associated to the lineage of Jesus while Esau couldn't have cared less. Since Esau did not value the spiritual birthright, he was willing to sell it to satisfy his stomach, losing the right to the inheritance that was also attached to it.

The truth is there is always the battle between the flesh and the spirit that often rages in us, but a good way to tell them apart is what is being valued, the things of this world or the things of God.

The battle between the flesh and the spirit can be seen throughout the Bible. The flesh is represented by the self-life and its infamous idol of pride. The self-life wants that which will feed selfish whims and ways that will make the flesh feel satisfied, while pride insists on being exalted in a place of supremacy and being right, ever calling the shots while expecting people in its world to orbit around it in adoration and obedience.

Self-will causes strife as it pushes against the will of others and pride will present opposition which will cause contention and accusation. A good example of this battle and how to handle it is found in *Genesis 26*.

Water was very important in the land that Isaac was residing in. However, every time his herdsmen dug a well the herdsmen of the land would fight against them. These contrary herdsmen represent the flesh. In the case of the first well they pushed against what was right and Isaac called the well Esek (strife) and in the case of the second well they were

277

contentious towards him, and he called that well Sitnah (opposition). The interesting part of this struggle is how Isaac responded to these herdsmen, he refused to give them audience regardless of what many would consider rights and a matter of honor, and went on to find another well.

The flesh wins when people give it any consideration or audience, even if the person tries to line the flesh up to reform or change it. The flesh is the flesh and the only way to deal with it is to mortify it by crucifying it every time it raises its head as a means to silence it and leave it behind.

There are various things that can enslave us in this age. The Bible tells us that where the Spirit of God is, there is liberty. When I do not feel the liberty of the Spirit in my life to advance forward in my walk, I know that there is some type of bondage in my life.

The Bible is clear that we must test or discern the spirit in operation (Holy Spirit, natural spirit of man, and the spirit of the world, Satan). *(See 1 Corinthians 2:10-14.)* Our flesh tempts and takes us captive through lusts, the world entices and enslaves us through attractions, and the devil seduces with lies to ensnare us into his traps. The pride of our flesh often puts unbearable standards on us that will keep us feeling defeated, the world erects ridiculous images that cause us to feel that we will never make the grade, often flinging us into a tormenting morbid reality, and Satan gives a false hope that we can have it all if we will simply sell our soul here and there. This simply means we will bow down and worship him.

How do you discern the point of bondage? If you feel great burdens based on personal standards, remember that Jesus' burden is light; therefore, do an exchange with Him. Are you struggling with the entangling spider web of the world, look to the One who was victorious over the world, Jesus Christ and put your faith and reliance squarely on and in Him to help you come out and truly be separated from it as you set your affections on the things above? Are you ensnared in one of his traps, pick up the sword of the Word of God and choose to believe it and not Satan's lies? Declare that Satan lost at the cross of Christ, and that you have been redeemed and he must respect his Creator's Word, which you are submitting to in faith.

Faith towards God and confidence in His Word ensures you are more than a conqueror and that in the end you will be an overcomer.

I live in the rural part of Idaho and, since the Corona situation hit, for the most part, life has gone on except for some businesses being closed, the inconvenience of waiting to drive through the window at the bank to do deposits, signs that read, "If you are sick, stop and go home," some wearing masks here and there, and silent churches on Wednesday and Sunday.

Yesterday I went to what we call the "big city" and when I saw the line outside of a certain store, I thought of Communism, and while listening to this young woman explaining how they are trying to keep us safe and as a result they have upcoming policies we needed to beware of that spoke of control and oppression, I thought of how quickly a society can be taken down by an overexaggerated crisis. My friend, Jeannette, was quick to verbally express that it was all "Communism" and she would never darken their store again.

Needless to say, the young enthusiastic lady's balloon was suddenly popped, and the man we were talking to in front of us hailed Jeannette's boldness, but the woman standing six feet behind us with her mask in place told her to shut up and let the lady speak. The lady who had the air taken out of her balloon was mad and the belligerent woman behind us gave us dirty looks until we entered the building at which time, I looked her right straight into her eyes and she looked down.

I grew up in the 60's where we understood the great threat of Communism to our nation, while feeling the tension of the cold war and watching our men, such as my uncle march off to war to push this Satanically inspired religion with its wicked philosophy of Socialism and its doctrine of Humanism back in East Asia. At the time we even had statements like, "Better dead than red" (the color of Communism).

Yesterday in the big city there was a darkness of oppression, life for the most part had been sucked out people, while stores everywhere remained closed. People were afraid to interact and some looked at us

279

with great suspicion because we were not playing along, making it clear how easy it is to get neighbor to turn on neighbor without any real reason or cause. During my time there I heard the warning from years ago, that Communism would take us without one shot being fired.

We are living in perilous times, but may I remind every believer, you are hid in Christ and your physical life is in God's hands, your mission is set, your weapon sure, your course already laid out before you, and the war won, but we must not surrender our faith out of fear, propagate the darkness by partaking of the lie, promote its death by drinking its poisonous Kool-Aide to get by, and above all we must not strive to save our present life here that is fading while selling our soul. We must always be willing to count the life the world promises as dung and be ever ready to offer up our bodies for God's use and glory on the battlefields of this world.

The question I have had to answer is how can I make sure that I finish the course. The Apostle Paul declared that he fought a good fight, kept the faith, and finished the course. We are told we are running a race and to finish the course we must lay aside every sin that "so easily besets" us. It is clear that we will not finish the course without having some battles along the way.

The Bible tells us to endure as good soldiers who avoid becoming entangled with this world. I have known people who made a commitment to serve the Lord when they had their earthly life in order, but when they finally felt they could serve the Lord, they admitted they did not have the strength and the wherewithal to do so.

Jesus was clear that we must first seek His kingdom before our earthly lives will fall into place and actually make sense. If we are honest with ourselves, we seek to first ensure our earthly wellbeing so we can control how we serve the Lord instead of trusting Him to guide us to the right places while taking the necessary steps of faith of obedience that will lead to true service and worship that will glorify Him.

FAITH

Only the Lord Jesus Christ is our sure footing,
but many people want to use Christ by tacking Him on
to their life and activities to keep them out of hell,
while pursuing the world that will ultimately
keep them out of heaven.
(Rayola Kelley)

What is faith? Faith is hard to describe because it begins as a gift from God, that becomes a choice of an open heart. This heart has been prepared to believe a matter is trustworthy because it comes from the One who is true and faithful. Once the heart receives it, then it can be embraced by the will as being true and at that point one is ready to walk it out in assurance that it is so.

The Bible's example of true faith was the man, Abraham. His faith was counted FOR righteousness. It is important to note the word FOR because it is not in place of righteousness but in light of the fact that the purpose of faith was being realized and fulfilled in Abraham. And, what is the purpose of faith: to line a believer up in attitude, spirit, and conduct as to what is right and acceptable to God so He can bring forth the promise.

Romans 4:19-21 describes Abraham's faith. The first thing we are told is that Abraham's faith was not weak, but strong for it was established on God, ending with God being glorified in his life. True faith will always bring proper glory to God.

Abraham's attitude was that he was dead or incapable of bringing forth the promise of a son. He chose to believe God as to what He promised him, and as a result he never staggered at whether it would happen or not, but rested in the One who promised it, the One who never lies. In fact, we are told he was FULLY PERSUADED knowing God would do the miraculous to bring it forth because He is able to perform it.

This is a beautiful picture of faith, but we need to note one important fact. People stand on what they consider to be promises, but are they

281

from God for that time, in order to bring forth His plan and purpose in a matter? As believers we have been given promises but some will never be fully realized until eternity. Meanwhile, we walk in this present world in light of those promises already being true and fulfilled in our lives. This is faith, and that is why at the end of it, Christians discover the fullness of their salvation.

It is easy to claim we have faith, but faith can be a doctrine, an idea, or a sentimental notion, but genuine faith is a seed that is planted when one chooses to believe that which is trustworthy. This seed becomes the necessary measure that begins to take root when activated and cultivated through obedience.

Faith becomes a gift that serves as a token that a matter will be brought forth as promised; therefore, we can hold on with assurance. This assurance serves as stepping stones that allows and guides our steps through the terrain, while withstanding the elements, and walking around the obstacles.

We can walk in such confidence because we know we can and will finish the course as long as we hold onto what is true, right, and eternal. The Bible brings faith into a concise perspective. We are told in *2 Corinthians 13:5*, that if our faith is not in the right Jesus, it will prove to be reprobate, useless, something that will fail us.

True, active faith comes by hearing and hearing by the Word of God. This means we are to walk by faith in what God has established as being true and not according to our understanding. Personal understanding points to the natural light we prefer to walk in and according to, but faith is not the light; rather, it is the inner assurance that enables us to walk according to the Word of God, which simply lights the dark path enough to step into what we know is true with confidence. However, we can't walk by faith if we try to confirm something according to our understanding and not the Word of God.

Our need to understand before we choose to believe God will end in unbelief, our insistence to see where we are going will cause us to walk in a false light that leads us into spiritual darkness, and our unwillingness to step into the darkness until we can see will cause us to become paralyzed by fear or cause us to grope our way without any ability to discern where we are.

As Christians we have the light of Christ's life within, the light of His Word as our "flashlight" to guide us through the darkness, and the light of His promises waiting to greet us at the end of the valley, canyon, or tunnel we are walking through. The challenge for each of us, is to realize we do have a choice as to what light we walk in; therefore, let us willingly and with great expectation and joy walk in the true light that heaven has indeed provided for us.

Jesus asked if He would find faith when He came back *(Luke 18:8)*. Faith is a matter I have greatly wrestled with through my Christian walk *(Jude 3)*. I began with romantic notions about faith because I had a certain knowledge of what I believed, but when my theology failed to answer the "whys" behind my many, overwhelming challenges, my faith digressed to a certain logic as to why God, who is capable of doing the impossible, remained silent and unresponsive to what I considered my great need.

Since there was no conviction of sin in my life that would result in chastisement or judgment, the best my logic accomplished was that it began to judge God as being indifferent and unfair. When I realized my logic was leading me into greater despair and hopelessness, my pathetic faith gave way to morbid self-pity that made me feel I was forgotten by God, which caused me to feel like a pawn in circumstances that comprised nothing more than a sick game that I greatly resented.

When I realized that my digression in faith was actually leading me into the sin of unbelief towards God, I realized that faith was a choice that I made when my understanding about God ceased. And, what choice did I make? To trust the righteous character of God to work out His perfect ways according to His timing *(Hebrews 11:6)*.

The reality of personal faith is that it is a pseudo faith that allows us to be independent of truly trusting God, but will eventually fail us during great testing because it is conditional and often based on what God can do, and not who God is. The fiery test of faith is what will bring you to the end of your faith to reveal to you that you do not possess true faith.

The measure of faith comes from God, and is given to us when personal notions, ideas, judgements, and any unbelief towards Him is exposed, and rendered into ashes along with any strength, personal will, and independence from trusting Him with all matters of our life.

It is out of ashes that real faith towards God will emerge to state as Job did in *Job 13:15, "Though he slay me, yet will I trust in him: but I will maintain mine own ways before him."*

What does it mean for one's faith to be tested, refined, and enlarged? It means walking through a wilderness where all false dependency on the world, man, personal philosophies, theologies, and conclusions fall to the wayside. It is being stripped of all false hope that is based on unfounded expectation, leaving a person uncertain about what they believe or understand. It is about being left in puddles of disappointments created by tears of betrayal and the quicksand of disillusionment because nothing pans out and the horizon offers no hope; and, if there is a slight appearance of deliverance, it proves to be nothing more than a fading mirage.

The test of faith is about being brought to the abyss of skepticism where all will be weighed in the balance and what is false will fall into the pit of destruction, while what is real is anchored to the Rock of Ages. If one does take a wrong step, they are pulled back to a place of safety and it they accidentally fall, the wings of hope will be caught by the current of the Spirit to ensure the person lands on the place of rest.

Perhaps this does not describe your experience with faith, but it does mine. Our faith is always brought to the crisis point so we can see what true faith is and what is nothing more than wishful thinking that swings from the branches of delusional nonsense. As stated, I trust God 100 percent of the time. I trust His timing is perfect, His ways are righteous, His plans designed by eternal wisdom, and He has the power to bring it about according to His will and glory.

Through the years I have met men of integrity and I know I can trust what they say, but I also know they have limitations that might hinder them for a season, obstacles that may cause them to change course, battles that will determine their next strategy, and the unknown that will cause them to learn how to listen for and become dependent on that which is greater than themselves.

Sadly, man wants to dictate to God as to what to do, how to do it, and when to do it to believe He is GOD, while ironically and in some cases desperately believing and holding man to his word as if he IS God, capable of bringing all matters together.

Today people are finding reasons to not believe, not because God failed them, but because man proved what is inevitable, that he is not God and such individuals' dependence is still firmly on what is seen and not the unseen realm of heaven.

It is natural for people who base their hope on what they see to operate according to an upside-down perspective. The main reason for this inverted perspective for most of us is that the flesh wants to avoid the testing of personal character and faith. We want man to be right when we have a place of agreement, but if he fails to do as he predicted or speculated, it becomes an excuse for the feeble in character to become insolent and angry towards God, the weak in faith to become skeptics and mocking towards truth, and the frail in mind to cower in some corner of self-pity that declares all is a sick joke after all.

It is natural for each of us to want to circumvent the barren wilderness of being brought to the end of self-reliance. We want to jump over the pinnacles of testing to land on the mountain tops of growth and revelation without learning to be mountain climbers so we can come to maturity, appreciate the view and properly discern it. We want to swing over the canyons of uncertainty to avoid facing our ineptness to change the terrain or the circumstances. And since many want their own reality, they will not accept what is in order to face it to learn real dependency on God.

The testing of faith requires one to trust God in the darkness, the trials of faith reveal that in a genuine state it is capable of enduring in the storms because it is founded on what is eternal, and the fiery ovens refine faith in order to reflect the face and ability of the Potter to bring forth a vessel fit for His use and glory. The Bible tells us that the enemy of God would wear out the patience of the saints.

Patience points to the ability to wait on the Lord, trust Him until He moves, and hold onto His promises when our faith is being rocked by the storms of uncertainty. The problem is that as Americans, we live in an instant society and are spoiled enough that we can't imagine being tested in the area of waiting and patience. We do not expect to be tested, to have any real tolerance in waiting, and have not disciplined ourselves enough to possess our souls in patience.

The truth is that if we avoid the testing, trials and fiery ovens of our faith, we will not be able to stand with any authority, withstand with abiding assurance, and continue to stand with the knowledge that Jesus Christ is indeed our all in all.

We are told about the fiery test of our faith. Faith is not based on what we can see or understand, but on who we know we can trust. Faith is tested and refined in two ways. The first thing that is tested in the crises of faith is what we think we know to be true. When I think about the best way to describe this test is the story of the wolf and the three pigs.

Each pig built different structures to protect themselves from the wolf who arrogantly stated that he could blow down each structure. No doubt as each one looked at their structure, they perceived there was no way the mere breath of the wolf could blow it down. However, the wolf managed to blow down the straw structure of vain and wishful thinking and the sticks of foolish opinions, but when he got to the bricks of truth, he was left breathless and without strength. This is true for Christians.

There are Christians that are in despair about what they are seeing as far as the events taking place on the national scene but you must remember when it comes to the world it is all about image and posturing and not what is true or revealing. Consider your reaction towards the testing of what you think you know, because the first test will reveal your real source of dependency. We often are banking on what we think is true based on our understanding, and when it falls, we must not cower in some corner while being swallowed by a sense of betrayal or disillusionment towards God.

At that point, we must out of love for truth seek the One who is the Truth, knowing that He will not be moved from what is so, as well as what has clearly established as being true. In the end, all that has been proclaimed will confirm that our God is trustworthy and true to all He has declared.

Yesterday I talked about the two tests of our faith. The first test is centered on what we think we know, and reveals our source of dependency. The zeal or inspiration behind our first test often proves to be misplaced expectancy (hope) that starts from the wrong premise.

It is natural to struggle with fitting certain theories of a matter into what we understand, but it sets us up to crash land when reality refutes it, because true faith never comes down to what we think we know. The second test will be aimed at what we know is true.

The best way to describe this test is like putting a puzzle together. When I put a puzzle together, I first seek out the straight edge pieces that identify the outlining framework of the picture, and once the frame is in place, I separate pieces according to color and shape. When it comes to shape, I look for something that will distinguish the piece in order to fit it in the right place.

I remember working on one puzzle and I was making great head way, but when it came to connecting certain parts of the puzzle together, something proved to be amiss. I had to finally examine each piece and I found there was one piece that looked like it fit, but it left a slight space. I put it aside and found the correct piece bringing much of the puzzle together.

As Christians, we know the truth because we have the framework of God's Word, but we know in part. We find ourselves being inundated with different pieces of the puzzle. We do our best to try to fit each piece in the design to make sense of it, but at times we find something is amiss causing confusion that can quickly turn into skepticism. Do we throw our hands up and walk away in unbelief that it is all a joke, or do we examine what we know is true in order to fit each piece in the right place that will bring clarity instead of confusion?

One might wonder why bother with the pieces when you already know what the picture looks like. Each puzzle I put together sharpened my discernment and when I was finished, I realized how each properly placed piece brought such dimension, beauty, and meaning to the picture that it created awe and wonderment in me.

We can always settle for a one-dimensional picture, but If we want a greater revelation of Christ, we must deal with the pieces of what has been placed before us, discern where they might fit, be open to cast pieces aside if they fail to properly fit, while knowing that when it all finally comes together, that is where we will understand the uniqueness that each piece added to the whole picture. And, what will be our declaration, "I knew in part, but now that I see clearly with the eyes of faith, and now I understand how it all works together for His glory."

As believers, the one thing we can be assured of is our faith will be tested, often bringing it to a point of crisis. Through the years I learned a few things about faith when being tested. The first thing is that the crisis of faith would always bring me to a narrow pinnacle that was propped up by great expectancy that always led to the heights of anxiousness and dread. It is when I began to suspect that my expectation was propped up by nothing more than vain imagination and speculation that I would come crashing down through the debris of nonsense.

After falling off a few pinnacles, I began to resent the inevitable discovery in each test of my faith, that I did not have the faith at that time to trust God with the details and truly come to a place of rest in Him as I waited for Him to bring forth the promise. I not only went into despair but I began to resent the test. Needless to say, it was not very Christian of me to give way to the resentment that God would never see it my way or do it the way I thought He should.

In order to address my resentment, I had to address my selfish attitude and when I did, I learned another important lesson about the testing of my faith. I am the one who created the pinnacle of anxiety and dread that always brought my faith to the point of crisis. Even though the Lord showed me the reality of the promise, I wanted to control the narrative of how it was to play out so that people would know that my God was not a liar.

The truth is I didn't want people to think I was a nut for believing Him in the first place about what He promised. It is true our faith towards God can make us a spectacle to an unbelieving, doomed world, but we need to realize that our conclusion of how something will play out has nothing to do with God's reputation, but rather with revealing our level of maturity and discernment. We must remember God's ways and thoughts are not our ways and thoughts and we must hold any personal conclusions lightly.

I occasionally shared the possibilities of what could or might happen at different times, but I never use them to prop me up to the point that I find myself dangling on the pinnacle of dread instead of hanging onto the sure Rock of Jesus. A couple of reasons I share the possibilities is to highlight what might be, but also to bring the contrast that can sharpen one's discernment.

Many times, the possibilities fall to the wayside because they are man's speculations, but at such times, a person must go back to the promise in order to appreciate what God does do to bring a matter to fruition. Man can speculate, but God will confirm what is truly from Him, enlarging the faith of His followers and instilling a greater ability to discern. In the end, when God finally does what He promises, it is always so simple, smooth, and clear that it renews the spirit of man as it brings humility, awe, and worship to his soul.

It is easy for our faith to become shipwrecked. There are a few things that will cause faith to become stranded. There is the rogue wave of pride, sands of complacency, the hard reefs of unbelief, the rocks of idolatry and heresy, and the shoreline of fear. There are two types of faith God gives a person. There is the MEASURE of faith mentioned in *Romans 12:3* and the GIFT of faith, which is the gift of the Spirit that is brought out in *1 Corinthians 12:9*.

The measure of faith is given to us when obedience is required, while the gift of faith is given to us to endure challenges until God brings forth a matter. Trust results in obedience and assurance becomes an avenue in which the gift of faith has freedom to see something through to the end, knowing God never lies or reneges on His Word or a promise.

What we need to recognize is that even our faith comes from above. One of the first things I had to learn about faith is that I did not have any real faith and that it comes from God when I needed it. Each type of faith always begins with me believing God and His Word. I have to believe the Word about what it says about the character of God and believe that God said it, therefore, it is established in stone as being so.

Faith is our shield for a reason; therefore, I had to, by faith, face the giants head on, as well as any mountains and tsunamis before me, while avoiding looking for that which would fit into my finite, intellectual understanding or to the horizon for the answer to my challenge. I had to train myself to always look up to the only One who could really solve the problem. When challenged, my belief must translate into choosing to believe God and His Word regardless of circumstances and feelings, which involves the will. Once the determination is there to trust the Lord, I must count everything else as being insignificant, focus ahead and walk out what has been set before me.

Today there is much darkness upon us and many lying voices and endless rhetoric bombarding us. Fear is causing many to faint, while others are raging, and some are falling into a puddle of hopelessness. As believers, we must not allow the circumstances to cause fear or hopelessness; rather, we have the light of God's truth to walk through the present darkness until we reach the light. Author Jerry Sittser summarized it best, "The quickest way for anyone to reach the sun and the light of day is not to run west, chasing after the setting sun, but to head east, plunging into the darkness until one comes to the sunrise."

Yesterday I mentioned the measure of faith. To measure something is to make sure the right proportion is given in order to ensure the right results. A good illustration of this are miracles. Faith and miracles walk hand in hand. God's miracles are measured according to the need. For example, God parted the Red Sea for the children of Israel to cross through, while He gave Peter permission to walk on water through stormy waves. Imagine if you switch these two miracles around, they would prove to be impractical.

God is practical and simply brings forth the extraordinary and miraculous according to the need, but always in surprising ways that create awe. However, in a time where people have been entertained with unrealistic sensationalism, they are looking for God to part the obstacle of the Red Sea for a few instead of realizing God will always call the few to walk on water.

The other aspect of miracles is that people want God to prove Himself by performing some intervention before believing rather than believing that God is and can do it if it is according to His will. Such faith allows Him to be God and move according to who He is to confirm the person's faith towards Him. We can see this example in *John 4:45-54* when Jesus did His second miracle.

A nobleman saw what Jesus did at the first miracle and believed, and came to Him to ask Him to heal his son. Jesus confirmed the nobleman's faith by healing His son, but not before speaking about those that seek the proof of signs and wonders. He later referred to these individuals as being part of a wicked generation.

A good example of one who sought a sign was Herod who wanted Christ to entertain Him with a miracle on the night He was betrayed. People like Herod have no intention of believing that God is who He says He is. Unbelief demands God "earn" trust by proving He is God, and anytime a person demands proof before they believe God, they will never be satisfied with one miracle. They will inevitably demand God to ever be the performer that will serve personal, self-serving benefits to continually earn their "trust." Needless to say, this is opposite of faith that is best defined in *Hebrews 11:1, "Now faith is the substance of things hoped for, the evidence of things not seen."*

Faith is not inspired by what we see but who we believe, and when it comes to God, we choose to believe that He is and is a rewarder of those who diligently seek Him for Himself and not some sign *(Hebrews 11:6)*.

The next time you need God's intervention, avoid looking for Him to part the Red Sea, which would allow you to walk on dry ground; instead, be prepared to listen for His voice to see if He is calling you to walk on water.

One of the great lessons of faith towards God is that until it ceases to be our last option in facing a matter, and it actually becomes our first choice in seeking God's will, we will never really benefit from it. Faith in its innocence can receive something such as forgiveness and eternal life, but for it to grow it must be challenged to let go of worldly solutions in order to look beyond personal fears, preferences, and desires to that which is eternal for real wisdom, guidance, and the right results. Faith ultimately trusts God with the end results, knowing He will work out details for His glory and our benefit.

Faith does not move us against our will; rather, it allows God to be God and becomes the avenue in which we can witness, embrace, or experience God's faithfulness, power, and abiding care in our lives. Many times, people will say "I trust God with this matter, but...." Wherever there is a "but" inserted into a situation, that is when the person is admitting they are not going to seek God's will because they want to have it their way according to their will. In some cases where people want their way, God might not even take issue with it, but, and there is that "but" again they don't want to seek Him just in case He might throw a wrench into their plans.

Sadly, people hijack the concept of faith, hide behind the word "faith", or use it as a screen to justify their fear, unbelief, and independence in order to have their life on their terms at that time. In most cases, we get away with our faith remaining weak in certain areas, our determination to do it our way intact, and our will firmly in place to carry out personal preferences, maintain any wishful thinking, hold to silly notions towards the quality of our faith, and hide behind a type of ignorance that comes from self-delusion. However, we need to be honest as to whether we are walking according to faith towards God.

If we are not walking by faith towards God and His promises, we can't be assured that we are where God wants us to be, and that in the end He will be able to bless us in a beneficial way that will ultimately bring glory to Him. We need to be honest with ourselves that as soon as we use the word "but" in relationship to faith and obedience, we need to stop ourselves and examine what is behind that "but." Is it fear, unbelief, some type of self-delusion, or independence? Until we honestly determine our point of unbelief, we will not be able to commit our way to Him, nor surrender our will to His will to bring Him the proper glory He deserves.

As believers we are called to walk in the light. But, what does this mean? As stated, there are different lights operating in this world. There is the natural light which represents our understanding of matters. It is natural to walk according to our idea of reality, whether it is reality or not. Jesus warned that what may seem like light to us is in fact spiritual darkness that will end in our spiritual ruin.

We can walk according to the philosophies or enlightenment of this present age, but they prove contrary to God's Word and will end in destruction. We can walk according to some religious creed but such creeds can't lead us through the great storms and challenges of life without bringing us to dead ends where nothing will make sense. Or, we can walk by faith.

God is light but what many fail to realize is that God's light becomes darkness to carnal understanding, formidable to the fearful and unbelieving, and foolish to the intellectual skeptic. It is for this reason the faith walk does not walk according to what it sees because in most cases the faith walk is exercised and enlarged when being tested by the formidable darkness that is consuming the terrain of our soul.

Faith walks according to what it knows about God. It grabs a hold of His Word as being true while holding on to hope that has been grounded on what has been promised. Its steps of expectation put trust in the assurance that God guides our steps through the most difficult terrain in order to lead us to havens of rest in storms, to the clefts of the rock when the winds are raging, and to places of refuge when weary and overwhelmed.

Right now, darkness is totally engulfing the age in which we live, presenting a great opportunity for our faith to be tested, enlarged, and refined as we hold to what we know is true, sure, and righteous.

It is easy to romanticize the idea of faith moving mountains, to cling to wishful thinking that faith is a magic wand that will miraculously set us above the storms, or that we can conjure it up to part any Rea Sea, but the truth is the way of faith is chosen at the darkest point in order to walk through the greatest storm.

Faith is developed in storms as one take steps of trust that God is leading him and her up the paths of righteousness in obedience. Obedience in the right spirit constantly proves for the believer that it is the only natural way of a matter in the faith walk because nothing else makes sense except to do what is right.

Years ago, a missionary's faith walk inspired me to tell the Lord that I wanted to learn what it meant to walk by true faith. I had no idea what I was in for, but I knew it was in my heart to experience God. From the missionary's testimony, I realized if I wanted to see God part the Rea Seas, calm the storms, and move the mountains that the different obstacles had to be present. The problem is I had romantic notions that when the test came that my faith was great enough to endure. However, when the challenges came, I realized I did not have faith; rather, I had romantic notions about faith and worldly options that gave me a way out just in case God failed.

The first lesson I learned on my faith walk is that my first response to my first test was to choose to believe that God is God and sitting on the throne regardless of what I am facing. This meant I could not let the fear initially created by the challenge define my reality or response, I had to choose to believe His Word. Faith comes by hearing and hearing by the Word of God.

The next lesson is that it is God who gives me the measure of faith to walk through the challenge, but I must step into it from the premise of child-like trust in obedience to walk in what I know is true. The third lesson is that it is God who parts the seas, moves the mountains, and calm the storms, and not our faith. Our faith simply allows Him to be God in a matter. These are simple lessons, but it is easy to fail the test at the initial point where we fail to choose the way of faith by choosing to believe that GOD IS.

I have acquired many precious nuggets along the way. One of those nuggets I have obtained is that genuine, abiding faith is never found on the surface, only in deep dark places of testing and adversity. Faith has different stages.

There is that infant stage of faith where you simply believe the Gospel and as a result you are born anew. The next stage is the crawling stage where you begin to experience the liberty of truth as you learn about the Christian faith. From the crawling stage you learn to stand on the truth of God's Word in order to balance yourself and from there one learns to walk by faith in simple obedience as he or she puts his or her focus on Jesus.

The next stage is the marathon where one must learn to run the race of faith through the challenging terrain of this world. This is where faith is tested, enlarged, and refined as precious gold. It is in the race that believers learn the disciplines of faith as they must endure like a good soldier in order to stay the course while maintaining the integrity of faith to see a matter through until they gain the prize.

The challenge for some Christians is that they come so far in their faith experience, but then fail to finish the course because of the challenges that confront them. They may learn to crawl, stand, and even take some steps of faith, but they fail to run the course because it may seem too uncertain, too long, and they do not have the vision to see the finish line and the prize.

Genuine faith trusts that the course set before a person will guide their steps to the finish line, which is heaven in order to gain the ultimate prize, and that is the Lord Jesus Christ in all of His glory.

One of the challenges of a Christian is to simply let things be. Some people are so busy trying to direct lives and events they become frustrated and miserable when their expectations crash land as others refuse to fall into line with the roles they are to act out, while circumstances continue to impede the mental script.

I have watched these so-called "directors" become bitter as guilt and regrets take hold of their life because their attempts often leave an unpleasant fallout that produce fruits of failure, bitterness, and anger. People who can't let things be never learn to enjoy what is. The treasures of life often pass them by because these people are all caught up with seeing their idea for their life play out to their specifications instead of being able to recognize the blessings before them.

The truth of the matter is, life is not another Hollywood that rarely deals in reality, and it never plays according to anyone's scripts. Life is what it is and it is only by accepting the reality of it that people can be liberated from unrealistic expectations and find the beauty of it. The things that bring us the most joy are those things that are often spontaneous, genuine, and pure. The faith walk does not immune us from the challenges and sorrows of life; rather, it enables us to walk in expectation of the real hope that awaits us beyond this world.

The one quality I appreciate about faith is that it accepts what is in life in order to embrace the truth and beauty that can be found in the gift of life. We know that the center of our faith is the Lord, the inspiration of faith is the joy that has been set before us, and the expectation of faith is that my life may not be according to some script on earth, but it is according to God's heavenly plan.

I don't know about you, but I can't count the times that I tried to jump in the middle of something to try to make sure it worked out the way I thought it should. After all, I told myself I just wanted to see everyone happy and at peace with one another, and I knew that under my "expert" direction it would all come together just as I had imagined. At times, I must admit I even became giddy over the possibilities of how it would all work out and how I would look and feel in the end.

I later learned that my notions were fantasy at best, silly at the least, and self-serving at the most. It is natural to want to fix things, but we often get in the way of what needs to happen for something to be fixed. I had to learn that any personal involvement on my part into matters that were not my business or beyond my abilities simply revealed a lack of faith towards the only one who can fix it, the Lord.

Faith is a walk but it is not a walk through the park; rather, it is a walk through the challenges of the world. Faith does not make us immune from the trials of the world, but it enables each of us, as believers, to endure them to the end where our deliverance awaits, because genuine faith is grounded in who the Lord is and not in what He does.

My walk of faith has proved to be adventurous but the one lesson I had to constantly remind myself of, and when required, relearn, is that I simply need to let things be to allow God to be God in a matter. It is not my faith that moves the mountains; rather, it is genuine faith that chooses to trust God to move, rearrange, or show me a way through or around each mountain.

Hebrews 11:6 summarizes it best, *"But without faith it is impossible to please him: for he that cometh to God must believe that he is, and that he is a rewarder of them that diligently seek him."*

An evangelist once told me that people love to get excited about the fruits and victory of the Gospel, but few want to consider the walk that brings them to a place of witnessing such glorious results. It is important to point out that this same evangelist had witnessed thousands of people coming to Christ in such places as India and South America.

It is true we want to hop over obstacles with expectation towards seeing great moves of God, while skipping the test of our faith and then jumping the Grand Canyon to great victory instead of taking steps of obedience to come to the place of overcoming.

We cannot lead people any further than we have come. If we are not willing to experience the challenges that build personal character and endure testing that refines and enlarges our faith, how can we possibly lead others up the narrow paths that will test every aspect of their character to a place where their faith endures until victory comes?

It's true that other people's faith walk will inspire us and their victories will cause our hope to soar, but as the Apostle Paul reminds us in *Romans 5:1-5, "Therefore being justified by faith, we have peace with God through our Lord Jesus Christ: By whom also we have access by faith into this grace wherein we stand, and rejoice in hope of the glory of God. And not only so, but we glory in tribulations also: knowing that tribulation worketh patience; And patience, experience; and experience, hope: And hope maketh not ashamed; because the love of God is shed abroad in our hearts by the Holy Ghost which is given unto us."*

Do you have true faith? Jesus asked this question in *Luke 18:8* in regard to His coming. There are various presentations of faith from formulas and methods that are aimed to control God and claim promises without meeting Biblical conditions. However, faith is not a formula or method but a doctrine that puts it into the camp of properly applying it in obedience to our Christian walk *(Hebrews 6:1, 2)*.

Active faith ensures right standing with the Lord, for what is done in faith and by faith is counted for righteousness or as being righteous, and will prove pleasing to God *(Hebrews 11:6)*. Faith is not something we conjure up. It begins with a choice to believe God's Word and will act upon it with child-like confidence. After all, God said it and I believe it for it is so *(Romans 10:17)*.

Once we choose to believe, we are given a measure of faith by God to walk a matter out, trusting that God will take care of the details *(Romans 12:3)*.

It is natural for believers to want great faith, but I have learned that real faith abides in confidence in light of a great God, who will be faithful, just, and perfect in all He does. In other words, true faith allows God to be God.

In *Hebrews 11:13* we are given special insight into genuine faith. First, faith has the ability to see beyond this world to the next. It is the spiritual eyesight of faith that we are to walk by in this present age and not by what we see happening around us or understand.

Faith walks according to the promises given by God and not by the circumstances that looms before the person. To faith the unseen world is more real than the physical world that is temporary and under judgment. Faith does not take stock in the logic of the present predominate philosophy but in the hope of the next.

Faith inspires the soul to not faint when the storms and challenges become too great and causes the heart to live in expectation that the present is temporary and that the eternity awaiting every believer is forever.

When people talk about the Old Testament and the New Testament, they point out that the Old Testament is about judgment while the New Testament is about grace. However, God never changes. The God of the Old Testament is full of grace and the God of the New Testament is still holy and Judge of all, and His wrath still abides on children of disobedience.

The difference between the Old and New Testament is that God in the New Testament simply put a face on grace. We are told in *John 1:16, 17* which states, *"And of his fulness have all we received, and grace for grace. For the law was given by Moses, but grace and truth came by Jesus Christ."*

Jesus Christ is the face of grace in the New Testament, but God's grace has always served as an avenue in which man could experience the promises and blessings of God, and the reason I know this is because of the one statement that is made in *Genesis 5:8, "But Noah found grace in the eyes of the LORD."*

The reason Noah found grace is the same reason we can experience His grace in Jesus, because of faith. We walk by faith and not by personal understanding and we are told that Noah walked with God in *Genesis 5:9*, and *Hebrews 11:7* tells us he was a man of faith. We know that acts of obedience that come out of faith are accounted to us by God as being righteous, and it is through righteousness that grace reigns *(Romans 5:21)*.

Last night we lost our electricity for a few hours, water too, and our internet for the rest of the night and a good part of today. We are so dependent on the systems of this world! I would like to say I have such an awareness of my dependency on the Lord as much as I have on these systems. We take for granted what we have and do not realize how much we are dependent on them until we are without them.

Sadly, we are unaware that we desperately need the Lord, and we are not always aware of whether He is present in a situation. We can assume, presume, and wish He was, but the real issue is, is He in a situation or have we left Him behind to do our own thing.

I often examine my attitude to see if I'm walking in some presumption about my relationship with the Lord, as well as see if I'm giving way to any assumption that what I'm doing in "His name" is acceptable to Him. I can't tell you how many times I must pull myself back to what is true (His Word) and right (His Spirit).

The systems of the world have one goal and that is to replace any dependency we have on God with dependency on it as far as seeking our purpose, happiness, and finding our potential. It wants each of us to serve it with great devotion and ultimately bow down before it as we worship the god of this world, Satan.

We can't afford to be flippant about where our dependency rests. It is easy to assume that we are dependent on the Lord, but it is only when we are tested in personal storms that we find out just how dependent we are. I remember when my faith was first tested in an obvious way. I was shocked to find out I had none and that it was only as I looked to Him that I was given a necessary measure of faith to walk through and out of the storm.

True faith has spiritual eyesight that looks beyond this world because it is persuaded that a matter is so. When you think about the word "persuaded," what comes to mind? Persuaded is the opposite of being fickle and uncertain about a matter. The words associated with persuaded are "convinced" and "converted."

Believers who walk by faith are persuaded that everything God says and all His promises are true. There is no shred of doubt in their understanding that a matter is already so even if they have not seen it. In fact, they have such confidence in it that they are actually "converted" to walk in it and to walk it out.

Conversion has to do with transformation. These people's lives and minds have been transformed by what has been promised by God and it has become embedded in what they look for and what they know they will see.

The breakdown for some Christians in their walk before the Lord comes down to being persuaded that what God has said and promised is true, converting them in how they see a matter and what they look for. I am not almost persuaded that what God says is true, causing me to take on an attitude of waiting "to see more evidence until I am finally converted," because there will never be enough evidence to silence fleshly skepticism.

I am persuaded because of who God is; therefore, choosing to believe He is not a liar. The result is I have been converted by what He has declared and promised.

Persuasion entails our thinking process. When one is in a debate or standing in a courtroom, the orators are trying to persuade the listeners that a matter is so, but when you look at the next word that is used to describe the faith walk of the saints in *Hebrews 11:13* it is the word "embraced."

Once a person is persuaded that something is true, then they will embrace it which points to believing it or reckoning it as being so, and where do we reckon a matter as being so? We reckon it in our will area by choosing to believe it.

Many people can agree with a matter, but do they believe or embrace it as truth that must be instituted in their very walk? Facts are tangible, but a truth must be received by faith in the heart as being so. At such a point there are no debates about whether truth is truth. Truth will never bow down to personal realities, making us comfortable in our present fantasy, and it will go against the grain of our future hope to make such reality adjust to our way of thinking. We can reject, refuse, and rage against truth but as *2 Corinthians 13:8 reminds us, "For we can do nothing against the truth, but for the truth."*

The final word associated with the faith described in *Hebrews 11:13* is "confessed." In *Romans 10:9* we are told that we must confess with our mouth the Lord Jesus. What does it mean to confess? Is it a simple verbal acknowledgement or does it entail more?

We often just think this word has to do with a verbal confession, but true confession entails more than a verbal declaration. When you look up the word "confession" it has three main aspects to it. The first one is we confess a matter is true. To confess something that is not true is a type of fraud and a point of betrayal to one's character and reputation.

The second aspect of confession is that it is associated with a deep conviction of FACTS. Our faith is not blind because it is based on facts that can be considered and reasoned out as to whether they can be verified and are consistent as to what is known to be true. Facts do not verify a matter is true; rather, truth testifies whether facts are truly lining up to what is obvious and so.

The final aspect of confessing something has to do with acknowledging one's allegiance as to who his or her master and lord is. A person's master and lord will determine who he or she is faithfully worshipping and serving. When we confess that Jesus is Lord, we are declaring who we belong to, who we will believe at all times, who we worship, and who we will serve.

Do you know walking by faith will always lead you into the unknown? I remember hearing an evangelist speak about his adventures in Russia six years before the iron curtain came down. As I listened to God's glorious, miraculous intervention on his behalf, I realized that the miraculous happened because he was walking by faith, trusting God to get him where he needed to be under incredible circumstances. I also recognized that the evangelist had a greater witness of the Lord because of his faith walk and I remember thinking, I want to obtain a greater witness of the Lord, but I knew I had to be willing to walk through the unknown, choosing to trust Him with the outcome.

I decided at that time in my church pew that I did not want to settle for experiencing God's intervention when in the middle of some trial, but

I wanted to walk by faith in the calling I felt He was putting on my heart to witness Him moving the mountains of obstacles out of the way in order for the calling to be fulfilled in my life.

I want to stress that everyone has a different calling, but I realized at the time mine was changing and I was being called out to the harvest field of the world. I did not know how it would translate but I knew the only way I was going to experience God's incredible intervention was by stepping out by faith into the unknown and trusting God that He would bring me to that which He had planned for me.

I have to admit some of my adventures proved to be a bit unnerving, but the Lord never failed to get me where I needed to be, while showing Himself capable of doing the practical and the miraculous in such wonderful ways.

Is the Lord bringing you to greater points of reliance? I never fully realized that my reliance was on what I thought I knew; that is, on my strength, and/or on the world until I started to walk by faith. When I started the new adventure of walking by faith I was willing to work in society, but He instructed me that He would provide for me financially because He wanted me available.

I began to write in order to fulfill a vision He had given me, but found that my writing was capable of driving a sane person insane. I wanted to be about His business, but I was confused about what it was. My co-laborer in the Gospel and I looked for open doors and only found small windows that we could crawl through, but never seemed to produce lasting fruit.

It was through the initial testing of my faith that I found that I did not rely on the Lord for my provision and that I trusted in what I thought I knew to get me around and out of situations. I also learned that the Lord had to prepare me while I learned to wait for doors to open.

My biggest struggle was simply letting God be God by trusting Him to be the God of the Bible. As I looked back at my life, I could see how He had been preparing me to take the steps into the unknown so He could create a greater reliance on Him in preparation to fulfill my calling and potential.

Rayola Kelley

There were many small steps but one of the biggest steps took place on the back of a Goldwing 1000 Motorcycle. I looked at all the things I possessed in order to enjoy life and realized that none of it added to my life from an eternal perspective. At the time I told the Lord, "If I can't serve you, take me home right now."

On that day at that time, I consecrated myself and within a year my world was turned upside down and I was being ushered into an unknown world to walk my life out by faith, to realize my calling, and reach my potential.

In what way does the Lord want to use you? It is natural to want to give God options as to how we think He should use us. After all, we perceive we know what is best for us, but the reality is what we consider as right for us is often based on what we would like to see happen, what we are comfortable with, or what we can control so that we can ensure we come out looking a certain way. However, our ways are not God's ways and our thoughts are not God thoughts.

We see from a limited plain and He sees from an eternal perspective. He often has to take us out of our comfort zones in order to use us. The reason for such a maneuver is that all matters done in His kingdom will be according to His Spirit and not personal strength. The Lord must place us in the uncomfortable places so we will fling ourselves on Him.

I remember when I first started my faith walk that He took me out of every comfort zone I had ever known to bring me to places where I would trust Him to prepare me to take the next step into unknown terrain. I cannot begin to describe the different, strange challenges that I encountered along the way. There to meet me at every unknown turn was fear to test my resolve to advance forward, to paralyze any waning trust, and to drive me back into my comfort zones to lick my sense of failures with silly excuses.

It took a while for me to realize that my faith walk was not about me trying to conjure up faith; rather, it was my opportunity to let God be God so that He could show Himself faithful and mighty on my behalf. It was at such times He enlarged my faith to take greater steps into the unknown to experience not only His power to ensure the end results, but His faithfulness to see me through to the end.

An evangelist once said that people see the end results of faith because it allows God to show Himself mighty in certain situations, but few know about the different challenges or trials that come with the steps of faith that lead to that moment of greatness on God's part.

Romans 12:3 tells us, we must respond according to the measure of faith given us to carry out a particular matter. Such faith is not placed in God based on what He can do; rather, it is placed on who God is, trusting that He knows how to bring about His plan for the benefit of those involved and His glory.

Sometimes the measure of faith He gives us seems small but I have discovered that such a measure gives us the front row seat to see His greatness. I remember a time when we knew we needed a new vehicle but we had no money and the pickup I had was fairly new and in nice condition but I was aware that it had depreciated greatly in value.

We went to the car dealership where the manager was a cousin of our friend. We were thinking big (a van), but the manager caused us to think on a more practical plane (a station wagon). Jeannette was a stickler for American cars, but the Lord challenged her to think outside of the limitations she had put on herself before going to the car dealership. We ended up with a choice between two station wagons.

The American built station wagon was in bad shape but a Japanese made station wagon seemed perfect in every way. We realized that the Japanese car had a great resale and I sat there wondering what was God's plan? Jeannette than told me that God gave her the amount we were to spend on the car along with the trade in of the pickup. I asked her the amount and when I heard it, I said, "No way is that going to happen." The amount she was given was $20.00. I shook my head and waited. The manager came out of his office and began to name off all that was included in the sale, which included sales tax. As I held my breath, he said you owe us $14.77!

God often uses small things to reveal His ability to work out the impossible. So regardless of how small your faith is in order to stand, remember if your faith is as a grain of mustard seed, it will allow God to move mountains.

Is the main pursuit of your faith walk to discover the Lord? It is not unusual for Christians to put their faith in theology, church affiliation, religious leaders, good works, experiences, and an assortment of other religious activities. However, such misdirected faith turns out to be "wishful thinking", which is not directed at the one who can move mountains of challenges, knock down giant obstacles, quiet the raging storms in souls, still the contrary winds of life, or save your soul.

Misdirected faith will eventually face some type of crises that will either bring the person to the realization his or her faith is a pseudo faith and that it needs to be directed towards God, or causes the individual to walk away from God altogether in total unbelief. We are to walk by faith towards God because of who He is and a faith that fails to cause a person to walk towards the God of the Bible is a pseudo faith.

Unfeigned faith is not something we conjure up; rather it is something we choose to walk towards and in the ways of God through obedience to His Word. Such a walk does not entail becoming more religious; rather, it will end with us having a greater confidence in the Lord because we have discovered that His abiding faithfulness is the attribute that reminds us He will never leave or forsake us.

Do you have an enduring faith? *Hebrews 6:11-12* tells us, *"And we desire that every one of you do shew the same diligence to the full assurance of hope unto the end: That ye be not slothful, but followers of them who through faith and patience inherit the promises."*

When I officially started my faith walk I did so with the desire to see God move in a mighty way, but I did not realize that my faith would have to be brought to some type of crisis before I would be prepared to see His intervention.

I had romantic notions about such a walk, but it did not take long for the crisis of my faith to knock such notions down. I did not understand that when it came to faith, hope was the key, not some sentimental nonsense that harbor at best wishful thinking. Hope in faith is that expectation that what God has said in His Word is so and I am to walk in light of that expectation happening.

Faith without expectation will not endure the crisis that will come to all those who are trying to stand in storms. The purpose for crisis in our faith is to enlarge it to endure the next challenge.

As we stand in the storm or challenge, we are given the measure of faith and as we withstand, we are given the gift of faith. And, as we continue to stand we are given the assurance of faith that will enable us to endure so that we can see the promises of God brought to fruition.

RIGHTEOUSNESS & OBEDIENCE

Faith towards God is the choice of the will,
trust is the preference of the wisdom of the intellect,
and assurance is the place where all
undisciplined emotions have landed
on the pathway of righteousness.
(Rayola Kelley)

Are you benefitting from the total work of salvation? *Philippians 2:12* tells us to work out our salvation with fear and trembling. I must state that salvation is a gift, but like any gift it is not meant to be left in some neat package; rather, it must be used.

Working out our salvation simply means to work in the life of Christ. Believers all start from the premise of believing God about their need for salvation and receiving Christ as Lord and Savior. To identify or seal us to salvation, God gives us the gift of the Holy Spirit. We must allow the Holy Spirit to work Jesus' life in us by submitting to His sanctifying work.

Submission is giving way to that which is worthy of consideration. Once the Spirit begins the work of imparting new life to us, we must work it out through obedience to God's Word. Such obedience is also a matter of faith, *"Faith comes by hearing, and hearing by the Word of God"* *(Romans 10:17).*

As we can see each response on our part is a matter of faith, and as noted God must either give us a gift of faith or a measure of faith to walk in this new life *(Romans 12:3; 1 Corinthians 12:7-10; 2 Corinthians 5:7).* To "believe" is a matter of receiving the gift of salvation. It has the same implication behind it as saying "Amen."

"Amen" points to that which has already been established as being true in heaven, but it must still be worked out on earth; therefore, once a matter is established as being true it is "Amen, so be it, for it is so."

Such faith points to trust that will stand because a matter is so, withstand because of being backed up by the authority of heaven, and continue to stand because of ever-lasting promises. The question is, are we allowing, assimilating, and activating the life of Christ in and out of us by faith through obedience to God's Word?

When I first started out on my Christian journey, I was zealous about being saved. The freedom I experienced was so precious to my soul after being weighed down from the burden of sin, I wanted the world to know about this great freedom. I felt myself flying high with such ecstasy. However, as with all honeymoons, the excitement wore off and I had to face the fact that Christianity is not a sensational trapeze act filled with ongoing adventure, but a life that must be lived out in the valleys of this age.

This life must find eternal purpose in everyday drudgery, inspiration in great darkness, hope when the blanket of depression weighs heavily upon the soul, and endurance when the storms come. If we as believers are to successfully live this life, we must learn how to bodily walk in this world, while keeping our hearts open and pure towards God in the midst of skepticism, our minds uncluttered and filled with the truth when the voices of propaganda are bombarding us from every direction, our souls prepared to face the uncertainty of the age, and our spirit free of worldly concerns so that we can soar on the currents of the Spirit to gain His perspective.

This may sound like a balancing act but the key to walking the Christian walk is to keep our focus on Christ. At times He will become hidden, and when He does, that is when we each must choose to stay on the path of Scriptural obedience and allow it to guide our steps until we come to the place where the light once again dawns upon our weary souls.

⤙⤚

What do you rely on to get on top of a matter: God or your intellect? My initial years of the Christian life was about trying to figure out how to be a good Christian rather than being a Christian by exercising godliness.

We make Christianity about us and our attempts of trying to be good, rather than giving way to the work of God by simply obeying what we know to be Scripturally right. I realized that what it came down to was our trying to logic out the Christian life instead of living it according to Scriptural instruction and example. It is for this reason that God never uses the term "logic," in Scripture only the term "reasoning" because His ways and thoughts are higher than our comprehension.

When God reasons with us, He never brings us to a point of progression in our understanding, but one of regression so we can receive His evaluation of a matter with child-like faith. We see this when it comes to sin in *Isaiah 1:18*. The truth is, real reasoning goes beyond man's logic.

Logic is man's way of substantiating what he has already deemed as true, while reasoning is God's way of bringing one to an understanding. Logic deems all that it cannot grasp as foolishness, but reasoning declares there is always more to discover about a matter, but it takes child-like faith to see and receive it.

This is what *Matthew 18:2-4* states, "*Verily I say unto you, Except ye be converted, and become as little children, ye shall not enter into the kingdom of heaven. Whosoever therefore shall humble himself as this little child, the same is greatest in the kingdom of heaven.*"

⤙⤚

One of the misunderstandings is the role "obedience" plays in our salvation. I have often mentioned *Hebrews 5:9* about how Jesus in His humanity was made perfect through obedience and as a result became the author of eternal salvation UNTO ALL THEM THAT OBEY HIM.

When you mention "obedience" there are those who say you can't earn your salvation. I totally agree, but "obedience" has nothing to do with earning salvation; rather, it is a natural response of love, faith, and expectation. *Hebrews 6:9* is clear that there are those things that accompany salvation. Notice the word "accompanying." Accompanying has nothing to do with earning anything; rather, it is like a supplementary that follows, confirms, explains, and serves as a form of manifestation of what exists or has been presented. Remember, it was Jesus who said if you love me, you will obey me.

James 2 tells us if our faith is not exercised in obedience, it will prove lifeless. Paul tells us to work out our salvation in fear and trembling. Faith operates in three arenas. The first arena is understanding.

Faith reveals and confirms in our spirit the truth about a matter so that we can believe that it is so. In fact, that is where the word "amen" comes from. It means "I believe it is so, so be it." The second arena has to do with receiving it as truth. We can intellectually agree that something is true, but if we do not receive it in our hearts as a conviction we must live by, then it will have no effect on our lives. The third arena is obedience.

Obedience is a natural response of genuine faith. If a matter is so, then it must be true and I must line up to it and live according to it. My response may be labeled obedience, but to me it is the least I can do out of love for my Lord, the natural response of a godly heart conviction, and the right response according to my faith towards the Lord. In a sense, my right response is a manifestation of my conversion towards the ways of righteousness.

A Christian's obedience should never be labeled or mistaken as a way to earn brownie points or salvation, but a natural loving response of faith towards what is true, right, and acceptable to our Lord.

Painting my office was one of my spring cleaning projects. I know how to paint but I forgot the method that I used to do an efficient job. I had to remember the method of the past to relearn what I needed to do to if the job was to come out right.

It is easy to assume that something you did in the past will automatically work as before. It's like riding a bike after many years. Yes, you can get back on it and start to ride it, but then you realize you've lost your familiarity with the actual experience of riding it, and so crashing or falling can easily happen. The truth is we must regularly do something in order to maintain the most productive procedure, or method of doing it, or we will find ourselves having to do some relearning as we discover that we're now unfamiliar with it.

This is true for God's Word. It is not enough to know it, we must daily practice what it says through obedience to make sure we maintain its effectiveness in our lives. Past experiences with God are great, but present application of God's Word is what makes it living, applicable, and beneficial for our lives and the times we live in.

A word we can become confused about is "holiness." Holiness points to being set apart. God is holy and we are to be holy if we are going to see the Lord, but what does that mean? Holiness has to do with purity, which is hard for us to grasp in our fallen condition and world. (See *Matthew 5:8, Hebrews 12:14* and *1 Peter 1:15-16*.)

Holiness is complete transparency that can be consuming fire to that which is profane and purifying to that which is exposed to its intense light. Some will say holiness is impossible, but the Lord would not command something if it was impossible, and there are those who try to be holy in their own power, but often end up taking on a cloak of self-righteousness that makes them judgmental, cruel, and tyrannical.

For the saint (a person set apart), holiness becomes a state where he or she is pliable in God's hands to ensure pure motives that keeps him or her responsive to His ways to maintain the integrity of actions. The main goal or intent of a saint being set apart is to please God by doing His will. Such a state begins with humility, a type of consecration, which is an ACT of holiness.

This is where one sets self apart so God can have His way. Humility will take on an attitude of righteousness as the person gives way to the WORK of holiness, which is sanctification that is done by the Holy Spirit. The complete work of holiness, the ACT (consecration) of being set apart or the WORK (sanctification) of being set apart by the Holy Spirit is for the purpose of bringing forth the image of Christ in and through us so that we will stand separate from this world in attitude, conduct, service, and worship.

What have you done with opportunities? There are a couple of things I have learned about opportunities: 1) they are not always obvious, 2) they present a small opening in which we have to take advantage of before the door is closed to us, and 3) when they come, we are not given days, hours, and minutes to take advantage of them but mere moments.

Every spiritual opportunity that has come to me, came by way of crossroads in my life. It has become clear that we do not carve out opportunities for ourselves like those of the world unless we are willing to sell our soul along the way; rather, as Christians, we are brought to a crossroad where we are given a slight glimpse into the opportunity that lays before us.

Opportunities influence our decisions and decisions determine the way we will walk. I remember the moment I was given choices as to where I would begin my new Christian walk. I wanted to go one way, but I also wanted to please God so I admitted my dilemma, and He graciously revealed the way He prepared for me that which was contrary to my way. I submitted to it and walked in it, and I must say I have never regretted it.

I can tell you the time He invited me to sit at His table of fellowship. I wanted to be about what I thought was His business and He wanted me to sit at His table and learn of Him. At that moment I chose to sit at His table and have been satisfied ever sense.

There was the time I consecrated my life to Him on the back of a motorcycle after seeing the vanity of this life. The life I knew went up in the air, but ultimately, I found my life in Christ.

There was another time that after working hard to promote our ministry, I was faced with watching it in the throes of "death", to be hidden away in a "grave" from all, but I embraced it because I knew greater fruit would come forth.

Spiritual opportunities afford us a moment where we can catch glimpses into eternity and if we choose to walk in light of the glimpses we receive, we will end up possessing heavenly treasures. It is easy to waste time. Each year passes us by, days get by us without much happening, and minutes slip by through various activities, but let us note the moments when opportunity meets us at some crossroad, giving us a quick glimpse into God's heart, mind, and will for our lives.

It is hard for people to realize that what they give into will become their master unless you study people like Cain and take it to heart. Consider what the Lord said to Cain in *Genesis 4:7, "If thou doest well, shalt thou not be accepted? And if thou doest not well, sin lieth at the door. And unto thee shall be his desire, and thou shalt rule over him."* The Lord was telling Cain that if he did what was right by offering the correct offering, it would go well for him, but if he failed to pull himself back from his wrong attitude that sin was waiting at his door to take him captive, and in the end his desires/emotions would end up ruling over him.

Under such rule, Cain would become a man out of control, defined by his desires. We know what happened. He would let his anger rule and as a result, he became the first murderer and ended up being a spiritual vagabond. As I have stated before, "Cain was the first man to built a city, but he had to leave the presence of the Lord to do so."

We all become Cain's at times when we want to nurse a right to feel jealous, offended, or angry, but we must not let the sun go down on such feelings, because darkness will give them the necessary cover to take root. We must quickly become reasonable and agree with the Lord about what is right and acceptable and then DO IT.

Jesus said, *"Blessed are those who hunger and thirst after righteousness."* I have spoken about desperation in past posts. Desperation is brought on by great need. The more needy we become, the more our desperation level grows. Humanity is in great need of salvation, but those who do not possess the eternal life of Jesus do not realize it. Such people often lean back on their laurels of good works, personal piousness, or wishful thinking to silence any spiritual hunger and thirst.

The one thing I have learned from the physical realm is that one must develop a taste for the spiritual. How many of you drink enough water, this does not include tea, coffee, or pop? How many of you eat the right foods, which will exclude junk food? Through the years, I had to change much of my drinking and eating habits due to gluten intolerance and allergies to such foods as onions and eggs. I had to discipline my food preferences and taste buds in order to acquire a thirst for water and a taste for the right foods.

This is also true for the things of God. We must discipline ourselves enough to acquire a taste for them so that we will hunger and thirst after them in desperation to satisfy our soul and spirit with righteousness. The acceptable and spiritual diets and pursuits of today have sadly left many feeling spiritually miserable, dissatisfied, anemic, and malnutrition.

It is clear that in God's Kingdom a certain spiritual diet will not meet everyone's needs and for this reason it is up to each of us to acquire the necessary taste for that which is pure and needful for our spiritual maintenance and growth.

Are you thirsting after righteousness? *Amos 8:11-12* tells that there will be a famine in the land, not a famine of bread, nor a thirst for water, but of hearing the words of the Lord. Clearly, people are seeking for something as they run here and there to find it, but they are not sure of what they are looking for. They see streams in the wilderness, only to find they are foul. They hear of cisterns only to discover they are broken and worthless.

As Christians, we must avoid the traps and foul waters of this age. The challenge for each of us is that we must not come near the poison waters of heresy because it tickles our ears with "positive New Age" lies. We must avoid the contaminated waters of the philosophies of the world due to popularity, or settling for stagnant waters taken out of the dead-letter, broken cisterns of man's religion. We must remember that the wells of salvation point to Jesus and it is His desire to uncap the Living Waters of His Spirit into our lives so that we can be revived, refreshed, and reenergized to run the race before us.

We need to truly partake of the Living Waters to avoid becoming like the Dead Sea, where we are taking things in but not becoming a conduit to make the Living Waters available to those who would accept the invitation found in *Revelations 22:17, "And the Spirit and the bride say, Come. And let him that heareth say, Come. And le him that is athirst come. And whosoever will, let him take the water of life freely."*

I mentioned that when it comes to the matters of doing right according to God and His Word that we must simply DO IT--not debate it. It is clear that in the case of Cain, he wanted to debate his offering of an unacceptable sacrifice to God and make it right in his own eyes.

Debate will never change the mind of someone who is already set in his or her understanding and ways; rather, debate is for those who are trying to reason a matter out that might prove to be contrary to their present reality or prove unjustifiable in the end. However, doing right is not a matter of debate but faith that believes and responds according to God's Word.

Righteousness is not a confusing matter in light of truth, and only becomes confusing when man does not want to obey. *Romans 3:12* warns us that in our fallen state we are prone to go our way and prove to be unprofitable in our works for none can do good in such a state. As Christians, we have been born again and have the Spirit of God in us but we must flee the dictates of youthful lusts and follow after righteousness as we walk after the Spirit (*2 Timothy 2:22; Romans 8:1*).

Righteousness will put us on the path to doing right in a matter to ensure an upright relationship with the Lord. For Cain his sin was lying at the door, ready to take him captive but *James 4:17* summarizes what happens when a person knows to do right but fails to properly walk in it, *"Therefore to him that knoweth to do good and doeth it not, to him it is sin."*

God was Israel's king but they wanted to be like the pagan nations around them and have a human king over them. *Jeremiah 17:5* tells us, *"Cursed be the man that trusted in man, and maketh flesh his arm, and whose heart departeth from the LORD."*

As I consider how imperfect man is in light of God, I shake my head at the prospect of what it will mean for any person when he or she desires the leadership of man over God, but the truth is we all have a tendency to desire such rule. If man in his fallen state lacks integrity in leadership positions, he can easily become corrupt because of power and will become a cruel tyrant or an indifferent despot.

We see this in Jesus' day. The religious leaders of that time would rather subject themselves to Caesar as king than Jesus Christ, only to set up Israel for future destruction (*John 19:14-17*). Sadly, the Jews have tasted the bitterness of being under Gentile rule until 1948.

As Christians we have a Lord because we are part of a household, but we are also citizens of an unseen kingdom, a kingdom in which Jesus is King. The question is how much do we allow Jesus to rule over our lives and how much reliance do we put on man?

What I have discovered is that there are very few righteous leaders that prove trustworthy and honorable, while our God never changes and is righteous and just. He can't be pressured, corrupted, bribed, or wrongly influenced, and yet how many of us as Christians, at times have rejected Jesus as king because we have failed to come under His lordship in service, while subjecting ourselves to His kingship in obedience?

What does it mean to do right by God? Once again, we must stop short of thinking that doing right where God is concerned is a matter of "good works," because it is not. Doing right is reckoned by God as being righteous, but in simple terms it simply comes down to doing what is honorable in light of God and in relationship to others.

Doing that which is honorable is a matter of reasonable service to God where others are concerned. Being honorable will choose the way of integrity and doing what is honorable will choose that which excellent to ensure the integrity of what is done. To properly honor others means you must naturally prefer them over self, and any action taken by the one who is honorable will be looked upon by them as the least they can do in a situation.

There will be no room for fake nobility or unwarranted opportunity to glory in what is done. For this reason, doing right is not a matter of sacrifice, but one that is simply the moral and proper thing to do. Being honorable pretty much means that when all is said and done, there will be no deviation in motive, no way in which regret can creep in, no fear about looking into the mirror, and no second guessing as to how God regards it.

That which is honorable can often turn into that which is sacrificial. When you do what is honorable it becomes what is acceptable to God and when you do that which is excellent it becomes that which can be considered "good" before God, but when that which is honorable becomes a sacrifice to God, it will be considered that which is perfect and worthy of consideration.

We must always strive to come to a place of perfection, ever being honorable in our motives in what we do, excellent in our ways, and sacrificial in our service to the Lord, knowing no matter how upright our motive is, how first rate our actions are, and how selfless our service may prove to be, it will always be the least we can do in light of Jesus' great sacrifice on the cross.

It is important to understand what is honorable. Many people try to be right instead of being honorable. The problem is trying to be right in matters is often based on what they perceive to be right, while being honorable is based on doing the right thing according to what the Word of God says.

Rayola Kelley

Being right about something finds its springboard in pride and can prove to be petty, judgmental, and accusing, while doing right in matters is not interested in any type of competition because the real test for honor has to do with personal character. As you can see from these examples, there is a big difference between these two approaches.

Being right is all about person coming out on top looking noble in some way, while being honorable is about doing what is necessary because it is simply the right thing to do. When it comes to being right, I have often tried to convince others in order to receive some type of accolades, or agreement that always justifies my judgmental attitude, or recognition that it is self-centered and is not Christ inspired. The difference is being honorable is void of self-glory because it is doing what is reasonable and there is no fanfare in doing what one must do to ensure a right outcome.

It took me a few years to understand the difference between these two approaches. I thought myself quite noble when I was operating from the premise of proving my personal worth by being "right." Later, after tasting the disappointment of fading glory that is associated with such self-serving nobility, I was able to learn that a place of real honor in God's kingdom is found in brokenness, humility, submission, and obedience before Him.

As I watch some people in Christendom looking for band wagons upon which to exalt themselves because they perceive themselves as being right or the expert on something, I remember what the Apostle Paul instructed in *Philippians 2:3, "Let nothing be done through strife or vainglory; but in lowliness of mind let each esteem other better than themselves."*

Many of us know the parable of the "Good Samaritan," but what we can miss when considering this parable is the reason the Lord shared it. It began with a question from a lawyer or scribe who in those days would interpret the Law of Moses.

This lawyer was trying to trip Jesus up, but found himself being exposed by the Truth. It is important to keep in mind that in Jesus' day the interpretations of the scribes became law as to whether they lined up to the intent of the Law of Moses. And, just what was the question this lawyer asked in *Luke 10:25, "Master, what shall I do to inherit eternal life?"*

Jesus simply quoted the two commandments that summarize the keeping of the Law—to love the Lord thy God with all our heart, soul, strength, and mind and to love thy neighbor as thyself. This lawyer had to admit that Jesus answered well, and he saw himself as loving God but not all of his neighbors.

To justify his lack of love for certain people such as the controversial, hated Samaritans, he asked Jesus, "And who is my neighbor?" Jesus told the parable of the "Good Samaritan."

Like the man left for dead in the story, it took the love of God to provide the way to enter in with mankind to save each of us in our lost state, the love of the Son to prepare the way of redemption so we could be healed and saved, and the same sacrificial love for us to walk in the way of true worship and service to others regardless of personal biases and prejudices in order to walk out our life in Christ. True love looks at the need of the soul and not the outer status of a person.

When Jesus asked the Lawyer who he thought showed the appropriate response in the story, the priest who turned his head so he could play ignorant, the Levite who came up to the victim to judge whether he had responsibility to do something, or the Samaritan who took responsibility to care for the man, the lawyer responded that the one who showed mercy. I had to wonder if it was cultural response or if he would not allow himself to openly say the "Samaritan." Upon the lawyer's admission, Jesus' response to him was, *"Go and do thou likewise."*

ISSUES OF THE HEART

The mind grows by what it takes in,
and the heart grows by what it gives out.
(Unknown)

Second Chronicles 16:9 says, *"For the eyes of the LORD run to and fro throughout the whole earth, to shew himself strong in the behalf of them whose heart is perfect toward him. Herein thou hast done foolishly; therefore from henceforth thou shalt have wars."* At this point the Lord is talking to King Asa of Judah. This king started out on the right track, but his focus and dependency turned from God to Syria and as a result he would find himself in one war after another.

The question is where is your focus and dependency right now? The eyes of the Lord are looking for those who He can show Himself strong through but if your heart, focus, and dependency is NOT on the Lord, you will never be a candidate in which the Lord can show Himself mighty. He does not use the strongest vessel, but the weakest one to reveal His grace is sufficient in any arena. He does not use someone who is hiding in some corner, He uses those who out of faith are willing to stand for truth to penetrate the great darkness of deception. He is not looking for the one who constantly brings attention to their greatness, He looks for the one, who although ever available to do His bidding when called, is more comfortable in quietly sitting at the end of the table of insignificance while being content in being overlooked and ignored.

As we face this great darkness, as believers we have an extraordinary opportunity to become an insignificant instrument, a rod in the hand of God. At such times He can show Himself mighty as He parts the darkness with His light and moves mightily upon hearts, in events, and through circumstances to show HE IS LORD.

Who or what holds your heart? The Bible emphasizes the heart because if the heart attitude is not right, the rest of our spiritual life will be off as to the spirit that we operate in along with our priorities, agendas, and what we value.

We know according to the parable of the Sower and the Seed, about the hard heart that is closed to the seeds of the Gospel and has no real inclination towards spiritual truths and matters, the stony heart that is full of the rocks of the self-life that prevents the seed from taking root, and the worldly heart that has divided loyalties.

The Bible also tells us that the heart can be greatly deceptive due to wicked influences. I am sure when you encounter discrepancies in a Christian's walk, you have heard statements like, "Well, the person has a heart for God." In other words, the hard heart can take consolation in the fact it has been exposed to the seed and has somewhat considered God, the selfish heart can fall back on its sentiments towards God, and the worldly heart can take comfort in religious affiliations and activities, but just because a person may display a heart towards God, it is the level of commitment towards God that reveals whether He owns their heart.

Jesus stated where your treasure is that is where your heart will be as well. You may have certain "noble" aspirations, inclinations, and goals when it comes to God, but if your heart belongs to anyone or anything else, the Lord, along with His will, calling, and plan for your life will be given a backseat to what really holds the desires and affections of your life.

The fruits of the wrong heart reveal who holds the heart. For example, when the hard heart is challenged to become open to God, it becomes indifferent and when the selfish heart is cornered to give way to the Spirit, resentment can take root. And, when the worldly heart must choose who it will ultimately serve, it can become confused and eventually the root of bitterness can take hold.

To be a true follower of Jesus, our love for anything in and of this world must pale in comparison to our love for Jesus. Our face must be set towards heaven, our heart steadfast towards Christ, our emotions tempered by the commitment to do the will of God, and our main desire must be to bring glory to Him in all we do.

As disciples of God, we can't settle with the idea we have a heart for God, we must make sure that our heart belongs to the Lord to avoid becoming indifferent to His truth, resentful of His ways, and bitter towards the fact that He alone deserves to be the center of our life and service. In essence, He must be sitting on the throne of our heart, as well as the focus of our affections and worship.

The Bible talks about believers being perfect; however, we must stipulate what it means for imperfect man to be a perfect man in this wicked world. Perfection in the kingdom of God has a couple of implications to it.

The first one is coming to "full age" or "spiritual maturity." This implies you are becoming the spiritual man *1 Corinthians 15* makes reference to according to your high calling while reaching your potential in God's kingdom. The second aspect of perfection has to do with possessing a pure heart. I admit, it is difficult to keep our heart pure in such an evil environment, but I believe certain responsibilities that were set forth to the man, Adam reveals what we need to do to guard our heart in order to maintain its purity before God. This responsibility is found in Genesis 2:15. "And the LORD God took man, and put him into the garden of Eden to dress it and to keep it."

There are two things we must note, 1) the garden for the most part was free of needing any real tending and 2) man was given a responsibility. When you look up the word, "dress" in the Strong's Concordance it points to service that serves as worship and the word "keep" means to guard.

Man was never meant to be "idle," or free of responsibilities, but his most important responsibility that gives him clarity as to a pure motive, purpose as to right agenda, and pursuit as far as an acceptable priority is to guard his heart in order to maintain an inner environment of worshipful service before the Lord to ensure a place of unhindered communion.

People are people and it is easy to cause fear and panic among them. The greatest tool to control, direct, and use people is something called "ignorance." The Bible is clear that people will perish for lack of knowledge or another way to put it "in their ignorance," they will perish.

Ignorance allows people to settle for less by accepting their opinions as "gospel" instead of challenging themselves to step outside of the box. This requires them to cease from getting by or being complacent towards what is truth as they realize they must stir themselves up to know the truth. Often these individuals hide behind indoctrination that has created misdirected loyalties and prejudices, while sliding into a state of hostility towards what is right by hiding the great "arrogance of ignorance" behind sentiment and passion.

Their unwillingness to allow their understanding of a matter to be tested gives them the means to claim ignorance or innocence that they didn't know what was so and therefore, they can't be held accountable for being or doing wrong. However, the Bible is clear we will all be held accountable for our attitude towards truth, what we can know based on the information made available, and how we handle what is true once it is presented to us.

Once again, we must consider the heart attitude towards truth. If one loves the truth of who Jesus is and the truth of God's Word, they will never settle for the shades of gray and darkness that ignorance produces in the mind of a person.

Yesterday I mentioned ignorance. It is a type of darkness that possesses shades of gray, but also dark shadows of superstition, fear, and delusion. However, in the end man will have no excuse for hiding in, or behind, ignorance.

The Lord gave us a moral conscience that knows there is a just God and Judge; therefore, to ignore the indictment of the conscience is a choice and not a state of ignorance. We have been entrusted with God's Word and whether we believe it, love its truth, live according to it, and abide in it is a choice of the heart, and to desire the truth makes it a preference and a pursuit that God will honor by revealing it to those who are truly seeking it.

As you can see, there will be no excuse for ignorance. The truth will not be popular, politically correct, and adjusted to the culture, but it will be moral, sure, immovable, and standing in the end. The truth will set those who seek it free, but for those who knock it to the side, adjust it, or crucify it, it will be hidden in plain sight because such individuals have chosen to be blinded to it, but in the end, all will know the truth.

As Christians, we know the truth, JESUS, we possess the truth, GOD'S WORD, and we have been given the discerner of all truth, the HOLY SPIRIT. It is for this reason we are told in *Acts 17:30-31, "And the times of this ignorance God winked at; but now commandeth all men everywhere to repent: Because he hath appointed a day, in the which he will judge the world in righteousness by that man (Jesus) whom he hath ordained; whereof he hath given assurance unto all men, in that he hath raised him from the dead." (Parenthesis added.)*

I have talked about facts and truth. As stated, facts are tangible, but can prove untrustworthy when it comes to possessing truth. Facts can be observed, but truth must be discerned because it requires faith on our part to receive it as being so. In other words, God said this and I believe it and will adjust and act accordingly to it.

Truth is from God, of God, and will uphold every aspect of who God is and His Word. Since truth is a matter of Spirit, it can't be handled as a mere fact, but rightly divided in order to develop sound judgments that will uphold it in integrity.

In a world where truth is ignored, shunned, mocked, and raged against, what must we look for to discern if something is from God. To properly discern something, you must lay aside personal feelings, evaluations, and conclusions, and determine in your heart that you want the truth and nothing but the truth. In essence, you have made a commitment of the heart to love truth and to walk in it as being absolute, complete, and eternal.

The next thing you must keep in mind is that God has already spoken what is true. In my experience with the truth, God has in someway shown me what is coming down the line and from that point, I begin to watch the pattern that signals that the Lord is bringing forth what He has already revealed to me. Truth will always be confirmed in due time, but we must trust the timing by holding onto the Lord and waiting for Him to bring forth what He has promised according to His plan.

One of the things we need to do during these trying days is to remember that a merry heart is like a good medicine for the soul. God gave us the gift of laughter that becomes a type of dance in the heart that lifts it to blessed heights where the blessings of God can be simply embraced. Through the years I learned that a merry heart is a light heart because of its ability to enjoy the Lord, embrace life as a gift, and learn to laugh at oneself and with others over light, comical situations.

It is easy to lose your sense of humor in times such as these. We have a tendency to become morbid rather than sober, skeptical instead of realistic, paranoid rather than reasonable, pessimistic rather than hopeful, and take on a foul mood instead of looking at it from a heavenly perspective to see what God is doing in it. After all, God shows Himself mighty in such times.

In the house I live in, it is not unusual to hear laughter. Out of the three of us, Jeannette is the person who is witty and delivers one-liners that can bring the house down in laughter. Carrie has a great sense of humor which serves her well because she is often the one teased, but such times becomes a pleasant break for us because she loves to laugh, and possesses a laughter that rings throughout the house. As for me, I can be tickled by a funny meme or a commercial, laugh at a humorous story, smile at cute actions, and even laugh a bit too loud at hilarious presentations.

Let's face it most of life is serious, but God gave us the ability to have a merry heart that allows frustration to be taken away with the mirth of laughter, anger to be defused by clever one-liners, and depression and sorrow to be lifted enough to let some light penetrate the darkness. At this time does your heart need to learn to dance to the gift of merriment in order to make your present mood light, the day hopeful, and life pleasant?

Rayola Kelley

We live in a time when it seems that some in the generation we refer to as the millennials have lost their way. The reason people of this age lose their way when they should be pursuing dreams, seeking out adventures, and finding their place in society is because they have no sense of destiny.

When I was in high school, I had a sense of destiny. Granted, I didn't know what it was, but I sensed it, and because of this I knew there was some target I needed to locate and aim at to understand my purpose for being. I realize looking back I had a sense of purpose for a couple of reasons.

The first one is I had a history that allowed me to see that destiny is bigger than one person and will ultimately embrace what is honorable and right in the end. If you don't believe me consider the founding fathers of this nation. The second thing I had to acknowledge is destiny had to be something that was a heart matter if I was going to see it through to the end. The third aspect of destiny is that you first must become lost in the magnitude of it before you can actually find it. For me, my destiny found its origins in a rugged cross.

It was Christ and His work on the cross that became my heart's passion, allowing me to discover that it has always been in my heart to know the true God of the universe. Finally, it was when I became lost to the old life and dead to the old ways and raised up in the newness of Jesus' life that I realized my real destiny.

As Christians, we have one destiny, one direction, and one destination and because of God's Spirit and His Word, let it not be said of any of us that we have become lost, aimless, and wandering in the barren terrain of this present world.

There is one aspect about snow that I confront when considering the condition it produces, and that is coldness. When I first go out to snow-blow and shovel the snow the first thing I usually become aware of is that my fingers are growing cold. Even though I have warm gloves, my fingertips feel as if they're individually standing out in the cold and are the first to feel the affront of the weather. This is a type of shock that comes from the extreme "change of climate."

One of the things that can bring coldness to our spiritual lives is isolation. Things happen that make us want to ether withdraw into ourselves or withdraw from everyone. Satan loves such isolation because he can bombard us with lies, doubts, and loneliness. The fruit of such isolation is fear, depression, and self-pity.

The way I combat the physical cold is to pull my fingers out of their slots and put them close to the palm of my hand that has maintained the heat of my body. It is amazing how within seconds warmth returns to them, and I can put them back in their places and they will remain warm until the job is done. This is true for our spiritual lives.

The Bible tells us to draw near to God and He will draw near to us. Our natural response to fearful, overwhelming challenges is to withdraw and isolate ourselves, but God has prepared such a simple way to avoid the coldness of isolation by simply drawing near to Him, trusting He can meet us in every circumstance, and He can replace our fear with His love, our depression with hope, and our self-pity with joy and confidence.

Next time you feel the coldness of isolation nipping at you, remember what *John 10:29* says, *"And I give unto them eternal life; and they shall never perish, neither shall any man pluck them out of my hand."* In summation, come back to the palm of God's hand where you will experience His warmth of love and life once again.

We are living in times that can make the heart grow cold. Hearts grow cold because of unabated fear. This is the reason people must take stock of how they are responding to the days we are living in.

Matthew 24 warns of hearts growing cold because of the occurrences that have been clearly laid out in Scripture. In other words, the fear created by the events of the days will be so overwhelming that man will become calculating and indifferent in order to survive. As I watch the trends in this nation, we have come out of a time of testing that produced great hopelessness in us, only to be ushered into a time of blessing and hope. Now we have had the first shock wave hit our bow as a nation, a warning shot to awaken us as to the serious times we are living in. How much time we have until the next great wave comes our way is anyone's guess, but we must take the opportunity to prepare ourselves.

Keep in mind, unabated fear is nothing but worship. The question is how do we deal with fear? Like everyone else, I have had my share of fear. I know how it can affect me, and in the past, I had to decide whether I was going to crawl up into a fetal position and whimper, or if I was going to face it head on. I have learned that it is not fear that will destroy a person; rather, it is the lack of character that will set the person up to be led away to the slaughter without any resistance by that which instills fear.

It was by standing up to fear and learning to resist it that I developed character to stand when confronted by it. I found out that the power in fear was in its deception that it already had won and I would be found to be a failure in standing against it. Once I decided to face it regardless of whether I failed or not, is when it lost its hold on me, and when I stepped back and looked up to my real Deliverer, instead of trying to push through it with my own power, it dissipated.

Great catastrophe is not the result of actually failing, the real failure comes when we fail to face fear, knowing we are already overcomers because our Lord has secured the victory on our behalf.

The Bible talks about the hearts of men growing cold in fearful, dark times. There are different elements that can cause a cold heart. Yesterday, I pointed out how isolation causes a coldness to settle upon our souls. There is a second way that coldness can settle on the soul: Inaction.

When you are working in the snow, inaction is the worst pose you can take because there is no action to generate heat in your body. The more active you are in shoveling or pushing the snowblower, the less chance there is for the coldness to overcome you. This is true in our Christian walk.

Jesus paid the complete price for our redemption, but redemption opens the way for reconciliation which allows us to enter into a viable relationship with God. Healthy relationships only occur when the necessary parties involved are participating in building a strong relationship together.

The problem is some Christians become inactive in their walk upon redemption, thinking grace is the end of all spiritual matters, when in fact we are told salvation will be found at the end of our faith (*1 Peter 1:9*). We are to walk out our Christian life by faith, and genuine faith is active, ever advancing forward towards the prize of one's high calling. I love what the Apostle Paul clearly pointed out in *Galatians 2:20*, *"I am crucified with Christ; nevertheless I live; yet not I, but Christ liveth in me: and the life which I now live in the flesh I live by the faith of the Son of God, who loved me, and gave himself for me."*

A relationship that is neglected becomes ineffective, a relationship ignored becomes stagnant, a relationship that is abused becomes toxic, and a relationship that is taken for granted often becomes dull, lifeless, and cold.

We are being called into a relationship with God through Jesus Christ and faith towards our God is what will cause us to walk towards Him, hope of future glory will put expectation in each of our steps, and taking up our cross to follow Him will ensure us of being led into a rich and full life of communion with our Lord and acceptable worship of Him.

The next element that can cause coldness to settle on our soul is indifference towards God and the matters of His kingdom. Indifference is a type of complacency that borders on either hopelessness or delusion, but it is also something far more sinister: It is a form of hatred.

Being lukewarm is often the emotional expression of indifference, but godly love can never be lukewarm because if it was, Jesus would have never felt the need to go to the cross and die on our behalf. It is God's love that demands a godly response in to all matters and will express itself in kindness, forgiveness, compassion, and sacrifice.

Luke-warmness comes from being half-hearted towards the Lord because there is divided devotion present. Often this divided devotion is between the idolatrous world and the consecrated-sold out life to God. At such a point, people wrestle with confusion as the Spirit and flesh struggle against each other in the arena of the soul as to where they will direct their devotion, set their affections upon, and ultimately serve.

Jesus said it best when he warned that such divided loyalties and the conflicts it will bring will eventually cause one to love one and hate of the other due to the great inner unrest it brings with it. Sadly, the people give way to that which is fleshly and worldly, and end up hating what is associated with God.

This hatred can find its roots in resentment and bitterness that comes down to the simple reality that to be a Christian means you can't openly pursue the preference of the flesh, while giving way to enticing lusts, which will end with frustration that causes one to fling self into the current of the world.

Indifference is love that has grown cold towards God and will express itself as being intolerant, judgmental, cruel, and mean. The next time you feel complacent or indifferent towards righteousness, examine yourself to make sure there are no divided loyalties in your life.

What kind of heart do you have towards the Lord and His Word? Jesus told a popular parable about the sower and the seed (*Matthew 13:1-23*). We know the seed comes down to the Word of God which includes the Gospel. The ground represents the heart and there are only four heart conditions. Out of the four heart conditions, there is only one condition that will receive God's Word properly.

When the Bible talks about God's people, the term it often uses is "remnant." When we consider out of 100%, only 25% possess a right heart, we might begin to understand why the word "remnant" is realistic, especially since it is God's will that none perish and all come to repentance. Let us consider the first three heart conditions.

The first one is a hard heart that is completely unreceptive towards God's Word. Since this type of heart will not allow the Word to penetrate and break it, it will eventually be crushed by some type of judgment (*Matthew 21:42-44*). A stony heart represents a selfish heart that only will receive that which serves its purpose, but since God's Word will not bow down to the different self-serving, self-seeking, self-centered ways,

His Word will not find any real place to take root in, and when the trials come this type of spiritual life will writher.

The third heart is a worldly divided heart where the weeds of worldly influence will take root and eventually drown out the good seed. Under the new covenant, we have been promised a new Spirit and a new heart. The problem is that some Christians have forgotten that even good ground must be constantly cultivated with God's Word and watered with the Holy Spirit.

Are you making the necessary spiritual investment to ensure your heart remains receptive and good towards God and His Word?

Yesterday I mentioned the heart conditions. It is clear that three heart conditions will not be able to properly handle the seeds of God's Word. The challenge is that at different times I have discovered these different heart conditions within myself.

It is the Lord's heart to make our heart truly a ground that is receptive to the work of His Spirit and Word. He has also provided the means to bring about a right heart condition; therefore, taking away any excuse on the Day of Judgment.

For the hard heart, it must be plowed up by truth, but a person must choose to love and prefer the truth over his or her present reality. For the stony heart the stones of self must be removed before it can be properly plowed. This requires one to honestly face their selfishness with the intent of refusing it any more audience that justifies its presence, ignore it shallowness, and flows unabated with its whims. When it comes to a worldly heart the weeds need to be pulled out, down to the root to ensure they can no longer influence the good seed, hinder the fruit, and undermine a Christian's testimony.

The ground of the heart must be worked by faith, sown with the truth of the Word, cultivated through obedience, and watered by His Spirit to ensure the integrity of the fruit. *James 1:21-24* states, *"Wherefore lay apart all filthiness and superfluity of naughtiness, and receive with meekness the engrafted word, which is able to save your souls. But be ye doers of the word, and not hearers only, deceiving your own selves. For if any be a hearer of the word, and not a doer, he is like unto a man beholding his natural face in a glass: For he beholdeth himself, and goeth his way, and straightway forgetteth what manner of man he was."*

↯↙➛↙

We often hear *Psalm 37:4* being quoted, *"Delight thyself also in the LORD; and he shall give thee the desires of thine heart."* It is natural to love this Scripture, but there is a condition in receiving the desires of our heart. The condition is we must first, "delight ourselves in the Lord."

"Delight" has to do with taking pleasure in something. We take pleasure in the Lord because we love Him and if we love Him, we will desire to know what will bring great delight or pleasure to Him. As we discover what brings pleasure to Him, it will become our heart desire to see it come to fruition.

Sadly, most people consider this Scripture in light of fleshly pleasure and not in light of bringing pleasure to the Lord so that they can share in His delight. If our desires line up to God's desires, we can be assured of receiving them, resulting in worship and communion.

↯↙➛↙

Yesterday, I wrote about the Lord giving us the desires of the heart. It is vital we line up to the desires of God in order to delight in, and with Him in His many blessings and gifts to us. A Facebook friend reminded me that God is also the one who puts the right desires in our hearts. How right she is.

As a teenager I had sensed within my heart for years that I had a destiny. I had no idea what it was until I met the Lord Jesus Christ. As I gained some things of the world in my Christian walk, I suddenly felt a desperation in my heart that if the essence of my life consisted of this world, I no longer wanted to be here. I knew then that only by making Christ my prize, my pursuit, and the desire of my heart that I would find real satisfaction.

It is vital that we discern what God has put in our hearts. Sometimes it is buried beneath lost dreams, sitting on dusty shelves of what could be because of the demands of this world, or left back in some maze due to the detours we take in our life. However, all we need to do is ask the

Lord to revive those sweet desires and choose to pursue them, knowing with confidence that they will lead us right back to Him in greater measure.

I have long ago learned this is the secret to the victorious walk. It is all about gaining more of Christ at each turn, through each valley, and in each storm.

Some of you know that I lived on the beautiful Priest River for a couple of years where I could observe the different changes of seasons on the landscape. Even though Priest River is fast moving, during the winter time the river was slowed down by the cold temperatures.

The Bible talks about men's hearts growing faint with fear and cold with the darkness of despair. Fear will always chill any hope we may have and the darkness will become iced over with indifference. There is clearly heaviness that seems to plague many, but Jesus is the light and His Spirit the fire.

Light can penetrate coldness of the heart with love from above and the fire with expectation and excitement. The key to experience both the light and the fire is to look up, ask the Lord to thaw out the coldness of our heart and give us one of flesh that will become consumed with His love and joy.

It is not unusual for people to try to bargain with God, but bargaining with God and making a vow with the Lord are two different acts. Bargaining with God comes out of desperation and sadly many easily forget or excuse their part of the bargain away when a matter turns out right, but a vow puts teeth of sincerity and commitment into the mix.

Jacob had vowed to make God his God if He brought him back to his father's land and ensured peace with his brother. As many know, God kept His part and as a result it was up to Jacob to keep his part. It is interesting to see where Jacob was called back to, to confirm his part: Bethel, the place where he made the vow (Genesis 35). This is true for Christians.

The Lord will often bring us back to important places or times when we made a vow or committed our life to Him to remind us. One of the things Jacob had to do to make God his God was to get rid of all idols. He commanded his family to bring him all the idols, which would include the idols that Rachel had taken from her father. It was there that Jacob hid them under the oak by Shechem.

It is important to keep in mind if the Lord is going to be our God, we must rid ourselves of all idols and be prepared to build an altar to remind us of our commitment to believe, worship, and serve no other God but the one true Lord God, Creator of heaven and earth, ruler and judge over all.

When was the last time you purged your house and temple (inner life) of all idols so that you could erect an altar in your heart to remember your commitment, and worship the Lord with all of your heart?

Is the Lord Jesus Christ your all in all? An author made a statement that the big problem in the church is that many of its members do not understand what it means for Jesus to be their all in all. As a result, they do not understand the potential, inheritance, and authority they have in Jesus. It took a whole book for this author to present his case but the reality is we can't, in our human limitations, begin to understand the extent of what it means for Christ to be all in all. However, we can experience Him becoming more and more to us as we abide in Him by faith and walk out His life in obedience.

For some people, Christ is a religious notion but we cannot interact or walk with a notion. We must take the Lord out of the foggy, misty flats of dead-letter doctrine and theology and come to a place of not only understanding what it means for Christ to be our all in all and to be all in our lives, but to work towards accomplishing that goal.

The Apostle Paul gives us the first insight in making the Lord our all in all in *1 Corinthians 15:28*. We must bring all aspects of our life under subjection to the Lord Jesus Christ. This means committing all to Him for His instruction and approval. After bringing all things under subjection to Him, we must ask and desire that all areas of our lives be filled with the cleansing water of His Spirit (*Ephesians 1:23*).

Finally, we need to put off the old and daily put on the new man, which will be renewed in the knowledge after the image of the One who created us, knowing there are no boundaries that can prevent Jesus from becoming our all in all, except unbelief, ignorance, and rebellion (*Colossians 3:10, 11*).

How do I make Jesus my all in all? The Apostle Paul gives us insight into this in *Philippians 3:7-11*. He had to count all things of this present world as being dung.

We are in this world, but our heart, thoughts, and affections must be directed heavenward. We must remember in Paul's time he had much influence among the Jews because of who he was and he had rights because he also was a citizen of Rome but in light of heaven, he counted all such things as residue in light of winning the prize of the excellency of the knowledge of Christ Jesus. Once he counted his identification with the world as being loss to him, he was able to make the great exchange and embrace the righteousness of Christ.

We cannot gain Christ as long as we are holding tightly to the things and matters of the world. In letting go of the world to possess Christ's righteousness, Paul made four declarations. The first one is that he would know Jesus. How many times does the Word exhort us to come to the knowledge of Christ?

In my early years of being a Christian, I pursued understanding by way of doctrine and theology. Seven years later I was hit with the harsh reality that I knew of Jesus in certain references and I knew about Jesus, but I did not know Jesus. It was at that time I was reminded that Jesus invited me to come to Him and that I was to learn of Him, not about Him. I needed to be a Mary sitting at the feet of Jesus.

It is easy to settle for information in our world of technology, but good relationships entail more than information about someone, it requires an investment that will produce a growing relationship. As believers we must make sure we are not settling for what will prove to be nothing more than a puff of smoke in the end.

Has your heart been properly circumcised? One of the tokens of God's covenant with the Jewish people was circumcision of the men. The foreskin represented the works of the flesh and it pointed to the need of every Israelite to cut away that which was associated to the flesh to stand distinct.

It is important to point out the idea of covenant involved a cutting, where blood established the covenant. Circumcision was to remind the Israelite people that they were part of a covenant with God and they were to be a separated people among the pagan nations. They were called to be a peculiar (special) people, a kingdom of priests and a holy nation (Exodus 19:5, 6).

The problem with outward tokens is that they can lack heart. They may give the appearance but they will lack the power to live it. It is for this reason *Deuteronomy 10:16 states, "Circumcise therefore, the foreskin of your heart, and be no more stiffnecked."* Hearts can become callus before the Lord, making one stiffnecked, rebellious towards God's authority, stubborn in his or her fleshly ways, and arrogant in attitude.

So many times, an outward token of a covenant with God was, and is, to remind us that there must be an inward response and work that will line us up to keeping our part in such an agreement. Jesus' blood was shed to establish the New Testament covenant, but are we keeping our part of it by loving Him with our whole heart and obeying His Word?

WAITING & RESTING

*Silence of the heart can prove to be a time of rest,
silence of the soul a time of peace, and silence in
our activities a test. If silence is not properly
appropriated, it will cause one's heart to become
anxious, the soul to become irritable, and the mind to faint.*
Rayola Kelley

The hardest challenge for mankind is to wait. Waiting involves trust, patience, and endurance. For Christians we learn to wait for three reasons. A time of waiting on the Lord is to test our level of trust towards the Lord with the purpose of fine-tuning and enlarging it.

The second reason is one of preparation. God does not entrust or command something unless He first prepares us to carry it out during a time of waiting. The final reason has to do with timing. If a matter has not been ordained, anointed (separated and prepared), and in accordance with His timing, He will not be properly glorified.

Patience is a virtue of the Holy Spirit. Patience manifests itself in four ways: long-suffering, meekness, compassion, and pity. When the Lord refrains from judging us, it is not because of love, but because He is long-suffering with us. Long-suffering points to being patient with someone even when they are abusing grace, using love in a perverted, self-serving way, being disobedient, and neglecting their real blessings and calling. God shows long-suffering as a means to give time to the sinner to repent before tasting judgment, consequences, or wrath.

You can't be patient unless meekness is present. The Bible talks about tribulation that works patience and patience experience. Tribulation is to work meekness in us so that we can be patient in waiting for the time where we experience the blessing or the promise. Meekness points to strength, power, and rage being under control. There can't be self-control without meekness.

We develop meekness in learning to wait before the Lord and it is for this reason, we are clothed with meekness and in meekness we will inherit the earth. Compassion is the ability to enter in with someone in order to possess the necessary pity to minister to them.

Most ministry lacks patience and therefore will lack compassion and pity, and will fail to be a source of consolation to others. This is why we are told to possess our souls in patience by faith to endure to the end. *Matthew 24:13* gives us this promise, *"But he that shall endure unto the end, the same shall be saved."*

"Waiting" is a terrible word when it comes to those who are impatient, selfish, spoiled, and controlling. Sadly, any of us can fall into any one of these four categories. The impatient have pressing things to do, the selfish have other things they prefer to do, the spoiled are too restless to be bothered with such inconveniences, and the controlling want to make sure their narratives come out on top in such times.

However, "waiting" is part of the preparation when it comes to the testing of faith, the refinement of our calling, and the forging of good character to see a matter through to the end. This type of waiting is not the same as being complacent, lazy, apathetic, and complicit; rather, it is a learned virtue to ensure that God's will is adhered to, His ways maintained, and His plan brought forth according to His timing.

To be complacent is to have an indifferent attitude towards God because one lacks understanding and laziness will display a casualness or agitation towards God because it can't be immediately satisfied. Apathy is an excuse to close down and be angry about the life God has given and complicity is the art of throwing crumbs at the distress of barking dogs to keep them unsuspecting and quiet, while cleverly stroking the egos of the arrogant to keep them corporative. This allows the complicit individual to do their own thing.

Waiting on, before, and with God is a state of readiness not indifference. It is listening for the instruction, not waiting for the right feeling that will stir one up, and it is watching for the right door to open, not angrily counting the doors that remain closed. Waiting is not complicit because it is not trying to give the impression of meekness and being agreeable to hide the dishonorable need to control; rather, it is meek because it is under the control of the Holy Spirit.

As Christians we must wait until we gain the right perspective, learn to be content in whatever state we are in, knowing it not only prepares us, and will allot us the tools to serve the Lord. We must ever be on alert for any open door of service and never forget we are representing our Lord and not ourselves.

My flesh hates to wait, my pride becomes offended and uncertain in waiting, my soul can become anxious, and my mind tormented, but when "waiting" has had its way in my life, my spirit soars, my soul is satisfied, and my mind is at peace with the Lord.

How many of you are waiting on God to fulfill a promise in your life? Abraham waited for 25 years before God gave him Isaac. I remember the Lord impressed upon me that I was to write a book. From the time He gave me that impression to the time I held my first published book in my hands was a span of 18 years.

I realized the years in between was a time of preparation and testing of my faith. After the publication of my first book, a missionary told me I would write more books. I was shocked because I had no intention of writing another book. We have just published my 53rd book.

The one valuable lesson I have learned is that somewhere along the line, God will ask you to offer His promises back to Him. You must in good faith give back to Him what He has entrusted to you, knowing whether it is consumed or purified in His fires, you are still going to love and serve Him because He is worthy.

How many times in your Christian walk or ministry did you feel you were pressing against a gate waiting for it to open and when it did, you found yourself falling through it instead of running the race? There are so many times that I have felt like my nose was pressed against some closed door or gate. I thought of myself as a race horse that was chomping at the bit to have the opportunity to show my capabilities in God's kingdom. I knew I could do nothing but wait until the door opened, but I could not understand why the way was not being opened to me for my zeal was great, my dreams electrifying, and my strength at its peak.

I felt hindered and frustrated. I wrestled before the Lord with questions as to His timing. Finally, when the gate did open, I found myself not only falling through the gate but I felt like I was floundering; and, due to the prior wrestling within the gate, I had little energy to actually run the race. It was at such times I learned a lesson that I was not meant to run the race in my own strength but in the Lord's.

Much of waiting on the Lord for me was to learn important disciplines so that I would not get ahead of Him and would follow the lead of His Spirit while coming into step with His yoke. Sometimes when we are waiting on the Lord, we question whether He is disciplining us for something we are not aware of instead of discerning whether He is establishing godly discipline in us in order to line us up to His will and pace us according to His perfect timing. We must remind ourselves of *Isaiah 40:31, "But they that wait upon the LORD shall renew their strength; they shall mount up with wings as eagles; they shall run, and not be weary; and they shall walk and not faint."*

Must we always wait on the Lord before we will ever see a matter come to fruition? There will always be a waiting period, but some are short, some are trying, and some seem like eternity. The key in waiting is to be faithful with what is in front of you. Without even realizing it the Lord will bring you to that place where He will use you to bring about His will and purpose.

The idea of faithfulness comes from doing something in good faith until a verbal, legal, contract, promise, or obligation is fulfilled. Faithfulness to God will often prepare you to be ready to stand in faith.

There was a time we were given a $6,000 promotional package to promote our book for free, but we had to travel to Rome, Georgia from Seattle, Washington to partake of it. We didn't have the funds to make such a trip, but yet I felt the Lord wanted us to go. I told the Lord He would have to solve the problem.

My friend who co-authored the book with me felt led to call a Christian couple who she had done a religious painting for to ask them to pray. The wife agreed to do so. The next morning when we walked into the office, the phone was ringing. It was the husband of the Christian couple. He told me because of his profession that he flew all over the world and that very morning the airlines had called him to inform him he had over 100,000 free flyer miles and that he was giving 50,000 of it to us so we could fly to Rome, Georgia.

Sometimes answered prayers happen quickly, sometimes you must wait for the answer, other times you might find yourself in a wrestling match in prayer to secure it, and there are times He must give you the gift of faith to know that He will bring a promised matter about in His timing.

Meanwhile, we occupy out of love for Him where we are and encourage ourselves in light of who He is, while trusting Him with the details of fulfilling the matters of heaven according to His purpose and will.

Yesterday a big wind storm came through and our power was out from 4pm to 8:30am, but I was thankful it lasted a short time compared to what happened in Texas. It is this time of the year to do spring house cleaning and that means I will not be on Facebook for the next two weeks, and I will miss my interaction with you.

In this case, I am not just talking about housecleaning, but yard work. It was suggested that I ask for your prayers because I could end up being buried by "stuff." I know I must avoid the great desire to accomplish such a task in one day because it is not possible.

I will be painting, alleviating "stuff", and cleaning. I don't know about you but I have a hard time pacing myself when it comes to projects. I want to get in there and do them so that I can go on to the next project and get it done. However, when you are waiting on God for the right timing in a matter, you must, and will learn the discipline of pacing yourself in patience.

We are told to possess our souls in patience. Much of possessing our soul is spiritually pacing ourselves. We must learn to recognize our limitations, take time to discern our obligations according to calling and burden, and be faithful to carry them out to completion. We much recognize that if God is not behind a matter, it will prove to be useless; after all, we are limited by our human strength, our restricted talents, and our partial knowledge of things.

Although we are subject to time and often feel pressed and pushed as if running out of time to do something, God is not. In the dimension of eternity there is no time. He alone has the power to carry out His plan for our lives. He can see this plan in light of the beginning of a matter to the end of it.

As we wrestle with the days we live in, the projects that seem endless, and the time that, like sand, slowly runs through an hour glass, we must remember when it comes to our time a matter never seems to come to fruition fast enough, but when timeless eternity steps on the scene, everything can fall into place in the twinkling of an eye.

Meanwhile, let us possess our souls in patience as we learn to pace ourselves according to God's open and closed doors while trusting Him to work out the details of His plan for our lives in uncertain days.

God provided Israel with six refuge cities. These cities were for the sojourner to rest in, those who accidentally killed someone to flee to, to avoid repercussions, and a place of safety from enemies. As Christians we are sojourners in this world and we must know the place of refuge if we are going to finish the course.

The reason why is because as sojourners we must be on constant guard against the robbers of our age who operate in the night, and the place of refuge allows us to simply rest in our faith, knowing that the thieves are outside of the gate. For the manslayer who seeks refuge in such a place, he had to remain in the place of refuge until the High Priest died and then he could once again return to his inheritance, free of paying consequences.

As Christians, we started out like a manslayer that had committed an offense against God and we sought the refuge provided by redemption. Since our High Priest, Jesus died on the cross, we now have the freedom to pursue our spiritual inheritance that has been secured for us. This brings us to our enemies.

We are soldiers, but soldiers must be able to come to a place of refuge where the war ceases outside of the gate, allowing us to be revived, refreshed, and renewed to continue to fight on until we reach our destination.

The Bible is clear that we are positionally hid in our Ark, Jesus Christ, and that it is the Rock that serves as our refuge from the storms, our high tower that places us out of the reach of our enemy, and our pavilion that is impenetrable, but the problem is there are those who come up to the gate of refuge, Jesus Christ's redemption, but fail to enter in.

There was the incident of Abner in *2 Samuel 3* that reminds me that many will be so close to experiencing God's abiding protection, but will fail to because they did not enter into it or left it to pursue other matters before resolving the matter of their soul. For Abner he had killed the brother of Joab, David's general in wartime, but Joab wanted revenge.

Abner came to the refuge city of Hebron to meet with David to make peace, but left it and it was on his way back to his home that Joab beckoned for him to come back under false pretense. It was outside of the gate of the refuge city, as well as the protection of the king, that Joab executed vengeance on Abner.

Some souls will fail to enter in because they want to hold onto their old life and others will taste some sweetness of Jesus' peace through some religious experience, but will go back into the world without the authority and abiding protection of the King. As Christians we must never pass by our refuge without entering in and being renewed and sent out by our Lord and Savior, Jesus Christ.

I must ask myself am I striving or pressing forward in my Christian life. In the past I have often found myself striving to reach a certain goal, to satisfy some illusive standard and appease certain people's expectations only to find myself becoming weary with it all. To strive for something often points to doing something in one's strength.

My personal strength through the years has greatly ebbed out with the tides of years. Recently, I was struggling with certain matters and when I sought the Lord, He simply instructed me to let things be. For years I have been striving to reach some mark, only to be knocked back by the realization, I would never reach that mark in my own strength.

Coming to a place of rest in the Lord has constantly reinforced the truth that the greatest thing I can do to advance in my spiritual life is to quit striving in my flesh, let go of worldly standards and selfish expectations, and like Paul press forward towards my high calling. In summation, I need to set aside the things that so easily beset me in order to press through the challenges of this present age to reach my high calling.

It has taken me years to realize that striving has more to do with personal accomplishments and goals and very little to do with reaching my high calling in the Lord. Obviously, before I can press forward against the challenging winds of the times, I first must cease striving with myself by letting go so that I can freely and successfully run the course that is set before me.

For the last couple of days, I have not been feeling well. I have flu-like symptoms that make life a bit miserable. I don't know about you but I hate feeling bad. I am not so sick that I must lay in bed, but I am miserable enough everything seems unimportant and I question if I have enough strength to do what is needed.

I have many things I need to do. I am in a race at times, in a battle at other times, on call most of the time, and always busy with some project. When you are not feeling good, you realize how you take for granted the strength and energy you have when you are not being physically hindered.

Our spiritual life is a lot like our physical challenges. We can become somewhat spiritually anemic and even though our souls are restless, we experience lethargy where nothing that is godly interests us. We know there is more to do, but we don't have the energy to stir ourselves up and the strength to do much except be a bit on edge. The question is, what must a body do at such a time?

The answer is simple, a person should come out from the demands of life, put aside the projects, and learn to rest in the source of all strength, Jesus. Being a busy person, I can tell you it is hard to rest when there is time to do this or that, but this and that can wait, but taking the opportunity to learn what it means to rest in Jesus is a necessity in life if we are going to learn to stand in His strength.

Right now, much in this world seems sick and restless, but the world knows nothing of the rest of Jesus, but how many Christians understand it? I have learned it is okay not to feel good sometimes because it presents its own opportunity to remember, learn, or discover what it means to rest in Jesus.

I don't know about you but it is the "little foxes" of irritations that get me the most. There is something about big being better, but in my world, it is the small, everyday mundane responsibilities that keep everything moving forward. Without the small details being worked out daily, there would be no big accomplishments.

Every book I ever wrote required me to walk through mundane days of struggling with words, organizing themes, reorganizing sentences, comparing words with words, and doing my best to proofread and edit it. In my many writing projects, I am reminded that a good stony path is made up of different layers of rocks of different sizes so the water can properly drain and the path can remain sturdy under the feet of those who walk upon it.

The real test that "little foxes" brings to our spiritual life may seem insignificant, but it is of the utmost importance as to whether God will entrust us with more. The test is faithfulness. I have mentioned this many times, but it is easy to forget that when the world stresses quantity, we can get caught up with the size, the feats, and the accomplishments while ignoring whether one's character would prove able to meet the feat and even use it as a springboard to reach heights of excellence and potential.

As believers we can't afford to let the matters of our life be thrown up by the winds of time and hope that somehow it will all fall into place. Most of the time we must take our lives back from the winds and demands of the world and come back to the altar of commitment and once again consecrate all to the Lord.

After consecration we need to wait before the Lord until He shows us the way through the spiritual wilderness, parts the Red Sea, put darkness between us and the enemy, and gives us the Water of the Holy Spirit to enrich and empower us before we proceed forward.

Many people are holding on until we as a nation return to normal, but what is normal? Normal means different things for different people. It's clear that right now our country is in limbo. It's almost as if we have been thrown down on some mat and the world is waiting to see how we rebound from it.

For Christians, limbo is an active time because it points to waiting and it is not waiting to see what happens, but waiting on the Lord because His is the next move. His move depends on what we as His people do in this time of waiting.

"Waiting" for the Christian entails the three "**Ps**," **pondering** upon His Word, **preparation** to stand, and **prayer** to seek God's will and endure, but for the world it is where the three "**Vs**," are revealed, **vanity** that falls into a great **vortex** that reveals there is **no value** to what it pursues.

It is a time such as this that Christians have the opportunity to not only shine in the darkness created by a spiritual vacuum, but to penetrate the darkness of despair with truth and hope. It's time to set the record straight as to what is true and to become the example of what is real in order to establish the hope that is eternal.

May we press towards this high calling with abiding confidence in the boldness and power of the Holy Spirit with assurance of hitting the mark.

Have you ever felt like sitting in the middle of a road in resignation, knowing that the current of life will never stop and that you will be either swept to the roadside or run over, settling your dilemma once and for all? I have been there a couple of times.

In my first experience of being in this state, I had to face that I was spiritually, emotionally, and physically tired and as a result I was totally out of perspective. In my quandary I felt I couldn't go any further, but at the same time I had come too far to go back to my former life.

I remember sitting there just waiting, and the Lord actually inserted Himself into my plight and gave me a choice. It was simple, choose the lush valleys of Sodom and Gomorrah or the fiery oven of Shadrach, Meshach, and Abednego. Since I had no intention of going backward to what already had been judged, there was only one right, sane decision to make. It would be the oven.

The oven has a way of putting matters in perspective. I knew that there needed to be purging in my life and that my faith needed to be enlarged and the oven would do both, but I was also reminded that the oven was the safest place for Shadrach, Meshach, and Abednego to be because the Son of God was also in that oven with them. I had the assurance He would be with me as well.

On this day of rest, how many of us as believers have truly come to a place of rest? Consider those who are in a panic about saving their lives, paranoid about what tomorrow will bring, and anxious about the future. Real rest is not a particular day, some practice, or a feeling; rather, it is a place we must come to in our soul and spirit.

How do we get to this place? We mount upon the wings of hope and allow the promises of God's Word to lift us up above the present troubled terrain of this age until we find ourselves in the current of praise where thanksgiving and expectation thrusts us forward until we see the place of refuge.

Once we come to this place, we must let go of the burdens that weigh our soul down while exhaling the heavy defiled air of this world and inhaling deeply the sweet breath of God's Spirit as we land on the runway of faith. One might ask how will we recognize this place.

Jesus talked about preparing places for us in *John 14:1-3*, but Matthew is the Gospel that identifies this glorious place in *Matthew 11:28-30, "Come unto me, all ye that labour and are heavy laden, and I will give you rest. Take my yoke upon you, and learn of me; for I am meek and lowly in heart: and ye shall find rest unto your souls. For my yoke is easy, and my burden is light."*

Jesus is our place of rest. When was the last time you came seeking Him as a place of sweet communion, causing your spirit to succumb to sweet peace and your soul to rest in assurance that all is "well with my soul"?

As we embark into uncertain times, it is important to remember that God is our helper. We must keep in mind that as our helper, He is not above us, below us, indifferent to us, or fickle in what He does on our behalf; rather, He is beside us.

347

He will encourage us during frightening times, comfort us during grave challenges and loss, guide us through darkness, and will take our hand and lead us up the narrow path of righteousness. To think that God, our Creator and Redeemer, offers Himself as our helper is incredible.

It is His goal to lead us to a place of complete rest in Him, but to reach this place, we must trust His words, obey His instructions, and walk through the situation according to His promises. It is vital that we keep looking up as we guard our hearts in these dark times, knowing that our solution is not of this world and that the real glory we desire will be found in the next age yet to come.

Do you need rest in your soul? It recently came to my attention the need to learn how to come to a place of being still in my relationship with the Lord and receive from Him, His precious peace. I realize that my soul must come to a place of rest in Christ and my spirit must be quiet before the Lord.

The only way I can be still in my unsettled mind is to put my mind on Christ. The only way I can be still in my soul is to come to a place of inner assurance that the Lord is in control and He is trustworthy. The way I can quiet my spirit is by worshipping and communing with Him in Spirit and truth.

But I must become still in my mind and soul before I still my spirit enough to enter into worship and communion. It is in the stillness of soul and spirit that I have walked away with a greater awe of the Lord which brings me out of the depths of uncertainty to the heights of soaring in the Spirit.

What does it mean to rest? In fact, sometimes we must rest from the activities we do while "resting." I had to learn what real rest entailed after experiencing a health crisis brought on by physical exhaustion.

First, I had to come to a place of rest. That meant laying aside all the activities of life. Then I had to come to a calmness in my soul and a quietness in my spirit to experience the fruit of rest: revival.

As believers, we know our place of rest is Jesus Christ, and I have found the one way to calm my soul is meditate on God's Word and the way to quiet my spirit is to think on the beauty and greatness of my Lord. When I land on who the Lord is, then my spirit is lifted up in worship which refreshes my inner man to meet the demands of life and to continue to run the race set before me.

SPIRITUAL SEASONS

The purpose of the desert (valley) season
is that we be given the opportunity
to build a highway in our hearts for
God. If we build Him a highway, it will
be the pathway upon which He will
lead us out of the valley.
(Bob Sorge)

Do you need some healing in your life before you embark into a new season? There are three types of healings that need to happen before we humans can know wholeness. The most popular one we often focus on is physical healing.

The Lord healed many people of their ailments, but He also has used them as a thorn in people's sides to temper the soul, discipline the walk, and keep personal strength in check. There is emotional healing that needs to occur due to mental anguish over such things as great losses, trauma, and tormenting regrets. God must heal the memory of such things in order to take the power hold it has on our lives. However, people for different reasons want to hold onto such memories, whether it is to protect themselves from the impact of like events in the future, as a right to hold onto certain unproductive feelings such as anger and self-pity, or maintain some type of shrine to avoid feeling the sharpness of what would be considered as betrayal to them.

Rayola Kelley

The final healing is spiritual healing, which includes such things as a broken heart, bondage to sins, and unresolved issues. The challenge is that most people are more tuned into how something makes them feel physically and emotionally while failing to discern the spiritual aspect of how a matter is actually affecting their attitude towards God, life, and others.

The truth is there can be physical challenges and a person can have spiritual wholeness because he or she is right before the Lord. If a person is struggling with emotional issues, it implies one of two things, he or she has not been truly born again or the person has some type of breakdown in his or her relationship with the Lord.

The reason I say this is because the Lord wants to heal the emotional aspect of the soul to not only make us whole but to prevent us from being inconsistent in our walk before Him. There is nothing that makes Christians more inconsistent in their walk or testimony than emotions that have personal rights attached to them, ultimately making them fickle and unpredictable.

I want to thank everyone for their prayers concerning the weather around here. The wind quietly came, leaving no evidence that it was even here. In fact, the snow is beautifully covering the tree branches proving the disturbance was very slight, but we have plenty of snow.

It has been snowing for over 24 hours and will continue to snow and there is another snow storm behind this one. A friend of ours showed the snow measuring over 13 inches high. I love snow in moderation. In other words, I love what I can enjoy and handle, but if it becomes too overwhelming for me, then it becomes an enemy, a curse.

The truth is we live in a world where what is natural and necessary can become an extreme that can greatly challenge us, and there are those who for adventure sake, seek extremes that operate on the precipice of destruction, which for some has sadly cost them their lives.

As I was thinking about the extremes, I am reminded that sin operates in the same way. It often takes us into extremes with our pride and lusts. We are in this world, but the goal of the world is to ultimately own our soul, and the way to do that is to entice us with what is moderate, needful, and natural to make it a pursuit of the heart, while capturing our affections that drive us into the absolute extremes.

In the past I have operated in extremes, and I can tell you it leaves you empty, miserable, and hopeless. There is a term in *Haggai 1:5, 7* that is significant when it comes to avoiding the traps of personal extremes, *"Consider your ways."* When you look up the word, "consider" in Strong's Concordance, it means "center."

Every time I read this, I realize that I need to consider if my ways are taking me into the extreme left fields of a matter or whether they are lining me up to that which needs to be the center of my life: the Lord. Life will occasionally bring the extremes our way, but we must remain close to the center of all that is true and right to make sure we are not caught up with the extreme winds and storms of this age that will end up bringing destruction in some way to our soul.

Winter has definitely hit the scene in Northern, Idaho. We had snow every day last week. I love the whiteness of the snow. It dresses up the different fir trees around us in glorious array. It allows the sun to reflect off of it, giving the impression of a treasure chest of diamonds, all ready to highlight the glory of the Creator.

At night, it reflects the light of the moon in greater ways that expose the terrain around it. One of the first Scriptures I learned as a new Christian used the illustration of snow, *"Come now, and let us reason together, saith the LORD: though your sins be as scarlet, they shall be as white as snow; through they be red like crimson, they shall be as wool" (Isaiah 1:18).*

This Scripture has often been used to encourage man to reason with man but it is important to understand who wants to reason with man and why. The Lord is the one who wants to reason with us about an important matter—sin. We often judge the intensity of sin according to who is doing it, and as a result we either logically justify it away or confirm the unmerciful pose we take about it.

If man lacks integrity, he can be quite partial about all matters pertaining to the kingdom of God, but God is not partial. He has no favorites and the cross of Christ and death proves that very fact. I often state, "When are we going to agree with God about sin?" We can't face a matter until we are honest about it and we can't address it in our lives until we take on the attitude of the judge about it.

As I consider this Scripture, the use of snow is not about covering sin, but cleansing us of it. The Lord wants to ever reason with me at the point of my sin so it can be addressed. Sin represents a spiritual type of winter where there is a dormancy taking place in my walk due to sin, and I cannot be cleansed of it until I honestly face it, and then repent and confess it. It is important to remember, wherever sin is present or reigning in your life, darkness will reside and you will fail to reflect the Lord at that point.

It is beautiful how snow dresses up our trees in the winter time. It appears to contain numerous diamonds, and at night reflects the terrain around us. As we are aware, the light that snow reflects can cause snow blindness.

Sometimes the transparent light of God can cause great darkness in our soul as it exposes the reality of our spiritual plight and our great need to be cleansed by Jesus' blood and the washing of His Word. While snow covers up various objects that can be offensive and discouraging to the physical eye, but when it comes to sin, even though we may try to cover it up the same way snow blankets the landscape, we must be cleansed from it. Thereby, we can be clothed in the righteousness of Christ and reflect His beauty and glory.

Cleansing can only take place when we bring our sins to the Lord seeking His forgiveness. As we humble ourselves before the Lord to deal with our sins, a wonderous exchange takes place, He imparts His eternal life to us and we are given salvation. In salvation we are made part of an incredible family and heirs of an eternal inheritance.

The treasure chest of these gifts and promises associated to this inheritance are like priceless diamonds that are meant to enrich our lives in this world and in the next to come. Do you possess the treasure chest of gifts and promises because, if not, you can by allowing God to reason with you about your sin and addressing it through the redemption of Jesus? And if you possess such treasure, are you utilizing it in such a way that your life is being enriched in abundance daily by that which is heavenly and eternal?

Last night I heard the most comforting sound: rain. The wind blew and the sky gave us its own version of fireworks and we prayed that neither left their mark on the land, but then came the rain.

I don't like working out in the rain, but I do love to hear the sound of it at night on the roof and terrain of the land. It reminds me of the rain from heaven, the Holy Spirit. So many times, my soul is left barren by the purging that is now taking place in the land, and my spirit is waning because of the intense heat and wind of our times that are spewing out the smoke and fire of hatred and violence, along with the fact that some of the activities taking place are indeed sucking the life out every fiber of morality and decency in America. Such activities speak of the great evilness that can take hold of hearts, the despairing wickedness that has taken captive the imaginations of man, and the ongoing saga of the digression that sin constantly works within the hearts of the disobedient and rebellious.

As a result, it can prove to be difficult to walk through the world without one's spirit being vexed, without the soul being weighed down by the despair caused by this world's perversion, and one becoming more and more aware that there is no way out of this world unless one walks through the door of eternity.

Rain reminds me that at times the spirit needs to be revived and refreshed by the Holy Spirit, the soul needs to be cleansed by the washing of the Word and the regeneration of the Spirit, and the body needs to be strengthened to finish the course set before every believer. I know once I seek the Lord to renew the inner man within me that, like the aftermath of rain upon the land, I will once again smell the fresh air of God's glorious promises: that soon all of this will past, bringing us into that which was ordained before the foundation of the world.

Rayola Kelley

We have been Scripturally told and warned about the times we are living in. As believers we know we are living in the age of the church, the times of the Gentiles, and the dispensation of grace. We know this age is coming to an end, as the times of the Gentiles gives way to the reign of an eternal kingdom, and that the dispensation of grace will give way to the next dispensation.

This time is also referred to as the last days by the Apostle Peter in *Acts 2:16-18*. If I understand what Peter was saying in these Scriptures, the last days started on the day of Pentecost when the Spirit was poured out upon all flesh. If this is correct, for the last 20 centuries the church has been living in the last days, knowing that its time will come to a conclusion when Christ comes for His body.

It is for this reason that Christians in every generation have been looking for His coming. With this in mind, what season are we in regard to these last days? Jesus said it best in *John 4:35, "Say not ye, There are yet four months, and then cometh harvest? Behold, I say unto you, Lift up your eyes, and look on the fields; for they are white already to harvest."*

For the last 20 centuries the church has been commissioned to work in the season of harvest. Granted, personally we experience different seasons of growth as do the members of the church body, but when it comes to the spiritual season we are in, it is the harvest season of souls. It is for this reason we have been given the same commission to plant the seed of the Gospel.

I worked in seed potatoes during the harvest and the work was hard and demanding, and the days long. There was no quitting until the harvest was completed. Keep in mind, in the harvest season, you can find yourself working in all kinds of weather but you can't let anything deter you from that one responsibility of ensuring the harvest is brought in.

Some of us have been faithful in planting the seeds of life in others, while others cultivate them to grow through sound Biblical teaching and some nurture them to maturity through discipling. The truth is we all have our part in the harvest and our responsibilities may vary as to our place in this last day harvest, but as Scripture reminds us, we are co-laborers with the Lord in this great harvest field.

As believers, we need to see the seriousness of the season, the hour, and the times we are living in and avail ourselves to do the Lord's bidding so that when souls are brought into the kingdom of God in these last days, we can be part of the extraordinary, witness the miraculous, and truly fulfill our high calling and commission.

The word that came to me this morning as I meditated on what to share was "sobriety." I have to admit I have not heard this world used much in my Christian walk. There is a tendency to lean towards that which sounds "positive" in order to avoid that which may come across as too harsh or negative.

Sobriety is a word that takes the silliness out of the positive and the extreme adverseness out of the negative to cause people to land on what is, and become grounded as a means to face the reality of something in order to prepare for what is looming on the horizon.

We are living in prophetic days and anyone who reads and knows the Bible will not dispute that we are in a season of testing, trials, and sorrows, but the problem is too many are trying to predict the day of deliverance according to how they interpret events, while failing to warn the people of their need to prepare for the particular season we are in. As believers, we are confident that the sky will part one day as Jesus gathers the redeemed, but meanwhile the instructions are the same. We must not be caught unaware of what is looming before us, but we must be ready to stand in the season, withstand its trials, and continue to stand even when it appears as if the promise of the blessed hope is a hoax.

Remember, there were ten virgins who were looking for the bridegroom, but only five were prepared to meet Him. We must note He came when least expected, at the darkest time of the night, catching those unprepared off guard.

Sobriety is what causes us to stand guard over our lives in Christ. With soberness, we stand against the advances of Satan with the belt of truth that upholds our testimony, our hearts covered by the breastplate of righteousness that ensures our authority, while withstanding as we advance forward with the Gospel, ever defending ourselves with the shield of faith, and trusting that the helmet of salvation will maintain a right attitude in the battle as we continue to stand with the sword of the Word.

The question remains, as God's soldiers, who are to endure to the end, while possessing our souls in patience, are we sober enough to be vigilant as we stand ready to face the battles that are yet before us until our Commander, King, and Lord calls us and comes to lead us home?

The smoke is being pushed out by a storm front, and today we are beginning to see the mountains around us. Most people prefer good days where the sun shines and the temperature is moderate so they can enjoy the gift of life. However, the current of life brings many storm fronts.

These fronts are important. Granted, they may disrupt our plans but spiritually they will bring the sweet breezes of refreshment to us, winds that clear the stagnant air of complacency, part the stifling heat of oppression, lift the humidity of uncertainty, and at different times usher in a new season of personal growth and refinement.

Last week when we entered the gray world of smoke, we had just gone through a couple of hot days, but as the smoke parts today, we are seeing more and more signs of autumn. I have not always enjoyed the different storm fronts that have blown through my life, but I have ended up appreciating how God has used them to change, and at times, completely transform the landscape of my soul.

Due to the season of time we are living in, there are many advancing storm fronts coming at us. We must not fear them; rather, we must face them and realize that God is the one who plans the storm fronts that will hit our lives. We can trust that He is using such fronts to change the landscape of our soul so that we can come to a place of truly enjoying the pure light of His Son, the fresh wind of His Spirit, the new season of refreshment and growth, and the heavenly life He is establishing in us.

Part of being in the fall season is about preparing for the winter season. In our situation on the home front there is a lot of work to do to prepare for it. For Christians, we have indeed come out of a hot season of purging where there has been much challenged by scorching circumstances that weigh heavily upon our souls. However, this is not the time to become stagnant from isolation or dormant because of hopelessness.

We are in an intense spiritual battle that calls for real courage and resolve to not succumb to the times. We must not allow the intensity of the circumstances to determine our passion, our resolve, or devotion towards the Lord.

The intensity of our faith is not determined by circumstances, but our level of love for God. If we possess a fickle love that swings with sentiment, we will find ourselves lying bruised and disillusioned in some pit of despair. If we are half-hearted in our love for God, we will find that we have no resolve to see our spiritual journey through to the end. If our love is based on God's responding the way we think He should, we will find ourselves walking away in total skepticism and unbelief.

Fall is a time to prepare for the long nights of darkness that are coming. Like our preparation, much has to do with preparing the ground and storing away that which is attached to the spring and fall to preserve it for next year. In this fall season, may each of us who are believers prepare the ground of our heart to become more tender towards the Lord, begin to tie up all the loose ends of our commitments and responsibilities to ensure we preserve the integrity of our faith and our Christian witness before others, and make sure that we are being realistic about the season we are in, the times we are facing, and resolve that our life in Christ will define how we respond to each circumstance. It is important to remember what *Matthew 24:13 states, "But he that shall endure unto the end, the same shall be saved."*

We had our first snowstorm this season. It is not unusual to see snow at this time of the year but we always expect snowstorms in November, around Thanksgiving. We often see October as the month of preparation

357

for winter. We put everything away from the summer months, but this storm may have caught some people off guard. After all, this is not the end of October and last year at this same time we were still mowing lawns, counting down the fact that we would be putting our lawnmowers away for the season and preparing our snowblowers.

Another problem with heavy snow falling this time of the year is that many trees have not yet shed their leaves, and the wet snow can cause the leaves to become so heavy on the branches that it can split trees and cause them to fall. As I was considering how this storm revealed just how prepared people are, I was reminded that we try to calculate matters based on seasons, but there are always those unexpected storms of life that reveal we are often unprepared.

We are living through a tough season when it comes to national and international events. As a nation, we must ask ourselves if we were prepared for them and what has this revealed about the caliber of our character as a nation and as a people. Now I am not trying to cause some debate as people have the tendency to point a finger at everyone else for the state of affairs. Pointing fingers is an immature practice that has never solved any problem. As Christians we are told to take responsibility for our spiritual lives.

A wise person will look beyond the present to see what must be done to prepare, a responsible watchman will see what is coming and warn others, people who operate in wishful thinking will ignore the signs and hope it passes without causing too much inconvenience, and the indifferent will turn a judgmental eye and use it as some type of platform where self, personal agenda, causes, and etc. are being exalted.

As a believer, I can read my Bible and know the season we are in and as one who loves God's truth, I will do my best to be a watchman and warn others of what is on the horizon, but I do not want to be one who operates in wishful thinking or indifference. The only way I can be sure if I am ready for this season is to shed all the weights that so easily beset me in my walk and be sure I possess enough oil of the Holy Spirit that I will be enabled to stand in the darkness.

This means I can't foolishly squander my time, energy, and spiritual gifts on that which has no eternal significance. *Ephesians 5:15-17* tells us, *"See then that ye walk circumspectly, not as fools, but as wise.*

Redeeming the time, because the days are evil, Wherefore be ye not unwise, but understanding what the will of the Lord is."

PREPARATION

*The watchword against temptations of
the flesh is: **flight.***
*The watchword against the world is: **faith**.*
*The watchword against temptations
from the devil is: **fight.***
(Donald Barnhouse)

We are expecting dear friends today. There has been much preparation going on in the home front to be ready for their visit. We are looking forward to seeing their faces and fellowshipping with them. As preparation was being made, I had to wonder if I have the same expectation in regard to Jesus' coming.

Am I preparing for Him? Clearly, I must have a viable relationship with Him to be waiting in expectation while preparing the inner tabernacle of my soul to meet with Him as my Friend, Savior, Lord, and God.

The apostle Paul talked about those who love Jesus' appearing in *1 Timothy 4:8* and goes on to say in Titus, *"Looking for that blessed hope, and the glorious appearing of the great God and our Saviour Jesus Christ (Titus 2:13).* Are you living in expectation and preparation for that great day?

As we live in times that seem uncertain and almost insane, we must not forget the Lord is the one who is in control. Uncertainty can make us feel vulnerable and it is true we are powerless to change circumstances, hearts, minds, or push back the tidal waves that hit the shorelines of our worlds.

As believers let us resign ourselves to remember our hope is not here, our home is in a far distant land, and our life hidden in the eternal refuge of heaven, our Lord Jesus Christ.

I recently heard the term, "Get your house in order." A person once confessed to me she thought, "getting your house in order," meant to get your physical house in order.

When the Bible talks about being ready for the days we are living in or "getting our house in order," it has to do with personal spiritual preparation. We have been living at our present location for seven years and it remains a work in progress because it is not only redoing some things here and there but maintaining it.

For Christians, "Getting their house in order," is about getting their lives right with the Lord and maintaining their relationship with Him at all times. We are the temple of God and every temple needs a good house cleaning once in a while where there is a thorough examination to see if there is any disrepair occurring in our relationship with the Lord. Perhaps there are weeds in the gardens of our heart that are choking out the importance of the Word and crowding out the passion and conviction we once held, and maybe there are tares of arrogance that have been planted in the field of our souls that could cause disruption in the amount of fruit that could be produced in and through our lives.

Perhaps our foundation has a crack in it because the ground of our theology has been challenged in some way and shifted off of center. And, we must not forget the structure, our inward Christian disciplines that define the character of our inner life and the countenance and conduct of our outer life that manifests the spirit, attitudes, and temperament we are operating according to.

The Bible is clear we do need to honestly examine the different aspects of the temples of our bodies, beginning with the inside and working to the outside to be sure we are ready to stand when the storms of life confront us. Keep in mind, the Pharisees were beautiful white-washed tombs with dead and decaying religion within.

We must rid ourselves of inward defilement before we can become a temple that properly represents a holy God at this time of great darkness. The Apostle Paul said it best in 1 Corinthians 3:16-17, "Know ye not that ye are the temple of God, and *that* the Spirit of God dwelleth in you? If any man defile the temple of God, him shall God destroy; for the temple of God is holy, which *temple* ye are?"

To me, spring house cleaning means to clean every nook and cranny in the home. To do this you have to expose everything to the light to see what needs to be cleaned and how to clean it. For me it requires me to occasionally get on my knees to shine the light on every area to do a "sufficient" job.

We are told in *Proverbs 16:2* that all of our ways seem clean to us, but God has a different view of all matters and for this reason. David asked God to turn on the searchlight on his heart to see if there was any wicked way in him in *Psalm 139:23-24*.

It is for this reason we are instructed by God's Word to examine our motives, test our spirit, and be honest about our fruit to make sure we are in the true faith. Examination of this type requires us to bend our knees in humility, flex our necks in submission, open our hearts to allow the heavenly light to freely shine, and be prepared to repent and ask God to do the cleaning necessary in our lives that will ensure we are cleansed and holy temples in which to worship and commune with Him.

As mentioned yesterday when cleaning you need light. Dust particles with different allergens that can stir up weaknesses in immune systems collect in darkness, cobwebs are allowed to begin to weave their own bewitching form of covering over what are considered valuable objects laying some type of claim to it, and non-essential stuff begins to fill every vacant spot. It is in darkness that mice and rats can find places to reside; therefore, every room must be opened and exposed to the light (including the garage).

It is easy as humans to have small closets of rights that will cause weakness in our character, dark corners where cobwebs of neglect collect which create an unattractive covering over that which should be prized, vacant spots where the world has filled it with empty things and activities, and the "rats" and "mice" of our age can freely operate and undermine through deception, indoctrination, and unbelief. I admit, when I encounter such a space in my life, I often want to shut the door and ignore it, but the truth is such spaces take away from the value and effectiveness of my spiritual life.

Before the priests went into the Holy Place to do service, they had to stop at the laver which was before the door of the Holy Place to clean away any spot or blemish from the world or the work done at the Altar of Burnt Offering. The laver was made of women's looking glasses which were made of bronze (brass) that had been brought to such a shine they could see their reflection in it *(Exodus 38:8)*. The laver pointed to the Word of God and the bronze, judgment on sin.

The Word of God judges sin and cleanses us from it in order to ensure we see the reflection of Christ in our lives *(Ephesians 5:26-27; 2 Corinthians 3:18; James 1:21-26)*. The next time you open God's Word, allow it to reveal what you are reflecting to those around you, the best of the self-life, the false glitter of the world, or the Light of heaven that came into the world to take the various cloaks away to reveal our great need for a Savior who will forgive, cleanse and set us free to be all that heaven ordained us to be *(John 15:22; Romans 8:29; 1 John 3:2)*.

I will be taking a slight pause away from technology for a couple of days. Granted, I may be popping in and out of Facebook, but for the most part I will be involved with other activities. As I was thinking about taking a pause, I realized how significant this activity is in every function of life.

In the weather there are pauses. For example, in hurricanes there is the eye of the storm and for other storms it is the quiet before the storm. In breathing, the pause can be a sigh, in singing it is taking a deep breath, in a sentence it is certain punctuation marks, and in music it is a symbol that represents a resting in the music before continuing on. We even see in the Psalms where the pause is identified with the word "Selah."

Pauses point to preparation that ensures that the appropriate emphasis follows. The calm before the storm is a space before greater

362

intensity of winds hit, and in singing it takes air to properly execute the tone and length of notes. As we can see, pauses are necessary. They may only represent a moment, but that moment is valuable to ensure the functioning or integrity of what follows.

In our Christian walk pauses point to stopping to hear, ponder, and meditate. It is in the pauses that the profound can be highlighted, the spirit can land, the soul can come to a place of rest, and the mind can become still. We daily take many pauses for granted, but we need to stop and consider when was the last time we paused long enough for God to speak to our spirit, reveal His heart, and fellowship with us.

A good cleansing of the inner sanctuary of our lives is of the uttermost importance. It is a matter of taking care of business as to the character of our faith towards the Lord, for without it we can't please Him. In fact, we are told by the Apostle Paul to examine ourselves and see if we are in the faith (*2 Corinthians 13:5*).

The whole purpose of self-examination in regard to our spiritual lives is a matter of doing business with God so that we can properly do His business on His behalf in this world. It is easy to instruct Christians to, "Get their house or temples in order," but how many understand what that means. Sadly, we have left too many Christians to figure out such matters without proper discipling.

Paul tells us that what happened in the Old Testament serves as our example. When I was first challenged with the idea of cleansing my temple, I figured the best place to go was the happenings and practices surrounding the Old Testament temple and guess what, I found an incident in *2 Kings 18:1-7* and *2 Chronicles 29 & 30* where the temple was cleansed and prepared for true service and worship.

Before I studied the whole process of cleansing, I asked the Lord to show me how to apply it to my life, and the nuggets He unveiled to me were incredible. The first thing we must do is to ensure our own heart attitude is right before the Lord.

As priests that are responsible for the environment of our own temples, we must make sure every entrance is open to God, allowing His penetrating light to reveal the condition of our inner sanctuary. We must make sure there is no musky smell of stagnation due to complacency, no dust of neglect where His Word is concerned, no decay of indifference for lack of godly love, and no ruin of defilement present due to unholy agreements. This allows us to identify and bring down all idols (high places-vain imaginations) and secret places (heart—misdirected affections).

All that is in the inner sanctuary of our lives must be brought to the place of sacrifice to either be consumed in the fire or refined and brought forth for service. The place of sacrifice also points to the shedding of blood and as believers we can have the assurance that the blood of Jesus cleanses us from all unrighteousness, and now we can have both the confidence and liberty to ask the Lord to fill up every vacated area of our temple with the presence of His Spirit to ensure the complete work of sanctification.

After all, what has not been sanctified by the Spirit cannot be used by Him. After the cleansing comes the freedom to celebrate before the Lord the life and blessings He has given us as we worship Him in Spirit and truth.

How do you look at crises? As a nation, we are in a state of emergency, but the question is how many of us would even realize that there was an emergency happening in our nation if we had not been told by our President and the media? Most people go their way without any concern about what is happening elsewhere. They may hear of tragedies, but as long as their lives are not personally touched, they may feel a few twinges of sympathy up front, but after that they pretty much go on without a lot of thought about it afterwards.

It is important to realize this type of emergency tests the readiness of the nation and the people as to how well they are prepared for a crisis. If we could grade our nation's preparedness on how the people responded to this crisis, I believe we might receive a failing grade. An emergency will also test the wisdom (foresight), the character, and the preparedness of the individual.

Wise people see what is coming down the line and prepare for it; therefore, they are not caught off guard. People who have true character will be prepared to face the crisis and become part of the solution and not the problem. As Christians we should not be caught off guard by any crises because we have been told in the Bible how to discern the times we live in and be prepared for the test. However, the sad thing is our nation has been in a moral crisis for years and has been crumbling within, our families have been ravaged by the idols and are being consumed by godless philosophies of this age, our societies are in utter chaos due to lawlessness, and our churches have been lulled to sleep by worldliness, rendered powerless by watered-down versions of the Bible and gospels, as well as lifeless doctrines and leaders who lack calling and vision.

These self-serving thieves prove to be nothing more than wolves who are building up their own personal kingdoms on earth or hireling shepherds who will leave the sheep to become prey to whoever and whatever as they preserve their own welfare. As a nation, society, and church we have been in a crisis for years, and even though there have been a few voices along the way crying out from the wildernesses and pulpits, for the most part it appears their warnings have fallen on deaf ears, with the exception of a few here and there taking heed.

I have a saying, "God never wastes a good crisis." May this be true for His people. What has this crisis revealed about you? If you find that you would receive a failing grade in any area, what steps do you need to take to be prepared? After all, the Bible is clear we are in a time of grave testing that will shake the whole world, and we can be assured that our faith, character, and preparedness will be tested.

There is so much depression surrounding us that it is easy to become weary with life. This is why we must be prepared to possess our souls in patience. When I think of patience in light of *Luke 21:19*, I think of what Job had to endure. Keep in mind it was James who reminds us in light of our faith to consider the patience of Job. Considering the example of Job in this way always signaled to me that it is time to discern the attitude of my heart.

Rayola Kelley

Righteousness involves three aspects of our Christian life. It is a place where we have right standing in the Lord. We are placed in Christ who serves as our righteousness and when God sees us, He sees His Son and is able to accept us. The second aspect of righteousness has to do with being right before the Lord and the third is doing right. Being right before the Lord is where attitude comes in. The one ingredient that is necessary to ensure righteousness is the fear of the Lord. When you have a healthy fear of God, you first of all dread displeasing Him because of your love for Him; secondly, you fear doing wrong due to consequences where you might bring a reproach on Him, and third you want to avoid any anxiety or terror about being separated from Him for eternity.

To dread displeasing Him is what disciplines your walk with obedience, fearing consequences is what brings sobriety to your ways before the Lord, and being realistic about the two choices of where man spends eternity is what keeps you in the straight narrow way of righteousness. Never forget the way to Christ, His life and His promises are hard and challenging according to *Matthew 7:13-14*.

My prayer is simple, "Lord reveal the attitude of my heart because we are living in days that try the patience of saints, the resolve of those steadfast in their hearts, and the godly who are courageous in the ways of righteousness."

Is there any area in which fallen man can arrive at and consider a matter completely finished or completed? We can complete worldly projects that are attached to building, literature, art and etc., but I have lived around artists and they are never satisfied with the completed product. There is always something they would change or do over. This is true for me and my books and posts. I can always find room for improvement.

Consider our daily activities. We have to maintain what we own, whether it is a home or a car. There is never a place where we can say with confidence about our various activities—it is finished to a point of complete perfection. This brings me to salvation.

Jesus was clear that His redemption on the cross was completed but for those who are believers, we will never enter into completion until the day we enter into His glory. We may be born again and stand justified, but we have not arrived at the place of perfection.

The Apostle John pointed out the three stages of Christianity in *1 John 2:12-14*. Clearly, we need to graduate from being children who live on the pure milk of doctrine, to the teenage stage where we are overcoming the enemy with the sword of the Lord's Word, and coming to full age as those who wisely lead and guide others in their Christian walk.

We are told to go on to perfection in *Hebrews 6:1*, which entails working out our salvation in fear and trembling (submission to the Holy Spirit work of sanctification and obedience to His Word), while picking up our cross daily and dying to the influence of the flesh as we fight the good fight taking place between the flesh and the Spirit, and the unseen realm of Satan.

We must contend for the faith first delivered to the saints and exhort each other to choose what is excellent, especially as we see the day of the blessed hope of Jesus' return drawing near (*Luke 9:23-25; Galatians 5:16-18; Ephesians 6:10-18; Philippians 2:12; Hebrews 5:12-6:2; 10:25; Jude 3*).

Those who think they have arrived in their Christian walk are very immature, are operating from wishful thinking, or are deluded. As believers, we stand justified which opens the door to a new life, as disciples we enter through that door to follow Christ into that life, as saints we are being sanctified by the Spirit as we live and walk out the life of Christ, and it is all in light of preparing us to be ultimately glorified with Christ, bringing us into His perfection.

Can we trust the Lord, our potter to put us in the right place when we encounter the fiery ovens? It amazed me to discover up until the ovens, clay could be broken down and reshaped. I don't know about you, but I would rather be broken down many times and prepared and shaped according to God's plans before He puts me in the ovens where brokenness means the end for a vessel.

The clay vessels had to go through two firings. The first firing was to rid them of excess water that would expand and bust them in intense heat. How we need to be rid of the self-life that is still reigning before being exposed to the intense testing of our faith and character.

The Lord is aware of this reality and knows exactly what trial to set us in to cause us to let go of the former to embrace God's plan. The second fire was the intense heat that would establish the vessel in its final form. If you are following Jesus, you probably have experienced the different stages of this process.

No doubt some of you might be experiencing the weather, pounding, or being shaped and others of you might feel the heat of the ovens, but take heart. Remember, the Lord is making you a vessel fit for His use and like Shadrach, Meshach, and Abednego in *Daniel 3*, you can be confident that He is doing the work and that you are not alone if you are in such fiery ovens because the Son of God will be with you.

THE DAYS WE LIVE IN

If the world is to get back on its feet,
the church has to get on its knees.
(Unknown)

As a believer what are you looking for? Many people are looking for certain events to happen. However, the Bible does not instruct us to consider the times we live in according to events because they can be misinterpreted, but according to the signs that Jesus laid out in Scripture.

Case in point, many are looking for a great revival to happen. Revival is about reviving something that is dead, or in a comatose state, or indifferent to its environment. The question is, is the visible church in America in such a state that it clearly needs to be revived?

Some would disagree with such a conclusion and they would point out the number of people attending their church. But revival has nothing to do with numbers, but with spiritual life and growth. I have to admit as I study the Scriptures concerning the times I'm living in, I am not preparing for or looking for certain events like a great revival; rather, I am looking and preparing for what the Bible has promised is so: I am looking for the coming of our blessed hope, Jesus Christ.

We are living in the times that both Paul and Peter warned us about in their epistles. It is not a surprise, but the lawlessness and corruption will cause great vexation to a saint's spirit. I realized there are only two aspects of this life that will limit man when it comes to his digression into the depths of wickedness and that is God's grace and the grave.

I am so thankful God's grace is stopping my descent into the depths of a depressing, tormenting, and hopeless reality. As we watch mankind spiral out of control, we must seek to see the bigger picture. First of all, we had a spiritual vacuum in this world and now we see the results of it.

Man is raging not against institutions but against God. Man screams great obscenities because hell is his inspiration, he hides behind injustice because he is lawless at heart and resents and rejects all righteous authority. He is a murderer because he is doing the bidding of his father, Satan who is a murderer. These people are liars and no truth can be found in them because they are Satan's mouthpiece.

The question is what is the goal of Satan in relationship to his systems of the world? If you know Scripture, the answer to that question is that it has, and always will be, to bring every human being under the umbrella of a one-world government, economic, and religious system ruled by him. Will Satan and cohorts succeed? As more and more facts come out about this "pandemic," it is obvious it is nothing more than a wicked agenda to set the world up for such a takeover, which is anti-God, anti-family, and anti-capitalism ideology.

However, the Bible tells us God laughs at the nations that rage against Him, the meek will inherit the earth, the righteous will be preserved, God's truth will be standing when all else collapses, and in the end, HE will be the Judge of all. As Christians we need to stand in light of what was foretold about this time. We need to stand on the truth of what we have been told, lean on the promises we know are true, and stay the course that has been set before us, knowing we are on the right side of reality, truth, and eternity.

Rayola Kelley

How many of you experienced childhood diseases? Before I reached third grade, I had survived Mumps, Chicken Pox, German Measles, and etc. Today children are vaccinated against many of these diseases, and we perceive it as doing them a favor, but are we? I had a bout with shingles a couple of years back. I knew about dull pain, pulsating pain, and sharp pain, but shingles exposed me to an intense (relentless) and unbearable pain, leaving me with scars to prove it.

Shingles is a mutation of Chicken Pox, and I learned the reason shingles has gained such momentum in our society is because children are being vaccinated against Chicken Pox. Apparently, if a childhood disease such as Chicken Pox is not allowed to run its course in society among the young to build a type of block, allowing the immune systems of others to be compromised because they are not being revved up to produce antibodies to push back such diseases as shingles.

I remembered hearing the story of a mother making sure her child was brought up in a germ-free environment and when her little girl was five, she died of some minor thing such as the common cold. The moral of the story was to let your children "eat dirt," because some of the strongest immune systems are found in children who live in garbage dumps.

A report came out that the reason there were so many deaths among the elderly in Italy due to coronavirus is because of vaccinations. These people had been vaccinated against many diseases due to the influx of refugees to a point that it actually compromised their immune system and they had no means to fight Corvid 19.

Have you ever looked at what they put in our vaccinations? They put in mercury (they will not allow this in the garbage dumps and yet they put it in our bodies), aborted baby parts, animal parts, fluorine (poison), aluminum, formaldehyde and various other things that no doubt are unnecessary or counterproductive. Vaccines, by the way, are so toxic that the used needles must be carefully sealed and disposed of as dangerous toxic waste. And, have you heard the latest, this next vaccine will have a chip in it that will store information about you, and keep track of you.

This chip may well be the mark of the beast mentioned in *Revelation 13:16-18* that we are warned about. God gave us a wonderful immune system that if encouraged and allowed to work proves effective, but the key is it must be encouraged and allowed to work by exposing it to the different viruses and bacteria of our environment. This is true for our spiritual life.

Many Christians want to be immune from the things of this world, but what God has given us to survive this world does not immune us from it but enables us to walk through it. Like the virus and bacteria that is all around us, it is unseen, but once it is given the right environment, it will manifest itself. And, what is this unseen source? It is our faith.

I have made mentioned about the latest cult in my posts. This cult is being greatly promoted by the left and the media, and sadly in some cases its wave of delusion and destruction is catching up well-meaning people into its current, but there are those who are also standing against it.

We as believers must remember the spirit and legitimacy of something comes down to the fruit it produces, and it is obvious whose bidding this latest cult is doing. It is important as believers that we initially stand back and discern every movement regardless of who it is associated with.

You can tell what cults are hiding behind their claims by what they emphasize, for the accuser is always the abuser. If they are hiding moral deviation, they promote outward moral goodness. If they are hiding seduction or delusion, they promote some form of truth that is wrapped up in propaganda and warning to watch out for the "wolves." If they are hiding greed, they promote charity and benevolence, and if they are hiding the worst type of biases and prejudices, they cry of racial injustice.

Keep in mind, that while you are caught up with what they are proclaiming, their actions are telling the real story. Perhaps some of you know the name of the latest cult. It is known as "Black Lives Matter."

This movement is capitalizing on a grave injustice by demanding that all fall down before it in sick submission and confess allegiance to something that is insanely racial, unjust, and evil. This cause is clearly serving as a front for untold injustices to take place everywhere, regardless of color, to create anarchy as a means to bring America down, and the "anti" in its name confirms this very fact.

The "anti" is against all order and establishment in America, which points to the complete breakdown and fall of society. The vacuum it leaves with be filled with the seeds and destruction of hell itself.

Satan is after worship and told Jesus that if He would bow down and worship him that he would give Him the kingdoms of the world. For Jesus to bow before Satan would have required Him to deny His glory as Creator while turning all dominion over to him in order to rule over doomed kingdoms.

We are warned in the end days of great delusion, and if possible, even the elect would be deceived. Never let it be said that any believer allows the causes of this world to bring him or her to a place where he or she bows their knees to the god of this world to somehow make peace with the idols, the serpents, the scorpions, and the devils of it.

As we confront the insanity of our age, it is easy to see why people who are part of the delusion of our time are totally seduced by demons, indoctrinated into a hellish reality, and deceived into believing the initial lie presented in the garden by the serpent. The Bible is clear in *Titus 1:15* that to the pure all things are pure, but to the profane and defiled all things are perverted.

What we see is determined by the filter we are looking through and that filter comes down to the spirit that is influencing us. How we often interpret something comes down to the attitude we are taking on because of the spirit that is motivating us.

It is impossible for the pure to comprehend the great evil of our days and it explains why the profane will mock, scoff at, and rage at the pure for their so-called "foolishness, stupidity, and naiveness." The pure can't imagine man being part of something that is so wicked that their conscience can't be pricked by the suffering and destruction that is being inflicted on the innocent, while the profane see purity as something that must be perverted, righteousness a virtue that must be silenced, and true freedom as an enemy to their agendas.

As I become more aware of how Satan's minions operate in dark, secret places everything from occultic practices to Babylonian paganism (idolatry), being part of the Cabal, the latest medical scams to control us, reset the world's economy to serve their greed and appetites, doing all they can to depopulate the world, and committing the worst, unimaginable atrocities to continue to possess and partake of the fountain of youth (Adrenochrome), I realize that we can know what a reprobate who no longer retains any real knowledge of God looks like.

It is clear these individuals have no conscience about their abominable actions, no real soul to care about the great sorrow and pain they leave behind, and why they believe they are part of the enlightened, the elite, and the infallible who will be victorious in the end over the one true God and His people.

Every time I get a small glimpse into the sick, profane, insane, hellish reality of these people, I thank the Lord, He saved me from all earthly claims on me, put His light in my inner man with His life, put my feet on the narrow path with His Word, keeps my mind clear with His truth, my soul sober with reality of His promises, and my spirit free to soar above the present world. Meanwhile, I stand in confidence of Jesus, knowing all the enemies will be brought under His sweet feet for He has already secured and sealed the necessary victory at the cross, and will bring it to full fruition when He comes back as Judge and King.

Our world is proving to be very upside down. I used to wonder how is it only eight people were saved during the flood, or how ten righteous men could not be found in Sodom to spare it from utter destruction, and how Elijah felt that he was the only one who stood for Jehovah in His day until the Lord revealed that 7,000 people had not yet bowed to Baal before his altars.

As I watch the happenings around me, it is easy to see that like the Bible states, "a little leaven corrupts the whole lump." It is clear we have had the leaven of the present corruption of this world take root and practically consume the different systems of our nation. Lies are now reality, injustice is justice, evil is good, rebellion is necessary, lawlessness is promoted, and wickedness is the accepted way. I believe many Americans are beginning to see the corruption that clearly is tearing our nation apart, but as Christians, are we beginning to see the danger of the church coming into agreement with the world?

The seeds of corruption have been planted in the church and the results are devastating. The real Gospel has been watered down to a mere social activity of good deeds, the call to holiness is ignored and labeled as being unloving, righteousness is redefined by tolerance towards sin, attitudes lack the fear of the Lord, service is often man-centered, religious experiences and fickle feelings supersede the Word of God, and worship is often nothing more than emotional hype. The results of this corruption have left some of the church without authority, power, and a distinct testimony to make the necessary impact on lost, hurting, seeking souls.

The Bible calls us to come out and be separate from this world. I can't tell you how many times I have heard the platitude, "We are in the world, but not part of it." The problem for some of the church is that the world is in it, and for some Christians, they had to sadly come out of their local church to once again hear the voice of the true Shepherd.

As believers we must discern how much of the world's spirit has corrupted how we look at God, our attitude towards His Word, our love towards one another, our devotion to God, and our life before Him. Perhaps as we approach a new year, we can truly ask God to turn on the searchlight, knowing that the only one who is able to turn our personal worlds right side up in an upside-down world is the Lord Jesus Christ.

Jesus talked about two matters that concerned Him the most in the end days. The first one was that of deception, but the second one was faith. He asked if He would find faith when He came back.

Faith can be used in different ways. It is a noun that identifies an attitude, a descriptive adjective that will produce a certain state, and an action word that, for the believer, is expressed in obedience to God's Word. The Bible is clear there is only one faith and that it is the only faith that pleases God.

It seems faith has been, in some cases, rendered into some formula, declaration, or wishful thinking. When you study the way of faith, there are four things you must recognize. It is a personal walk that no one else can do for you. The second thing faith does is line us up to the ways of righteousness. The third aspect of faith is that it begins where our own human understanding, strength, and abilities cease. And finally, faith is to lead us to the place where we actually inherit the promises of God. That is why faith is referred to as a walk.

It allows us to encounter God in His glory, experience God in His ways, witness Him doing the extraordinary in and through the ordinary, and cause our testimony to grow when we become part of His miraculous interventions. Sadly, Christians stop at faith being simply a noun. They hear the Gospel, accept its message and happily go on their way back into the world without understanding that it is a gift from God given to us that has the goal of making us true heirs to what is eternal in order to obtain our spiritual inheritance.

The question is, is faith a noun to you or an adjective that you try to conjure up on your own in order to get God to move on your behalf instead of walking in faith towards God? The only thing that is going to enable us to stand in these days is genuine faith that withstands with truth and will continue to stand according to eternal promises.

As Bible believing Christians, we recognize that the signs around us signal the season that will end with the coming of Jesus for His church. There is no need to debate that Jesus, Paul, and Peter's description of these particular days are playing out before our eyes. The question is what will our response be?

Are we going to sit around and wait for the sky to part when the Bible is clear we are to occupy, work until the night is too great, be watching for Him, ready to heed His call at all times, and praying that we be found worthy to escape such a time (possessing the oil of the Spirit) when He does come?

I love the promise of His coming, but I also personally take seriously the warnings and instructions that surround this blessed hope that have been resonating among believers for over 20 centuries. The Bible was written for my edification and not for me to pick and choose what will serve my particular mood or preferred reality (fantasy) for the day.

To me we are living in these precarious times that require us to be vigilant towards what is happening, sober about our responses, and living out our lives in expectation of our King and Lord's visitation. Such knowledge should cause every one of us to drop casual practices of skipping from one Scriptural promise to another, swinging from one branch of fanciful notion about Christianity to another hyperbolic branch, or hanging on to a rope of wishful thinking that is not attached to the eternal Rock.

We must make sure that we are spiritually preparing ourselves to not simply get by in these times, but to make sure we are prepared to stand on truth regardless of what it costs, withstand by faith towards God in spite of the mockery and possible persecution, and continue to stand because His promises are "Amen, "so be it on earth, for it is so in heaven."

Today we live in dark times. This darkness has nothing to do with Covid 19, but with the spiritual depravity that clearly exists in our nation. There are three types of darkness: the natural darkness, the darkness of understanding, and spiritual darkness. Natural darkness for the Christian is a time of rest and preparation to properly walk in the light of the day. The darkness of understanding requires the believer to choose the way of faith until God shines His light on a matter. In such darkness, we as believers take steps of obedience to what we know is Scripturally true to walk the narrow unseen path of righteousness in order to come to the light of God's revelation where He often reveals Himself to us in greater ways.

For believers, spiritual darkness serves as a heavy hand upon the soul. At such times our soul must learn to wait upon the Lord until He lifts it, which often reveals the priceless, eternal work He has been doing in our lives. However, when it comes to the unsaved and the wicked, darkness is different for them.

These people prefer it because it hides their unbelief, rebellious independence from God, and their wicked deeds. For the unredeemed sinner, darkness is a quasi-state where assumptions and wishful thinking allow them to walk in some false light, whether it is man-made religion, secularism, or worldly decency. Sadly, each false light is void of any real salvation. Their light of understanding is a dim light of wishful thinking that will fail them, while spiritual darkness causes them to grope in the endless caverns of spiritual hopelessness and defeat where they eventually experience leanness of spirit and judgment.

For the wicked they love the darkness because they can scheme to rob the vulnerable, attempt to kill the truth, and figure out how to destroy all righteousness. They smile at the vulnerable while they steal from them, they talk out of both sides of their mouth in order to hide their murderous intensions, and they rage against all righteousness in order to destroy it. They are tools of Satan, sons of Belial, and the children of the age which are designated to taste God's cup of wrath to the bitter end.

As believers, we must not let the darkness of this world bury us under despair, cause us to hide out of fear, or swallow us up in hopelessness. After all, we possess the very light of heaven, and although we can't see it, we need to remember it is always there, and one day it will part the darkness and we will become aware that the eyes of our faith have indeed been fine-tuned to see into that which is unseen and eternal.

The question is how are we to wade through these times? If I asked you what is the greatest problem we are facing, I would probably be given various answers from pestilence that is being used to usher in tyrannical control at every governmental level, corruption in our government where our politicians are for sale, lawlessness in our society that is allowed and encouraged to disrupt order, burn cities and destroy the quality of our life, the breakdown of our family, unregulated technology, and etc. However, these are not the problems, these are the symptoms of the problem.

What is the real problem? The problem is three-fold: 1) God has been kicked out of most arenas, 2) truth is being sacrificed in every area, and 3) man's heart. God presence and intervention is needed to bring and ensure order in any productive society and He does it through truth, which is absolute in authority, final in judgment, ensures integrity in godly love, upholds the witness of genuine faith, and sets the captive free while putting the enemy on notice.

However, when the true God of the Bible is missing from the equation there is no real moral gauge and without truth there are no absolutes that man can test and discern a matter to see if it is real in order to properly address it. The question is why is God and truth missing? It is because sinful man wants to control his understanding of God and determine his own reality as a means to have his own way.

Man's way is perverse, contrary, unacceptable, and hypocritical to God. As believers we must not get caught up with the many ruses orchestrated by the clowns of our time; rather, we must stand for truth when given the opportunity to do so. However, beware, when you stand for truth, you set up a mirror that will bring contrast to the one who comes face to face with it. Such a contrast usually will cause rebellious, unrepentant man to hate you, rage against the standard, and aggressively attempt to wipe out any witness of it.

People are looking to various things to either encourage themselves in these trying times, or numb their feelings with artificial measures, or feed their wishful thinking with fantasy. However, the reality of today is hitting us head on and is bringing discouragement, awakening feelings of uncertainty and fear, and causing wishful thinking to faint in its tracks.

We can hunker down into some dark corner, trying to think positive as we look around at that which seems hopeless, or convince ourselves that all will be alright in the end. The truth is there is a shaking going on in our nation and it is meant to wake us up to reality.

We can't address what is until we are willing to face it as it is. We can't be part of the solution until we are willing to admit the problem and take responsibility for what our part could be if we cared to.

Much of what has happened to us as a nation is because people have been asleep, while some are aware but due to hopelessness became complacent, and some lived in denial as they simply got by. As a nation we will never return to normalcy, and I don't know about you but my spirit has become vexed over the moral and spiritual condition of what has been shoved down our throats as being "normal."

Clearly, what has become "normal" to the psychology of this nation and to a visible church, where there is no real distinction between the world and it, must NOT be allowed to return to such "normalcy." As a nation, we must begin to come back to the strong roots that made this nation a nation of opportunity and not oppression. As a people, we must not settle for the crumbs of the elite and the false promises of the politician that is drunk on greed and power, and as Christians we must begin to choose the way of excellence which includes separation from this present age and sacrifice of the old in order to gain and reflect that which is the light of heaven.

My grandfather was a farmer and we have been blessed with brothers in the Lord who are also farmers. They are, for the most part, great weathermen because for them success depends on properly gauging and monitoring the weather. Nature has a way of telling you what the weather will be by how it is reacting and even by different smells.

In certain dry environments rain has a particular smell and so does the air in autumn. Dew in the morning means the day will be hot, while leaves closing up means plant life is bracing itself against the chilly spring weather or an approaching storm. The latest bit of information I learned is that carpenter ants come out when the weather hits 70 degrees and will fly until their wings fall off.

When it comes to the spiritual season we are now in, we are being bombarded by signs that the prophetic warnings found in such Scriptures as *Matthew 24; 2 Timothy 3:1-7; 4:1-4; 1 Thessalonians 5:1-6;* and *2 Thessalonians 2* are coming at us in waves that are slamming against us, testing our patience and resolve. These signs are not given to cause our hearts to faint; rather, they are to alert us that we need to spiritually prepare for what is about to come.

The present realities of the day are clearly prophetical as we watch some people's hearts grow cold, others go into utter despair; some lose any semblance of faith, and the rest experiencing grave brokenness and vexation of spirit; but as believers, we are told not to cower in the corner but to occupy until the return of our Lord. Just as prophesied in Daniel, the patience of the saints is being tested as the anti-Christ systems try to wear that patience down, and it is for this reason Jesus asked if He would find true faith when He came back. He also warned that only those who endure to the end will be saved.

This is why we are instructed to possess our souls in patience. To possess our souls in patience means we have to be watchmen, ever guarding the place of communion with our Lord, as well as the integrity of the sanctuary of our inner lives and homes, and ready at all times to respond like a good soldier to anything that would disrupt our life in the Lord. Revelation 14:12 actually summarizes what the patience of the saint is, "Here is the patience of the saints: here are they that keep the commandments of God and the faith of Jesus."

Another instruction that we have been given concerning the trying times of the last days is to pray we will be found worthy to escape. What does it mean to be worthy to escape such days?

Again, we are told we can't be like children of darkness that will be spiritually asleep when Jesus comes. We must be watchmen, ever guarding the gates, watching for enemies that are trying to gain access within, and from the walls for when the great armies come in order to warn others of the pending danger. We can't be careless servants that live like the devil, while thinking we will straighten up our act just before our Lord comes, for we do not know when He will come.

The crux of the matter is that we need to make sure we are like the five virgins in Matthew 25:1-13 that possessed the oil of the Holy Spirit to see us through these dark times in preparation of meeting our Bridegroom who is coming for a chaste, ready, prepared bride.

The question is what are you doing in these times? There is no need to cower for we know who wins in the end, and there is no reason to grow cold, wallow in despair, or lose faith because we know who owns our heart, serves as our hope and is the author and finisher of our faith. Therefore, let us faithfully occupy as we stand as faithful saints, withstand as good soldiers, and continue to stand in expectation of seeing the return of our blessed hope, Jesus Christ.

As we walk through these times, we need to remember the promises that have been given to us by God's Word. What we remember and how we remember is also a choice. We choose what we remember and it is often based on the emotional impact it made on us and we also choose how we want to remember it.

Good memories can become a point of sentimentality that can be exalted to the place of fantasy or legend. Bad memories can be used as an avenue to become an excuse for bad feelings or become the means to justify unseen walls of protection and wrong behavior. I must never let memories wall me in because my world will become small, and instead of becoming an adventurer to discover life, I will end up living in a morbid, depressing reality. Memories must be kept in perspective. Sentimental memories will never be again and they must never become fanciful to the extent I think I can live them once again, and only God can heal the bad memories to prevent them from running roughshod over my life.

The reality of reminiscing when it comes to my spiritual walk is to remember the lessons I have learned to gain both experience and wisdom and to be able to gauge personal growth. Some great lessons that I constantly need to remind myself of is that God is God and He is sovereign in all that is happening. He has both His eye and hand on me and I need to first of all let Him be God, second of all trust Him to be God, and third of all let matters be what they are so that I can see the adventure in them to honestly face the emotional tides associated with them, for only truth will set me free.

What are you choosing to remember when threatening storms are on the horizon, challenging terrain lays before you, and failure and defeat seem inevitable? I, for one, know they are a test of my character and faith and I have had to come to the place where I say, "Let them be what they are for I know my God is who He is and nothing is too great for Him for His work to be hindered in my life and nothing too small that He will allow me to trip into some great abyss where I will become lost to Him."

Rayola Kelley

It is getting hard to listen to what seems like ludicrous nonsense. Today the matters confronting this world reminds us that the glory of the world is at best temporary, but at worst it is a false glitter that hides its darkness. As I watch the events happening around us that glitter is clearly giving way to fear that causes confusion, control that creates anger, and oppression that produces despair.

I see people struggling with what is true as some politicians and media with wicked agendas use fear tactics of life and death issues to control them. Politicians along with some cronies have been entrusted with a sacred position to protect the citizenry from anything encroaching their basic rights, but are now threatening such rights by using this opportunity to abuse their power, becoming tyrants and despots.

People for the most part want to be left alone to pursue life, liberty, and property, but now they are being oppressed by politicians that in the name of fear are stripping them of their lifestyles. It is a sad state of affairs, but as a believer, I must remember that Satan is the god of this world and that I am not looking to this world to provide me with life, liberty, purpose, or happiness. It is true, I can become quite overwhelmed by what I see and hear, but as a believer I can rejoice and look up knowing that my redemption draws near.

But meanwhile, whether we like it or not, we are in a battle for the souls of people and this nation. As being part of the kingdom of light, I need to stand against the deception of the kingdom of darkness that is totally engulfing this world with the light of God's truth and Gospel. Some of the battles are intense and prove wearisome to the soul, but as soldiers of the cross, we must avoid becoming weary in doing what we need to do because in due season we shall reap.

May we as believers, be clear and urgent about our mission here, and be prayerful but bold in declaring the message that is the power of God unto salvation. Let us rejoice that in such troubling times, that people who now know their vulnerability and sense their need to be saved, will begin to look towards heaven and call upon the name of the Lord.

THE HIGH CALLING

*I am not my own, nor would I choose
for myself. Let God employ me where
He thinks fit.
(William Carey)*

In the new year the question we must answer to ensure we are on the right course is what or who are we going to live for as we count the cost. Remember, Jesus said we must be willing to count the cost of true discipleship.

Even in our religious pursuits, we can live FOR the flesh while putting on a religious robe, to find ourselves in bondage to something that can prove to be obsessive, tormenting, and defeating. We can live ACCORDING to the world while tacking Jesus on to justify our inconsistencies and our ineptness to overcome, only to discover it is nothing more than a façade that is temporary, empty, and illusive. Our final and only right choice is to live UNTO the Lord.

This points to living the consecrated life. In countries where there is great persecution, the choice that such Christians are faced with, is Jesus worth dying for? Many have answered that question and have paid the ultimate price with their very lives.

In America, until recently, the persecution against our faith has been subtle, but it is becoming more aggressive. When you are in the midst of freedom and abundance the necessary choice is not obvious, but for believers in such an environment, there is only one right choice and that is to live FOR Christ.

To live for Christ is to live ACCORDING to His Word in order to live UNTO Him as a living, consecrated sacrifice. The cost is simple, but it means dying daily to that which is attached to the dictates of the flesh and the strong lures of the world. The Apostle Paul talked about beating the members of his body into subjection so he could fight the fight and run the race without becoming a castaway.

He also told how he counted the things of the world as being dung, and that he became crucified to the world's influence and the world crucified to him. This is the cost of true discipleship, but it is the type of cost that will ensure you stay on the course, and keep your focus right, while maintaining the sure way of being a conqueror of the flesh and an overcomer of the world.

Are you simply PRESENTING AN IMAGE of Christianity or are you REFLECTING THE IMAGE of Christianity, the Lord Jesus Christ? The struggle for some people is trying to determine what true Christianity is. To many it is living according to a certain code, ordinance, theology, or doctrine, but Christianity is not about outward compliance, performance, conformation, or reformation. It is about transformation, where one is inwardly conformed to the image of Christ.

Being a Christian means you have become identified with Christ and His life, and Christianity implies walking out the life of Christ. The end result is that you live the life of Christ in order to be inwardly conformed to His image.

It is easy to complicate the simplicity of Christ in us by trying to define Christianity by our ideas and actions, instead of giving way to the transforming work of the Spirit so the life of Christ can be established in us, thereby causing us to become identified and defined by His life. I have complicated Christianity by making it about impressing God by what I do and how I live, but when I realized that the real work of the Christian life is done by God and He is only pleased when I give way to it, I could finally come to the place of rest and quit striving to enter into a place of perfection and submit to the One who will bring me to perfection.

I cannot tell you what a great relief it was when I could declare Galatians 2:20, *"I am crucified with Christ: nevertheless I live; yet not I but Christ liveth in me: and the life which I now live in the flesh I love by the faith of the Son of God, who loved me, and gave himself for me."* It was living the life of Christ that enabled me to understand what real Christianity was all about.

What does God desire the most from us as believers? That is the question I ask myself so I can avoid assuming too much about my Creator, my life in Christ, and my priorities.

Since we are selfish creatures, we all start out with our main concern being about self, as many in our world cater to us in our infancy. As we grow from childhood, we realize we are not the only duck in the pond, and that we need relationships with people so our world somewhat enlarges as we learn to interact with others through family relationships and friendships. As we hit the teenage years, we start discovering what the Bible refers to as youthful lusts that can turn our secure world upside down and cause some of us to be rendered into an emotional puddle of insecurities, vulnerabilities, and outright foolishness. If we make it to adulthood as a somewhat balanced person, we will know that to keep our sanity in this world we have to make it about the well-being of others.

The Bible tells us to deny ourselves while the world tells us to esteem ourselves, and to emotionally survive our relationships with others, we must learn the simple truth of self-denial. It is in self-denial we realize that the most satisfying place is found in serving others, the most rewarding time is in being instrumental in bringing some type of joy to others, and the most restful times are when we know all is well in our relationships, especially with God.

Man has everything backwards. He lives in an upside-down world because he begins with loving self rather than loving God. He has a world turned inside out because he begins with preferring self over others. He has a world upended by chaos because it is out of order when it comes to personal priorities, agendas, and pursuits.

To begin with God, we must trust Him with all details of our lives, to prefer others over self, we must see that our greatest calling and honor is to become a means of blessing through service to them, and to make sure our world is not chaotic, our main goal in all we do must be to bring glory to our Creator.

God desires to see our world in order but that requires us to trust Him with our lives, offer our bodies as living sacrifices for His use in regard to others, and to offer all priorities, agendas, and pursuits on the altar of consecration and let the fire of God purify what He wants to do through us, sanctify what He wants to use in regard to others, and refine what will ultimately bring glory to Him.

The challenge of our times is to keep our sanity and sense of humor, knowing that our future is secure in Christ as we press forward towards the ultimate goal of our high calling: to reach the unhindered glory of the next age. As believers we are people of hope, as citizens of heaven we are people with a future and inheritance, and as saints of the Most High we are people with position and promise.

We must not allow the waves of the fear of this age to sweep us into the riptides of hopelessness. We must not allow the present circumstances to take our eyes off of that which is heavenly and eternal. We must not slide into the cesspool of despondency as the hearts of many around us grow cold and indifferent.

As believers we need to remember that we stand on an immovable Rock, as citizens we are also ambassadors, which means we have the authority of heaven behind us to carry out our mission, as saints we have the power of heaven, the Holy Spirit who enables us to carry out our calling, and as soldiers of the cross, we not only are under the command of our victorious Lord and Savior, but we have the most powerful weapon to bring utter defeat to our enemies.

The next time the condition of the world is getting you down, just remember, you are not of this world, you do not belong to this time, and you are not a citizen of this world; therefore, you are not under the foot of the leaders of this age. Let it never be said of the army of God, that we have laid down our weapons in surrender, fled the battle while flinging our armor aside to hide in some dark cave of despondency as if our great Commander is not capable of victory or worthy of sacrificial service. We must remember He enables us to withstand with His truth while counting this life as dung as we continue to stand on His promises in light of greater hope, a wondrous future, and an unending heavenly glory.

It is a tendency to overlook the small details in light of any big mission ahead of us. We often get caught up with the possibilities of great feats while missing small details that have to do with personal obedience to God. Moses was called to lead Israel into the Promised Land, but before he could, he had to take care of family matters—that of circumcising his sons (*Exodus 4:24-26*).

Apparently, it was not important to him to make sure his sons were identified to the covenant that identified the Jewish people to Yahweh, but it was to God. The fact that Moses failed to take care of business with his sons almost cost him his life and stripped him of valuable authority before the Lord to stand. It was his wife who circumcised their sons, called him a bloody husband, a term associated with the fact that his lack of action was worthy of death.

We think God is into the big things, but it is God who does the big things and what He is interested in is whether we do our part by taking care of those things He has entrusted to us. If Moses could not oversee the small details that are of the utmost importance to God, how could he be entrusted to be an obedient, faithful instrument in the hand of God to stand and be part of the impossible and miraculous?

What kind of expectation do you have when it comes to your calling? When I first realized I had some type of calling, I was ready to go out to conquer the world to fulfill it. In my mind since God called me, I had all of the authority and power of heaven behind me, but I failed to realize that God had to first prepare me as His vessel with not so pleasant measures in order to form and strengthen me in a way in which my calling could be brought forth for His glory.

It is hard in our humanness to remember that it is in the waiting on the Lord that the greatest preparation takes place. We fail to understand it is the silence of the Lord that causes us to choose to trust Him even more with what is going on. It is the restlessness in our spirit that inspires us to become more established on the Rock to ensure excellence in our

Christian walk, and it is the battle in our soul that creates the endurance in us to see the process through to the end.

It is vital that we as believers remember our hope is Christ in us and when we direct it in any other direction and for any other purpose than to see Him glorified, our hope is being set up to be deferred, bringing us into a place of complete discouragement. Such discouragement becomes a place of temptation where some end up walking away from their calling in utter defeat.

There are many things that must walk hand in hand with calling. We often start out with zeal when it comes to the initial discovery of our calling. This zeal is often a product of unbridled enthusiasm, unrealistic ideas that are grandiose in scope, and youthful strength that seems infallible. What is lacking is a true understanding of God's righteousness, a grounding in the Word of God, a sobriety about the battle ahead, and vision.

At the height of my zeal for God, I suddenly found myself in a spiritual wilderness where unbridled enthusiasm was doused by spiritual drought, my grandiose ideas left in the dust of vanity, and my strength no match to stand against the trying elements of the barren land. However, it was in the wilderness I discovered the sustaining care of God, the oasis of Living Waters, and clarity as to what my calling really was.

The wilderness is where we leave the "old man" behind in order for the new man to be established, founded on His Word, and ready to walk out our calling according to God purpose. The wilderness is clearly a place of preparation.

Jesus went there to be tempted before going forth in the world to fulfill His mission, Moses was prepared there before leading the people out of Egypt, Elijah was fed there before filling the next task, and John's voice came out of the wilderness to prepare people for Jesus.

In my walk I have been led out to the wilderness many times, but I have learned to embrace it more and more through the years. We must not forget that in the midst of the wilderness is where the tabernacle was erected and for believers it is where we will find the sanctuary where our life of worship is established, our communion made sweet, and our service clearly defined.

Are you a temple of God? We know that we are in Christ, but Christ is also in us. We are not living our life, but the life of Christ by faith. We have been considering what Christ is to us because we are in Him, but what must we be to Jesus because He is in us? After all, He is to be ALL TO US, but He must also become ALL IN US.

The Bible is clear that we are the temple of God and it goes on to explain that the person of the Godhead that resides in us is the Holy Spirit (*1 Corinthians 3:16, 17; 6:19*). In order to understand the significance of what it means to be a temple, you have to consider the tabernacle of old.

The purpose for establishing the tabernacle was so God could reveal Himself as "Emmanuel," God with us. One of His promises to the people of Israel is that He would reside in their midst, He would be with them. The tabernacle was a dwelling place for God's presence and glory in the midst of the barren wilderness.

The world is the wilderness and as believers we are earthly tabernacles that house the very presence of God. The tabernacle of old blended into the countryside and likewise we blend in with the rest of humanity, but if God's presence is in us and we are reflecting the life of Jesus, we will stand distinct in the midst of humanity.

Are you a walking tabernacle that reflects the presence of the Spirit and the glory of the Son?

Is your body serving as God's tabernacle? The New Testament temple was designed after the Old Testament tabernacle. God gave Moses clear instructions on Mount Sinai how the tabernacle was to be constructed. It would serve as a bit of heaven on earth as it was to house His presence and a pattern of His heavenly dwelling place (Hebrews 8:5).

The Lord's light at night was to remind the children of Israel of His constant abiding protection on their lives, and the pillar of cloud by day not only led them but was preparing the way for them to enter into all that the Lord had promised them. The Apostle Paul made this statement in *Acts 17:24* and *25*, *"God that made the world and all things therein, seeing that he is Lord of heaven and earth, dwelleth not in temples made with hands; Neither is worshipped with men's hands, as though he needed any thing, seeing he giveth to all life, and breath, and all things."*

God allowed Israel to construct a temple but it was eventually destroyed because of their disobedience. Since redemption was paid in full, the Lord has a different temple to reside in. This temple He created, formed, and now works in is the believer.

As believers, we are a fulfillment of the Lord to be "Emmanuel," among His people and in this world" Now I want you to meditate on this reality. You are the avenue in which the Lord wants to fulfill a very important promise and prophecy found back in *Isaiah 7:14*. It is important that as believers we are not settling for being spectators as to what God is doing, but that we become part of the great move of God.

Let's start by realizing we are His temples and that we possess His presence (His Spirit) and His glory (His life), thereby we need to be availing ourselves to become the temple that is worthy for Him to reside in.

What condition is your temple in? Our bodies house a spirit and a soul (*1 Thessalonians 5:23*). The spirit was put into man to interact with God in worship and communion, while the soul was to lift God up in praise, and our body was to serve as a witness of the His abiding presence in our spirit and His glory (light) that should fill our souls.

Sin caused man to fall from the state of being a spiritual man that could interact with God who is spirit and truth, into a soulish state that would pursue the things of the flesh and the world. The real present issue comes down to what spirit is influencing us the most and what kind of light is filling our souls.

There is the natural spirit who is motivated by the self life and the spirit of the world (Satan) who robs us from any real life (*1 Corinthians*

2:10-14). The light of the world is the darkness of sin and the light of Satan is often a false light that deceives us as to the great darkness of the abyss of spiritual death that awaits those who reject salvation. Sin defiles the temple of man and renders it useless where God is concerned while Satan destroys it.

This brings us back to whether we, as believers, are being a true temple of God. In the Old Testament God established that one temple was to be built in Jerusalem, but He allowed that temple to be destroyed because of sin. We know a new temple will be once again established in Jerusalem during the one-thousand--year reign of Christ, but meanwhile He has ordained that the bodies of His believers are to serve as His modern-day temple; but, when the self-life has been allowed to erect idols and Satan has established altars in our lives, God's presence will withdraw from such arenas and His glory will depart.

The question remains. What condition is your temple in?

Are you serving as God's temple? In the last three posts I have been talking about how we as believers are the temples of God. We, as a many-membered church, comprise a spiritual household, but individually we are temples of God. This means we are places of worship where service is rendered before God, prayers are to be offered up to Him, and ministry is to be done on behalf of Him.

The Bible clearly lays out how we are to carry out these different activities in and from our temples. We are to worship in spirit and truth, serve in love, and minister in meekness. But, to be effective in obtaining and maintaining a life of worship, we must avoid corrupting our bodies with unholy agreements and our lives with the defilement of the world and the perversion of the self-life.

In *1 Corinthians 3:16, 17,* we are told, *"Know ye not that ye are the temple of God, and that the Spirit of God dwelleth in you? If any man defile the temple of God, him shall God destroy; for the temple of God is holy, which temple ye are"?*

The problem is we sometimes are more interested in the outside of our temples than the inside of them. It is easy to give the appearance of holiness but have defilement going on within. Since the Spirit is in us as the Living Waters He can bring about the cleansing work of sanctification, but we must repent of sin, whether it is selfishness, rebellion, idolatry, or unbelief, sincerely seek the Lord to ask Him to uncap the Rivers of Living Waters to bring about any necessary cleansing. This is the only way to ensure that God's presence will be evident in our life.

How much time do you spend on your inner life? Most people are interested in dressing their outer temple, but fail to preserve their inner life. In the wilderness the tabernacle looked like part of the scenery, but inside the Holy Place and Most Holy Place the beauty was heavenly.

Ezekiel 8:12 talks about the idols of the mind and *14:2-5* talks about idols of the heart. The problem with idols of the mind (imagery) is that they can be very much a part of the landscape and hard to discern, and it is for this reason I refer to such idolatry as idolatry in high places, but when it comes to the heart, I refer to that particular idolatry as idolatry in secret chambers. The idols of the heart can also be subtle, but if we examine the direction of our affections they are easy enough to identify.

The Apostle Paul spoke of bringing the strongholds down that are in our imagination in *2 Corinthians 10:3-5* and King David asked the Lord to create a clean heart and renew a right spirit in him (*Psalm 51:10*). It is important that we make sure that we rid our inner lives of all idolatry by repenting and turning to the Lord and sincerely asking Him to not only expose all idols but to cleanse us from their presence and influence in our lives.

I have been thinking about life. Through the years I have discovered three types of life. There is a physical life which has to do with one's existence, the world's idea of life which is nothing more than a lifestyle, and then there is life itself where one breathes it in and out in order to experience it.

The quality of our physical existence determines how we function in the present world. Most of us get by as we strive to survive in the midst of challenge, disappointment, uncertainty, loss, and sorrow. We sense there is more to life, but it often eludes us. We want to experience love, peace, and joy but often find ourselves being robbed of all three through betrayal, conflict, disappointment, and misery. Since satisfaction often eludes us on a physical level, we seek it by establishing some lifestyle.

The world falsely promises us that if we pursue and attain to a certain lifestyle, we will be happy and satisfied. It tempts us to fill our lives with activities, things, and "noble" causes, but no matter the attainment, life eventually becomes hollow because the world's presentation of life is nothing more than a lifeless image, leaving us emptier and more dissatisfied.

The Bible is clear the only place you can find life is in the One who gives life. To know real life is to experience the life man was designed to live out by His Creator. This life entails breathing in God's Spirit through the born-again experience, exhaling out that breath in praise and worship, and interacting with this environment through intimate communion with the Lord and acceptable service.

Clearly, at the core of this life is relationship which determines who or what we interact with. For the physical life it comes down to our relationship with our fleshly environment and when it comes to the world it comes down to playing some game to get ahead, but when it comes to real life it always comes back to the type of relationship we have with God. The man who lacks a growing relationship with God, may possess bits and pieces of the self-life and the world, but will possess a lean spirit and a restless soul, but those who have found and continue to ever seek their life in Christ, will know and experience this eternal, abundant life because they will possess the breath (Spirit), the heartbeat (love), the peace (reconciliation), and the joy (salvation) of God.

Rayola Kelley

TIME

*God is not in a hurry. He cannot
do things with us until we are
trained and ready for them.
(James Fraser)*

We are about to enter a New Year. We always hope the New Year will bring better opportunities, and that certain expectations regarding our life will be finally realized.

However, what I have come to realize is that every year seems like the last year with seconds quickly passing by, minutes fleeing, hours becoming lost, days forgotten, and months running together, becoming one big blur. Granted, I can look back on some days and years and see accomplishments but accomplishments can become like trophies that tarnish with time as the excitement of them becomes a distant memory of bygone days.

I realized that as a believer each passing year means I am getting closer to experiencing all the expectations of the hope I have in my heart. The Bible tells me that today is the day of salvation and I took advantage of being born again back in 1976.

The fact that I am still here reminds me of the opportunity to redeem the time, work out my salvation as I avail myself to do the work of God knowing as Paul did in *2 Corinthians 5:9, 10, "Wherefore we labour, that whether present or absent, we may be accepted of him. For we must all appear before the judgment seat of Christ; that every one may receive the things done in his body, according to that he hath done, whether it be good or bad."*

This brings me to my hope that should be every believer's hope and it is found in *Colossians 2:27, "To whom God would make known what is the riches of the glory of this mystery among the Gentiles; which is Christ in you, the hope of glory."* The only real hope I have that will be fully realized and ever remembered is the hope I have surrounding my salvation and life in Christ.

As a Christian, I know I am to live my days in the light of my sustaining, lasting hope, Jesus Christ and not in light of wishing for some type utopia on this dying earth that will never be.

Life is challenging, and as a result, years can prove to be a blur in the rear mirror, days for the most part too short, minutes are like vapors, seconds a quick flash like lightning, and moments a blink of an eye. When I was a child time seemed to never move, especially if I was waiting for some special event and when I was teenager time proved to be a bit sporadic or chaotic depending on activities.

As a young adult, I felt I had all the time in the world to conquer the world. Now I am in my "golden" years. I have often wondered why they attached "golden" to this time of life. To me "gold" points to that which is of value, is a substance that has survived the process, and when it is formed and shining, can actually reflect what is important.

Time has proven one thing, that my body is not meant to last forever, the strength of my youth is clearly waning, and the dreams of my past are like the ghost towns of yesteryear, once exciting, but now silently collecting dust as cobwebs blow in the winds of time.

Hitting my "golden" years has caused me to become more reflective about the past. I am not talking about regrets, missed opportunities, and great failures due to sin, for the cross of Christ turned my regrets into lessons learned, missed opportunities into wisdom to recognize new prospects, and my failures into stepping stones that strengthened my inner character. Rather, I am talking about the type of reflection I am putting forth and the hope of my future.

Without Christ, I would be facing the downward slide towards the grave, that might be marked by some stone that will either be covered by moss or wiped clean by the wind; but with Christ, I realize my life has become more defined as it serves as a conduit of His life in me.

It is the life of Christ in me who strengthens me to run the course for the day. It is in Him the inner man is renewed and I possess the wisdom to avoid the detours of regrets, the curves of missed opportunities, and the ditches and destructive ruts of great failures. Presently, I may not be running as fast as I once did towards the finish line of glory, but I have been assured that as long as I keep my focus steadfastly on Him, I will finish the course and hopefully when I look into the glorious face and eyes of my Lord, I will see His reflection coming forth from my life.

As many know, I've taken two weeks off to do some spring-cleaning. Even though I was not on my computer much, I still wanted to record some of the important Scriptural lessons I was reminded of during my experiences. Jesus said, "Count the cost."

Before I started my spring cleaning, I had to estimate the cost of my time, energy, and endurance. Although never certain of time in my busy life, I still had to estimate the time it would take me to do the right job while honestly facing the fact that my energy is fickle, and if I even had the endurance to see it through.

I realized I would have to go the extra mile if I was going to accomplish it. It is never easy to estimate the cost up front because past experiences tell you that you never know what challenges you will run into. That is why when you go to count such a cost, it is in light of everything that needs to be done to do a sufficient job.

As Christians, we can't begin to count the cost of our Christian life and it is for this reason Jesus instructed us to deny ourselves first of maintaining any personal rights to drop the ball if it gets too hard, and pick up our cross as a means to offer the necessary sacrifice to ensure we endure until it is accomplished. However, to count the cost we have to honestly face our limitations, admit our lack of ability to see it through, and be willing to offer up everything we have to endure to the end.

I have learned that honesty up front is necessary, but it must be followed by integrity if I am to realistically consider the cost, and then it must be established in truth that only God's strength will carry me to the finish line. The walk of faith for a Christian is never based on the estimation of the Christian's ability to carry out a matter but on the reality that without Christ, nothing of significance will be accomplished or properly carried out to the end.

We must always count the cost, knowing that we do not have what it takes to pay it, the strength to carry it out, and the means to endure unless we come to the end of our very limited abilities, and look up seeking God's capabilities.

Even though some days seem like drudgery, we are in a current that keeps us in a constant flux, but many of the changes are expected such as in the case of seasons. However, in Scripture it talks about those who try to change the times and seasons.

I have been aware that our calendar has changed. According to a recent article when it came to the Roman calendar, the names of the months September to December mean nothing more than the number 7 to 10 in Latin, and when it came to January and February, they were actually the 11th and 12th month, pointing to the fact that the New Year in the Roman calendar originally started on the 1st of March.

The Romans changed the start of the New Year to January in 154 to 153 BC, and it was done for political reasons. This was the time the new consul took office and due to an uprising by the Spanish people against Rome, they could not wait until March to bring in the new leadership to address the situation.

In our dimension time will always march on signaling days and seasons will be determined by the sun and the tides by the moon, while man ever tries to adjust calendar dates to comply to his plans, his ways, and his whims. Man does much to slow time, adjust time, and direct time, but in the end, he will discover what I know, God is the One who will have His way in all matters in the end.

Events, political changes, and judgments will be in compliance with His plans, marching according to His timing, and coming to full fruition based on His will. God is Creator and He is sovereign, and it is for this reason I choose to trust His timing in all matters, knowing that the righteous will be vindicated and upheld, the wicked will be judged, the meek will inherit the earth, and God's promises to His people will be fulfilled.

Rayola Kelley

Every day I am reminded in one way or another that life is fragile, short, and uncertain. As Christians we can only count on the present day to get things right and lightly plan for the future to faithfully stay the course, while preparing for eternity. We know we are immortal until the Lord calls us home, but we must redeem the present time in order to keep our focus on the true prize of heaven, Jesus Christ.

As a believer, I remind myself this world is a temporary place, where believers are simply passing through because they are citizens of an unseen kingdom. To determine how this present world is going to affect me as a spiritual sojourner, I must see the world as a barren wilderness and myself as a truth seeker looking for my heavenly portion. I must be prepared to confront this age as a confusing maze that only the Holy Spirit can guide me through. As a student of righteousness, I must keep in mind that this world is a harsh testing ground, and as soldier a battlefield.

It is important to remember these simple truths if we are to effectively walk through this world in preparation for the next world. As a citizen of heaven, we owe our loyalty to our king, as a seeker of true treasures, we must not settle for temporary riches, as students we must recognize our true teacher and example, and as effective soldiers we must not become entangled with the affairs of this world.

As sojourners we must have a set destination to keep each of us in the way, and as seekers we must know what type of life we are looking for to avoid being enslaved by the vanity of this age. As students, we must apply what we have learned, and as soldiers we must make sure our armor is in place with the belt of truth, our weapon sharpened, our ears tuned into the Holy Spirit, our shield of faith in front, and prepared to advance forward upon receiving commands from our Commander and Chief.

Today is the day the Lord has made, and the question is what will our response be to the gift of life and time He has given us? For some people this day is shrouded in darkness due to crises, loss, and devastation, while to other people the day is gray because of ongoing struggles, uncertainty, and despair, while others are emotionally hiding in some safe mental corner while mechanically taking steps to simply get through the day.

As Christians, we are told that we must run the race set before us, but to beware that tribulation awaits us, giant circumstances will mockingly stand before us, and that which seems impossible will force us to stop in our tracks. Life is a course and a flowing river that can't be controlled, changed, or tamed by man.

This course can be overwhelming due to being wrought with potholes of hindrances, speed bumps of difficulties, cracked surfaces of uncertainties, and great gaps of destruction and disillusionment that brings into question whether one will ever reach his or her destination. It is at the point of challenges, hindrances, difficult surfaces, and impossible obstacles that we can discover there is a way through challenges, over hindrances, and around obstacles but to discover it we must look beyond challenges, never let hindrances cause us to resign, or impossibilities to result in surrender.

Since the Lord has gone before us and has designed our personal course, we must trust He is in control of what lies in the path, and we must always choose to look up, seek His face and wait for the Light of the world to guide us through challenges, put hindrances in perspective, and reveal the way through impossible terrain. As Christians we must not consider each day as another day, but as an opportunity to discover the warmth, comfort, treasures, and new revelations of that which is clothed in majesty, whose beauty is indescribable, whose ways are perfect, and whose glory is ever unfolding before us while enfolding us in perfect love, blessed peace, glorious promises and hope of Jesus Christ.

The sky this morning is incredible. We have had a few days of wind and rain. This morning as I looked out to enjoy God's way of highlighting the canvas of the landscape by situating the lighting of the sky, I was awestruck by how the sky displayed drama with dark clouds and a change of scene with blue sky where the sun was clearly breaking through to expose the beauty of creation. However, such displays remind you weather is unpredictable as to whether the light will give way to the force of dark clouds or whether the clouds will finally be dispelled and move on.

Before the weather changes, the winds always come first as a warning sign to prepare for a change, followed by the clouds. Depending on the force of the wind, it will determine how fast the clouds march across the sky, while the amount of water they are carrying will determine their color and how low they are.

Today we live in what seems to be the constant change of weather on all fronts, and unlike the past, many are discovering they are in the path of these changes. *Ephesians 4:14* tells us we must no more be children tossed to and fro, carried about with every wind of doctrine, by the sleight of men, and the cunning craftiness whereby they lie in wait to deceive.

The fronts that are colliding in the political, religious, and personal arenas are producing dark, formidable moods to hang over many. It appears as if the light of truth, decency, and reason is being completely squelched by the heavy darkness of deception that is descending upon our nation and the world like a funnel cloud. *1 Thessalonians 2:10-12* tells us because people do not love the truth God is sending a strong delusion so that they will believe a lie in order to bring damnation on them.

Today we are watching people being tossed to and fro by foolish sentiment, insane hypocrisy, ruthless deduction, lawless movements, and destructive forces, but as Christians we can choose to not get caught up with the storms of our time by choosing to love the truth and avoid getting ensnared in the lies. By choosing the light of God's truth, we may see the dark clouds come, but we will always be assured of standing in the light that will dispel the clouds before such storm consume us.

The Apostle Paul instructed us to redeem the time for the days are evil. I have squandered time in the past, let its opportunities pass me by, and wished I could step outside of it and change the fallout of bad decisions.

It is easy to look ahead concerning what is happening and fall into despair about the present. We can look behind knowing that there is no reason to linger in the past because there is no means to change what has been. We must learn to consider and embrace one day at a time.

We are not meant to live in any other tense but the present. The present may seem overwhelming, but it is a gift and the only time we have to work with truth, work within faith, and come to terms with the life God has given to us.

It is clear that the Lord must insert Himself into time to meet with us. No doubt time will part and give way to that which is eternal. For Jacob, the Lord inserted Himself into an unexpected place to meet with him (*Genesis 28*). Many people want to encounter or see God, but Scripture is clear that when the Lord inserts Himself into time to meet with mere man, it is not a time of celebration but one of undoing.

As for Jacob, he had a dream of a ladder set up on earth and the top of it reached to heaven and the angels of God ascended and descended on it. At the top of this ladder the LORD stood above it and introduced Himself to Jacob. Even though the Lord reaffirmed his covenant with Jacob that He had made with Abraham and Isaac, he was completely unnerved by it, which caused great fear and dread to fall on him.

Seeing the Lord usually does not create celebration, but great sobriety in a person because God is holy. It is easy for man in his limited reality to forget the implications of God's holiness, but as *Hebrews 10:31* reminds us, "It is a fearful thing to fall into the hands of the living God."

Jesus identified this ladder in *John 1:51, "Verily, verily, I say unto you, Hereafter ye shall see heaven open, and the angels of God ascending and descending upon the Son of man."* Jesus is the ladder that connects the man of earth to the God of heaven through redemption, and it is on Him that all blessings and promises descend on man as they ascend upward through praise, worship, and service for the glory of God.

REACHING OUR POTENTIAL

Sickness may be before us, but the Lord will
give grace; poverty may happen to us,
but grace will surely be afforded; death
must come but grace will light a candle
in the darkest hour.
(Charles Spurgeon)

What does it mean to be placed in high places with Jesus (*Ephesians 2:6*)? The idea of being placed in high places reveals that we are not of this world and that we have been raised above the judgment and wrath that abides on it.

The challenge for most Christians is that we live in this world and are physically bound to this earth. We deal with worldly demands and are struggling to get above the earthy hold the world has on us to clearly see the reality of the next. I have struggled with my perspective of trying to realize my heavenly status in Christ and be realistic about my earthy existence.

As we are reminded in *Proverbs 3:5,6, "Trust in the LORD with all thine heart; and lean not unto thine own understanding. In all thy ways acknowledge him, and he shall direct thy paths."* It took a few years but I discovered the heavenly places in Christ have to do with my perspective. I needed to quit leaning on what I thought I knew and search for real understanding from above.

The Bible talks about the eagle seeing afar off. For most of us we can only see from a very limited perspective, which consists of the small world we live in that is hedged in by opinions, ideas, and philosophies. We are sometimes faced with forests of problems, weeds of challenge that often stand taller than our head, and a jungle of irritations that seem to abound. We are clearly earthbound by our perspective, but the Lord wants to lift us out and above our small worlds and give us a heavenly perspective.

I have realized as far as my perspective goes, I can be like a domestic turkey who may never get higher than a fence in my perspective and a goat who acts as if small mounds are mountains as long as it stands above the others, or I can become like a lone eagle who searches for the wind of the Holy Spirit so that I can be lifted above this world and given a heavenly perspective.

～✝～

What kind of water do you possess? I was once told our bodies, although made of dust are also made up of over 90% water. If you are truly born again, you are also a vessel that carries the Living Water of the Spirit.

One of the great claims aimed at many Americans is that they do not drink enough water, which points to dehydration. This lack of water can cause a series of health issues. Sadly, many Americans have substituted caffeine, soda, and protein drinks for water but health challenges prove these substitutes cannot replace water.

Likewise, the water of the Holy Spirit is necessary to ensure our spiritual life does not become barren and unfruitful. We must keep in mind that there is no substitution for this spiritual water such as sentimental notions about God, fleshly worship, or worldly religious activities.

We must examine ourselves and make sure we are not accepting any substitution for the presence and work of the Holy Spirit in our vessel, because any such substitution will leave us either dry or contaminated, rendering us as useless vessels to God.

～✝～

John in his first epistle tells us if we are going abide or continue in Jesus we must walk as He walked (*1 John 2:6*). The instruction is clear but how many understand what it means to walk as Jesus walked?

As believers, we understand that we walk by faith but TOWARDS what and ACCORDING to who? It is natural to fill in the blanks of such matters with assumed beliefs that can become presumptuous, self-willed, rigid, and lifeless, outward piousness without any real inward transformation. We know a butterfly starts out as a caterpillar before a miraculous transformation takes place where it comes out as a beautiful, new creation.

Jesus was clear if we are to walk as He walked, we must follow Him into a new life. The Apostle Paul admitted he was living the life of Jesus in him by faith in the Son of God. There is that word, "faith." We are told we are to have faith TOWARDS God. This type of faith is a passive faith where we choose to believe and direct all of our trust in the person, word, work, and will of God on our behalf.

Believing starts from the premise of being persuaded that something is so, thereby, choosing to believe it is truth, but the next phase entails active faith by actually responding to Jesus. His command is to follow Him into this new life.

It is active faith that gives us assurance of our direction because we are walking as He walked and confidence in the right choices we make because we are walking ACCORDING to His Word. It is obvious, that if we are going to reach our potential of reflecting Jesus in this world to others, we must follow Him into a godly life and down the paths of righteousness, to ensure the unveiling and unfolding of His glory in our lives.

In past posts I talked about the type of glory we reflect and that it is determined by what glory we expose ourselves to the most. If we expose ourselves to the world's glory, we will discover it is temporary because it has no real substance behind it. If we walk in the personal glory of self, it will prove to be vain and fading. If we expose ourselves to the false glory of man-centered and inspired religion, we will find that it is a false light that hides much darkness behind it but will crumble in the light of truth and judgment.

When we consider Moses' exposure to the glory of God, it caused him to reflect the glory of the first ministration which was the Law. The Law could only reveal sin but had no way for man to be pardoned or justified before it, since its glory revealed holiness and clearly proved to be overwhelming to the people of Israel who stood undone and guilty before it.

The second ministration came by way of Christ. Man could look into its face and find forgiveness and grace. In fact, we are told in *2 Corinthians 3:14*, *"But their minds were blinded: for until this day remaineth the same vail untaken away in the reading of the old testament; which vail is done away in Christ."*

The first ministration of the law put a veil of darkness upon man's mind and heart because he stood condemned, but the Lord Jesus Christ takes that veil away from those who come under His ministration of grace. The more we expose ourselves to Jesus' glory in His Word, prayer, and fellowship, the more we will reflect His glory.

The Apostle Paul put it this way in *2 Corinthians 3:17-18*, *"Now the Lord is that Spirit: and where the Spirit of the Lord is, there is liberty. But we all, with open face beholding as in a glass the glory of the Lord, are changed into the same image from glory to glory, even as by the Spirit of the Lord."*

What glory are you reflecting the most in your life?

We have all been gifted with talents to enable us to reach our potential, but what are we doing with them? Some are trying to utilize them in a proper way, others are squandering them, and some have buried them.

It seems people struggle with realizing their true potential. They have become lost because dreams have been shattered by reality, initiative swallowed by disillusionment, zeal lost in indifference, talents buried by discouragement, and hope left in the dust of failures.

However, as Christians we know our life is hid in Jesus and His life is what is being developed in us. I have learned that if I allow the life of Jesus to refine and define me my talents will be revealed, and I will reach my potential according to the design of my Creator. This is what will bring satisfaction to the seeking soul who does not want to "simply" get by in this present age.

Rayola Kelley

As a Christian what are you reaching for? It is easy to become sidetracked or take detours in our religious pursuits. It is for this reason we must stop and consider what we are reaching for.

Some are reaching to grasp some mound of religious standards, others for pinnacles of perfection, and there are those who are ever climbing a mountain of religious piousness. Sadly, those who seek a certain religious standard find there are other heights that arise, making it further and harder to obtain, making them feel hopeless.

Individuals who seek pinnacles of perfection find that they aren't only teetering on them, they are falling off of them in complete frustration and anger because they are trying so hard. Those who are ever climbing mountains of personal piousness are met with other mountaintops, often causing them to conclude they are high enough, thus they settle on the mountaintop of religious arrogance and delusion.

I know about all of these so-called "elevated" places because I have pursued them and was met with the harsh reality that I miserably failed to obtain what I was pursuing. I'm glad that the Apostle Paul dealt with this issue in *Philippians 3*.

As a boy he was set apart to pursue the mounds of religious standards, as a Hebrew he was striving to reach pinnacles of perfection according to the Law, and as a zealous Pharisee he was motivated to reach mountain peaks of religious accomplishment as a means to fulfill what he thought to be his calling and mission.

The thing I love the most is reading about the incident where Paul actually encountered what he should be pursuing in order to fulfill his real calling. He met Jesus Christ on the road to Damascus while on his way to persecute Christians.

As Christians we need to quit pursuing high places and begin to realize what we are striving to gain is the person of Jesus Christ and where we will actually encounter Him are in the low places of great need, humility, brokenness, and repentance.

Yesterday I asked about what are you reaching for. We often start out with great aspirations to reach the highest points we can in our life. Whether we think the peak has to do with material wealth, power, or success. Sadly, people who venture into the world's idea of success either fall through the cracks because the price of their soul and dignity are too high a price to pay or they have to betray themselves in some way to get to the top, leaving them with a hollow victory at best. I have rarely seen people who chose the ways of the world and reached the "heights" happy or really satisfied.

In Christianity there are times we may feel buried under various challenges, enfolded in a stifling darkness, struggling against a strong current, and walking through mud, but we can always come to a place of satisfaction and rest when we remember to direct our focus and attention in the right direction.

The Apostle Paul counted his aspirations attached to the world as being dung and desired to become identified with Jesus in every way. He knew that it required him to know the power of his resurrection to possess authority and the fellowship of his sufferings to attain his real inheritance, while being made conformable unto his death so that Jesus' life could be brought forth. It was clear Paul understood that he would have to press through the present age he was living in if he was going to attain his real high calling, which was to reflect the glory of Jesus.

What is greatness? The age we live in marks surface things such as titles, positions, abilities, and wealth as a sign of greatness, but our Lord had a different take on it. To be great you had to have the virtue and attitude of a humble, meek, obedient servant. I don't know about you, but after you get past the spotlight the world may put on an individual, what leaves a lasting impression is the person's character and the type of attitude it wears.

True servitude comes with a price of much inward temperance. For me it came with the Lord taking various instruments to my pride, beginning with a spoon that stirred me up to face my pride, a shovel that buried me with embarrassment brought on by my pride, and a backhoe that left me with the gaping reality of how far-reaching pride is into every level of one's character. It was then that I learned greatness in God's kingdom is when the Lord Jesus Christ's attitude is shining in and through our character in times of challenges and service to others.

407

Have you ever considered how life is a current? We are constantly being moved through this age by an unseen current. Granted, there are different currents. For example, there are the fast currents of the world, the constant current of time, and the unpredictable currents of events.

As I look back at my years in this ministry, I realize that the current that moves me is the very life of Jesus in me. I am reminded that the life I live is not my life, and I must live this life according to faith (*Galatians 2:20*). I realize as a Christian I must choose daily to live this other person's life, a life contrary to my old life: I must live the life of Christ.

This is why it takes the Holy Spirit to enable each believer to live this life, but the key to living the victorious life is we must get in the current. *Ezekiel 47:3-5* reveals different levels that religious people can operate in when it comes to the current of the Holy Spirit.

There are those who only want to get ankle deep in religion, while some will go knee deep to check out the possibilities, and others will wade as far as the loins in regard to service, but the key to the victorious life is to fling self right into the current of the river of the Holy Spirit. This river is impassable and there will never be any way to resist the current, but let me state, it is a glorious adventure, one that will bring you to wondrous places of communion, spiritual growth, and worship.

As believers, we have been delivered from the power of darkness, and translated into the kingdom of his dear Son. We all know about the process of a butterfly. It begins as a caterpillar. There are no similarities initially; that is, the caterpillar and the final product, the butterfly. The caterpillar wraps itself up in a cocoon (grave) in submission to reach its ultimate potential, to come forth as a beautiful butterfly who will add its distinction of beauty to God's creation.

We are told to not be conformed to this world but to be transformed by the renewing of the mind. The key is that this transformation takes place away from prying eyes. Like the caterpillar, the miracle of transformation for the believer is done in obscure places. When we are first born again, the miracle of life takes place because the very life of Christ is implanted in us, but transformation can only take place when we become identified with Christ in His death and burial.

It is as we choose death to the old life that we become identified with Him in the grave where the old is left behind. It is at this point the real transformation can take place because it is from the grave that man can be raised in the newness of Christ's life, now capable of reflecting the beauty of the glory attached to His life.

Are you being made conformable to Jesus' death? This seems a dichotomy because as believers we offer eternal life to all who will come to Christ, but in this Scripture, Paul is talking about being conformed to Jesus' death.

The apostle understood that if he was to know Jesus in greater measure, he had to become identified with Jesus in the overcoming power of His resurrection as he fellowshipped with Him in suffering. Suffering can lead to death, and he knew that he was walking towards his demise in a couple of ways.

Physical death works in the members of our body and will claim it in due time if Jesus does not come first, but the second death had to do with the disciplined life of one dying to the self-life. Apostle Paul knew he had to walk towards the demise of his self-life in order to be conformed to Jesus' death.

To be conformed means to be fashioned according to something in order to make it similar; and, it is the old life that identifies us to this present world and it must be addressed and put off daily. The Apostle Paul stated he died daily to his old life. Through his epistles, he makes many references to mortifying the deeds of the flesh, by putting off the old so that he could put on the new. He made this statement as to why this particular death was necessary in *Galatians 6:14, "But God forbid that I should glory, save in the cross of our Lord Jesus Christ, by whom the world is crucified unto me, and I unto the world."* We must be fashioned in Jesus' death so that we can be raised in the newness of His life. The more the life of Christ is established in us the more we will have put off the old, allowing us to be conformed to His image, thereby, reflecting His glory.

Reflecting the Lord's glory is the ultimate potential of every person. Each one of us has been predestinated to be conformed to the image of Christ and to reflect His glory which is the essence of our calling and potential. It is a battle between the flesh and the Spirit to come to this place, but once we do, we will find completeness in our spirit and satisfaction in our soul.

Are you pressing toward the mark for the prize of the high calling of God in Christ Jesus (*Philippians 3:14*)? The Apostle Paul was focused on gaining the prize of heaven which he realized could only be found and obtained in Christ. He wanted to seize Christ and be completely apprehended by Him. He wanted to possess all that Christ had for him, find the eternal treasures of heaven that could only be obtained by faith, and comprehend mysteries that would forever change his vision. However, to gain the prize above entails considering all earthly and fleshly matters and functions as being insignificant in light of heaven.

There is a constant struggle between the responsibilities of this earth and the burdens of heaven. It is easy to major in earthly matters while minoring in heavenly responsibilities because they do not seem as urgent or pressing. After all, the world demands we respond right away, while heaven appears to give us an option to do it later.

Paul understood since heaven will not press us to possess the prize, it is up to each of us to press towards it ourselves. In order to accomplish such a feat, we must value Christ above all other earthly responsibilities and set our affections on Him, which will cause our minds to consider Him, as our hearts reach up towards the Lord with a desire to seek and find Him.

Matthew 6:33 says it best, *"But seek ye first the kingdom of God, and his righteousness; and all these things shall be added unto you."* What do you value the most, diligently seek after, and ultimately pursue? These three emphases will show you where your heart is.

What kind of footprints do you want to leave in this world? It is natural to want to make our life count for something. The problem is there are only three places we can leave our footprints in this world: in the sands of time that will be quickly taken away by wind or trampled under by those who follow us, history that can change or be forgotten according to the narrative of others, or people's hearts where such footprints will fade in a couple of generations.

When I was young, I knew I had some unknown destiny to fulfill. I had a sense of awe and wonderment about it. To me, destiny was associated with doing great things. After high school I found out there was nothing unique about me. Granted, left to myself I could think highly of myself but life's challenges revealed my lacking character, my inept abilities, and my silly notions. It revealed to me how naïve I was about life and the world.

When I received the Lord Jesus Christ as my Lord and Savior, the idea of destiny once again rose out of the ashes to cause me to consider the purpose of my life. It took a few years of going around the same mountain, recognizing similar failures, and coming face to face with my immaturity before I realized that my destiny was wrapped up in the person of Jesus Christ who did the greatest work on a cross by providing me with salvation.

I learned the heritage I was now part of was eternal, and that my footprints would be immortalized by the legacy and witness I would leave behind. "Witness" has the same implication as being a "martyr" (a sacrifice) (*Romans 12:1, 2*). *Hebrews 12:1 summarizes this witness, "Wherefore, seeing we also are compassed about with so great a cloud of witnesses, let us lay aside every weight, and the sin which doth so easily beset us, and let us run with patience the race that is set before us."*

The key here is I must run the race by following in footsteps bigger than life and larger than the world, Jesus Christ, and finish the course set before me. Even though my footprints will be overshadowed by those who have gone before me, I will leave them so others may follow the example of Christ right into infinity, right into His everlasting glory.

OVERCOMING

God reserves the greatest victories
for the vessels that have known
the greatest brokenness.
(Bob Sorge)

It has taken me awhile to understand that, as man, Jesus became our example. Although, He was a sinless man, He still had to be perfected in His humanity. To me this is the most extraordinary aspect about Jesus being our example. It is true He was sinless and we are born in a fallen state where our inclination is to do what is wrong. He may have started from eternity, and we from the baseness of sin and death, but His example shows us that the matter of doing right will come down, not to our original state, but to our heart attitude, character, and choices.

In His humanity Jesus had the choice to be very human and choose the way of independence, but yet He chose to live contrary to the desires of His flesh and the preference of the world, in order to please His Father. In light of His deity, He could have demanded His way as man, but instead He choose to come under the will of His Father and become the Lamb. He could have called a legion of angels to rescue Him from those who would unmercifully judge, abuse, and put Him on the cross, but instead He went to the cross, embraced it, and called upon the Father to forgive them for they "know not what they do." We can find comfort in the fact that God could do no less but out of love, mercy, and grace to provide us with a solution to our sin, but as man, Jesus had to choose the cross, and He did so out of honor and obedience to the Father. He did it on our behalf in order to become the face of grace to the outcast, the hope of life to the sinner, and the author of salvation to the lost.

We can use our human nature to justify our human failures, our iniquity, our sinful actions, and our deviant ways, but we are who we are and what we become will be based on choosing the right master, the upright state, and the ways of righteousness. These choices will cause our flesh to suffer, our pride to be stripped of its authority, our ways to

412

be disciplined, our inner man to be refined, and our faith to be tested, but in doing so, we will be brought to maturity or perfection.

By using parentheses and emphasizing the word "perfection" in *Hebrews 5:8* and *9*, I felt these two Scriptures give us a great example of what Jesus' in His humanity accomplished, *"Though he were a Son (of God), yet (in His humanity) learned he obedience by the things which he suffered; And being made PERFECT (as man), he became the author (Savior) of eternal salvation unto all them that obey him (in light of His example)."*

The trap I must avoid as a believer is that if I am at peace with my environment, whether it constitutes truth or righteousness, that all is well with my soul. My Bible tells me I do not find real peace in a fragile environment that is void of conflict and is nothing more than a house of cards that will collapse, but that I find peace when my relationship is right with God and others. This also means I have developed a right attitude towards the world.

Jesus told us we will have much tribulation in this world, and instead of trying to control our world with a false sense of peace, we must be prepared to walk through the tribulations and conflicts of this world by faith towards the One who is the Prince of Peace. The Apostle John put it best in *1 John 5:4-5, "For whatsoever is born of God overcometh the world: and this is the victory that overcometh the world, even our faith. Who is he that overcometh the world, but he that believeth that Jesus is the Son of God?"*

It is easy as a Christian to struggle with various matters of life. There has been an impression given by some Christian teachers that if you become a Christian, you will somehow be immune from the trials and tribulations that come with life. Even though the Lord is clear that there will be much tribulation in the world, we are not to fear it for He has overcome it.

However, there are some that fiercely cling to this false premise and unfairly judge those who are struggling with the challenges that come from being in this world. The function of the world is Satan's domain and our bodies are under a curse of death due to sin. We must not cling to that which constitutes the false hope that if we think, say, and do the right things we will keep God off our backs and we will be spared from grave trials; rather, we must cling to the reality that we have been given the means to overcome the world.

The Apostle John gives us this insight in *1 John 5:5, "Who is he that overcometh the world, but he that believeth that Jesus is the Son of God?"* We overcome the world because we walk by faith towards God according to His Word and promises. We are not delivered from the world, but, like Noah, we will be delivered through the world, which means we will be spared from tasting the judgment that abides on the world and experiencing the wrath that abides on those who are disobedient towards the Gospel.

We cannot encourage ourselves when we are operating from a false premise; rather, the only way we can encourage ourselves is when our faith is directed at the right source, in the right way, and for the right reasons.

Christians live in an environment of contradictions and must discern their attitude and response to such paradoxes. For instance, we can't claim to be a victim of this age and blame our present attitude on the days we live in when we have all the necessary means to be victorious in Christ. We can't see ourselves as being poor in this world when we can be rich in faith in Christ. We can't live in self-pity or as if defeated when we are called to be more than conquerors and overcomers of this world. We can't live in a constant state of hopelessness when our real hope is not of this world. We can't keep looking around for the answers to the grave problems of life while failing to look upward towards the only answer, while setting our heart and focus on the solution. We have to quit fainting in our minds and letting our hearts grow cold in this age when we have the wonderful example of Jesus Christ enduring such contradictions as our Redeemer.

As believers, we need to recognize that the contradictions exist in our lives because we have believed some lie that is causing confusion in our minds about God and His Word. Whether we use the rulers of this world to judge a matter or use personal unrealistic standards that will keep us feeling deflated, we need to recognize the source of it is Satan and reject it. As believers we must believe God's Word and walk in the assurance that we are citizens of another world, and that what we are experiencing here is temporary in light of the eternal glory that awaits us.

If you are struggling with the many contradictions that you are seeing, remember Jesus. Jesus never walked according to the contradictions of the world but according to that which was excellent and eternal. The way He overcame the contradictions of this world was through submission to the Father's plan, standing on the sure Word of God, and carrying out His Father's perfect will.

As a Christian I have to examine myself at times to see if I am a squatter, an associate, a pleasure seeker, or a sojourner in this world. To be a squatter in this world means to stake out a piece of land that belongs to another, and to be an associate means that you will shrewdly use what you can in order to advance personal agendas without totally becoming beholden to the world, while to be a pleasure seeker is to seek those things that please the flesh according to the world, but when it comes to the spiritual sojourner, they are simply passing through.

I have to acknowledge that I have fit in all of these categories at one time or the other. As a godless person void of God's presence, I was a squatter in this world, making me subject to the god of this world, Satan. I had no intention of being wicked, but I failed to do what was right and simply tried to get by, by being decent and claiming rights to benefit from the destructive ways of the world.

At times I associated with the world, trying to figure out how to get the most out of the world without really selling my soul, but every attempt left me lost as to who I was and what life was about. Like every human I had my moral weaknesses of character that the world easily took captive so that the god of the age could bring accusation against me.

This was made possible because I betrayed my conscience to get along, compromised my moral convictions to fit in, and justified wrong attitudes and profane actions because everyone else did it, and upon comparing myself to others, I was not so bad.

When I first became a Christian, I did not realize the hold, claims, and power the world had over me, but through time the Lord exposed the inroads of the world upon my attitude, my ways, and my conduct. As I stated yesterday, the closer I get to the glory of the next world, the dimmer the light of this present age becomes. John stated in *1 John 1:5:4 & 5, "For whatsoever is born of God overcometh the world: and this is the victory that overcometh the world, even our faith. Who is he that overcometh the world, but he that believeth that Jesus is the Son of God?"*

There is much talk about unity today, but in some cases, it is not about godly unity but going with the flow and not challenging or disrupting the wicked agendas of the powers of the present darkness to live in some quasi state of peace. People think that unity means peace, but unity in God's kingdom really means having the same spirit, coming into agreement with what is honorable, necessary, and right, as well as possessing the same biblical convictions, being on the same page as to what is going on and what needs to be done.

People want peace at any cost, but peace that is void of true agreement will prove to be tyrannical, false, mocking, and tormenting. Why are people willing to accept a false peace instead of fleeing from that which is contrary to true unity?

The answer sometimes comes down to people want to settle back on their worldly laurels without worrying about the tidal wave of judgment that is heading for every shoreline of the world. They do not want to face that every foundation is about to be shaken and every way challenged. They do not want to have to stir themselves up to stand for that which may not be popular before men, withstand with truth that exposes the darkness to see the hatred, rage, and agendas of man, and continue to stand when all seems against them. However, if we are to stand on the right side of eternity, we must agree with God's evaluation of a matter, side with truth no matter the cost, and do what is honorable no matter how ridiculous it may seem to others.

To be overcomers of this present world, we must come out and be separate from the world's attitudes, ways, and practices. The way to true spiritual victory is the narrow way of the cross, the hard way of self-denial, and a foreign way because it often ends in sacrificing what is considered normal to our way of thinking, acceptable to the world, and popular with those who set the trends, and control the indoctrination and propaganda of the world.

Jesus stated that in the world there would be much tribulation, but be of good cheer for He has overcome the world. The type of attitude we take on and our response to a situation is a personal choice. It comes down to who we believe and what we believe. If I believe the world, then I must fear what I cannot see, fling all aside and blindly follow what is being said, and somehow save my life in the midst of chaos. However, as a Christian I must adhere to the example of Jesus.

The Lord overcame the world and so must I, but I can't do it if I am looking to the world for hope, looking within for inspiration and strength, and looking around for some lifeboat to keep me from drowning in the insanity of it all. As a Christian, I can encourage myself in the Lord because He is in control, He is aware of who I am and where I am at, and He is the one who holds my life in His hand and has saved my soul from the worst fate possible.

The Apostle John actually tells us how to overcome the world in *1 John 5:4, "For whatsoever is born of God overcometh the world: and this is the victory that overcometh the world, even our faith."* If you are a born again, you should be overcoming the world because of the spirit in you leading and guiding you through the darkness, knowing that the hope of victory is sure because your faith is firmly planted in and on the Rock of eternity.

Depending on your attitude about the days we live in, you may feel discouraged, anxious, vexed, or have a sense of rising expectation because Jesus is coming to set matters in order. We are living in the times the Bible calls perilous. Everything that was brought out about this time is being displayed in living color before our very eyes.

The Apostle Paul talked about the fact that men would be lovers of their own selves, covetous, boasters, proud, blasphemers, disobedient to parents, unthankful, unholy, without natural affection, trucebreakers, false accusers, incontinent, fierce, despisers of those that are good, traitors, heady, highminded, and lovers of pleasures more than lovers of God. Some will have a form of godliness but will deny the power thereof. Paul's instruction is clear, *"from such turn away" (2 Timothy 3:5)*.

As believers we are not to give such people any audience or come into agreement with them because all they will do is profane what is true, right, and acceptable to God. The truth is the wicked environment caused by these people can easily enough bury us, but as believers we are called to be overcomers and not victims of our times.

How do we overcome discouragement? We encourage ourselves in the Lord by seeking His face. How do we cease to be anxious? We must choose to trust God in His sovereignty, knowing that He never allows anything to touch our lives unless He is about to do a greater work in us. What about being vexed? Vexation points to one's spirit being stirred up and this stirring is to serve as a means in which one can honestly enter into the seriousness of a matter in order to effectively stand in the gap in prayer and supplication until the irritation lifts.

Those who are honest with the times know that our nation is in a precarious situation and that much is on the line. It does not matter what side of the political issue we stand on; we must make sure we are standing on the right side of truth, righteousness and eternity. Meanwhile, we know the signs Paul mentioned will be prominent in the day that Jesus returns. So instead of becoming discouraged by looking around for some light of hope, and being dismayed by the insanity taking place, we need to look up, knowing that the battle belongs to God, the real war has already been won at Calvary, and that as believers we need not look around for the light because the light is present within us. We need to discern, take courage in, and trust the path the light is illuminating and walk in obedience to it.

Lies, fears, and the intimidating threats of losses and death are three devices Satan uses to paralyze, drive, or make people run into his web of destruction or fall into his deadly snare. The questions we each need to ask are what is Satan's main target, what is he after, and what is his ultimate goal.

Satan's main target is our faith. Jude wanted to preach the Gospel but admitted he had to contend or wrestle for the faith that was first delivered to the saints. As *Hebrews 11:6* points out, you can't please God without faith, and when you study the hall of fame in *Hebrews 11* that names people of faith and their accomplishments, you realize that the key to overcoming and finishing the course is faith. *This is brought out in 1 John 5:4, "For whatsoever is born of God overcometh the world; and this is the victory that overc3ometh the world, even our faith."*

The problem is that there is confusion about what constitutes genuine faith. Some people think you can conjure it up with positive thinking, there are some who have associated some method to faith, and there are others who think faith is a feeling of self-sufficiency or infallibility, but faith is none of these things. Faith is one of the gifts of God and it is often given to us in the right measure to enable us to faithfully walk a matter out.

The Apostle Paul made reference to the law of faith in *Romans 3:27*. Law is about cause and effect and operates within principles that ensure the same results. When it comes to faith, the cause that puts it into operation is believing God, while it operates in the love of God and its effect is that of obedience.

Jesus stated if you love me, you will obey me, while Paul summarized the simplicity of true faith in *Romans 10:17, "Faith comes by hearing and hearing by the word of God."* The result is an overcoming life that walks in light of an eternal city, sees beyond this present world, and lives a life that becomes foreign, absurd, and insane to this present world. Genuine faith is a choice, but the choice is the same, it is ever ready to risk all associated with this present world to gain the glory of the next one.

I have been talking about consecration, the personal act of setting ourselves apart for one purpose, to bring honor and glory to the Lord. Christians sometimes wonder what sets Christians apart from each other in their walk. They have believed the same Gospel, received the same Christ, and possessed the same spirit, but the results vary when it comes to the overcoming, victorious Christian life.

The difference comes down to one word: Consecration. Consecration is best represented by the burnt offering in the Old Testament. A burnt offering spoke of total consecration that represented the sincere intent of the one offering it. Fire and smoke were associated with this offering and was used with the sin and trespass offerings. The fire of the burnt offering consumed the sin or trespass offering, pointing to the purging of sin and God's acceptance of it, while smoke pointed to holiness. It was the smoke that served as the sweet savor to God because the sin was no more, leaving only that which was pure.

The Apostle Paul tells us that we are to present our bodies as a living sacrifice—a burnt offering. The more you consecrate your life the more personal victory you will experience. People are like onions. They have layer on top of layer. For believers, each layer must be taken off to expose the real character of their faith and devotion to experience purging, while being refined and brought to perfection.

At salvation, the act of consecration is that of true repentance, where the person turns and faces that he or she is a sinner with a sin problem and needs to be saved. In the initial stages of the faith walk, consecration comes in the form of believing that the Word of God is true and assimilating it into their walk.

The next stage of consecration has to do with discipleship where the believer follows Christ into a life of service where each step of obedience to the Lord and Master sets them apart. The next stage is that of becoming a soldier who is seasoned and knows how to stand by faith, withstand with truth, and continue to stand because of the promises yet to come.

The next to the last stage has to do with knowing what is the good, acceptable, and perfect will of God. At this point of consecration all service whether sacrificial or not is considered reasonable by the servant and soldier, worship is assured of being acceptable to God, and communion is being perfected in the saint.

The final stage of consecration is glorification in and with Christ.

Are you in a bubble of denial, a limited frustrating box of theology, encased in a cement encloser of judgmental opinions, struggling in a deep pit of despair, depression, uncertainty, and hopelessness, or are you firmly hidden in Christ where your life is being sustained by the Bread from heaven and established by the Holy Spirit?

We are told the strongholds in our life are in our mind, in our way of thinking, hearing, and perceiving a matter. Man, clearly is limited by his finite state as to what he knows, what he sees, and what he understands. However, we have something called pride that will exalt us in our arrogance to believe we know more than we think we do, as well as possessing haughtiness that exalts our conceit to think highly of what we think we know, and we have high opinions about our nobility that keeps us from seeing just how base we can be.

People often quote the Scripture, "You shall know the truth and the truth shall make you free," but they do not know that it will cost them. Truth will pop "bubbles," shake "boxes" until they fall apart, cause "cement walls" to crumble, and cause the light to shine in the deepest pits, often revealing more than one wants to see. If God's truth is allowed to be the sword, the hammer, the fire, and the water, it will set captives free from the strongholds of their attitudes, opinions, small limited worlds, and insipid realities; but, for it to do that it must be preferred above all other realities, valued more than the greatest treasures, and desired more than the greatest knowledge of the world.

My prayer is that every believer will love God's truth, and regardless of the cost to possess it, it will not matter because it is worth it.

Rayola Kelley

What obstacle in your humanness are you trying to overcome? We live in dark, depressing times and we are often finding ourselves in various wrestling matches. Whether it is the injustice of our times, the mental debate taking place over the insanity that seems to rule, the grave iniquity that shakes all innocence and naivete to such a point it appears as if all will collapse in utter dismay, or the inner struggles with the flesh, the world, and Satan, we are being tested by the days we live in.

When things are going well, we can believe that we have great faith, are doing great things, and are being great in our Christian walk. As I have stated in the past, the world is a classroom, life is the teacher, and the tools that are used to reveal our level of faith, the depth of our character, and our devotion to God are suffering, adversity, failure, and desperation.

Suffering teaches us patience, adversity inner endurance, failure humility, and desperation what it means to seek the Lord with urgency, while holding on to His promises. It is important to remember that when you are attempting to come out on top in the flesh regardless of the results, it is selfishness. When you desire to have your way at all costs it is arrogance, and when you demand you are right, you are in a wrong spirit. When you justify or excuse away doing what is right, it is evil, and when you play games with others' pride and emotions it is wicked.

Genuine faith towards God will cause us to flee the traps of pride, while the application of the cross will address the self-life, and following Jesus will ensure we find and secure His life. We must remember there is only one gate, one right way and it is straight because the person and work of Jesus is the only entrance, the way hard and narrow because it entails a personal cross, and the challenges very measured because it is a disciplined walk in the ways of righteousness. For me, my Christian walk at times has felt like a tight rope, but I balance it out with Spirit and truth, knowing God is the one who directs my steps, the Word is my safety net, and His promises my focus.

Yesterday I talked about how my Christian life feels like walking a tightrope. When I was first a Christian, I perceived my walk as a climbing expedition up some religious pinnacle of dos and don'ts where I could revel in my Christian accomplishments once I hit the peak. When I was knocked off my miserable pinnacle of fantasy, I realized pinnacles were made of foolish notions that left you either teetering or dangling from crumbling peaks of nonsense.

I recognized that Christianity was not a pinnacle moment, but a life-time journey. This is when I became a mountain climber, but I found that mountain climbing was treacherous and I was tempted to either stay too long on the plateaus of normalcy or I would find myself falling into crevices of defeat. That is when I began to understand why God must sometimes move mountains because we have a tendency to climb such mountains in our own strength to accomplish great feats in our Christian life.

At such times it is easy to become emotionally stuck, unable to move up the mountain, and in our mind down is not optional because who wants to lose what has already been gained? We fail to realize we are clinging to our strength instead of activating our faith towards God and letting go so that He can move it out of the way to show Himself mighty on our behalf.

When it came to canyons, I was always looking for some shortcut over them and around them but I discovered that the thing I was avoiding was descending into such places of humility. In fact, I often resented such a notion because I knew I would have to look up and place all of my dependency on God to lead me through it. Keep in mind, only God can straighten out the crooked places.

The truth is we must be led through the barren wilderness of the soul, through the dark, formidable canyons and valleys of uncertainty due to the age we live in, and up the mountains of challenges, which point to a narrow path already designed by the Creator. That narrow path proves to be restrictive. It does not allow us to tout about some imaginary greatness on our part, use ropes of personal strength and cleverness to evade it altogether by climbing above it, or avoid the hard landings that come when we find ourselves in a freefall in our personal life into the pits and crevices of despair, depression, and darkness of the unknown. To me the narrow path is like a tightrope that requires me to trust Him to keep my feet from slipping as I ascend upwards towards the ultimate, promised destination of every blood-bought saint.

When I am in an unproductive mood, I must stop and realize that I am the only one who can change it. It is hard to give up a mood that justifies the way I feel about something, but if I am to encourage myself in the things of God, I first have to lose my foul mood by giving up my right to it.

Let's face it, we can all have these moods at times but we must never adopt them because we are nursing some insipid right to feel this way about this irritation or think this way about that matter. To be an overcoming Christian when it comes to the matters of the flesh requires each of us to understand we are responsible for the attitude behind all moods.

If you want to change a mood, you first have to own it so you can then change the attitude towards something. The Bible is clear we must take on the mind (attitude) of Christ about matters and if we do, we will find ourselves being lifted above the matter at hand and given an eternal perspective that will cause hope to rise up in us setting expectation free to bring wondrous encouragement to our souls.

How important is our testimony? We often take our testimony for granted; after all, it is there, but through the years I have asked people directly and indirectly about their testimony and you know the percentage of people who call themselves Christians I have encounter that actually understand what it means to have a testimony, maybe five percent.

Most tell me about their church, pastor, or what they are doing for the Lord. When I first got saved out of a cult, I realized that there was a bit of sensationalism attached to my testimony that could get people caught up with the idea that I was saved out of something. It is not unusual for people being saved out of drugs etc. to have a bit of sensationalism attached to their testimony. It can all be quite impressive, but the problem is we have a tendency to focus on the person who was miraculously saved instead of the One who accomplished the impressive, the impossible, and the incredible: The Lord Himself.

Through the years my testimony has grown, enlarged, and come to a place of sober maturity. The reason I say this is because my testimony is more about how God has faithfully met me in dire situations, guided me through dark times, held me during fearful times, and carried me in overwhelming times. A mature testimony does not come with age but experience where one has discovered the Lord in the dark places and realized His intervention when the light exposes all of His footprints. This incredible record is about hindsight that has become light in the present, while encouraging of erecting hope for the future.

The question is as a believer do you understand what a testimony is? It is the one sure record that can't be debated, argued, or defeated, and the beauty of it is that it belongs to YOU.

John summarized it best in *Revelation 12:11, "And they overcame him by the blood of the Lamb, and by the word of their testimony; and they loved not their lives unto the death."*

What is a testimony? I became a Christian at a time when some churches encouraged the congregation to share a testimony to edify the church. When you study Paul in Acts, he gave his testimony at various times and it was geared towards the people he was talking to. It reminds me of what he said in *1 Corinthians 9:22b, "...I am made all things to all men, that I might by all means save some."*

It has become obvious to me that the Lord has led me to certain places in my life to grow me up in order to entrust me with a greater testimony. Keep in mind our testimony cost God His Son and Jesus His life. When I approach a group to share my testimony I first wait before the Lord as to how I am to share it because I know I can choose and adjust the part of my testimony that is able to reach into their lives and personally touch the hearers.

Our initial testimony is about ourselves, how Christ reached down into our sin laden-life to save us from sin and death, but it must grow up to a place where it ceases to simply be about what Jesus saved us from to the place where we can share what Jesus has done in us. Salvation truly points to the great work Jesus did on our behalf on the cross, but as the testimony grows it becomes more about Jesus and who He is becoming to us because of what He is doing in us and through us.

The initial testimony is about the great victory of the cross of Christ over the reign of sin, but if it grows it will become about His victorious life in us that enables us to be overcomers over our lusts and more than conquerors over the enemies of our soul because of who He is, Kings of kings and Lord of lords.

The Bible declares that we as believers are more than conquerors because of His love and overcomers when it comes to those things that present the greatest challenges to our walk. Through the years I had to take stock of what was conquering me and what I was being overcome by as to the things of this world. Was I truly being conquered by the love of God in my attitudes and actions towards Him and others and was I overcoming the world with my faith as proclaimed by *1 John 5:4-5*?

There were a couple of obstacles that I found myself having to constantly be aware of. One obstacle was my notions of how things should be and the other one was my agendas. My notions seemed acceptable and righteous but they often became burdens that put undue pressure on me to be something or accomplish something that was unrealistic. I would become frustrated with myself that always flowed over to others in a judgmental way. Eventually the frustration would be turned inward causing depression because I tried so hard to live up to my notions without success. And, then there were those self-serving agendas.

I often tested myself based on my goals, but found myself being a hypocrite because my agendas and priorities were not in line with my goals, causing me to be doubleminded. The Bible tells us that everything we do will seem clean in our own eyes, but God weighs our motives or the spirit behind us and that we must cease to be doubleminded and truly apply real faith in all matters (*Proverbs 16:2; James 4:8*).

Jesus eventually showed me my notions were not His burden for His is light and the confusion and doublemindedness was not the yoke He put upon me to carry. It was not until I did the exchange of my notions with His burden to love, and allowed my personal cross to become a yoke in which He carried the heavier part, allowing me to simply come into step with Him that I understood what it meant for me to come into rest about all matters pertaining to the work in His kingdom and my life.

We often box ourselves in with personal notions and standards and allow the yoke of our cross to become too heavy of a burden to carry because we are trying to fit the things of God into our understanding and ways. It was after I learned, and, I might add, continue to learn, these two lessons that I understood what it meant to, "not personally sweat it," because He was indeed in control of all matters.

Are you overcoming the "fleshly man" in you so that you can become a spiritual man? The Apostle Paul talks about the earthly, fleshly man and the spiritual man in *1 Corinthians 15:42-50*. It is important to point out that at the core of man's will is pride. Pride is the great idol that demands an audience when it comes to lusts, insists on ruling from the throne of the self-life, and wants complete allegiance and worship when all is said and done because it sees itself as being RIGHT.

Pride also presents a dichotomy. It will justify your right to pursue life on your terms, but it will also turn around and harshly judge and condemn you when you go against your conscience on a matter. We can see the attitude of pride in *Isaiah 14:12-15*. This is my paraphrase of it in relationship to man's will, "I WILL control my reality, my world, and my life. I WILL ascend in my arrogance in the matters of life. I WILL exalt my ways in regard to life. I WILL sit on the throne, ruling over the ways of life, and in the end I WILL be like the Most High in the matters of life." Keep in mind this was the big temptation in the Garden of Eden, "to be as God."

If we do not recognize our pride and resist giving it audience, we will be ruled by it and it will become a tyrant to others who are in our life. It is vital we come to the place of humility so we can humble ourselves and submit our will to the will of God in all matters.

What are you willing to lose in order to gain heaven? It is quite noble to think of sacrificing in light of gaining recognition or something that will prove beneficial to your very person, but when it comes to gaining the real prize of heaven, there is nothing noble about the cost because such costs are necessary to gain the prize.

It is a known fact that to make money it will cost you money. To gain that which can't be seen will cost you what is seen and in essence you are gambling what you have in light of gaining uncertain riches.

Jesus counted the cost of redemption for us and He paid the complete price for our souls on the cross. But, to gain the unseen promises of heaven, what will it cost us—things that are attached to our flesh (lusts), the world (our lifestyle), and Satan (enlightenment).

It is important to realize whatever we gain will cost us. The flesh claims if you feed its lust, you will be satisfied, but you must sear your moral conscience so you can pursue it. The world advocates that if you gain a certain lifestyle, you will possess great status, happiness, and success but you must sell your soul, and Satan offers enlightenment that will either save you or make you a god, but you must become a reprobate and worship him, gambling with your soul that he is not the liar and murderer he is.

The question is what will it cost you to gain Christ? The answer is simple, it will require you to crucify the flesh, separate yourself from the false promises of the world, and flee the false light of Satan in order to whole-heartedly pursue the real prize of heaven, Jesus Christ.

One of the tormentors I had to overcome were regrets. Regrets are those things that are like little foxes that hinder the work God is presently doing, because like Lot's wife they have the ability to cause us to look back at what might have been but will always stand as is in the annual of our history.

Such things can cause us to second guess our decisions in light of circumstances that will always play out with the same ending. I know of people who try to avoid regrets only to find out that these little foxes will always find those who constantly operate in the "what ifs." The truth is, regrets exist because we are not God, who sovereignly controls circumstances, and Satan is quick to use this reality against us with accusations that he slams against our tender conscience as he props them up with tormenting possibilities that will never be.

We do not possess some crystal ball to look into the future to prepare our conscience for what we inevitably have no control over or could not change if we did know something was about to happen. The only way I make peace with regrets is to let them be a mirror that exposes any area of moral weakness in me or allow them to serve as a teacher that can give me some wise hindsight that ultimately brings me to the same conclusion; that is, I must learn from yesteryear, simply do right in a matter today to avoid future regrets, trust God to work it all out for His glory, and then let God be God.

God never intended us to be burdened down with regrets that weary us with the "what ifs" of yesterday. It is impossible to live life on the events of yesterday when we are looking back, because we will be missing the blessings God wants to give us today.

RESURRECTION

Sometimes the greatest darkness
of the soul can cause one to become
enlightened to the powerful
life-changing truths of heaven.
(Rayola Kelley)

We know that we are hid in Christ according to *Colossians 3:2*. This concept points to Christ being a type of ark.

There are two arks mentioned in the Old Testament, Noah's ark and Moses' ark that was made of bulrushes and daubed with slime and pitch to keep it afloat in the Nile River when he was just a babe *(Exodus 2:3)*. What most people do not realize is that both arks were a type of grave.

There must be some type of death before there can be resurrection into a new existence (*Romans 6:3-5*). Without the ark both individuals were doomed because of the death sentence placed upon their generation but the ark lifted Noah up above the waters, Moses' ark was drawn up and out of the water, and we know Jesus was lifted up on the cross (*Genesis 7:17; Exodus 2:5-6; John 12:32*).

As you study the ark, the construction of both pointed to an act of faith. Out of faith Noah built an ark and out of faith Moses' parents prepared his ark and as a result both were miraculously saved. The struggle that many Christians have is that they fail to remember that they are constantly walking towards their demise. On that day when they actually put off the fleshly tabernacle (body), they will do so possessing the expectation of being raised in newness of life with a new glorified body (*John 5:21-29; Daniel 12:1-3*).

We must remember that if we are in Christ, our old life is buried and we have been lifted up in Him to avoid the wrath to come. In fact, we have been brought through a type of spiritual baptism which guarantees us that we do possess a new life, a blessed hope, and a glorious future.

As believers we are strangers and pilgrims in this world. As strangers we are simply passing through and as pilgrims, we are looking for that place where we can worship God according to our conscience. The difference between those who belong to the world and those who are strangers is that we have recognized our need to seek out our spiritual refuge in this dangerous world.

God provided the Jews with six refuge cities that strangers could seek out and find protection in, and also for those who accidentally killed someone could find protection from the victim's family seeking revenge. The Bible is clear we all start out being enemies of God and we need to find a place of refuge from His wrath.

Like the refuge cities, God has provided the believer a place of refuge, the person of Jesus Christ. As believers, we are hidden in Him and will be spared from the wrath that will come upon this world, as well as those who are children of disobedience, but we must flee to this city, seeking such refuge.

The Apostle Paul put it in this way, *"And to wait for his Son from heaven, whom he raised from the dead, even Jesus which delivered us from the wrath to come" (1 Thessalonians 1:10).* Are you hidden in Christ because you have sought Him out as the only refuge from the judgment that abides on this present world and the wrath to come upon all disobedience?

When we consider the valley of the shadow of death, we often do so in light of the death of a person. However, there are three different types of death that this valley prepares people to walk through.

There is the physical death where the spirit and soul are separated from the physical body. It is at this time the temporary glory of the physical life is put off so that the spirit and soul can be ushered into the eternal glory of the next world.

The second death is the death to the self-life. This is where aspects of the "old man," are put off daily so that the believer can put on the new man of Christ Jesus. Death to the self-life entails denying self the right to life on its terms, picking up the cross to crucify the lusts of the flesh, while becoming crucified to the world, and begin to follow Jesus into a new life.

The final death is the spiritual death. Sin has already broken the relationship God desires with man. Christ came to restore that relationship, but if a person has not been reconciled back to God through Jesus' redemption, he or she stands condemned and has already been judged. If a person remains separated from God in this life, he or she will remain separated from Him in the next life.

Daniel 12:1 talks about the names in the Book of life and then goes on to say this in *Daniel 12:2-3, "And many of them that sleep in the dust of the earth shall awake, some to everlasting life, and some to shame and everlasting contempt. And they that be wise shall shine as the brightness of the firmament; and they that turn many to righteousness as the stars for ever and ever."*

For the most part all men will experience two of these deaths. For believers (that is until Jesus comes for His bride) they will experience the physical death as well as the death to the self-life. For unbelievers, they will experience both the physical and spiritual deaths.

As we as believers walk through the valleys, we can be confident that the Lord is preparing us for the glory of heaven and a greater resurrection, as the new man is unveiled in and through us in this life from His unveiling in His Word through revelation by the Spirit to the complete unveiling of the fulness of His glory in the next age to come.

We are walking either in the light of Christ or in the darkness of this present world. One of the biggest challenges we have in Christianity comes down to our attitude towards this age or the world.

Sadly, we are given the impression by some in Christendom that we can gain the world and possess heaven at the same time. The Bible is clear, you can't gain the world without selling your soul to it. The world with its wrong spirit, its lustful pursuits, its temporary glory, and its false promises is an enemy of God, and those who love the world will fail to do the will of God and will be found to be void of His love. Yes, we are of the world, but we are not to be part of it.

The world has its purpose when it comes to the Christian walk. For example, it is a big classroom where our faith will be tested by the currents of life, as well as a spiritual barren wilderness where there is no real life and it is up to us to establish our life in Christ in the midst of it. It is a tomb where the things of the flesh will fall away and be no more, covered up by the sands of time, and it is a place of death where it will serve as a door to eternity. When we consider the world as a classroom, we must realize that our goal is to learn the lessons of life in preparation for our graduation into a greater life, where we will cease to be identified to this world and become a spiritual man who is taking on the image of Christ.

When it comes to it being our barren wilderness, we must note that it stands between us and our real citizenship and spiritual inheritance. We must recognize we have been slaves to Egypt (the world) and God has miraculously delivered us from its tyrannical reign through the sacrificial death of Christ. He has indeed broken all the claims of this world upon our lives, but we need to acknowledge that our journey is just beginning and we are spiritual paupers who needs God's intervention every minute, hour, and day if we are to enter into our promised inheritance.

Finally, it is the passageway of death. I heard a statement one time that Christians are always walking towards their demise. It is true, as a classroom it teaches us that at our journey is filled with markers where different aspects of the self-life were cast aside, and as a wilderness it reminds us death works in us so we can gain what is eternal. As a tomb we are reminded we must leave the old behind in order to gain the new, and as a door of death we recognize that without death, there is no glorious resurrection.

I used to connect resurrection and life together, sometimes causing a bit of a blur that allowed me to operate in assumption. It is true that they walk hand in hand with each other, but one day I noted which word preceded which word. Consider what Jesus said to Martha in *John 11:25, 26, "I am the resurrection, and the life; he that believeth in me, though he were dead, yet shall he live: And whosoever liveth and believeth in me shall never die. Believest thou this?"*

God is the only One who can give life and He is the God of perfect order and we must note that resurrection comes first. There cannot be any real life without resurrection. The reason for this order is that resurrection is about raising up that which is dead into life.

We are all born spiritually dead in sin, and Jesus' redemption was about paying the price for our sin to satisfy the holy Law of God, but His resurrection was about quickening our spirit with His life (born again) to raise us up in a new life. Without His resurrection our faith in Him would prove worthless, the preaching of the Gospel would be in vain, and we would still be dead.

I am so thankful for our loving Savior who took our place on the cross and rose three days later as our Risen Lord and now serves as our High Priest in the courts of heaven and one day soon He is coming back as King, Lord, and Judge over all.

Martin Luther suffered with bouts of depression and such bouts will always express themselves in moods and in the countenance. One day his wise wife was dressed in black. When he asked her for the reason for her attire, her response was that God must be dead by the way he was acting.

How many of us are acting as if God is dead? As a believer, I serve a Savior that saved me and who is now a risen Lord sitting on the right hand of the Majesty in the heavens who will one day come back as King and Judge over all. Too many times we allow the morbid darkness of this world to determine our moods and countenance and as a result, we look like we have lost our best friend, Jesus, and that God is no more.

This time of season (Resurrection Sunday) reminds us that the cross is empty because redemption was paid in full and the grave is empty because our Lord is risen so that the empty, barren tombs of our lives could be filled with His eternal life. As believers we must cease to walk around in a state of hopeless despair due to the present darkness, but remember that all that matters and is necessary lives and is not embodied in a dead Savior but in our Risen Lord. Let us rejoice that we possess the same power of resurrection that raised up our Lord and that the life that is in us proved victorious over death and the grave.

〜〜〜〜

The wonderful promise of possessing eternal life is that within it is also resurrection power that one day will raise every believer up in a new body. Have you ever noticed how the word "resurrection" is used before the word "life?" Jesus said this in *John 11:25, "I am the resurrection, and the life: he that believeth in me, though he were dead, yet shall he live."*

There can't be any life without the power present to quicken the spirit. One of the miracles I marvel at is the raising of Lazarus in *John 11*. Jesus gave us a preview of how every believer's resurrection will look like in the raising of Lazarus. He simply called him forth from the grave and that will be true for us. *John 5:25, "Verily, verily, I say unto you, The hour is coming, and now is, when the dead shall hear the voice of the Son of God: and they that hear shall live."*

However, there is another aspect of the raising of Lazarus and that has to do with his graveclothes. When we are born again, we experience the quickening of our spirit just like Lazarus did in the grave. Salvation is certainly a miracle, but the other part of it is that when Lazarus came forth from the grave, the Lord instructed those around him to loose him from his graveclothes. This is also an important example.

When we are born again, we come out of our spiritual grave bound by the ragged clothes of the old life and we need others to loose us from them. To loose someone from the old takes the wise unwrapping with Scriptural instruction and the sharp cutting of the truth, with the intent to lovingly and carefully setting the person free to walk out their new life in Christ. Another word for loosing someone from the old is "discipleship."

Deliverance means different things to different people. There is deliverance FROM and THROUGH challenge, but there is also deliverance TO something. When it comes to salvation, deliverance presents a complete picture of a salvation that is not only free, but rich and complete.

We see this in the case of Israel, the people were delivered FROM Egypt, delivered THROUGH the wilderness, and delivered TO the Promised Land. Probably one of the great struggles Christians find themselves in is that they came to Christ, knowing they needed deliverance FROM their past sins, and as life becomes harder, they began to realize more and more that they needed deliverance THROUGH their present age. However, they often failed to realize that deliverance from the past and deliverance through the present is all about deliverance TO that which is greater, more excellent, and glorious. In essence, believers are being delivered TO receive the promises that is attached to the fullness of our redemption.

We appreciate the deliverance from the past, and know it is called JUSTIFICATION, while we wrestle to give way to our present deliverance known as SANCTIFICATION, but we can fail to see that for deliverance to be complete we must come into a place where we finally receive all that was promised to us. For the children of Israel, it was the Promised Land, but for Christian it is about something that is far more wondrous.

Deliverance for us as believers is clearly about being set free from the hold of the flesh and the designs of the world and prepared to come into a state of GLORIFICATION, where we are identified with and in Christ so that the fullness of our redemption will be realized. As we watch the world go mad and digress into a type of insanity where up is down and down is up, evil is good and good is evil, we must recognize that for us as believers we are, in essence, being prepared for what *Hebrews 11:35* refers to as a "better resurrection."

Are you walking in expectation of a glorious resurrection? *Hebrews 11* talks about the great victory of faith as well as the challenging reality of faith. It tells us that those who were tortured because they did not accept deliverance did so that they might obtain a better resurrection (*Hebrews 11:35*).

Our present walk through this age determines what we are preparing for as far as the next world to come. We can't live like the devil and expect to be comfortable in heaven and we can't live like a saint and think for one minute hell would embrace us. Since we are baptized into Jesus' death, we must die daily to fleshly and worldly influences like the Apostle Paul so we can be renewed daily in the inner man and raised up in newness of life on the great day of resurrection (*John 5:20-29; 1 Corinthians 15:31, 42-54*).

I remember sharing this great promise of a new, glorious body with a friend whose physical body was ravished by many different physical elements. She looked upward in such expectation with a peaceful smile, and it was as if heaven came down and enfolded her in its radiant light. Her face changed and she actually looked young. It was obvious she could hardly wait for that glorious day, and that very night she went home to be with the Lord.

Our physical body is dying and will be put off one day. In Christ we have become identified with His death in order to be raised up daily in newness of His life, and on the day He calls us forth from the grave, we will be raised with a new body that will never die.

Are you looking up and living in great expectation of that day? Are you getting homesick?

What does it mean to know the power of Jesus' resurrection? In *Philippians 3:10*, the Apostle Paul wanted to know Jesus, but He also wanted to know the power of His resurrection.

Jesus gave up the glories of heaven to become identified with man so that He could become the great substitute for him on the cross. Likewise, we must become identified with Jesus in His death, burial, and resurrection to be raised up in new life (*Romans 6:1-5*).

Jesus made an important statement in *John 11:25, "I am the resurrection, and the life, he that believeth in me, though he were dead, yet shall he live."* It is important to consider the order in Jesus' statement. Resurrection comes before life. This order is important because there can't be a resurrection without some type of death, and what comes out of resurrection is some type of life.

It is easy to get caught up with Jesus' great sacrifice, but if He had not risen from the grave to be victorious over death, the preaching of the Gospel and our faith in Him as believers would be in vain (*1 Corinthians 15:1-4, 12-22*). It is for this reason that *Romans 10:9* states, *"That if thou shalt confess with thy mouth the Lord Jesus and shalt believe in thine heart that God hath raised him from the dead, thou shalt be saved."* Notice we must believe in our heart Christ was raised from the grave. We do not serve a dead Savior; rather, we serve a risen Lord who will one day come back as King and Judge to rule over the all earth.

Meanwhile, what does resurrection mean for the believer: that the very life of Christ has been raised up in our once lifeless soul and now we possess eternal life. The more we put down the old life, the more we will advance forward to obtain a greater resurrection. The Apostle Paul understood this and that is why he wanted to know the power of His resurrection.

Right now, we only understand resurrection in part, but one day every believer will experience the fullness of it. The question that Jesus asked Martha in *John 11:26*, is one for us to honestly answer, *"And whosoever liveth and believeth in me shall never die. Believest thou this? "*

Other books by Rayola Kelley

Hidden Manna
Battle for the Soul
Stories of the Heart
Transforming Love & Beyond
The Great Debate
Post to Post (Walking in the Way)

Volume One: Establishing Our Life in Christ
My Words are Spirit and Life
The Anatomy of Sin
The Principles of the Abundant Life
The Place of Covenant
Unmasking the Cult Mentality

Volume Two: Putting on the Life of Christ
He Actually Thought It Not Robbery
Revelation of the Cross
In Search of Real Faith
Think on These Things
Follow the Pattern

Volume Three: Developing a Godly Environment
Godly Discipline
Prayer and Worship
Don't Touch That Dial
Face of Thankfulness
ABC's of Christianity

Volume Four: Issues of the Heart
Hidden Manna (Revised)
Bring Down the Sacred Cows
The Manual for the Single Christian Life
Parents are People Too

Volume Five: Challenging the Christian Life
The Issues of Life
Presentation of the Gospel
For the Purpose of Edification
Whatever Happened to the Church?
Women's Place in the Kingdom of God

Volume Six: Developing Our Christian Life
The Many Faces of Christianity
Possessing Our Souls
Experiencing the Christian Life
The Power of Our Testimonies
The Victorious Journey

Volume Seven: Discovering True Ministry
From Prisons and Dots to Christianity
So You Want to be in Ministry

Devotions:
Devotions of the Heart: Book One and Two
Daily Food for the Soul: OT and NT

Gentle Shepherd Ministries Devotion Series:
Being a Child of God
Disciplining the Strength of our Youth
Coming to Full Age

Nugget Books:
Nuggets From Heaven
More Nuggets From Heaven
Heavenly Gems
More Heavenly Gems
Heavenly Treasures

Gentle Shepherd Ministries Series:

The Christian Life Series:
What Matter Is This?
The Challenge of It
The Reality of It

The Leadership Series:
Overcoming
A Matter of Authority and Power
The Dynamics of True Leadership